NATURALISM AND THE HUMAN SPIRIT

Number 8 of the Columbia Studies
in Philosophy
Edited under the Department of Philosophy
Columbia University

EDITED BY YERVANT H. KRIKORIAN

NATURALISM
AND THE
HUMAN
SPIRIT

COLUMBIA UNIVERSITY PRESS

MORNINGSIDE HEIGHTS · NEW YORK

TO

MORRIS R. COHEN

PREFACE

Major philosophic attitudes never find complete expression, for such attitudes not only carry ideational twilight zones but, as time goes on, grow in their meaning and vary in the scope of their application. In the light of new experience and reflection they need restatement. This is especially true of naturalism. Naturalism as a philosophy has an ancient ancestry and older formulations; but its present vigorous growth in a world that has more secular interests and more scientific ideas than before demands new expression. The contributors to this volume are primarily representative of naturalism; many eminent names are not included. The essays that follow endeavor to state freshly the nature of naturalism; they range from its application to various fields to an account of its historical development in America. The aim of these essays is not rigid agreement or unanimity of belief; each writer expresses his own view and is solely responsible for it.

Yet in this co-operative work there are common agreements, not so much in specific ideas as in general attitudes. The method relied upon in seeking an understanding of the world is the empirical method of science as against allegedly superior methods; the world sought is the world of natural existence, since only this world can be empirically authenticated. These essays are also intensely concerned with the aspirations of the human spirit—its love of freedom, its sense of beauty, its hope of creating a better civilization. For the attainment of these ends a philosophy that is empirical, that relies on intelligence, that finds the good within actual existence without denying ideal possibilities may render its fair contribution.

It is a pleasure to acknolwedge the full and generous co-operation of the contributors. Special thanks are due to Professor Ernest Nagel for his valuable suggestions and to Professor John Randall, Jr., and to Professor Abraham Edel for their many helpful ideas. Several contributors are grateful to the editors of *Ethics*, *The Journal of Philosophy*, and the *Philosophy of Science* for their permission to make use of material which appeared in these journals.

YERVANT H. KRIKORIAN

New York
May, 1944

CONTENTS

1 ANTINATURALISM IN EXTREMIS

John Dewey, Columbia University 1

2 NATURALISM AND RELIGION

Sterling P. Lamprecht, Amherst College 17

3 NATURALISM AND DEMOCRACY

Sidney Hook, New York University 40

4 NATURALISM AND ETHICAL THEORY

Abraham Edel, College of the City of New York 65

5 A NATURAL HISTORY OF THE AESTHETIC
TRANSACTION

Eliseo Vivas, University of Wisconsin 96

6 THE UNNATURAL

Herbert W. Schneider, Columbia University 121

7 THE HISTORY OF PHILOSOPHY

George Boas, Johns Hopkins University 133

8 THE MATERIALS OF HISTORICAL KNOWLEDGE

Edward W. Strong, University of California 154

x   *Contents*

9 NATURALISM AND THE SOCIOLOGICAL ANALYSIS
   OF KNOWLEDGE

                      Thelma Z. Lavine, Wells College 183

10 LOGIC WITHOUT ONTOLOGY

                  Ernest Nagel, Columbia University 210

11 A NATURALISTIC VIEW OF MIND

     Yervant H. Krikorian, College of the City of New York 242

12 THE CATEGORIES OF NATURALISM

            William R. Dennes, University of California 270

13 THE NATURALISM OF FREDERICK WOODBRIDGE

              Harry Todd Costello, Trinity College 295

14 NATURALISM IN AMERICA

                  Harold A. Larrabee, Union College 319

15 EPILOGUE: THE NATURE OF NATURALISM

         John Herman Randall, Jr., Columbia University 354

     INDEX   383

I

ANTINATURALISM IN EXTREMIS

John Dewey

I

PHILOSOPHICAL naturalism has a more distinguished ancestry than is usually recognized; there are, for example, the names of Aristotle and Spinoza. However, the Aristotle who has exercised the greatest influence upon modern philosophy was one whose naturalism did not prevent him from regarding the physical as the lowest stratum in the hierarchical order of Being and from holding that pure intellect, pure because free from contamination by any trace of the material, is at the apex. It is to be doubted, however, whether the work of Aristotle would have inured, as it has done, to the credit of antinaturalism if he had not been adopted as the official philosopher of the Church and if his writings had not found their way into modern culture through a transformation they underwent in the medieval period.

For in this period the out-and-out supernaturalism of the Roman Catholic Church was injected whenever possible into interpretations of Aristotle. The naturalistic elements in his teaching were overlaid, covered up, with supernatural beliefs; or, if that was not possible, were slurred over as the views of a pagan not enlightened by the Hebraic-Christian revelation from on high. The supernaturalism thus read into Aristotle united with elements in him which are genuinely nonnaturalistic from the standpoint of present science, and the union resulted in his being held up by many modern writers as the founder, in conjunction with Plato, of spiritualistic antinaturalistic philosophy.

When, however, it is a question of moral theory, the naturalism of Aristotle lies so clearly on the face that medieval Christian theological philosophy was compelled to give it a radically different turn. How different was this turn may be inferred from words of Cardinal Newman that express the orthodox views: "The pattern man, the just, the upright, the generous, the honorable, the conscientious, if he is all this not from a supernatural power, but from *mere natural virtue*," has the pros-

pect of heaven "closed and refused to him." [1] When such measure is
meted out to virtues like honor, uprightness, justice, and generosity, one
readily gathers how conduct proceeding from appetite and desire will
be judged. For the latter are deeply dyed with the Pauline and Augustinian view of the total corruption of the body and lusts of carnal flesh.
The historic source of the doctrine of the corruption of nature and the
fallen estate of man is now often relegated to the background. But the
Western world was reared under the influence of the doctrines and
sacraments of the Church. Contrast between the old Adam, which is
"natural," and a higher self, which is "spiritual," remains the assumption
of philosophers who avowedly repudiated supernaturalism—as in the
striking case of Kant. The Church never forgot to remind its adherents
of their lost condition due to their fallen estate; otherwise there would
have been no need for the work of redemption supernaturally entrusted
to it. Similarly, the professedly nonsupernatural philosopher who is
antinaturalist never ceases to dwell upon the merely sensuous and self-
seeking character of the natural man, upon the morally seductive character of natural impulse and desire; for otherwise there would be no
place for the doctrine that the truly moral factors in human relations
are superimposed from a spiritual nonnatural source and authority.

It is needful to use such terms as "nonnaturalist" and "antinaturalist,"
because in addition to frank supernaturalism there are philosophers who
claim to rest their extra- (if not super-) naturalism upon a higher faculty
of Reason or Intuition, not upon a special divine revelation. While I am
personally convinced that their philosophy can be understood only as
a historical heritage from frank supernaturalism, I shall call attention to
a point of agreement and practical co-operation between the two antinaturalistic schools. Both of them identify naturalism with "materialism" and then employ the identification to charge naturalists with reduction of all distinctively human values, moral, aesthetic, logical, to
blind mechanical conjunctions of material entities—a reduction which
is in effect their complete destruction. The identification thus permits
antinaturalists to substitute name-calling for discussion of specific issues
in their own terms and in their connection with concrete evidence.

Regarding the identification in question, it suffices here to note that
the naturalist is one who has respect for the conclusion of natural
science. Hence he is quite aware that "matter" has in modern science

---

[1] The word "mere" plays a large role in antinaturalistic writings.

none of the low, base, inert properties assigned to it in classic Greek and medieval philosophy; properties that were the ground for setting it in stark opposition to all that is higher, to which eulogistic adjectives may be applied. In consequence, he is aware that since "matter" and "materialism" acquired their significance in contrast with something called "spirit" and "spiritualism," the fact that naturalism has no place for the latter also deprives the former epithets of all significance in philosophy. It would be difficult to find a greater distance between any two terms than that which separates "matter" in the Greek-medieval tradition and the technical signification, suitably expressed in mathematical symbols, that the word bears in science today.

Reference to science reminds us that nobody save, perhaps, the most dogmatic supernaturalist denies that modern methods of experimental observation have wrought a profound transformation in the subject matters of astronomy, physics, chemistry, and biology, that the change wrought in them has exercised the most profound influence upon human relations. To recognition of this fact the naturalist adds a further fact of fateful significance. He sees how antinaturalism has operated to prevent the application of scientific methods of inquiry in the field of human social subject matter. Antinaturalism has prevented science from completing its career and fulfilling its constructive potentialities. For it has held that this latter field is extranatural and hence is reserved for organs and methods which are radically different from those which have given man the command he now possesses in the affairs, issues, and questions acknowledged to be natural. It is beyond human imagination to estimate the extent to which undesirable features of the present human situation are connected with the split, the division, the confusion, and the conflict embodied in this half-way, mixed, unintegrated situation as respects knowledge and attainment of truth. Democracy cannot obtain adequate recognition of its own meaning or coherent practical realization as long as antinaturalism operates to delay and frustrate the use of the methods by which alone understanding and consequent ability to guide social relationships are attained.

In this connection it is appropriate to say something which is more-or-less apart from the main topic of this paper. Philosophic naturalism still has a work to do in a field that so far it has hardly done more than touch. Because of the influence of supernatural religion, first Catholic and then Protestant, it is not just "matter" which continues to reflect the beliefs of a prescientific and predemocratic period. Such words as "mind," "subject," "self," "person," "the individual," to say nothing of "value," are more than tinged in their current usage (which affects willy-nilly philosophical formulations) with significations they absorbed from beliefs of an extranatural character. There is almost no word employed in psychological and societal analysis and description that does not re-flect this influence.

Hence, draw the conclusion that the most pressing problem and the most urgent task of naturalism at the present time is to work out on the basis of available evidence a naturalistic interpretation of the things and events designated by words that now exert almost complete control of psychological and societal inquiry and report. For example, no issue is more basic for naturalistic theory than the nature of observation. A sur-vey of contemporary literature will, nevertheless, disclose that it is rarely discussed in its own terms—the terms, that is, of procedures employed by inquirers in astronomical observatories; in chemical, physical, and biological laboratories; in the examinations conducted by physicians; and in what is done in field excursions of botanists and zoologists. In-stead, it appears to be obligatory to substitute reduction to terms of sen-sations, sense, sense-data (the exact word is of little importance) which are affected by an inheritance of nonnaturalism.

The current discussion of language—also a topic of basic importance —affords another example. Students of this subject from a logical and a social point of view, who regard themselves as antimetaphysical scien-tific positivists, nevertheless write as if words consisted of an "inner" private, mentalistic core or substance and an "outer" physical shell by means of which a "subjective" intrinsically incommunicable somehow gets conveyed "trans-subjectively"! And they appear quite unaware of the extranatural origin and status of the postulate. Until naturalists have definitely applied their own principles, methods, and procedures to for-mulation of such topics as mind, consciousness, self, person, value, and so forth, they will be at a serious and regrettable disadvantage. For writers of the "rational" philosophical variety of antinaturalism almost base their premises upon alleged facts of and about mind, consciousness, self, and so forth. They suppose that the "facts" are accepted by natu-ralists. When they do not find the conclusions they expect, they usually accuse naturalists of holding an inconsistent, untenable and truncated position.

II

This topic, however, is much too large for discussion here. The rest of this paper, accordingly, is devoted to the contrast which exists between charges brought against naturalism (on the ground of its identification with materialism) and the facts of the case. At the present time there is a veritable eruption of accusations. Many nonnaturalists seem to regard the present tragic state of the world as a heaven-sent occasion for accusing naturalism of being the responsible cause of the manifold evils from which we are suffering. I begin by citing some specimen cases.

"Materialists, agnostics, behaviorists and their ilk can be sincere defenders of democracy only by being inconsistent; for their theories, whether they wish it or not, lead inevitably to justifying government by brute force and to denying all those rights and freedoms we term inalienable." [2] Naturalists are not included by name in the foregoing list. But a roll of miscellaneous names that follows shows that they fall within the "ilk" who bear this dire responsibility.

Kant and Carlyle, William James and Herbert Spencer, William McDougall and Henri Bergson, Arthur de Gobineau and Houstan Stewart Chamberlain —all of whom would have been horrified at the completed product of Naziism—made such a philosophy not only possible but almost inevitable by their denial of one or more of the fundamentals on which any free and humanitarian and Christian concept of society must be built. [3]

The grouping together of men whose philosophies have nothing, or next to nothing, in common except denial or neglect of the dogmas of Roman Catholic theological philosophy, which is held up by its adherents as providing the sole basis of a "free" as well as an ordered society, is a commentary on the careless intellectual criteria prevailing in this circle. For it is a serious kind of carelessness, which a naturalist would not dare to engage in. Only the confidence of one who thinks he is speaking for a divinely founded and divinely directed institution could think of lumping together men of such contrary beliefs. Even more to the point is the fact that among those who are regarded as causes of the present social disorder is Kant, who is definitely a philosophical antinaturalist; one who, among other things, formulated the doctrine that

[2] Thomas P. Neill, "Democracy's Intellectual Fifth Column," *The Catholic World*, CLV (May, 1942), 151.
[3] *Ibid.*, pp. 151-52.

every human person is an end in himself and is possessed of freedom because of membership in a realm above the natural world—the Kant who, moreover, regarded it as the function of history, with its gradual improvement of social institutions, to usher in republican government as the only one conforming to the philosophical principles he laid down.

In view of the fact that Bergson is included in the list, it is interesting that the following quotation is from a writer (held up to Protestants as a specimen of the liberalism of the Catholic Church) who has publicly expressed peculiar indebtedness to this very Bergson:

What the world and civilization have needed in modern times in the intellectual order, what the temporal good of man has needed for four centuries, is just Christian Philosophy. In their place arose a separate philosophy and an inhuman Humanism, a Humanism destructive of man because it wanted to be centered upon men and not upon God. We have drained the cup, we now see before our eyes that bloody anti-Humanism, that ferocious irrationalism and trend to slavery in which rationalistic Humanism finally winds up.[4]

A "mere" naturalist, even if he counted upon the ignorance or short memory of his audience, would hesitate to assume that the world was in a state of blissful order and peace, free from blood and ferocity before the rise of rationalism, naturalism, and humanism. Even the ordinary reader might recall that some of the bloodiest and most cruel events in human history occurred in the name of and with the explicit sanction of supernaturalism, including the ecclesiastic institution which dominated European culture until the last "four centuries," which are so significantly mentioned.

If, however, the reader is familiar with the contents of supernatural medieval philosophy, he will also recall that bloody and ferocious persecutions and oppressions are very different when they are carried on by the Church with its supernatural source and center. For in the latter case they are intended to save from eternal damnation the souls of believers in heresies; or, if that is not possible, at least to protect others from being contaminated by literally "damnable" heresies. The interpretation put by St. Thomas Aquinas (now the official philosopher of the Church) upon the Biblical injunction "Love thy neighbor as thyself" is proof for the orthodox that since the love in question is love of

[4] From J. Maritain, "Contemporary Renewals in Modern Thought," in Pennsylvania University, Bicentennial Conference, *Religion in the Modern World*, 1941, p. 14.

an immortal and nonnatural soul, which can be saved only by acceptance of the creed of the Church and by sharing in its sacraments, the injunction of Jesus is so far from having the meaning that would naturally be assigned to it that it expressly authorizes any and all means that may tend to save the soul from the tortures of hell. For what are peace, earthly and natural contentment, and a reasonable degree of happiness during a mere three score years and ten in comparison with reward and punishment in a supernatural eternity?

I come now to a statement which, if I mistake not, has both supernatural and philosophical antinaturalists as sponsors.

Many who hold to this naturalistic view in democratic countries are unaware of the dangers in their position. Influenced by the last remnants of philosophical Idealism, romantic Transcendentalism, or religious Theism in our day, they act as if they still believed in the spiritual conception of man which they have intellectually repudiated. They try to maintain their feeling for the dignity of man, while paying homage to an essentially materialistic philosophy according to which man is simply [*sic!*] a highly developed animal . . . they are living off the spiritual capital which has come down to them from their classical and religious heritage. . . . Since this contradiction will prove to be intellectually intolerable, scholars and teachers *must* recover and re-affirm the spiritual conception of man and his good which we have derived from Greek and Hebraic-Christian sources. If they fail to do this not only religious reverence and moral responsibility, but also the scholarly activities with which they are directly concerned, will be greatly endangered. Already, under totalitarian regimes and to a lesser extent in the democracies, these activities are being undermined.[5]

It is probable that the signers of this statement belong to both the supernatural and the rationalistic varieties of antinaturalism. Reference to our classic *and* religious heritage, to Greek *and* Hebraic-Christian sources, indicates that such is the case. They agree for purposes of attack. But cross-examination would disclose a fundamental incompatibility. For example, philosophical antinaturalists are obliged to confine themselves to dire prediction of terrible things to happen because of naturalism. Their companions of the supernatural variety are aware of

[5] From a statement signed by a group of Princeton professors, in the *Proceedings of the Conference on Science, Philosophy and Religion*, II, 255. Although "science" appears in the title, the meetings and discussions of this conference are chiefly devoted to asserting some aspect of antinaturalism; literary writers, being innocent of the philosophical issues involved, serve as cement of the amalgam.

active and forcible means that were once employed to stay the spread of heresies like naturalism so as to prevent the frightful consequences from happening; if they are literate in their faith, they know that such methods are still required and are prevented from being put into execution by the spread of naturalistic liberalism in civilized countries. When members of this group think of the pains that were taken when the Church had power to protect the faithful from "science falsely so-called" and from dangerous thoughts in scholarship, they may well have smiled at the innocence of their colleagues who imply that inquiry, scholarship, and teaching are completely unhampered where naturalism has not obtained a foothold. And they might certainly say of their merely philosophical *confrères* that they are living off a capital derived from a supernatural heritage. A mere naturalist will content himself with wondering whether ignorance of history, complacency, provincialism with respect to the non-Christian part of the world, or sheer rhetorical dogmatism is the outstanding trait of the pronunciamento. A historian of ideas could contribute some interesting information as to the persons who have done most in fact to make democracy and freedom of mind realities in the modern world as well as the persons who withstood their efforts at every turn—until the march of events forced at least a temporary abstinence from that particular line of obscurantic obstructionism.

I conclude these citations with a passage written some time before the crisis had reached its present intensity. In a book that G. K. Chesterton wrote after a visit to this country he spoke as follows of the prospects of democracy in the United States.

So far as that democracy becomes or remains Catholic and Christian, that democracy will remain democratic. . . . Men will more and more realise that there is no meaning in democracy if there is no meaning in anything . . . if the universe has not a centre of significance and an authority that is the author of our rights.[6]

I should not have supposed that an advance was to be expected in greater realization of the truism that if there is no meaning in anything there is none in democracy. The nub of the passage resides clearly in the assertion that the rights and freedom which constitute democracy have no validity or significance save as they are referred to some center

---

[6] Gilbert Chesterton, *What I Saw in America*, New York, 1922, p. 296.

and authority entirely outside nature—and outside men's natural social connections with one another. This intrinsically skeptical, cynical, and pessimistic view of human nature is at the bottom of all asseverations that naturalism is destructive of the values associated with democracy, including belief in the dignity of man and the worth of human life. This disparaging view (to put it mildly) of man is that upon which rests the whole enterprise of condemning naturalism, no matter in what fine philosophical language the condemnation is set forth. The fact of the case is that naturalism finds the values in question, the worth and dignity of men and women, residing in human nature itself, in the connections, actual and potential, that human beings sustain to one another in the natural environment. Not only that, but naturalism is ready at any time to maintain the thesis that foundation within man and nature is a much sounder basis than is or can be any foundation alleged to exist outside the constitution of man in nature.

I do not suppose it is a matter merely of expediency or of policy in order to win adherents that results in keeping in the dim background the historic origin of the view that human nature is inherently too depraved to be trusted. But it is well to recall that its source is the Pauline (and Augustinian) interpretation of an ancient Hebrew legend about Adam and Eve in the Paradise of Eden. Adherents of the Christian faith who have been influenced by geology, history, anthropology, and literary criticism may prefer, quite understandably, to relegate the story to the field of symbolism. But the view that all nature is somehow thoroughly corrupted and that mankind is collectively and individually in a fallen estate is the only ground upon which there can be urged the necessity of redemption by extranatural means. And the diluted philosophic version of historic supernaturalism, which goes by the name of "metaphysical spiritualism" or "idealism," has no basis upon which to erect its "higher" nonnatural organs and faculties and the supernatural (if not supranatural) truths they are said to reveal, without a correspondingly pessimistic view of human nature in its natural estate.

III

I now come to the moral and social consequences that flow from a base and degrading view of nature in general and human nature in particular, a view which inheres in every variety of antinaturalistic philosophy. The whole tendency of this view has been to put a heavy discount upon resources potentially available for the betterment of human life. In the case of any candid clear-eyed person, it should be enough to ask some simple questions: What is the inevitable effect of holding that anything remotely approaching basic and serious amelioration of the human estate must be based upon means and methods that lie outside the scope of the natural? What is the result of believing that human capacities are so low that reliance upon them can only make things worse? Science cannot help; industry and commerce cannot help; political and jural arrangements cannot help; ordinary human affections, sympathies, and friendships cannot help. Place these natural resources under the terrible handicap put upon them by every mode of antinaturalism, and what is the outcome likely to be? Probably not that these things have in fact accomplished nothing, but that their operation is weakened and frustrated in just the degree in which supernaturalism prevails.

Take the case of science as a case of "natural" knowledge obtained by "natural" means and methods; the conclusion, from the extranaturalistic point of view, is that mere natural knowledge must be placed in the most disparaging opposition to a higher realm of truths accessible only to extranatural organs. Does anyone believe that where this climate of opinion prevails scientific method and conclusions reached by its use will do what they are capable of? Denial of reasonable freedom and attendant responsibility to any group produces conditions which can then be cited as reasons why the members of the group cannot be entrusted with freedom and be given responsibility. Similarly, the low estimate put upon science, the idea that because it is occupied with the natural world it is incapacitated from exercising positive influence upon values to which the adjectives "ideal" and "higher" (or any adjectives having favorable connotation) can be applied, tends to restrict and deflect its influence. The very fruit of antinaturalism is made the ground of attack upon naturalism.

If I stated that this low opinion of science tends to lower the intellectual standards of antinaturalists, to dull their sense of the importance of evidence, to blunt their sensitivity to the need of accuracy of statement, and to encourage substitution of emotional rhetoric for analysis and discrimination, I might seem to follow too closely the model set by the aspersions—such as those quoted—of antinaturalists. It may be said, in any case, that while some writers of the antinaturalistic school say a good deal, following Aristotle, about the "intellectual virtues," evidence is lacking that they are aware of the way in which the rise of scientific methods has enlarged the range and sharpened the edge of these excellencies. How could they be aware of it when it is a necessary part of their system to depreciate scientific method in behalf of higher methods of and organs for attaining the extranatural truths which are said to be of infinitely higher import?

Aside from displaying systematic disrespect for scientific method, supernaturalists deny the findings of science when the latter conflict with any of the dogmas of their creed. The story of the conflict of theology and science is the well-known result. This warfare is played down at the present time. But, as already indicated, its existence throws a flood of light upon the charge (brought in the manifesto previously quoted) that naturalists are those who are endangering free scholarship. Philosophic antinaturalists are ambiguous in their treatment of certain scientific issues. For example, scientific workers in the biological field are agreed in accepting some form of genetic development of all species of plants and animals, mankind included. This conclusion puts man definitely and squarely within the natural world. What, it may be asked, is the attitude of theological antinaturalists toward this conclusion? Do the men, for example, who sign a statement saying that naturalists regard man as "simply a highly developed animal," mean to deny the scientific biological conclusion? Do they hold that philosophical naturalism, not scientific inquiry, originated and upholds the doctrine of development? Or do they wish to take advantage of the word "animal" to present naturalistic philosophers in a bad light?

The latter accept without discount and qualification facts that are authenticated by careful and thorough inquiry. Hence they recognize in their full force all the observed facts which constitute the differences that exist between man and other animals as well as those facts which constitute strands of continuity between the different modes of living. The idea that there is anything in naturalism to prevent acknowledgment of differential traits in their full significance or to compel "reduction" to traits characteristic of worms, clams, cats, or monkeys has no foundation. This lack of foundation is probably the reason antinaturalist critics find it advisable to represent naturalism as simply a variety of materialism. Otherwise the view attributed to naturalism is simply an instance of a procedure too common in philosophical controversy: namely, representation of the position of an opponent in the terms it would have *if* the critic held it; that is, not in its own terms, but *after* translation into the terms of another and opposed theory has taken place. Upon the whole, nonsupernatural antinaturalists are in such a dilemma that we should extend sympathetic pity to them. If they present the naturalistic position in its own terms, they have to take serious account of scientific method and its conclusions. But in that case they will be imbued with some of the ideas of the very philosophy they are committed to attack. Under these circumstances the ambivalence of their own attitude is readily understood.

Lack of respect for scientific method, which after all is but systematic, extensive, and carefully controlled use of alert and unprejudiced observation and experimentation in collecting, arranging, and testing evidence, is attended by a tendency toward finalism and dogmatism. Nontheological antinaturalists would quite probably deny that their views are marked by that quality of fanaticism which has marked the supernatural brand. And they have not displayed it in anything like the same intensity. But from the standpoint of logic it must be said that their failure in this respect is more creditable to their hearts than to their heads. For it is an essential part of their doctrine that there stands above the inquiring, patient, ever-learning, and tentative method of science an organ or faculty which reveals ultimate and immutable truths and that apart from the truths thus obtained there is no sure foundation for morals or for a moral order of society. As one critic of naturalism remarked (somewhat naïvely), without such absolute and final truths there would be in morals merely the kind of certainty that exists in physics and chemistry.

Nontheological antinaturalists write and speak as if there were complete agreement on the part of all absolutists as to the specific content of their ultimate truths with respect to standards, rules, and ideals. Supernaturalists know better. The latter are aware of the conflict that exists; they are aware that conflict between truths claiming ultimate and complete authority is the most fundamental kind of discord that can possibly exist. Hence their claim to supernatural guidance, and hence their fanaticism in carrying on a campaign to wipe out heresies which are the more dangerous if they claim to rest on possession of ultimate truths. The members of nonsupernatural variety, in the more humane attitude they usually take, are living upon a capital inherited from the modern liberal developments they professedly repudiate. Were they to yield to the demands of logic, they would see how much more secure is the position of those who hold that given a body of ultimate and immutable truths, without which there is only moral and social confusion and conflict, a special institution is required to make known and to enforce these truths.

During periods in which social customs were static, when isolation of groups from one another was the rule, it was comparatively easy for men to live in complacent assurance as to the finality of their own practices and beliefs. That time has gone. The problem of attaining mutual understanding and a reasonable degree of amicable co-operation among different peoples, races, and classes is bound up with the problem of reaching by peaceful and democratic means some workable adjustment of the values, standards, and ends which are now in a state of conflict. Dependence upon the absolutist and totalitarian factor, which is involved in every form of antinaturalism, adds to the difficulty of this already extremely difficult undertaking.

To represent naturalistic morals as if they involved denial of the existence and legitimacy of regulative ends and standards is but another case of translation of a disliked position into the terms of the view held by its opponents. The idea that unless standards and rules are absolute, and hence eternal and immutable, they are not rules and criteria at all is childish. If there is anything confirmed by observation it is that human beings naturally cherish certain ends and relationships, that, in short, they naturally institute values. Having desires and having to guide their conduct by aims and purposes, nothing else is possible. But it is likewise an abundantly confirmed fact that standards and ends which are now influential grew up and obtained their effectiveness over human behavior in all sorts of relatively accidental ways, particularly under conditions of geographical isolation, social segregation, and absence of scientific method. These conditions no longer obtain. It requires a good deal of pessimism to assume that vastly improved knowledge of nature, human nature included, cannot be employed or will not be employed to render human relationships more humane, just, and liberal. The notion that such knowledge and such application, the things for which naturalism stands, will increase misunderstanding and conflict is an extraordinary reversed charge of what the dogmatic absolutism of appeal to extranatural authority has in fact sanctioned.

Reference to the pessimism which is involved reminds one of the chorus of voices now proclaiming that naturalism is committed to a dangerously romantic, optimistic, and utopian view of human nature. This claim might be looked upon as a welcome variation of the charge that naturalism looks upon everything human as "merely" animal. But it happens also to be aside from the mark. It is probably "natural" for those who engage in sweeping rationalistic generalizations to match their own pessimism by attributing an equally unrestrained optimism to their opponents. But since naturalists are committed to basing conclusions upon evidence, they give equal weight to observed facts that point in the direction of either nonsocial behavior or of amity and cooperation. In neither case, however, are the facts taken to be final and fixed; they are treated as indications of things to be done.

Naturalism is certainly hopeful enough to reject the view expressed by Cardinal Newman when he said: "She [the Church] regards this world and all that is in it, as dust and ashes, compared with the value of a single soul. . . . She considers the action of this world and the action of the soul simply incommensurate." Naturalism rejects this view, because the "soul" and its action are put in opposition as supernatural to a natural world and its action, the latter being regarded as thoroughly corrupt—because of supernatural causes. But naturalism does not fly to the opposite extreme. It holds to the possibility of discovering by natural means those conditions in human nature and in the environment which work concretely toward production of concrete forms of social health and social disease—just as the possibility of knowledge and of control in action by adequate knowledge are in process of actual demonstration in the case of medicine. The chief difficulty is that in social and moral matters we are twenty-five hundred years behind the discovery of Hippocrates as to the natural quality of the causes of disease and health and behind his dictum that all events are equally sacred and equally natural.

I mention one further instance of the contrast between the relative bearings of antinaturalism and naturalism. Because of the influence of a low view of human nature and of matter, a sharp line has been drawn and has become generally current between the economic and the moral

—and this in spite of facts which demonstrate that at present industry and commerce have more influence upon the actual relations of human groups to one another than any other single factor. Now the "economic" was marked off as a separate nonmoral compartment because, on the one hand, it was supposed to spring from and to satisfy appetites and desires that are bodily and carnal and because, on the other hand, it has to do with mere "matter."

Whether or not Karl Marx originated the idea that economic factors are the only ultimate causative factors in production of social changes, he did not originate the notion that such factors are "materialistic." He accepted that notion from the current classic Greek-medieval-Christian tradition. I know of no way to judge how much of the remediable harshness and brutal inhumanity of social relationships in their economic aspect is connected with denial of intrinsic moral significance to them. I do not mean that antinaturalism is the original source of the evils that exist. But I do mean that the attitude that whatever is natural is submoral (and in tendency antimoral) has a great deal to do with perpetuating an evil state of affairs, especially since we now have natural means at command for rendering the situation more humane. Moreover, on the political side we usually fail to note that so-called laissez-faire individualism, with its extreme separatism and isolationism of human beings from one another, is in fact a secularized version of the inheritance of a supernatural soul, the latter having intrinsic connection only with God.

Fear and hate for what is feared accompany situations of great stress and strain. The philosophic attempt to hold the rise of naturalism accountable for the evils of the present situation, to treat it as the ideological incarnation of the enemy democratic peoples are fighting, is accentuated by the emotional perturbations that attend the present crisis. Intense emotion is an all-or-none event. It sees things in terms of only the blackest black or the purest shining white. Hence it is that persons of scholastic cultivation can write as if brutality, cruelty, savage intolerance were unknown until the rise of the group of factors which constitute the grounds for naturalism. A *diabolus ex machina* is the emotionalized dramatic counterpart of the *deus ex machina* of supernaturalism. A naturalistic writer, being human, may yield to the influence of fear and hate. But to that extent he abandons his humanistic naturalism, for the latter calls for observation of concrete natural causal conditions as controls of emotions that are aroused and for projection of aims and methods that are consonant with the social conditions which inquiry discloses. His philosophy commits him to continued use of all the methods of intelligent action which are potentially available. It commits him to aversion to the escapism and defeatism that inhere in antinaturalism.

As the war is a global war, so the peace must be a peace that has respect for all the peoples and "races" of the world. I mentioned earlier the provincialism which leaves the non-Christians of the world, especially of Asia (and later Africa will come into the scene) outside the fold, which philosophical nonsupernaturalism admits within the truly human compass only upon conditions dictated by its own metaphysics. A philosophic naturalist cannot approve or go along with those whose beliefs and whose actions (if the latter cohere with their theories) weaken dependence upon the natural agencies, cultural, economic, scientific, political, by which a more humane and friendly world can alone be built. On the contrary, to him the present tragic scene is a challenge to employ courageously, patiently, persistently, and with wholehearted devotion all the natural resources that are now potentially at command. He cannot conceal, no matter how charitable his disposition, what antinaturalism does to check and hamper the use of means that are admitted to be the only ones actually within the power of human beings in their natural environment.

2

NATURALISM AND RELIGION

Sterling P. Lamprecht

A NATURALISTIC philosophy and a religious view of the world are often taken to be incompatible or alternative attitudes between which men must choose. In a sense this is doubtless true. At least, it is true when naturalism is the theory that a final and complete philosophy can be worked out in terms of physical atomism or of blind and unconscious forces; and it is likewise true when religion is identified with some particular set of beliefs which, arising in the context of some special historic culture, are laid down as an authoritative orthodoxy to which men's thinking must strictly conform. The warfare which has been waged between science and religion at certain periods of history has been due to the fact that a premature naturalism or an antiquated religion or both have been current. That warfare, however, is a wearisome conflict that belongs to only certain periods of history. It is not intrinsic to the nature of either the advance of science or the vitality of religion, and fortunately it seems rather outmoded in most quarters in our own day. It may, of course, break out again with renewed vigor. But it would seem to have been entirely due either to an immature naturalism that tried to encompass the vast and complicated texture of the system of nature in some simple formula or to a theology that scorned empirical investigation and chose rather to lay down a priori propositions for the control of men's thinking. Whatever weaknesses the contemporary scene may exhibit, there are both philosophical and religious forces today that are free from these excesses.

In broader senses of the terms, such as current usage would seem to warrant, naturalism and religion may be more compatible. But one must be cautious of these terms. The term "naturalism" is ordinarily used very vaguely and perhaps has no established meaning that all who dub themselves naturalists would agree to accept. Likewise the term "religion," as Professor Gilbert Murray has pointed out, can hardly be defined so as to indicate the essential nature of all the diverse materials to which it is normally applied. No attempt to enforce arbitrarily chosen definitions could hope to satisfy everyone. Yet for the purposes of this essay some preliminary indication may well be given of the meanings here assigned to the two terms.

Suffice it to say that in this essay "naturalism" means a philosophical position, empirical in method, that regards everything that exists or occurs to be conditioned in its existence or occurrence by causal factors within one all-encompassing system of nature, however "spiritual" or purposeful or rational some of these things and events may in their functions and values prove to be. There are, of course, equivocal words in this definition. Not all can be analyzed here, but three may receive some comment.

The word "empirical," for instance, contains multitudes of controversies. Some philosophers, seemingly intrigued by the prestige which the empirical tradition today enjoys, want to call themselves empiricists merely because they consent to reject those beliefs that can be shown to contradict ascertained facts. Others accept a kind of empiricism for purposes of scientific procedure and practical affairs, but all the time hold that the existences and occurrences thus empirically found require some further "explanation" to make them "satisfactory" or "intelligible." Neither of these groups of would-be empiricists is empirical enough. Members of the former group sometimes consider themselves entitled to accept all sorts of beliefs that rest on emotional preferences or a priori moral or aesthetic taste. Those in the latter group are too condescending in their empirical professions, making empiricism a derivative methodology that rests on what some romanticism leads them to feel "satisfactory" or on what some rationalism leads them to find "intelligible." Naturalists, it is here maintained, take the empirical method more seriously. They seek by discipline to distinguish the varying degrees of probability which ideas seem to have, to accept as beliefs only those ideas that are well accredited, and to entertain any further ideas only as hypotheses or hopes or fancies. They reject satisfaction as a requisite test for truth, except such satisfaction as is found in the discovery of the strict conformity of idea to ascertained fact. They may well find whatever exists or occurs to be intelligible; but they do not permit themselves to interpret intelligibility as consonance with "principles" adduced *ad hoc* or from beyond what is experienced. The naturalist may not find that the world satisfies all his wishes; but he would rather use facts to support his ideas than suppose some favored idea to be a support for the facts.

The word "conditioned" is also equivocal. The point intended in the definition is that a distinction must be made between the causal factors by which the origin of things is properly described and the values to which the same things lend themselves. When one has discovered a thing's causes, he has not necessarily determined its values. "A thing is what it is and not another thing," however it may have been produced. The qualitative nature of a thing is what empirically it is found to be,[1] even though its causes were of different qualitative character. Life and purpose and beauty and knowledge have their conditions, that is, can occur only within certain types of situation and as the result of suitable efficient causes; but these efficient causes may not be living or purposeful or admirable or cognitive. It is a mistake, according to naturalism as here defined, to demote a result because its cause was lowly; it is likewise a mistake to attribute to causes the excellences of the effects. It is unjustified dogma to suppose with the Cartesian tradition that an effect may not contain more "perfection" than its cause. Materialists tend to slight many things because their origin lies in "matter in motion." Idealists tend to romanticize about ontological forces because their outcomes are often, or at least occasionally, of high moral or aesthetic value. Naturalists endeavor to avoid both errors by recognizing the validity of, but difference between, causal explanation and moral worth of things and events. What conditions a thing is not the measure of its value.

Then there is the word "system." The naturalist is not pledged to any particular theory of the degree of systematic connection among things and events. We find connections of many sorts, some close and others remote. In stating that the system of nature is all-encompassing, no supposition was intended to the effect that the world is a deductive system in which each part is related by implication to all other parts. The phrase "all-encompassing system" was used chiefly for negative reasons. Naturalists, both historically and also in contemporary discussion, have found it necessary to reject certain views which seem to them destructive of a sound position and hence have often had to be primarily negative in their preliminary approach. Naturalists, as the term is here employed, are opposed to all dualisms—Cartesian, Lockian, or such as "critical realism" offers—and to all subjectivisms that treat experience

---

[1] The nature of anything may, of course, be, and probably always is, much more than it is empirically found to be. But the point of the argument is that everything is at least what it is given as in experience.

as a private affair and thus make the very existence of an "external" world or objective order a matter of doubt. One can distinguish citrous fruits, for example, from all other things, or mental activity from purely spatial displacement. But such distinctions are hardly valid grounds for "dualisms." While no one has built up a dualism on the basis of the unique quality of citrous fruits, many have done so on the basis of the unique character of mental activity or mind. We empirically find both mind and matter, both ideas and things, both reflection and blind impulse; but the world still remains an interrelated whole without intrusions from some other "realm" or bifurcations or ontological gulfs. To suppose that mind, because it is distinguishable from matter and distinctive in its essential nature, did not have an origin in natural events antecedent to it, is to become at once mythological, to appeal to what has no possible empirical support, to turn the quality of an effect into an operating cause behind the effect. Naturalism is systematic therefore in this exact sense: that it would explain mind or purposiveness or any other thing or event or quality in the same way in which it would explain cyclones or wars or northern lights. One may often lack an explanation of some thing or event, as may indeed be the case with northern lights; but lack of explanation is surely not to be turned into an excuse for alleging a nonnatural origin. Piety toward some precious existence and reverence before some fine event may at times add to the beauty and the moral worth of men's lives. But as soon as such piety and reverence lead men to attribute an effect to an origin outside the natural world, they become deplorable occasions for obscurantism.

Religion is a term equally difficult to define without neglecting some of its frequent usages. But for the purposes of this essay it may be given a precise meaning. The religious life is here taken to mean a life in which multiple interests and diverse values are brought into effective and organic unity through central allegiance to some integrating ideal. Religion may at times mean more, and these further meanings may well be desirable in other contexts. But the sense here employed is one which both historically and philosophically seems legitimate. Life may at times be comparatively aimless, when men drift with changing currents and seek in turn incompatible ends. But men have often had some commitment to ends of allegedly supreme worth, some attitude which expresses their final loyalties, some set of dominant values (good or bad, as the case may be) to which they pay great devotion. When this happens, life is being lived on what is here meant by the religious level. At times religious devotion may be so extreme as to lead men to narrow their aspirations to some single aim which, even if legitimate, is not extensive with the moral possibilities they might well seek to attain; the religious life then becomes rigid, harsh, and even fanatic. But at its best the religious life is a kind of fulfillment of life's most urgent moral needs. The religious life is almost wholly a human characteristic; if it occur in partial form among beings other than human, it is (however interesting to students of comparative psychology) of slight general significance. But among men it is of great significance; it is that which, more, perhaps, than any other characteristic, is a distinguishing trait of human existence. Historically all societies of men have been largely molded by religious forces, and most individuals have shown the effect in their single lives of religious orientation. One may fairly say that the religious life, as here defined, is the measure of the worth which men have thought and hoped they could give to their lives.

The religious life in some gifted and inventive men has been in part a personal adventure. But normally it is found, like every important phase of human existence, embodied in institutions and built into the social forms through which men transmit to succeeding generations their customs, their purposes, their beliefs, and their sentiments. It is historically one of the most definitive phases of any human culture. It has been so dominating a phase that normally it is the phase by which we must seek to understand and appraise any culture as a whole. In it are expressed the regulative principles by which other phases of life are brought into some sort of adjustment to each other and are given their relative importance. It has been one of the most persistent and potent means by which successive generations have sought to maintain, transmit, and regularize the structural pattern of their entire culture. It has made its sponsors regard certain purposes and certain values as vital and real even without actual investigation of the degree of vitality and the genuineness of reality which those purposes and those values might justifiably be deemed to possess. Inspiring men to high endeavor, it yet often fastens upon them constraints that hinder them from further and perhaps higher values, even if it also subjects them to discipline that saves them from gross vices and stupidly parochial ambitions. Like every other phase of human existence, it is capable of both noble fulfillment and debasing use. Just as the advance of natural science, for instance, has both good and bad consequences, so with religion. The advance of science may release human energies from confinement to necessary but dull routine and open the way to participation in the various arts of civilized life (including the further advance of science itself); it may also be perverted into a technique of destruction, destruction of many homely arts that are superior to the machine processes that sweep them away, destruction even of the peaceful order that is one of the most essential prerequisites for civilization. So religion may enlighten and instruct and civilize hordes of men who otherwise would be without effective control, without noble impetus, without refinement of ideas or ideals; it may also frustrate men's lives by turning them to purely imaginary ends, vain hopes, false beliefs, and futile ambitions. "Religion" and "religious" ought never to be used as terms of eulogistic import; they are descriptive terms, indicative of a way in which human life may be organized around a dominating interest or unified set of interests. Whether the interests are genuinely good or bad, whether human life is thereby enriched or impoverished, whether, then, religion is uplifting or degrading,—these are further considerations which ought to be empirically determined in each case. No presumption ought to be entertained that the "religious" is the excellent any more than that all ideas are true or all social institutions are beneficial.

When just now a definition of religion was offered in terms of a certain way of living, no disparagement was intended of the doctrinal or credal developments which naturally occur in conjunction with the leading of the religious life. To define religion as a way of life is not an indication of anti-intellectualism. This point is worth some emphasis, just because there is much nonsense spoken and written today to the effect that we need more religion and less theology. Whether we need more religion or not depends upon the merits of the religion proffered. But at least we do not need less theology; rather we need better theology. Perhaps in a narrow (but etymologically justified) sense of the term "theology," a better theology would cease altogether to be theology. For it is a moot point (and one to which we shall return below) whether belief in God or gods or divine beings of any kind is warranted. And if theology be used to mean such belief together with its grounds and implications and systematized developments, then theology might need to be discarded. There need be no quarrel over words at this point. But it seems linguistically justified to retain the word "theology" in a broader sense than its etymological sense. Contemporary usage would certainly seem to warrant the employment of the term "theology" for any serious, thoughtful, sincere theorizing about the presuppositions, nature, and consequences of the religious way of life. If religion be a way of life, theology would, then, be the theory that explains and seeks to justify that way. But at least some intellectual clarification is demanded for the religious life, whether it be called theology or cosmology or philosophy of religion. All human attitudes, all human ideals and aspirations, all programs of action involve correlative beliefs, and these beliefs, when carefully formulated and maturely grasped, may be legitimately called doctrines (a word that has unjustly been handled with disparagement, as if it were a mark of arrogance to know what one really means or to say what one really believes). Any separation of the intellectual life from its requisite context in affairs is disastrous. It is, indeed, doubly disastrous. On the one hand it leaves practice to unregulated impulse and vain endeavor; on the other hand it so isolates intellect from the materials it would understand as to make it issue in futile fancies instead of sound knowledge. The intellectual life, in the sense of a life in which men seek sophisticatedly to understand what they are doing, why they are doing it, how they are thereby related to other things in the world around them, and what the grounds and consequences of their actions are,—the intellectual life in this sense is the only life which can be thoroughly and adequately good. The last statement may seem extreme; but it could not be challenged except on the theory that ignorance is bliss. Many men may lead lives that could not, under the above statement, be considered to illustrate the intellectual life, and these lives may be moderately decent, good to a degree, worthy of some modicum of praise and emulation. The contention made here is that none of these lives is as good as it would be if it were also raised to the level of the intellectual life.

Theology, then, in the sense of an effort to understand the grounds and consequences of the religious life, is a development without which the religious life is not merely incomplete but also seriously stunted. People today often enjoy collecting specimens of religion (perhaps under the influence of William James's indiscriminate enthusiasm for bizarre and exotic religious ideas and experiences) as others collect marriage customs or burial rites, and yet regard it as "academic" to inquire into the intellectual validity of the specimens collected. A few decades ago the study of religion needed to turn from exclusive pre-occupation with religious ideas to an examination of the rituals and other practices of which the ideas were the outcome; but the study of religion today needs to avoid the notion that only rituals are important and ideas may be ignored. Religion is more than quaint acts and picturesque ceremonies. It goes on in a world of which it comes to offer an interpretation, and in the light of the truth or error of this interpretation, as well as in the light of the benefit or harm of its practices, it must in the last analysis be judged.

The current disregard of the intellectual import of religion has been furthered by, perhaps occasioned by, a too-easy and insufficiently informed pragmatism. Ideas, we are told, are tools for action, the significance of which lies in the specific successes or failures to which they lead. Whether this statement is sound or unsound depends upon what is meant by specific successes and failures. Certainly one of the specific results to which the use of ideas as tools may lead is a general understanding, an increasingly adequate general understanding of the nature of that world within which action occurs and ideas serve as tools. Intelligence can do more than formulate ideas for immediate practice: it may succeed in gaining, as reflection occurs upon the entire course of using ideas in practice, an understanding of what the world in part is. Men ought to seek, in religion as in commerce or politics or art or agriculture, to formulate in explicit and clear fashion the beliefs which their practices imply, demand, and justify. However instrumental ideas may be in furthering effective action, ideas are also, certainly when sound and perhaps at certain times when not altogether sound, among the final goods and intrinsically valuable ends which men are entitled to seek, to possess, to enjoy. We do not merely entertain ideas in order to gain special ends, though this is true enough so far as it goes; we also find that one of the consequences of gaining special ends (even when, as is normal for most men, these special ends do not deliberately include the acquisition of true ideas) is the clarification of mind and increase of knowledge that may yet ensue. Life well lived is always the intellectual life, even if the intellectual life is not always well lived. Tentative ideas, entertained as leads in inquiry, may grow into world-views, into theologies or cosmologies; they may thus become an effective insight into some large section or important aspect of the world of which men and ideas are parts, but which stretches far beyond the immediate and the local. Understanding may never be adequate to the vastness of the world: it may remain sorely incomplete even when sound in its partial advance. But if taken with humility and not turned into an allegedly final and exhaustive account of the nature of things, it may yet be one of man's noblest achievements. And so, to return to the theme of this paper, religion ought never to be extolled while doctrine and belief are slighted. Rather, religion as a way of life requires doctrine and belief as among the fulfillments without which religion is not found in a wholly legitimate form. Surely, if religion be taken in the sense above defined, there is no phase of life which more urgently needs competent intellectual treatment. There is no phase of life which men more urgently need to free from error and to understand in its implications than that phase in which organization and effective centering are given to all the other phases of life.

The fact remains, however, that the religious way is chronologically and logically prior to theology and to any development of belief or doctrine which is formulated as explanation and justification of that way. It is chronologically prior, because it is what animates men to think along such lines. It is logically prior, because thinking does not occur in a rationalistic vacuum, but requires a subject-matter to which it is pertinent and with which it may be concerned. Thinking may, indeed ordinarily does, produce data which, once produced, belong to the texture of its subject-matter. This last fact the instrumentalists have well established. Instrumentalism, however, cannot properly be given an idealistic turn. If data are produced by the course of reflection, it does not follow that in general subject-matter is a consequence of reflection. Subject-matter is enlarged, is transformed, is significantly amplified, by reflection. But reflection, at each of its stages, rests on the subject-matter already at hand, even if at each stage it also participates in the creative production of the subject-matter with which some later stage may then be concerned. If the theological or doctrinal outcome of the religious way transforms the future course of that way (promoting it, perhaps, altering it often, annulling it sometimes by negative conclusions), it is yet a consequence of the initial occurrence of the activities and practices of the religious way in its earlier forms.

This relationship between the religious way, on the one hand, and doctrinal theories or beliefs, on the other, is what warrants Santayana's contention, now familiar in its phraseology, if not always grasped in its author's due intent, that religion contains two distinguishable elements, a moral consciousness and a poetic or mythological conception of things. The moral consciousness is the embracing purpose, the unifying ideal aspiration, whereby life becomes significantly centered and without which life cannot properly be called religious at all. The embracing purpose is not, of course, necessarily good. One has only to recall the nature of the religious life in its historical occurrences to realize that the moral consciousness is often vicious as well as often uplifting. Religion, in this its fundamental aspect, needs constant criticism, just as does every political program, every economic proposal, every social effort of any kind. Not simply may a religious ideal suitable for one culture and one situation be undesirable in another culture and another situation, but also the most admirable religious ideal which history discloses may yet fall short of the best potentialities of its own time and place. To say that religion embodies a moral consciousness is not to say that religion is of high moral worth; it is rather to say that religion has grave consequences for moral concerns. Religion must always be taken seriously, even if it can seldom be endorsed as morally adequate.

The poetic or mythological conception of things is the theological apologetic or doctrinal development to which the occurrence of the religious way leads men. The phrase Santayana uses, however happily coined for those who know his literary approach and philosophical background, has often been misunderstood. Many impatient readers, wanting only a defense for their own doctrines, have taken Santayana to be mocking their earnestness. There is no mocking intended. Were mocking intended, the phrase might still be not wholly unfair; for the most devout upholder of a fixed credal commitment must yet recognize the absurd and ridiculous tenets of many barbarous or crude religious beliefs. There is delicate appraisal rather than mocking in Santayana's phrase. Santayana's remark here, as often elsewhere, is deeply Platonic in its literary as well as philosophical affiliations. Plato uses "myths" without any implication of slight or scorn. The *Phaedrus* myth of the charioteer with his white and black steeds, the myth of Ur in the *Republic*, the scientific myth of the *Timaeus*, these and other myths are among Plato's moments of most crucial import. Words fail, and meanings cannot be literally set forth; but, as Plato himself says repeatedly, we may believe that some such thing as the myth suggests is true until we have a better form of stating things. The myth is not a finally satisfactory statement; but it appears to express, if not the true nature of things, at least some role which things play in human experience, some role which things seem to assume in human imagination. Exactly such are all human theologies. Unverified, yet cherished, they reflect more of the manner in which adherents approach the world than of the manner in which the world, independent of the human imagination, is constituted. They would, if true, justify their adherents in continuing to approach the world as these adherents are doing; but only time and experimental inquiry can justify the approach or serve through discipline to correct it.

The term "poetic" in Santayana's usage also echoes Plato. But possibly it is more directly related to Matthew Arnold. Theology and religious beliefs generally are poetic, not in the sense of being merely pretty fancies or felicitous phrases, but in Arnold's sense of poetry as "the criticism of life." To formulate a theology is to put into definite statement the propositions presupposed by and involved in a religious attitude. To submit such propositions to one's own scrutiny and others' examination is to begin to get beyond blind assumption and to initiate a critical standpoint. Every doctrine and belief is in this sense a criticism of some way of living or of some alleged existential things with which in the course of living men have come in contact. Even when beliefs are so tenaciously held as to be called dogmas, they still play the same poetic role. To speak of religion in terms of poetry is not to disparage religion, but to amplify the idea of poetry. That many critics of Santayana (including the late Paul Elmer More, whose tributes to Plato and respect for poetry ought to have safeguarded him against this error) have quite missed the point is evidence of partisan zeal rather than literary and philosophical acumen on the part of the critics. And one further remark ought here to be added. It is only when one properly grasps the poetic nature of religious beliefs that one can have a tolerable respect for many curious notions with which the historical study of religions acquaints us. The belief in the animal gods of ancient Egypt, the superstitions connected with primitive vegetation-cults, the eschatological pronouncements of many bizarre groups of former times and even of our own day, the ascetic convictions of many wild hermits,—these and other such notions too numerous to be listed are, when viewed externally and in isolation from the practices which gave rise to them, so much intellectual nonsense. As myths and poetry, however, they reveal both the pathos of certain phases of human life and the character of certain human aspirations. The study of the history of religions has usually been far too unsympathetic: it has not put religious beliefs properly into their context as by-products of the practices and purposes that antedate them. Taken as poetry, they would gain in dignity, even if, merely as beliefs, they continued to seem to many persons both barbarous and false.

It was said above that the older forms of naturalism were hostile to religion. Those older forms were sometimes, as in Herbert Spencer, militantly agnostic; but the agnosticism came from philosophical traditions that were not attached, except by historical accident, to the naturalistic approach. In spite of the well-known title of a book by the late James Ward, naturalism and agnosticism have no essential connections with each other. Naturalists ought properly to reject any general agnosticism. Though as free as any men to grant that there is much men do not know, they are surely pledged to support the position that men can gain a good deal of knowledge of nature. Another and older form of naturalism was, as in some of the French Encyclopaedists, aggressively atheistic; but the atheism was here almost an a priori dogma, with its animating force in antiecclesiastical social reasons, rather than a carefully established empirical conclusion. Again, and particularly in the last few decades, antireligious forms of naturalism were framed in terms of a contrast between the aspirations of men, which were said to be as futile as they were noble, and the ways of nature, which were said to be as destructive as they were indifferent. There has been much in this last kind of naturalism to appeal to certain minds, especially youthful minds: it is at least heroic in its defiances and uncompromising in its battle against cruelty and oppression. In its finest expression this type of naturalism is to be found in Huxley's deservedly famous essay *Evolution and Ethics;* and in a more flamboyant expression it appears in Bertrand Russell's equally well-known essay *A Free Man's Worship.* These and other such writings have given rise to a widely entertained supposition that naturalism is committed to the idea of "an alien world" in which ideals are sure to be crushed by "the trampling march of unconscious power." This view is no more an integral part of a sound naturalism than are militant agnosticism and aggressive atheism. But its associations with naturalism have recently been so close that it perhaps requires more extended treatment.

However naturalism be defined, it ought certainly to involve the position that man and his ways (including his moral aspirations and his rationally formulated ideals) are as "natural" as lightning and its ways, or as sunshine and its ways. Lightning is surely not to be contrasted with an alien world around it just because it distinctively differs from, perhaps, everything else in its surroundings; and sunshine is surely not to be regarded as imprisoned in a world indifferent to it because darkness and icy winds work to produce certain effects that run counter to its effects. Nature is full of contrasts and surprises. But at least nature is such that man has come about in the course of time, whatever his antecedents or causes; and man, once he appears, and like everything else, is part and parcel of nature. Certain things in nature threaten man's security, as indeed one man often threatens the security of his fellows. Certain other things in nature sustain, support, validate man's growth and purposes, as indeed men often work to each other's advantage and benefit. It is easy to say that man is a child of nature; but the remark is not particularly enlightening, because the same might be said of all other living things. Moreover, living things are "children" of nature in only the sense in which all things, nonliving as well as living, occur within the texture of conditions and causes that are requisite for their occurrence. The world may well be "alien" to some purposes and congenial to others. But to speak of the world as "alien" in some absolute sense is nonsense. The world is alien only to a point of view or an ambition or an interest; and surely the instruction of experience is that men ought to learn to take, then, some other point of view, to adopt some other ambition, to cherish some other interest. To hold rigorously to what is not possible in the kind of world in which we occur and our acts must therefore be performed is a mark, not of exalted morality that is "too good" for the natural realm, but of immature folly that has not yet discovered what morality really is. Morality is not like the pose of a melodramatic actor who learns his lines before he faces his audience and feels the audience to be hostile if they do not applaud him; it is rather the facing of actual situations as they confront us and of meeting the exigencies of those situations in the best ways in which we can handle them. The ethical implications of a theory of an "alien" world are that ideals are a priori in origin, that their validity does not depend upon their effectiveness in practice, and hence that they are not really the technique for the guidance of men living the good life. These ethical implications of the theory are as fantastic as the initial ontological suppositions that nature and man are alien to one another.

It is only fair to recognize, however, a residual element in the historical, if inadequate, expressions which have from time to time been given to the naturalistic standpoint. Naturalism must, in all its expressions, valid as well as invalid, so interpret the world as to make it seem "alien" to a certain type of theological commitment that is common to most established religious traditions of our Western culture. That is, naturalism makes the world seem "alien" to those whose beliefs center in a theistic interpretation of the world. In first saying this, however, one ought to guard against such overstatement concerning the theistic hypothesis as has been indulged in by many "naturalists." Not infrequently naturalists have been prone to toss off the remark that the existence of God is quite unimportant one way or the other. Such is surely not the case, and the allegation is fair to neither theism nor naturalism. Had man an ally of vast power to secure the victory of his ideals, had he an understanding companion in his sorrows, had he a guide to impose needed discipline upon his impulses, he ought to welcome such and to deem it of great worth. Men seek human allies and friends and are often brave enough to respect human judges and guides; and the divine would be as much more welcome than the human as the lasting is better than the transient or the strong is better than the weak. Theism is therefore a matter of great moment; and only the premature zeal of nontheists could dismiss it as of minor concern.

The existence of God therefore deserves the fairest consideration. But existence is always a matter of fact rather than a function of desire, whether it be God's existence or any other existence that is being investigated. And in considering the question, it is important to remark at the outset that the phrase "the existence of God" is highly ambiguous. The phrase has meant many different things to many different people. The presence of equivocation in the phrase is doubtless due to the curious fact that many who doubt the more traditional views yet wish to retain the term God in some Pickwickian sense, because of linguistic piety or timidity in acknowledging their honest views; but such linguistic warping of established usage is of questionable propriety. Of course there can be no review in one paper, there could hardly be review in a long book, of all the forms of theistic theory that have been proffered.

There seem, however, to be three meanings of the term that recur most frequently and so deserve attention here.

In the major sense of our Western culture God has been conceived as a person. This is properly to be called the anthropomorphic conception of God, though adherents of this theory often reject the term out of fear that whatever is anthropomorphic is superstitious. Even when God is conceived as a person, however, there are many different possibilities of regarding him. Some conceive him as omnipotent, some as limited in power; some as creator, some as "carpenter" or operator upon independently existing materials; some as omniscient, some as growing into fuller knowledge; some as having sentiments and feelings, some as a purely intellectual type of mind. But all theories of God as a person seem at least to attribute to him the power to act; to be a person is also surely to be an agent who does things. What he is supposed to do will vary with the defenders of the theory. In some of the old statements of deism, for instance, God is supposed merely to have started off the world long ago and then retired from the scene; but more commonly, both before and since the vogue of deism, men have believed in a theory of "particular providence," according to which God is continually acting so as to redirect the course of events in ways in which events would not occur without his special actions. Perhaps the most frequently held view is an evasive middle position that leaves the degree of God's activity too undefined to be pinned down in controversy. The last remark is unfair to the more orthodox theologians who stem from the scholastic tradition and still work to give precise definitions; but at least it applies to many so-called "liberal" theologians of contemporary Protestant groups.

The existence of God in the sense of a person is an open possibility. Whether God so defined exists or does not exist can be decided only by evidence. From the standpoint of any naturalism (and of a good many other philosophies too) all matters of existential status can be determined by no other than uncompromisingly empirical means. Measured by this test, the three traditional arguments for the existence of God and a current argument based on William James's will-to-believe all seem to fail to meet the requirement of empirical evidence. And these four arguments, though far from being all that might be listed, are the leading types of argument except that from revelation, which of course begs the point at issue at the outset. The three traditional arguments mentioned are the ontological, the cosmological, and the teleological. The ontological argument, rejected as unconvincing by even Saint Thomas, does not even claim to be empirical. The cosmological argument rests on the supposition that where there is order there is manifestation of mind; but for that supposition there is no empirical evidence, and indeed the supposition, being highly general, is more doubtful than the conclusion it is designed to support. The teleological argument depends considerably on the cosmological argument (as both Hume and Kant pointed out) or on a fundamental confusion between two quite different meanings of "purpose"—purpose as design or intent or plan, and purpose as utility or harmony or adaptation. The will-to-believe argument is both the weakest and yet the most popular today (which is in itself a commentary on the decadence of theology in our own time). William James said (in his reply to the questionnaire that Professor Pratt sent out many years ago and again in some of his books) that he believed in God because he needed some assurance that his own causes would triumph. Others follow the same type of argument when they assert that the existence of God is required in order to make the world "rational" or "satisfactory" or "intelligible." But in these last cases the rationality or satisfactoriness or intelligibility is required only to make it possible to carry out some other beliefs consistently, and these other beliefs (though the horde of them could not be considered here) are usually adduced arbitrarily and *ad hoc* and may be unsound when put to any empirical test. It is, perhaps, true that certain people find it psychologically requisite to believe in God, also that certain philosophical assumptions require the existence of God in order to be rounded out in a systematic way. But the entire will-to-believe argument is romanticism, not empiricism. Hume and Kant both dealt effectively with most of these considerations; and the repetition of the arguments since their time is evidence of the persistence of old beliefs and of the pathos of human hopes, but hardly of what is really at stake, namely, proof of the existence of God.

The influence of William James upon "liberal" theology has been so marked that it deserves further comment. James, it ought never to be forgotten, came to philosophy from psychology, and to psychology from medicine. He was fundamentally concerned, in a large part of his work and especially in his earlier work, to help people to live vigorously, optimistically, dynamically. He had many other interests, too, and an unswerving loyalty to truth. He shows, particularly in his later writings, a desire to work out the implications of a frank and unmitigated empirical method in handling all philosophical questions. But he never outgrew entirely an anxious concern for the noncognitive functions of ideas and beliefs. His was a therapeutic attitude. As a result, his writings are infested with many romantic elements. Without any evidence at all (unless one accepts as evidence the subjective fancies and cravings of abnormal people), he yet encouraged others to indulge in belief in "an unseen order" or a "spiritual world" that surrounds the natural order, if thereby they could gain the courage to face life's problems with resolute cheerfulness and heightened courage. Santayana may be correct in his comment that James "did not really believe; he merely believed that one had the right to believe that he might be right if he believed." More probably James believed at some times, in some moods, and for some purposes, and did not believe at other times, in other moods, and for other purposes. In any case, what kept his romanticism from becoming capricious and preserved the high moral integrity of the man was his personal quality rather than his philosophical tendencies. In other hands the consequences of the will-to-believe attitude has become more apparent. One might say, if willing to risk overstatement such as most sharp antitheses involve, that whereas Santayana's philosophy shows men how to live a spiritual life in a natural world, James's influence has been to encourage men to live a natural life in a spiritual world. James's influence has been to lead religious leaders to suppose that they can neglect objective evidence and rely on "deep feelings," which, they are prone to contend, cannot lead them astray. Thus we hear today in many quarters that whatever makes for man's emotional ease or comfort is true, or as "good as true," or at least worthy of being believed. There is here no facing of facts, no discipline in reflection, no recognition of intellectual standards. The older "dogmatic theology" seems by contrast a highly respectable affair; for there is always the open possibility that an alleged revelation is a genuine revelation and that a faith that claims no verification is yet a true faith. James, in spite of his charm and stimulus to philosophy in the United States, has also led to a serious decline in theological education. His formula that ideas are true if they work has become in other hands the apologetic that ideas may be believed if they please. How they please, and whether such pleasure as they bring is a licit pleasure in a world that cannot long be ignored without disaster, are questions that are often slighted.

A second sense in which the existence of God is affirmed is that God is the timeless ground of the temporal world. This is the position of Saint Thomas; it has been presented recently by Professor Whitehead and Professor A. E. Taylor. The world is contingent, so the argument runs; and the contingent necessarily involves some necessary ground relatively to which it is contingent. Now there is great authority in the tradition that so treats the theistic question. But in spite of the respect due its defenders, the argument does not seem empirically warranted. Every existence is contingent for its production upon both the materials that lend themselves to its production and also the efficient causes capable of so treating those materials as to bring about its production. Every event, as well as every existence, is contingent; for, however necessary it may be for us to accept events after they have occurred and to face them frankly for what they are as they are occurring, they are still, in advance of their occurrence, only among the possibilities that might happen contingently upon the prior occurrence of other requisite events. All this seems to be true, and an account of the world without recognition of contingency would be quite inadequate. But to go from existences and events that are contingent to an entire world that is contingent seems difficult and may be an instance of the fallacy of composition. At least it seems questionable whether the world-as-a-whole can ever be the subject of empirically justifiable propositions. We know what we mean by contingency, because we can point to many instances of it and then can define the characteristics of those instances by virtue of which they are so designated. But, applied to the world-as-a-whole, the word "contingency" (like any other word) is of dubious significance or perhaps of no significance. One might apply here the same sort of criticism that Hume in his *Dialogues concerning Natural Religion* applied effectively to the cosmological argument. As Hume pointed out, we can go from effects to their causes, when instructed sufficiently by experience, and we can likewise go from causes to effects; but the causes and effects we can handle in our reasonings are all specific causes and effects within the world. No one, he pointed out, knows just what is meant by the statement that the world-as-a-whole is an effect; and therefore one can hardly pass from the world-as-a-whole, taken as being an "effect," to some alleged cause that lies back of or beyond it.

Moreover, and even if one waives what has just been said, the necessary ground of the contingent world (whatever that phrase may mean) can hardly be said to exist. There may be some totality of truth of which the world is the expression, or some set of first principles of which the world is the development, or some system of "universals" of which the world, in Plato's language, is the "imitation" or in which the world "participates." But to identify God with such entities is hardly to have an existent God, and surely it is not to have a God of the qualities and character which religious men are prone to attribute to God. Professor Whitehead, it is only fair to add, does not treat God as an object of religious concern, but only as a metaphysical principle. But ordinarily advocates of this type of theistic argument do proceed from what strictly their argument would, if sound, enable them to conclude to a further elaboration of the conclusion such as nothing in the argument suggests to be in any way relevant or pertinent.

A third sense in which the existence of God is asserted is that God is an ideal or a supreme value. Naturalism and many other philosophies might well assent to what is in this case asserted. But it must be pointed out again that the language is hardly suited to the meaning intended. Santayana has said that "the existence of God is in one sense obvious and in another sense of no religious interest." Dissent has already been expressed earlier in this paper to the second part of Santayana's remark; for Santayana means to deny that the existence of God as a personal being and a great power in the world would be of religious interest, and such unconcern, as has been said above, is hardly warranted. The first part of his remark, however, is true enough; for he is meaning that God as a Platonic form or set of moral ideals is real as all ideal possibilities are real and can hardly be denied in that sense by those who understand what is meant. But, if the point be granted, the language used by Santayana and often similarly employed by many others seems undesirable. God in this sense does not "exist"; that is, God in this sense is not meant to be taken as anything within the spatial-temporal world of which alone "existence" can be affirmed. And just as it is linguistically undesirable to speak of existence in this way, so it may well be urged that it is undesirable to speak of God in this way. There is slight, if any, fault to be found with Santayana's remark in the context in which it occurs; for all that is here said is there indicated. But there is much reason to find fault with others who use similar phrases in other contexts, because these others often bank on the equivocation of their language to mislead their hearers or readers and to gain for their views the authority of the theistic tradition in its more normal sense. Of course language is fluid and may be used in many ways: as Hobbes said, "words are wise men's counters." But we reason by the instrumentality of words, both in making our own ideas clear to ourselves and in conveying our meanings to others. In case one wished to affirm that there is some significant ideal—nonexistent, but morally and religiously authoritative, a fairer statement of the position would explicitly avoid the phrase "the existence of God" and would employ other language less likely to be misunderstood. It would be much more fair as well as much more clear to say that whether God does or does not exist, we human beings yet have supreme values to cherish and noble ideals to pursue.

Whether naturalists generally will agree with the preceding paragraphs in detail or not, all will probably reject the arguments for the existence of God as failing in empirical warrant. Though God may exist, the arguments are all weak and evidence is lacking. Naturalism does not stand or fall with rejection of the arguments for the existence of God; indeed, its general theses would remain intact if God were discovered to exist, just as they remain intact when any other existence is discovered. But naturalism does stand or fall with its acceptance of a strictly empirical method and its refusal to believe a matter of great moment when no evidence can be found. Naturalism is certainly no more concerned to disprove the existence of God than to disprove the existence of another planet in the solar system. But as naturalism would rebel against the vain instructions that we human beings set our clocks by the movements of an undiscovered planet, so it rebels against the claim that life ought to be centered in and guided by divine will or providence. Until and unless the existence of God is shown by empirical evidence to be probable, it is not an article by which human values and human ideals may be significantly determined or advanced or enforced.

No more immoral advice could be given to our time than the not-infrequently uttered exhortation of some popular preachers that morality would be a sham unless God exists. Naturalists, like any other persons, might well grant that morality might be in some respects revised if the existence of God were known. If God exists, his will is either in accord with what is right for men to do on grounds independent of his existence, or it is not so in accord. In the former case, knowledge of his existence would have no bearing on the content of moral principles, but would add, at least for many people, certain religious sanctions. In the latter case, knowledge of his existence would change the content of moral principles; but to what extent and in what ways, it is useless to consider until both his existence and his will come to be known. Meanwhile, men continually have to act, and they may act rightly or wrongly, from sound ideals or from spurious ideals. To tell them that life has no meaning without belief in the existence of God, or to tell them that ideals are futile in a world in which God does not exist, is to throw away moral certainties [2] and moral probabilities in order to try by that absurd means to inveigle people into accepting a theology for which there is no evidence. Morality, in its vital matters, is much more certain and much more basic than any theological doctrine, true or false. We may remain uncommitted on the theory of the existence of God, without being in any way troubled about many important values and aims of human life.

Two points may receive brief concluding notice. These may both be stated without any attempt in this paper to build up a religious point of view, to state the principles by which life for men generally may be richly integrated, to seek to establish the truth of any set of ideals through which unity and harmony may prevail for any single man or any large society. There are many such religious points of view, and there will doubtless be more if human civilization endures. One has only to turn to the great religious leaders of the past and to the great institutionalized traditions built thereon. Or, if these be suspect because of their dependence or seeming dependence upon doctrinal definitions that lack empirical warrant, one may turn to other sources and suggestions. Santayana has summed up the virtues of the religious life in terms of piety, spirituality, and charity. Professor Whitehead has summed them up in terms of beauty, knowledge, peace, and adventure. Similar statements can and doubtless will appear many times. But it is fair to recognize that the doctrinal conclusions to which naturalists will be led by the course of their experience (religious and of other kinds) will probably be less picturesque, less dramatic, less immediately appealing to many men than the doctrines of the great traditional religions. Likewise, it is fair to add that these doctrinal conclusions may be more empirically warranted, more immediately fruitful in their bearing on affairs, more practical in

---

[2] "Certainties" may be a word that jars on the ears of many empiricists and naturalists. If so, it may be said that it is here used to mean the conclusions that are so well tested that they seem to be settled.

their significant interrelatedness to our knowledge of the world and of man's potentialities.

The first of the two points just alluded to is that there ought to be no expectation or even desire to formulate a universally acceptable religion. This does not mean that religion is a matter of merely subjective taste. It means that as complex a being as man and as intricate a career as human life can hardly be supposed to have one single best way of being organized. There will doubtless be religious movements in which large numbers of men will share, and probably there ought to be such. But goods are too pluralistic to be summed up in one formula, and sound ideals are too numerous to be collectively pursued in the course of any one human life. A physician, a politician, a merchant, a lawyer may well have different means by which to secure the best lives, different principles by which to organize their lives most effectively. Even within any one life it is doubtful whether complete integration would not be confining, narrow, fanatic. Religion, without being capricious, may yet be very personal. There may be as many personal religious convictions and as many corresponding religious forms of life as there are honest, devout, and good men. What is important to recognize is that any thoughtful and earnest life will be likely progressively to gain in religious quality. The wise man can neither cut himself off from historic forms (and all great historic forms of life have had religious centering) nor yield to historic pressures. The final religion is as absurd a dream as the final poem or the final symphony. The religious quest must forever remain a piece of "unfinished business" for openminded and sensitive men.

The other point is almost a corollary of the first. It is that there is danger in a too-intense religious zeal. Religion ought to be the ornament of a rich life, not the driving passion of a fixed commitment. History is full of stories of cases of immature religious commitments. Religious commitments ought never to be drilled into men; they ought never be made too early in life. If a youth adopts a definite religious point of view, he may, of course, lead a life of singleness of aim and powerful persistence of effort. But the odds are against any fine achievement by such means. The chances are, that he will either become intolerant, biased, and insensitive to all possibilities of development that lie beyond the range of his youthful mind or rebel against religion and become a secularized person with scorn for earnest moral endeavor. The middle way is, in religion as generally in life, the best way. The middle way is to take religion with a sense of humor, a light touch, and a sensitive appreciation for what has, at least for the time being, no apparent religious import. The convert is usually the bigot, because he swings into his new way of life with the intensity of one-sided passion. The man who grows into a religious position gradually, imperceptibly, with consciously tentative or even hesitant assent, is much more likely to reach a sound stand and a generous degree of truth. Hence one should seek to postpone religious commitment and to accept it, not as authoritative over the whole of life, but as experimental over only certain parts of life. In that way a religious way of life might coexist, as it has too seldom coexisted, with the emancipated mind.

3

NATURALISM AND DEMOCRACY

Sidney Hook

I

In the famous third chapter of his *Four Stages of Greek Religion* Gilbert Murray characterizes the period from 300 B.C. through the first century of the Christian era as marked by a "failure of nerve." This failure of nerve exhibited itself in "a rise of asceticism, of mysticism, in a sense, of pessimism; a loss of self-confidence, of hope in this life and of faith in normal human efforts; a despair of patient inquiry, a cry for infallible revelation; an indifference to the welfare of the state, a conversion of the soul to God."

A survey of the cultural tendencies of our times shows many signs pointing to a new failure of nerve in Western civilization. The revival of the doctrine of the original depravity of human nature; prophecies of doom for Western culture, no matter who wins the war or peace; the search for a center of value that transcends human interest; the mystical apotheosis of "the leader"; contempt for all social programs and philosophies, because of the obvious failure of some of them; violent attacks against secularism; posturing about the cultivation of spiritual purity; a concern with mystery rather than problems and the belief that myth and mysteries are modes of knowledge—these are only some of the secondary evidences of the new failure of nerve.

The primary evidence of the new failure of nerve is to be found in an attitude which accompanies all the movements and views listed in the previous paragraph and many others as well. It exhibits itself as a loss of confidence in scientific method and in varied quests for a "knowledge" and "truth" which are uniquely different from those won by the processes of scientific inquiry. Often, with no great regard for consistency, these uniquely different truths are regarded as "superior" to the common garden variety of science and good sense. This distrust of scientific method is often concealed by statements to the effect that science, of course, has a certain validity in its proper place and sphere, that only the pretensions of scientific philosophy—naturalism, empiricism, positivism

—are being criticized. Yet it is not to the actual procedures of scientific inquiry that such critics go to correct this or that formulation of scientific philosophy; rather do they invoke the claims of some rival method to give us knowledge of what is beyond the competence of scientific method. Occasionally they boldly assert that their substitute method gives a more reliable and complete knowledge even of the matters that the sciences report. What an eloquent revelation is contained in Reinhold Niebuhr's words, "Science which is only science cannot be scientifically accurate."

Distrust of scientific method is transformed into open hostility whenever some privileged "private" truth pleads for exemption from the tests set up to safeguard the intelligence from illusion. The pleas for exemption take many forms. They are rarely direct and above board. Usually they are presented as corollaries of special *theories* of knowledge, being, or experience. There are some who interpret science and discursive knowledge generally as merely a method of confirming what we *already* know, in a dim but sure way, by other modes of experience. If the methods of scientific inquiry do not yield this confirmation, they are held to be at fault; some other way must be found of validating and communicating primal wisdom. Others maintain that scientific method can give us only partial truths, which become less partial, not by subjecting them to more careful scientific scrutiny, but by incorporating them into a theological or metaphysical system. Still others openly declare it to be axiomatic that every experience, every feeling and motion, directly reports a truth that cannot be warranted and does not need to be warranted by experiment or inference.

These, bluntly put, are gateways to intellectual and moral irresponsibility. But of the view that every mode of experience gives direct authentic knowledge it would, perhaps, be more accurate to say that it carries us far beyond the gateways. For frequently it is a defense of willful obscurantism. It starts from the assumption that *every* experience gives us an authentic report of the objective world instead of material for judgment. It makes our viscera an organ of knowledge. It justifies every passionate prejudice by asserting that if only we feel deeply enough about anything, our feeling must declare some truth about the object which provokes it that is just as legitimate as the considered judgment which discovers the root of the feeling in a personal aberration. After all, is it not the case that every heresy-hunting bigot and hallucinated fanatic is convinced that there is a truth in the feelings, visions, and passions that run riot within him? Hitler is not the only one for whom questions of evidence are incidental when they are not dismissed as impertinent. If the voice of feeling cannot be mistaken, every difference would be an invitation to battle, every insane mind could set itself up as a prophet. It is not only as a defense against the marginally sane that we need the safeguards of critical, scientific method. Every vested interest in social life, every inequitable privilege, every "truth" promulgated as a national, class, or racial truth likewise denies the competence of scientific inquiry to evaluate its claims. Nor are our own normal selves free from the tendency to mistake intensity of the feeling or conviction with which beliefs are held as indubitable evidence of their validity.

Sometimes the demand that the revelations of feeling, intuition, and emotion meet scientific canons of evidence is rejected as an arbitrary legislative decree concerning what visions are permissible and what may or may not exist. The complaint is made that such a demand impoverishes the imaginative resources and chokes off the vision, without which there is no growth of new knowledge, but at most a blind fooling with canons and methods. As far as seeing visions and winning new truths are concerned, such an interpretation is nothing short of grotesque. The essential point, where the question of knowledge or truth arises, is whether we have seen a vision or been a victim of a delusion; or, to avoid the appearance of question-begging, whether we have beheld a trustworthy or untrustworthy vision. Some people claim to see things that we know are not there. If seeing were believing, men could be perpetually duped.

The intelligent demand for evidence need not paralyze the pioneers of truth who catch glimpses of what may until then be undreamed of. For the sciences themselves do not demand complete or exact confirmation of an hypothesis to begin with, but only enough to institute further inquiries; and the history of science is sufficient evidence that the discipline of its method, far from being a bar against the discovery of new truths, is a positive aid in acquiring them. As for decreeing what does or can *exist*, there is nothing in scientific method that *forbids* anything to exist. It concerns itself only with the responsibility of the assertions that proclaim the existence of anything. It does not jeer at the mystical swoon of rapture; it only denies the mystic's retrospective cognitive claims for which no evidence is offered except the fact of the trance.

Scientific method does not entail any metaphysical theory of existence, and certainly not metaphysical materialism. The attack upon scientific method, in order to be free to believe whatever voice speaks to us, is really a flight from responsibility. This is the dominant characteristic of the failure of nerve.

II

The causes of the failure of nerve in our time are multiple and obvious. Economic crises, world war, a bad peace, tragically inept statesmanship, the tidal wave of fascism tell the story of the twentieth century. It is important not to ignore or minimize this. The "arguments" of those who have been panicked into embracing refurbished varieties of transcendental consolation may be met a thousand times over. But not until a stable, democratic, freedom and welfare planning economy is built out of what is left of our world can we legitimately hope that these cultural reversions will subside from epidemic to episodic proportions. Until then we must strive to prevent emotional hysteria from infecting those who still cling to the principles of rational experiment and analysis as the only reliable instruments for riding out and mastering the cultural and social chaos of our age.

It is characteristic of the tendencies hostile to scientific method that they reject the view that the breakdown of capitalism and the rise of fascism are due primarily to a conjunction of material factors. Rather do they attribute the crisis of our culture to a specific faith or philosophy rooted in scientific method. They allege that the bankruptcy of Western European civilization is the direct result of the bankruptcy of the positivist and naturalistic spirit which, sprouting from seeds scattered during the Renaissance, came to full flower in our own time. They assert that science and the scientific attitude pervaded every sphere of culture and experience, that all truth-claims and values were submitted to them for final arbitration, and that they were employed not so much to reinterpret as to deny the existence of human intelligence, courage, and dignity.[1]

No empirical evidence is offered for these extreme statements or for the fantastic conclusion that modern ills are the consequence of our attempt to live by scientific theory and practice. On the contrary, a scien-

---

[1] These contentions run through the *Proceedings of the Conference on Science, Philosophy and Religion in Their Relation to the Democratic Way of Life*. The neo-Thomists are most vociferous in their promulgation. Other religious and metaphysical groups are now echoing them. See Hallowell, *Ethics*, III, No. 3 (1942), 337.

tific analysis of modern history—and I am assuming that history is an empirical discipline—reveals that the chief causes of our maladjustments and suicidal conflicts are to be found precisely in those areas of social life in which *the rationale of scientific method has not been persistently employed.* Where is the evidence that any state ever attempted to meet scientifically the challenge of poverty, unemployment, the distribution of raw materials, the impact of technology either in government or in industry? The belief that we have grappled with these problems in a rational and scientific spirit is a myth. The principles which have controlled our response to basic social problems have been drawn in the main from outworn traditions hostile or indifferent to the ethics and the logic of scientific inquiry. It is only by courtesy that we can call them principles at all. Drift and improvisation have been the rule. Enthusiasm for the bare *results* of the physical sciences—which undoubtedly did reach a high pitch in the nineteenth century—does not betoken an acceptance of a scientific or experimental philosophy of life in which all values are tested by their causes and consequences. The cry that a set of "laboratory techniques" cannot determine the basic values in a philosophy of life betrays the literary man's illusion that the laboratory procedures of the natural sciences are the be-all and end-all of scientific method instead of restricted applications of it in special fields. Wisdom is counterposed to knowledge as if it were a superior organ or faculty or method instead of a variety of knowledge, namely, knowledge of the nature, origin, and careers of human values.

Perhaps the most malicious expression of the attack upon naturalism in contemporary American thought is the attempt to prove that a consistent naturalist or positivist cannot in principle accept the philosophy of democracy. Sometimes it is even charged that naturalists and positivists constitute the philosophical fifth column of Western civilization and that their doctrines have paved the way for the triumph of totalitarianism. Usually this charge is coupled with the assertion that the philosophy of democracy *must* be based upon the specific dogmas of one or another theologic-metaphysical school.

The bulk of this essay will be devoted to the analysis of the democratic faith in order to discover whether it necessarily rests upon theological or metaphysical truths or whether an adequate justification of democracy can be made from a naturalistic standpoint.

A few preliminary remarks are necessary in order to indicate in what sense the term "naturalism" is to be understood. Despite the variety of specific doctrines which naturalists have professed from Democritus to Dewey, what unites them all is the wholehearted acceptance of scientific method as the only reliable way of reaching truths about the world of nature, society, and man. The differences between naturalists in the history of thought can easily be explained in terms of (1) varying historical conceptions of what fields and problems are amenable to scientific treatment and (2) progressive refinements in the methods of inquiry themselves. All their differences can in principle be resolved by appealing to the *method* to which they give common allegiance, except for those temperamental differences of emphasis and selective bias which no naturalist claims to be an avenue to truth. The least common denominator of all historic naturalisms, therefore, is not so much a set of specific doctrines as the method of scientific or rational empiricism.

Naturalism is opposed to all known forms of supernaturalism, not because it rules out a priori what may or may not exist, but because no plausible evidence has been found to warrant belief in the entities and powers to which supernatural status has been attributed. The existence of God, immortality, disembodied spirits, cosmic purpose and design, as these have been customarily interpreted by the great institutional religions, are denied by naturalists for the same generic reasons that they deny the existence of fairies, elves, and leprechauns. There are other conceptions of God, to be sure, and provided they are not self-contradictory in meaning, the naturalist is prepared in principle to consider their claims to validity. All he asks is that the conception be sufficiently definite to make possible specific inferences of the determinate conditions—the *how, when,* and *where* of His operation. The trouble with most conceptions of God which differ from the conventional ones is that either they are so vague that no one can tell what they mean or else they designate something in experience for which a perfectly suitable term already exists.

I do not see that anything is gained by blinking the fact that the naturalist denies the existence of supernatural powers. Nor need he pass as an agnostic except in those situations in which the weight of evidence is equally balanced and he suspends judgment until such time as more evidence is available. But if he is faithful to his method, he must assert that for every traditional conception of God, the weight of evidence so far is decidedly in the negative. So long as no self-contradictory notions are advanced, he will not rule out the abstract logical possibility that angelic creatures push the planets any more than that there exists a gingerbread castle on the other side of the moon. All he demands is the presence of sufficient precision of meaning to make it possible to test, let us say—taking an illustration disputed by the doctrinal findings of past naturalisms—the existence of extrasensory perception. The possibility of extrasensory perception cannot be ruled out a priori. Here, as elsewhere, the naturalist must follow the preponderance of scientific evidence. He therefore welcomes those who talk about the experiential evidence for religious beliefs as distinct from those who begin with mystery and end in mystery. He only asks to be given an opportunity to examine the evidence and to evaluate it by the same general canons which have led to the great triumphs of knowledge in the past. It is natural in this case, as in the case of extrasensory perception, that he should scrutinize with great care reports which if true would lead him radically to modify some of his earlier generalizations. The unusual must clear a higher hurdle of credibility than the usual. But only on its first jump. Unfortunately, for all their talk of appeal to experience, direct or indirect, religious experientialists dare not appeal to any experience of sufficiently determinate character to permit of definite tests. There is a certain wisdom in this reluctance. For if experience can confirm a belief, it can also invalidate it. But to most supernaturalists this is an inadmissible possibility. We therefore find that the kind of experience to which reference is made is not only unique but also uniquely self-authenticating. Those who are not blessed by the experiences are regarded as blind or deaf or worse! But is it not odd that those who worship Zeus on the ground of a unique experience should deny to others the right to worship Odin on the ground of a different unique experience?

I have deliberately sharpened the antisupernatural doctrinal conclusions of naturalism in order to meet squarely the challenge to naturalism to find a consistent and rational defense of democratic belief on the basis of scientific method.

III

The successful defense of democracy does not rest primarily upon the analysis of its nature and presuppositions. Nonetheless, some clarification of the meaning of democracy, of the ground upon which we hold it, and of the procedure by which we arrive at conclusions for the class of problems and decisions of this kind is necessary if our choice to defend democracy is to be intelligent. In so far as intelligent choice makes a difference to events, analysis is not without ultimate bearing upon conduct. Particularly today, when the allegiances of large numbers have become unhinged and even larger numbers are more certain of what they want to believe than of the reasons for their belief, the answers to our questions may be of some practical moment. It is noteworthy that in an age not conspicuous for its appeal to reason, few will give assent to doctrines which they admit to be demonstrably false or out of line with verifiable fact.

Perhaps more dangerous to democracy than arguments against it is the feeling that analysis or reflection is irrelevant to those "beliefs" for which we are prepared to suffer, to fight, and sometimes to die. They are then regarded either as automatic consequences of conditioning—social or biological—or as sacred commands from a divine source, or as the irresistible cry of conscience. Once the rational nerve of belief is paralyzed, action may still be vigorous in behalf of expressed goals, but it cannot be intelligent. For whatever else intelligence is, it is sensitiveness to, and awareness of, the presence of *alternate means* which in fact determine the realized content of the goals we profess. Belief without reasons blinds us to the presence of alternate means. That is why the action it inspires is so often self-defeating. There are many causes in history of which we can say that they have been betrayed by their own successes.

IV

It is hard to separate a discussion of democracy from a discussion of its philosophical presuppositions, for the nature of democracy is itself often in dispute. In addition, the meaning of the word "presuppositions" is not univocal. Its customary usage includes "consequences" and "implications," as well as "assumptions." What I propose to do, therefore, in order to facilitate the joining of issues, is to ask and answer three generic questions. The first is: What is democracy? The second is: What are the grounds or reasons on which we can justify our belief in democracy? The third is: Are there any facts of a cosmic, historical, or psychological kind which stand in the way of our acceptance of democracy, that is, which make democracy an impracticable ideal? It is apparent that the last two questions are related, since if any ideal is demonstrably impractica-ble—in a sense other than completely realizable, for no ideal can be com-pletely realized—this would have some bearing upon its desirability or upon the grounds of our choice.

V

Any adequate description of the nature of democracy must at the very least do justice to customary usage, which distinguishes between democratic and nondemocratic societies and between historic phases within any one society, regarded as more or less democratic with rela-tion to each other. Although for propaganda purposes even totalitarian states claim to be democratic "in a higher sense," their canonic writings recognize the differences between the structure of these states and those considered democratic in a less esoteric sense. This is often betrayed in the adjectives prefixed to the latter, such as "so-called," "alleged," "par-liamentary," or "bourgeois." Germany and Russia and Italy are not democratic states; England and the United States are. And when his-torians examine the development of English and American society they unanimously acknowledge, although they evaluate the fact differently, that these societies were less democratic when property, racial, or reli-gious qualifications were set for citizenship than they are today, when these qualifications have been eliminated or reduced.

What principle is expressed in these customary distinctions? The prin-ciple may be stated in various ways, but for our purposes we may say that a democratic state is one in which the basic decisions of government rest upon the freely given consent of the governed.[2] This obviously is only a beginning. For as soon as we begin to investigate the conditions which must be present before we grant that a state lives up to this prin-ciple, we are carried beyond the sphere of political considerations into the domain of ethics. Thus, if information has been withheld or with-drawn before consent is assessed; if the opposition is muzzled or sup-pressed so that consent is as unanimous as a totalitarian plebiscite; or if economic sanctions are threatened against a section of the community

[2] Although the chief terms in this statement are vague, they can be made more precise (see my *Reason, Social Myths, and Democracy*, New York, 1941, p. 285). On the basis of the analysis a set of important conditions is enumerated, in the ab-sence of which democracy cannot exist; in addition, a set of conditions is described on the *presence* of which the effective functioning of democracy depends.

in the event that consent takes one form or another, we declare that the "spirit" or "logic" or "rationale" of democracy is absent from its political forms. If birth does not give divine right, neither do numbers. We are all acquainted with situations in which we say that a political democracy has traduced its own ideals. Whenever we criticize existing states which conform to the political definition of democracy on the ground that they are not democratic enough; whenever we point out that Athenian democracy was limited only to free men or that in some parts of the American South it is limited only to white men, or that in some countries it is limited only to men, we are invoking a broader principle of democracy as a controlling reference in our judgments of comparison. This principle is an ethical one.

What is this principle of ethical democracy? It is the principle of equality—an equality, not of status or origin, but of opportunity, relevant functions, and social participation. The enormous literature and bitter controversy which center around the concept of equality indicate that it is only a little less ambiguous than the concept of democracy. It is necessary, therefore, to block it off from some current notions before developing the argument.

1. The principle of equality is not a *description* of fact about men's physical or intellectual natures. It is a *prescription* or policy for treating men.

2. It is not a prescription for treating men in identical ways who are unequal in their physical or intellectual nature. It is a policy of equality of concern or consideration for men whose different needs may require differential treatment.

3. It is not a mechanical policy of equal opportunity for everyone at any time and in all respects. A musical genius is entitled to greater opportunities to develop his musical talents than someone who is tone deaf. It is equality of opportunity for all individuals to develop whatever personal and socially desirable talents they possess and to make whatever unique contributions their capacities permit.

4. It is not a demand for absolute uniformity of living conditions or even for arithmetically equal compensation for socially useful work. It demands that when the productive forces of a society makes possible the gratification of basic human needs (which are, of course, historical variables), no one should be deprived of necessities in order to provide others with luxuries.

5. It is not a policy of restricting the freedom of being different or becoming different. It is a policy of *encouraging* the freedom to be different, restricting only that exercise of freedom which converts talents or possessions into a monopoly that frustrates the emergence of other free personalities.

6. It is not a demand that all people be leaders or that none should be. It does demand that the career of leadership, like all other careers, be open to all whose natural or acquired talents qualify them; that everyone have a say in the process of selecting leaders; that the initiative of leaders operate within a framework of basic laws; and that these laws in turn ultimately rest upon the freely given consent of the persons who constitute the community.

7. It does not make the assumption of sentimental humanitarianism that all men are naturally good. It does assume that men, treated as equals in a community of persons, may become better. The emphasis upon respect for the personality of all individuals, the attitude which treats the personality, not as something fixed, but as a growing, developing pattern, is unique to the philosophy of democracy.

What I have been trying to show is that the logic of the democrat's position compels him to go beyond the limited conception of political democracy—the equality of freedom—to a broader attitude extending to those other phases of social existence that bear upon the effective exercise of equality of freedom. This in fact has been the historical tendency observable wherever democratic principles and programs are permitted to operate. Perhaps the synoptic phrase "social equality," whose connotations encompass political, educational, and economic democracy, may be taken as the most appropriate expression of the meaning of democracy in the broadest sense.

It is clear that the principle of equality, like any principle of justice, cannot by itself determine what is specifically right or good in each concrete case. But whatever the right is discovered to be, from the point of view of democracy it is the result of an analysis which considers equally the needs of all the persons involved in the situation; and, furthermore, whatever the good is, it becomes better to the extent that it is shared among other members of the community. It is also clear that in concrete situations there will be conflicts between various demands for equality and that in negotiating these conflicts the methods of intelligence are indispensable for a functioning democracy. If "naturalism" and "scientific empiricism" be generic terms for the philosophic attitude which submits *all* claims of fact and value to test by experience, then scientific empiricism as a philosophy is more congenial to a democratic than to an antidemocratic community, for it brings into the open light of criticism the interests in which moral values and social institutions are rooted.[3] *Empiricism so conceived is commitment to a procedure, not to a theory of metaphysics.*

In this brief account of the nature of democracy as a way of life I have not aimed at an exhaustive analysis of the *forms* in which it may be expressed, but have tried to indicate the basic ideals which are involved in the customary usage of the term and in the implications of that usage.

VI

We now come to the problem which is of primary concern to philosophers. What are the grounds upon which acceptance of democracy in contradistinction to other modes of social life can be justified? So far as I can see, there are four generic types of justification which have been or can be offered.

The first asserts that the rational foundation of democratic belief consists in a set of supernatural religious truths in the sense that there can be no intelligent ground for choosing between democracy and other forms of society which does not logically commit us to some kind of theology.

The second asserts the same thing about metaphysics understood as a theory of "reality." Usually these two approaches go hand in hand.

The third maintains that the choice of democracy is a nonrational preference rooted in the constitution of our natures and brought to flower by nurture and education.

The fourth affirms that the belief in democracy is an hypothesis controlled by the same general pattern of inquiry which we apply to any scientific hypothesis, but referring to different subject matter, that is, our evaluations.

1. *Democracy and religion.*—Does democracy as a way of life rest upon belief in supernatural religious truths in the sense that if the latter are denied, the former must necessarily be denied? It is becoming increasingly fashionable to maintain this. Were historical considerations

[3] For further elaboration of the connections between empiricism and democracy see my "Metaphysics and Social Attitudes," *Social Frontier,* IV, No. 32 (February, 1938), 153–58.

relevant here, I think it could be conclusively established that the great institutional religions, with the possible exception of some forms of Protestantism, have tended in fact to support theocratic forms of government. Nor is this surprising if the Kingdom of Heaven be taken as a model or inspiration for the Kingdom of Earth. Whoever heard of a democratically organized Paradise? Walt Whitman in heaven would meet with the same fate as Lucifer, but for different reasons. Not only is the notion of a democratically organized heaven blasphemous, but the proposal to reform along democratic lines a hierarchically organized church would lead to excommunication. If we examine the actual behavior which has been sanctified by the maxim: "Render unto Caesar what is Caesar's and to God what is God's," we will discover that historical, institutional religion has always been able to adapt itself to any form of government or society which will tolerate its existence.

But our concern is not with historical questions, fascinating as they are, but with the logic of the position. We must consequently rephrase the question to read: Does belief in democracy logically rest upon any theological propositions in the sense that the denial of the second entails the denial of the first? And for this discussion I shall take as illustrative of theological propositions the two cardinal propositions of natural theology, namely, "God exists" and "Man has an immortal soul." To assert that whoever has no grounds for affirming the existence of God and immortality has no grounds for affirming the validity of democracy is to claim that the former are at least necessary conditions of the latter. I shall argue that they constitute neither necessary nor sufficient conditions.

a) Before examining this claim, let us note the tremendous risk it involves. Were those who advance it ever compelled to admit that these theological propositions are indemonstrable or false, they would have to surrender their belief in democracy. But this, I submit, very few of them are prepared to do. They would search for other reasons and grounds. Like those who would make the validity of moral judgments dependent upon the existence of God and immortality, the theological defenders of democracy shift from a problem in which, although difficult, it is possible to reach an agreement on the basis of some empirical evidence, to one in which the nature of the terms and sphere of discourse makes such agreement much more difficult. Confirmed democrats, it seems to me, are much more convinced of the validity of the democratic ideal than they are of the theological propositions upon which it presumably depends. They would no more exonerate from the obligation of accepting the democratic ideal an atheist or agnostic who pleads that he has no reason to believe in God and the hereafter than they would exempt him from the obligation of living honestly.

b) Aside from the difficulties of establishing God's existence, how can we get from the fact of his existence to the desirability of the democratic way of life? None of the attributes of God, save the moral attributes, can serve as a premise justifying one way of life rather than another. And if the moral attributes of God can serve as premises, necessary or sufficient, for the democratic way of life, it is only because *we* regard them as worthy, that is, as truly moral. Obviously any theology which makes God's power the justification or source of his goodness is worse than useless for purposes of deriving democracy. The attribution of moral qualities to God is an expression of what we think his qualities ought to be. And this is a problem of precisely the same order as that which we are called upon to answer when we ask for the grounds of our democratic allegiance.

c) The situation is the same if we grant that human beings have immortal souls. In what way is this a necessary or sufficient presupposition of democracy? The brotherhood of man may be a theological fact as it is a biological fact, but what makes it wrong for Cain to kill his brother Abel and right, under certain circumstances, for us to kill Cain is a moral principle which can no more be derived from theology than from biology—unless, of course, the moral principle is one of the premises of our theological (or biological) system. In this case we are no further along than we were when we raised the question about the democratic way of life. In passing it should be observed that belief in the immortality of the soul can be, and has been, used (in the Hindu doctrines of *samtra* and *karma*) to sanctify the tightest system of antidemocratic social stratification the world has ever seen.[4]

2. *Democracy and metaphysics.*—The problem of the metaphysical foundation of democracy is more difficult because of varying concep-

---

[4] See Max Weber, *Religionssoziologie*, Tübingen, 1920, II, 119–20. The lot of the Hindu in this life is a consequence of his sins or virtues in a previous life. Therefore, he cannot complain about the injustice of any "accident of birth" or station. But, no matter how unclean his caste, he has the hope that, by exemplary observance of the caste rituals and cheerful acceptance of his present lot, he may improve his social position in the next cycle of rebirth.

tions of metaphysics. By "metaphysics" I shall understand the discipline designated by the term "ontology" or any theory of "being *überhaupt.*" The evidence seems to me to be overwhelming that there is a definite historical connection between the social movements of a period and its dominant metaphysical teachings; furthermore, I am prepared to defend as a historically true proposition that systems of idealistic metaphysics, because of the semiofficial roles they have played in their respective cultures, have been more generally employed to bolster antidemocratic social movements than systems of empirical or materialistic metaphysics. Whether there is *always* an intrinsic personal or psychological relation between a philosopher's metaphysics and his ethics or politics is a more difficult question, but one which seems to me to require an answer in the negative. More germane to our present concern is my contention that there is no necessary logical connection between a theory of being or becoming and any particular theory of ethics or politics. Stated more accurately, it seems to me demonstrable that no system of metaphysics *univocally* determines a system of ethics or politics. There may be certain facts about man and nature which might have a bearing upon our judgment about what social system is of the highest worth, but, as I shall argue later, these are facts concerning which the empirical sciences are qualified to report without benefit of metaphysics.

Two species of metaphysics are most often invoked in behalf of democracy. One asserts that the value of democracy or the values from which it may be derived are "grounded in reality," a phrase which is interpreted to mean that the universe "justifies" or "guarantees" both the validity and the ultimate supremacy of basic human ideals. I must confess that it is difficult for me to understand this view except as a shamefaced kind of theology. However that may be, there is no agreed-upon denotation of *the* universe. There are many universes. Nor is there any one basic human ideal, but there are many human ideals which are often in conflict with one another, even though they all invoke the universe as a ground of their validity and as a guaranty of their triumph. Finally, and most important, no matter what character the universe is alleged to have, no matter what the nature of the far-off event toward which it is moving, no matter who wins or loses, nothing logically compelling in the way of judgment follows unless *we* have already morally evaluated the character of events. For most metaphysicians the very word "reality" is an implicit value term. To be sure, history may be conceived as a struggle between the Prince of Darkness and the Prince of Light, but the latter is so named because he carries *our* moral flag.

The second metaphysical view to which resort is often made is at the same time a kind of rejoinder to our position. It distinguishes between a metaphysical realm of being and a metaphysical realm of values and grounds the democratic way of life in the latter. Just as the spectrum of colors is there to be beheld by all who are not color blind and would still be there even if man's ancestors had climbed no higher than the mole in the tree of evolution, so the spectrum of values is there to be beheld by all who are not value blind and would still be there even if human beings had never existed at all. The view that colors would still be there even if human beings had no eyes is not without its difficulties. But they do not begin to compare in difficulty with the view that values are essentially unrelated to an evaluator and his interests. Santayana has quite aptly remarked of this doctrine that there is much sense in saying that whiskey "is pervaded as it were, by an inherent intoxication, and stands dead drunk in its bottle."

The subject is vast, but it is enough to show that this view is question-begging in precisely the same way as other theological and metaphysical derivations. The existence of these absolute norms is presumably certified or authenticated at some point by an act of immediate intuition. If the testimony of the intuition is construed not merely from what individuals *say* they intuit but also from the conduct that flows from their intuition—and conduct counts more in any moral scheme than mere words—then it is clear that individuals intuit or "see" *different* values. The "great" visions are not all compatible with one another in what they command, not to mention the visions that we do not call great. Which visions are the authentic ones? Prior to every conclusion that these are the objective values of all eternity, or even of all time and existence, is the assumption that *this* is the trustworthy seer. In a dispute between two men, one of whom asserts that the other is color blind and the other that the first is "just seeing things," there are definite ways of determining who is right. In a dispute between two seers whose immediate intuitions report conflicting news about the nature and hierarchy of absolute values, there is no rational way of reaching a consensus. The true prophet cannot be distinguished from the false by invoking absolute values whose validity depends upon a prior assumption of the reliability of prophetic testimony. The complacency with which some writers have cut the Gordian knot by introducing reference to the intuitions of "the best people" or "the most cultured people" or "the saving remnant" is evidence either of parochialism or of snobbery.

The record of human error and cruelty shows what ghastly consequences often result from the conviction that one's moral insight cannot possibly be wrong and that it needs no further justification than its own incandescent purity. No more than a solipsist can make plausible on his own assumptions the existence of another solipsist, can an absolutist find a rightful place for another absolutist who disagrees with him. Absolutists face each other over an abyss which cannot be bridged even by their weapons of war.

3. *Democracy and preferences.*—The view that an acceptance of democracy is an expression of a preference does not carry us far until the kind of preference is indicated. A preference may express a passing whim or a deep natural bent; it may be impulsive or reflective. Preferences are rooted in our natures. Their forms, occasions, and objects are supplied by education, that is, broadly speaking, by social habits and intelligence. But either our natures can be changed, or the educators can be re-educated. If neither is possible, then the fact of moral choice becomes unintelligible. If we can offer no justification of a preference except that it is ours, obviously no point of intellectual or moral issue is raised; nor, a fortiori, can any be settled by the trial of arms. If we offer a justification of a preference, it will take one of the generic forms already discussed or about to be discussed.

4. *Democracy as a hypothesis.*—When democracy is taken strictly as a form of political government, its superiority over other forms of government can be established to the extent to which it achieves more security, freedom, and co-operative diversity than any of its alternatives. If we test the workings of political democracy by Paul's scheme of virtues or by Nietzsche's, we may perhaps reach another conclusion. So long as there is no dispute about observable effects and so long as we raise no question about the moral ideals by which we evaluate these effects, we have clear sailing.

But, as has already been made plain, by democracy as a way of life we mean a way of organizing human relationships which embodies a certain complex of moral ideals. Can these ideals be treated as hypotheses? The conventional reply has always been that no moral principle can be regarded as a hypothesis, for we must already have certain knowledge of what is good before we can evaluate the consequences of acting upon it. If any position is question-begging, surely this seems to be.

Were this a symposium on value theory, I would devote all my time to developing the general theory of moral ideals as hypotheses. But here I can only barely indicate that the notion is not viciously circular. A moral ideal is a prescription to act in a certain situation or class of situations in determinate ways that will organize the human needs and wants involved so as to fulfill a set of other values which are postulated as binding in relation to the problem in hand. No more than in other cases of inquiry do we start with an empty head. The cluster of values we bring to the situation is the result of prior experience and reflection. *They are not arbitrarily postulated.* The consequences of acting upon the hypothesis may lead us to challenge a postulated or assumed value. This in turn can become the subject of a similar investigation. Terminal values are always related to specific contexts; there is no absolute terminal value which is either self-evident or beyond the necessity of justifying itself if its credentials are challenged. There is no vicious infinite regress involved if we take our problems concretely and one at a time. Nor is the procedure narrowly circular. For if after a long history of raising and solving moral problems we postulate as a value in solving a later problem a value which had itself to be certified in an earlier problem, this would testify to the presence of a fruitful set of systematically related values in the structure of our moral behavior. New values would emerge or be discovered in the course of our attempt to act upon our ideals and from the necessity of mediating the conflict between the postulated values as they bear on concrete human needs in specific situations.

I should like, however, to make the general position take form out of the discussion of the theme before us. That theme is: *Why should we treat individuals of unequal talents and endowments as persons who are equally entitled to relevant consideration and care?* Short of a treatise, I can state only the reasons, without amplification of the concrete needs of the social situation which democracy seeks to meet and the institutional practices by which it must meet them.

1. This method of treating human beings is more successful than any other in evoking a maximum of creative, voluntary effort from all members of the community. Properly implemented, it gives all persons a stake in the community and elicits a maximum of intelligent loyalty.

2. It enlarges the scope of our experience by enabling us to acquire

insight into the needs, drives, and aspirations of others. Learning to understand how life is organized by other centers of experience is both a challenge and a discipline for our imagination. In aiding the growth of others, we aid our own growth.

3. The willingness to understand another man's point of view without necessarily surrendering to it makes it more likely that different points of view may negotiate their differences and learn to live peacefully with one another. A democratic community cannot be free from strife in a world where inequalities will always exist, but its ethics, when intelligently acted upon, makes more likely the diminution of strife or its transference to socially harmless forms than is the case when its principle of equality is denied. The consequences are less toadying, less fear, and less duplicity in the equalitarian community than there are in the non-equalitarian society.

4. In nurturing the capacities of each individual so that they may come to their greatest fulfillment we can best share our existing stores of truth and beauty and uncover new dimensions in these realms. How can anyone dedicated to the values of science and art consistently oppose a policy which maximizes the possibility of the discovery and widest dispersion of scientific truths and artistic meanings?

5. Regard for the potentialities of all individuals makes for less cruelty of man toward man, especially where cruelty is the result of blindness to, or ignorance of, the needs of others. A community organized along democratic lines is guilty of cruelty only at those points where it has failed to live up to its own ideals. A totalitarian community is systematically insensitive to the personal needs not only of members of the outlawed scapegoat group but also of the majority of its subjects who are excluded from policy-making discussions. At best, there is no way of determining these personal needs except by the interpretation of the dictator and his experts who act on the fateful dogma that they know the true interests of their subjects better than the subjects themselves. At worst, the dictator assumes not only that he speaks for his subjects but that in some mystic way he feels and thinks for them too. Despite the great limitations—limitations from the point of view of their own ideals —under which the nineteenth- and twentieth-century democracies of the Western world suffered, I think it is indisputable, on the evidence, that by and large their social life, in so far as this was the consequence

of policy, displayed less cruelty than the social life of any other historical period.

6. Reasonableness of conclusions, where attitudes and interests conflict, depends upon the degree of mutual consultation and free intellectual communication between the principals involved. The democratic way of life makes possible the widest forms of mutual consultation and communication. Conclusions reached by these processes have a quality that can never be found where conclusions are imposed by force or authority—even if they are our own. Let me illustrate what I mean by taking as an example an enterprise represented by a community of scholars, let us say the American Philosophical Association. Who among us, desirous as we may be of the possibility of philosophical agreement, would forego the methods of public discussion, criticism, argument, and rejoinder for a philosophical consensus imposed by a Gestapo or a G.P.U., even if by a strange quirk of affairs it was *our* philosophic position that the goon squads of orthodoxy sought to make the way of salvation? Who among us, knowing that outside the threshold of our meetings there stood an individual of foreign country, color, or faith, capable of making a contribution to our deliberations, would not open the door to him? These are not rhetorical questions framed to discover philosophical fifth columnists. They are designed to show that the procedures of critical discussion and discovery, which are pre-eminently exhibited in the work of a scientific community, take for granted that national, racial, or religious origins are irrelevant to the logic of the method by which reasonable conclusions are reached. Democracy as a way of life differs from its alternatives in that it makes possible the extension of this method of reaching reasonable conclusions from the fields of professional science and philosophy to all areas of human experience in which genuine problems arise.

There are other grounds that may be offered in justification of democracy as the most adequate social philosophy for our times. Every one of them, like the foregoing, postulates implicitly or explicitly values or desiderata. But I repeat: these postulates are ultimate only for the problem in hand. They may require justification. When we undertake such justification, we have undertaken a new inquiry into a new problem. Much is assumed on the basis of previously tested evidence: nothing is logically begged.

There are two important consequences of approaching democracy in this way. The first is that we avoid the temptation, which is rapidly gaining vogue, of making democracy absolutely valid in and for itself. There are many today who write as if they believe that democracy should prevail even though the heavens fall and say in so many words that "to question the validity of democracy is to disbelieve in it" [5] and that we can meet the blind fanatical faith of fascism only with a faith in democracy which is at least just as fanatical. This temptation, it seems to me, must be avoided, because, by counterposing subrational dogma to subrational dogma, we prepare the ground for an acceptance of a "might makes right" morality. Secondly, those who make of democracy an absolute value, which requires no justification but its inherent rightness, tend to identify this absolute democracy with whatever particular democratic *status quo* exists. On the other hand, the natural tendency of those who cannot distinguish between social philosophies on the ground of their inherent rightness is to test a social philosophy by the social institutions in which it is embodied. They are, therefore, more attentive to the actual workings and effects of democracy, more historical minded, and less likely to gloss over existing imperfections.

To those who say that human beings will not fight wholeheartedly except for certainties, and emphatically not for a hypothesis which is only probable, the reply must be made that this empirical proposition is highly dubious. Men have fought and do fight vigorously for causes on the basis of preponderant evidence. Vigorous action, indeed, is only desirable in troubled situations when we have first decided what *is* intelligent action. And intelligent action does not result when we assume that our ideas or ideals simply cannot be wrong. That both intelligence and resoluteness are compatible is clear in fields as far apart as military science and medicine. Once it is decided that the chances of one military action are relatively better than another or once it is decided that an operation gives a patient a better chance of surviving than no operation, wisdom demands that the best warranted alternative be pursued with all our heart and all our soul. Let us remember that when we are called upon to fight for democracy we are not asked to fight for an ideal which has just been proposed as a *merely possible* valid ideal for our times; we

---

[5] James Feibleman, *Positive Democracy*, Chapel Hill, N.C., 1940, p. 124: "Democracy requires the same unconscious belief in its rationality as does science. To question the validity of democracy is to disbelieve in it, for we must not even be aware of our belief if it is to be profound enough to mean anything."

already have considerable evidence in its behalf, the weight of which, unfortunately too often, is properly evaluated by some critics only when democracy is lost or imperiled. We have every reason to believe that we are fighting for a truth, and sometimes it is necessary to fight for it even though the fighting doesn't make it true. But in contradistinction to others who fight for their truths, we are prepared to establish to reasonable men that democracy is the better alternative. But not all men are reasonable, it will be objected. This brings us to the theme of our final section.

VII

We now turn to the question, Is democracy feasible? We can imagine someone who has accepted the tentative ends by which we evaluate ways of life criticizing us as follows: "If only the assertions made in the previous section could be established as true, the case for democracy would be convincing. But the nature of man as we know him, of history as scientifically understood, and of the larger world we live in precludes the possibility of ever achieving democracy. It runs counter to the facts. Although you may still choose to live or to die for democracy, the attempt to realize it, like any attempt to realize an ideal which has no natural basis, will be a ghastly failure. Its natural consequences will be worse than the evils it sets out to cure, and it will subvert the very ideals to which you have appealed in your argument. Democracy is an infirmity of noble but innocent minds who have never understood the world. It is not an intelligent option."

I have to consider briefly three types of objection to the feasibility of the democratic ideal.

1. The first is based upon the alleged psychological impossibility of democracy. It maintains that democracy is too good for men who are essentially evil, fallen creatures, dominated by the lust for power, property, and self. In less theological form it asserts that democracy makes too high a call upon human intelligence and disinterestedness.

It is true that the psychological nature of man is quite relevant to our problem. If most human beings were idiots or infantile or permanently incapable of self-development, the democratic ideal could hardly be defended on plausible grounds. But there is no evidence that most human beings are such, and *an intelligent attempt to find out whether they are would require that equalization of social opportunity which is of the essence of democracy.* Even without such an experiment, if we surrender the utopian expectation of the complete realization of the democratic ideal and bear in mind that the forms of democracy may be direct as well as indirect and that democracy is compatible with the delegation of powers and responsibilities, the evidence at hand could hardly justify the belief either in universal cretinism or in man's permanent ineducability. Nor do we have to counter with the assertion that men are *infinitely* perfectible to make our option for democracy reasonable. We require merely that they be sufficiently plastic, sufficiently capable of learning, improvement and intelligent self-criticism, to choose responsibly between alternatives of action whenever—and here is the rub—they have alternatives of choice. It is only the democratic community which will systematically give them the alternatives of choice on basic decisions. It is not without significance that no free people has ever voluntarily relinquished its democratic forms in favor of a government which has openly proclaimed as its aim the establishment of a permanent dictatorship. Principled dictatorships, as distinct from those that come in through the unguarded doors of democracy, always triumph by usurpation. As low as the human estate is today, there is no reason to believe that human beings belong to a psychological species inferior to that of their ancestors. Although history is rich in human stupidities and lost opportunities, in the face of men's achievements in the arts and sciences it would be simply foolish to read history as nothing but the record of human error.

The theological doctrine of man's essentially evil nature metaphorically expresses the truth that he is always limited, always tempted, and never free from his animal origins. But, taken literally, it makes any kind of moral virtue inconceivable except by interposition of divine grace or mystery. Here, too, we do not have to counter with a contrary theological proposition that man is essentially good. He is neither one nor the other, but he becomes good or evil depending upon his society, his habits, and his intelligence.

2. The most powerful arguments against the feasibility of democracy, strangely enough, have been neglected by most social philosophers. These are developed in the writings of Gaetano Mosca, Vilfredo Pareto, and Roberto Michels. Their common thesis, formulated on the basis of vast, detailed studies of political and social history, is that all historical

change, whether reform or revolution, consists of the substitution of one ruling minority for another. This rule rests upon three pillars: vital myths which cement human relationships and conceal differences of interest; fraud or manipulation which negotiates differences of interests; and force which ultimately settles differences of interest. The nature of social organization, they maintain, is such that democrats may be victorious, but democracy never. So it has been; so it is; and so it will be.

I have elsewhere tried to meet their arguments in detail.[6] But here I content myself with one consideration which points to the self-confessed inadequacy of their position. Despite this alleged law, every one of them admits, explicitly or implicitly, that some forms of society are better than others—and in every case it is the society which has a greater degree of democracy than the others. Thus Mosca, after maintaining the inescapability of minority rule, pays strong tribute to the superiority of parliamentary democracy over all other alternatives.[7]

Three basic errors, it seems to me, vitiate their conclusion. The first is that the amount of freedom and democracy in a society is determined by a law *already known*, or, as some would say today, by a historical wave. The truth is that the amount of freedom and democracy in the present and the future depends as much upon human willingness to fight for them as upon anything else. The second error is the belief, common not only to these thinkers but also to countless others, that human nature is unchangeable. In so far as this is neither a proposition of biology or of theology nor a logical tautology, but refers to psychological and social traits, it can be shown to be false. The third is their confusion between an organizing principle and the individual members of the series organized. Since no identification is possible between the principle of democracy and any one member of the series, they go from the true conclusion that the principle is incompletely realized in any one case to the false conclusion that there are no degrees of realization in the series of cases.

3. The third class of objections to the feasibility of the democratic ideal is derived from alleged cosmic or physico-chemical laws which contain the equations of doom for man and all his works. Even granting the validity of such laws, they would hold no matter what society exists,

---

[6] *Reason, Social Myths, and Democracy*, ch. vii.
[7] *The Ruling Classes*, Eng. trans. by H. D. Kahn; New York and London, 1939, p. 256.

and therefore they establish nothing about the relative superiority of one form of society over another. Such laws, as William James already pointed out in a definitive refutation of all views of this type, tell us about the *size of* "energy-rills," not their *significance.*[8]

VIII

That the cosmic home of man limits his power, if not his dreams, is, of course, true. It is a perennial source of his humility before the intractabilities of things and the transient character of what he builds. But it is also true that this limitation is the source of his opportunities and a necessary condition for all achievement. From these truths we cannot infer that nature is the guarantor of man's ideals, certainly not of the democratic ideal. But neither is it the enemy of human ideals. Man's friends and enemies are other men. To forget this is to go from natural piety to superstition. The cosmic scene against which men live out their lives will not be affected by Hitler's victory or by his defeat. Democracy needs no cosmic support other than the *chance* to make good. That chance it has, because man is part of nature. To ask for more is unreasonable, even if it is not unworthy. The way in which man acts upon his chances is additional evidence of the objective possibilities and novelties of existence. In so far as he is caught up in the flux of things, the intelligent democratic man honestly confronts the potentialities of existence, its futurities, its openness, its indeterminateness. He is free from the romantic madness which would seek to outlaw the truths of science and of the quaint conceit, permissible only as poetry, that nature is a democratic republic. He takes the world as science describes it. He employs his knowledge of the world to increase man's power over things, to decrease man's power over man, and to enlarge the fellowship of free and equal persons striving to achieve a more just and happier society.

[8] See his reply to Henry Adams, who tried to draw social and historical implications from the second law of thermodynamics (*The Letters of William James*, Boston, 1920, II, 344–47).

4

NATURALISM AND ETHICAL THEORY

Abraham Edel

IN our Western tradition ethical analysis has been far from naturalistic. The investigation of ethical values has not been considered an empirical project. The dominant stress has been on insight, introspection, and the immediate apprehension of essences. Results have been framed in the absolutes of conviction rather than the probabilities of science, for scientific method has been held to be inapplicable to the world of the spirit.

For these reasons present-day naturalism is bound to emphasize the need for extending empirical or scientific method to the treatment of values. A naturalistic approach involves reanalysis of ethical ideas in terms of our present logical equipment, designation of the empirical material with which ethics is concerned, and continual testing of the utility of ethical formulations in terms of this material. Insistence on such testing is part of the naturalistic stress on the primacy of matter; recognition that ethical formulations may require alteration is a consequence of noting the pervasiveness of change. Reliance on scientific method, together with an appreciation of the primacy of matter and the pervasiveness of change, I take to be the central points of naturalism as a philosophic outlook.

In constructing its ethical theory naturalism today may draw upon two major sources. One is the results of the sciences, especially the biological, psychological, and social studies. The other is the history of ethical theory in which a broad naturalistic current may be traced through portions of many theoretical writings. Thus we may draw upon the formal analysis of Aristotle, who built a structure upon the "nature" of man, which he filled in with biologic material and everyday observations and prejudices. The history of materialism from Democritus through Hobbes and the French materialists to the Marxian school provides a long tradition in which the naturalistic approach achieved maturity. In addition, there is the temporal stress of evolutionary ethical theory and the stubborn empiricism of much of the Utilitarian structure. In American philosophy of our own time Dewey in his various writings and Santayana in his *Life of Reason* have to some extent gathered the strands and produced substantially naturalistic ethical systems.

This essay aims both to characterize the approach of naturalism in ethical theory and at the same time to analyze more intensively a few of the problems that are crucial in the internal development of naturalistic ethics itself.

I · INTERPRETATION OF ETHICAL TERMS

The need for empirical interpretation of ethical terms has been strongly denied in nonnaturalistic ethics. For example, Hartmann has written: "The settlement of the matter depends upon demonstrating that there is a self-existent ideal sphere in which values are native, and that, as the contents of this sphere, values, self-subsistent and dependent upon no prior experience, are discerned a priori." [1] In the intuitionist tradition ethical concepts become clear, certain types of action are seen self-evidently to be right or good, to have some moral or value character. As W. D. Ross puts it:

We have no more direct way of access to the facts about rightness and goodness and about what things are right or good than by thinking about them; the moral convictions of thoughtful and well-educated people are the data of ethics just as sense-perceptions are the data of a natural science. . . . The verdicts of the moral consciousness of the best people are the foundation on which he must build; though he must first compare them with one another and eliminate any contradictions they may contain.[2]

Of course, as Aristotle says, "this is not evident except to the good man; for wickedness perverts us and causes us to be deceived about the starting-points of action." [3] Or, to quote Hartmann again,

But it is here just as it is with mathematical insight. Not everyone is capable of it; not everyone has the eye, the ethical maturity, the spiritual elevation, for seeing the situation as it is. Nevertheless the universality, necessity and objectivity of the valuational judgment hold good in idea. For this universality does not at all mean that everyone is capable of the insight in question. It only means that whoever is capable of it—that is, whoever has attained the adequate mentality—must necessarily feel and judge thus and not otherwise.[4]

[1] *Ethics* (English translation by Stanton Coit), 1, 165.
[2] *The Right and the Good*, pp. 40–41. [3] *Nicomachean Ethics* 1144a 34–36.
[4] *Ethics* (English translation by Stanton Coit), 1, 225.

In a naturalistic ethics, since ethical statements that are not analytic or conventional are to be empirically verifiable, there must be among ethical terms those capable of empirical interpretation. Thus Hobbes says, "Whatsoever is the object of any man's appetite or desire; that is it, which he for his part calleth *good*." Similarly, "good" has at various times been interpreted as productive of pleasure, an object of striving, of approval, of interest, of enjoyment, of active tension, and so forth. In all those cases the *ethical* term is being translated into *psychological* terms, and it is assumed that psychological science or common usage provides the empirical procedures by which statements containing the psychological terms may be tested. Or the ethical term may be translated into "what enables the group to survive"; here the empirical identifications of the constituent terms are left to sociology and biology, and so forth.

Where in a system or a statement such terms are used and no empirical interpretation given—even where empirical interpretation is ruled out— a naturalistic ethics will examine the specific ways in which the term is applied and from these contexts discover what is in fact being employed as an interpretation. Thus Aristotle constantly defines the virtues as ways of organizing the raw materials of character according to the mean, and the mean as an ability to act in the right fashion toward the right persons to the right extent, and so forth, and right is defined as what a man of practical wisdom would do in a particular context. We have thus a system worked out for possible application, but it can be applied only if men of practical wisdom are pointed out to us, so that we can learn empirically what right conduct is, or if the empirical procedures by which conduct may be judged right are given us so that we may identify empirically the men of practical wisdom. Ross takes "the moral convictions of thoughtful and well-educated people" as the data of ethics, so that ultimately his system finds its empirical interpretations in what such persons will say. However, precision would require specification of how "well-educated" is to be interpreted. Is it limited to graduation from Oxford or Cambridge, or does it include as well those who have gone to the special higher school reserved for first-born sons of the chiefs among the Maori? Similarly, when we examine Hartmann's *Ethics* we find we need to know the empirical marks of "ethical maturity" and "spiritual elevation." Again, when it is argued that things taken to be good have no common character, so that one may merely list them [5] (for example, pleasure, friendship), the interpretation of good is really reduced to "what is either pleasure or friendship, etc." Usually, however, there is implicit some vague mode of identification, such as "that towards which I have a certain feeling, a feeling grossly recognizable but not yet analyzed" or "that towards which I prefer to guide my conduct," or "that which I am ready to use as grounds for approving of conduct," or even "that which I have been taught to call good." On the other hand, it may be that "good" is being equivocally applied. A term of such wide usage frequently turns out to be equivocal. What is important is that eventually there be some empirical interpretation, whether one or several conjointly. If there is none whatsoever, then the statements containing the term belong to a system having no application.[6]

In the light of the variety of interpretations offered for "good" in the naturalistic tradition, must it be said that *any* interpretation is bound to be arbitrary? Logically, of course, the interpretation has the status of a convention. It is a kind of "co-ordinating definition," where it is not purely a "nominal definition." But to stress the conventional side overmuch is to lose sight of the mass of material (broadly speaking, man's evaluations) that is to be systematized. As in establishing the meaning for any term by the examination of usage, the result is a convention, but it is one which preserves a wide range of common usage and *thereafter* helps determine what usage will become common. Thus, the initial material does not remain completely fixed, but may at some points be altered in the process. The problem is the same as that faced in attempts to demarcate the subject matter of a science. Physics has been called the science of motion, or of bodies in motion. A more advanced physics may choose, however, to define its subject matter as what its most general formulas apply to and may shift the boundary lines as it finds application beyond for its laws. Thus, in time large portions of physics and chemistry have coalesced because laws have been discovered having consequences exemplified in both.

[5] G. E. Moore's view in *Principia Ethica* is an illustration of this position.

[6] The use of a metaphysical interpretation merely postpones the demand for an empirical one. "Good" may be translated into theological terms as "according to the nature God has implanted in man." The nonnaturalistic elements arise in the question of empirical procedures for identifying the translation. On the other hand, where "right" is equated with "what God wills" it has sometimes been argued that God wills it because it is right, and not that it is right because God wills it. This is, in effect, denying the correctness of "what God wills" as the primary interpretation of "right."

Similarly, ethics need have no finally delimited subject matter. We may start with any of the traditional interpretations of good—in terms of pleasure, desire, striving, interest, and so forth—and reject one in favor of another on a basis such as that it is too wide or too narrow for the domain we have implicitly or, if possible, explicitly accepted as a starting point. Shall we, for example, start with men's pleasures or men's desires as the material of ethics? That is, shall we decide on "pleasure" or "object of desire" as the interpretation of "good"? Since desire involves a state of deprivation and some pleasures may occur without antecedent deprivation or even anticipation, the two interpretations delimit different though overlapping fields for study. Shall we therefore say that "pleasure" as an interpretation of "good" gives us too wide a field, or that "object of desire" narrows too much the field of ethics? Clearly it does not matter too much which we do. If "pleasure" is taken as the interpretation of "good," we shall have to say that not all of ethics refers to conduct aiming at the satisfaction of desire; if "object of desire" is decided upon, we shall have to say that not all values in conduct are embraced in ethics. The results on any one set of conventions could be translated into the results on any other, if the whole field to which both refer is ordered, whether in one system or several conjointly. The choice between interpretations is therefore to be made in the hope of achieving the most systematic account of the field.

In contrast to a great part of the modern [7] naturalistic tradition I should like to present the view that the act of choosing is the existential material to which ethics most systematically refers, that choosing is not the secondary application of rules, but the primary material whose tendency ethical rules describe and delimit, in short, that ethical terms can best be interpreted as referring to phases and elements of choice.

Our attention is directed toward choice as soon as we begin to examine carefully the actual interpretation of the psychological and social terms into which traditional naturalistic ethics has translated "good." In most cases there is a direct or indirect reference to the initiation of conduct, that is, to choice or a series of choices. Frequently the test of A's being pleased by x is taken to be the fact that he prefers it or keeps on choosing it. The fundamental error of many critics of Bentham and Mill was to take them literally and to assume that the psychological properties of pleasure were crucial to Utilitarianism. In terms of their

[7] Choice does occupy a central position in the ethics of Plato and Aristotle.

actual procedure in concrete ethical discussion, "to be pleased" meant simply to choose or be ready to choose certain courses of action or sets of results.[8] Similarly, striving, active tension, desire, and enjoyment would be made manifest by actions and sets of choices. Approval and interest might more likely issue in discourse on a person's part, and in the case of pleasure, too, he might report on his feelings. We have, therefore, to decide between a material of ethics that is discovered merely by introspection, or one in which introspective materials will be a part correlated with and checked up by more readily observable conduct. The decision need not be forced upon us. We may try both and see which produces a more systematic science.

Our preference for an interpretation in terms of choice is based on several factors. There is the fact, just noted, that many traditional interpretations are themselves indirect appeals to sets of choices. Again, choice is the beginning of conduct, and ethics, interested in guiding conduct, should pay attention to starting points where control is rendered possible. It is also more objectively discoverable. The reliability of direct inspection of the self and its attitudes may be seriously questioned. The traditional emphasis upon it is a consequence of the dualist's dichotomy of the realm of mind and the realm of nature. Of course, if one of the traditional notions can be rendered more precise and capable of refined distinctions and manipulation, especially if it permit of quantitative measurement, it might be used as the material of ethics even if it be correlated only roughly with choice. But in spite of the hopes of the hedonistic calculus, it cannot be said that present-day studies in the psychology of feeling have achieved results comparable, for example, to the substitution of thermometer readings for sensations of hot and cold in determining therapy.

The task of giving ethical terms an interpretation with reference to choice is an elaborate one. We may illustrate it with the fundamental notion of *good* or *ethical value*, turning our attention in "*x* is good" to the typical case in which *x* is a general term. The problem is tremendously clarified when we compare it to many similar issues in the field of legal theory, where the ethical statement is writ large in the legal statement.

If we take rules of law to be the rules manifest or discoverable as general trends in judicial decisions (a position of growing importance since

[8] Cf. the standard Latin form *placuit senatui* for "the senate decided."

Gray's classic work *The Nature and Sources of the Law*), we get an interpretation that has the following advantages:

1. It provides a *descriptive* meaning to "a law." Whether such-and-such is law becomes a question for empirical investigation in a clearly designated material.

2. It preserves a *normative* character for a rule of law in two senses, first with reference to the judge who may feel obligated to consider seriously an established rule, and second with reference to the public, who may investigate what they must or must not do, at what cost to themselves.

3. It guarantees no theoretical certainty which does not exist in fact, since it indicates the creative role of judges, in whose decisions even established rules may be weakened or sharply broken.

4. It preserves a fundamental point in permitting the *criticism* of decisions on legal grounds, not merely on moral ones. Thus any one decision may be declared legally wrong in the light of a trend of decisions, while a whole trend may be estimated in the light of its consistency with prevailing rules in the body of law.

5. It distinguishes between law and the sources of law. Sources may have two senses—what judges in fact look to in rendering decision (statute, precedent, custom, and so forth) and what the causes of decision may be in so far as they lie in the judge and in circumstances.

There is no reason why the analysis of an ethical rule such as *"x is good"* should be simpler than the analysis of the legal rule. An ethical rule thus interpreted states the general trends discoverable in acts of choice, both in the initiation of conduct and in reflection thereon. This interpretation presents the same advantages as its analogue in legal philosophy:

1. It makes the statement that such-and-such is good an empirical proposition referring to the forms of choice in the conduct and reflection of some implicitly specified individual or group.

2. It preserves a normative character, because it is a fact that men often guide themselves in present choice by the character of their previous acts of choice and the results of their reflection upon them. Similarly, in many relationships (child-parent, pupil-teacher, and so forth) people guide their conduct by the choices that others make.

3. It does not guarantee a theoretical certainty even concerning one's own values or judgments of goodness. In spite of the old notion that a man can read off his values from within himself, it is pretty clear that we are frequently mistaken. The interpretation likewise makes manifest the creative

role of present choice. It is not simply a point at which a man struggles with himself to follow some pre-existent moral rule, but is a genuine pivot for weakening, breaking, continuing or strengthening values, beginning new paths, offering new suggestions, and so forth.

4. It meets the superficial objection that men choose something because it is good, and it is not good because they choose it. For the interpretation allows for the *criticism* of choices, which it could not do if it identified "good" simply with "object of choice" and made ethics identical with psychology. Thus a man's or group's particular choice can be estimated in the light of his or their accepted trend of choice, and any trend of choice can be criticized in the light of the consistency with the whole body of trends of choice of that individual or group. Finally, corresponding to moral criticism of rules of law is the possibility of extraneous criticism in the light of the trends of choice of some other individual or group than the one concerned.

5. It can distinguish between good and the "sources" of good. Again sources may have two senses—what the person judging looks to (whether it pleases or attracts, whether it is what he has always done, or what venerable people have done, and so forth) and what the causes of choice may be (psychological, social and cultural, physiological, and so forth).

The interpretation offered enables us to resolve two traditional disputes about ethical statements, whether they are "normative" or "descriptive" and whether there are any distinctively ethical statements. In both cases the difficulties are seen to be due to the demand for an absolute answer.

As was pointed out above, ethical statements are descriptive in one context and normative in another. They are descriptive in that they tell about someone's or some group's trend of choice. They are normative to the person or group adopting them as rules of choice. This adoption may be implicit in conduct, or it may be explicit in reflection on conduct. Such adoption in reflection is itself really a choice—*a choice of a class of choices to be made in subsequent conduct on relevant occasions.* Such reflection on conduct, frequently a process of justification for action performed or of analysis of implicit adoption of a rule, may thus be viewed as a second-order choice.[9]

---

[9] A first-order choice is thus a direct initiation of conduct, a second-order choice an indirect one. That first-order choices do not thereafter always manifest the second-order choice shows simply that a good intention or firm conviction may falter on a specific occasion. Neither does a first-order choice always get carried through with its initial ardor.

The ethical statement which is normative in respect to each of the first-order choices is descriptive when seen as a second-order choice. Similarly, another second-order choice may function normatively in respect to this one. For example, I may choose in a particular case to persist in a course of action in spite of difficulties and justify myself by saying that strength of character is a good. This rule reflectively adopted functions normatively for my particular choice. Descriptively it is, according to our analysis, a second-order choice, to issue in a whole class of kindred actions if I do not falter or retract it. Now, if I justify strength of character by saying that it is an integral element in the achievement of "success" and that success is a good, this latter second-order choice functions normatively in respect to my evaluation of strength of character, and may itself in turn be descriptively considered. There need be no theoretical end to this process, although for any person or group at any one time there probably is.

The second question—whether there are any distinctively ethical statements—is settled in a similar fashion. Absolutely, there are not, since the implied reference to a particular individual or group enables us to investigate whether these are in fact his or its values (trends of choice). But clearly in each context there are distinctly ethical statements, since any statement such as "I desire this" can be intelligibly countered with "But is it good?" and even "I find this good" can be met with "But is it good?" Aristotle described this part of the ethical process in a fashion which corresponds closely to everyday ethical exhortation. The good in a particular act of choice he called the apparent good. When he did not approve of the choice, it could be called mistaken. Now while this tended to neglect the genuinely pivotal character of the particular act of choice, we may readily rewrite the Aristotelian description in the light of a fuller naturalism. The distinction between my apparent good and my real good becomes that between the object of choice in any single act of choice or reflection on conduct and the object of choice when reflection is ideally complete. Expanding reflection frequently shows the relation of the present particular goods to wider goods. It does not necessarily reduce them to a subsidiary role, but examines whether they are permitted by, compatible with, and part of a complex pattern of organized pervasive goods which constitutes my "general good." I may thus come to see that what appeared to me to be my good really is my good, or in other cases, really is not my good. First-order choices thus become strengthened or rejected in second-order choices, just as conversely second-order choices are tested and completed or discarded in first-order choices. If a man's analysis of his aims, activities, and role could be furnished with entire certainty, he would be able to follow the advice of Socrates to its conclusion; he would know himself and his real good.[10] The notion of a man's real good is therefore to be understood as the organized system of his choices in an ideally completed process of reflection on choice, anything short of which is his apparent good. Now, since this ideal represents and allows of indefinite perfection, what a man has in mind when he offers principles of what men should do, is the widest system on which he operates at present.

So far we have dealt with "good" as a single term. To complete its interpretation, even for illustrative purposes, we should recognize such differences as are intended by "good" and "a good" on the one hand, and "good for" on the other. This emerges in ethical discourse as the contrast of "end" and "means" or "valuable" and "instrumental." Because so much controversy has centered and still centers in such questions as whether ends and means can be divorced, whether the end justifies the means, and so forth, it is useful to examine the interpretation of these distinctions. This is aided by a closer inspection of choice as an act.

Choice implies that an individual in a definite situation is adopting one of alternative courses of action. He need not be standing still about to embark on one or another path; he may be in the midst of action, choosing whether to continue on one path or turn toward another.[11] A choice is not the occurrence of an action, but its beginning. Hence a choice determines conduct only as part of an act determines the act— that is, by limiting the variety of possible completions. But for the most part that is important enough to determine the direction of the act. Now, since the act of choice is a beginning, it is also capable of analysis with reference to its projected middle and end. This is the source of the categories of means and ends.

It follows on such an approach that "means" and "ends" should not be taken out of the context of a process and made to characterize things or events or actions in themselves. To say that something is an end is to

[10] This enables us also to understand why Socrates stubbornly adhered to the view that no one voluntarily chooses evil; for to choose is to evaluate. Of course his assertion could not be proved, since its logical status was that of a proposed interpretation.

[11] Hence, frequently "to avoid a choice" is itself to make a choice.

say that it occupies the position of projected terminus in a process involving a means. To say that something is a means is to say that there is a process for which a terminus is projected beyond the means. Whenever ambiguity arises it is always salutary to go back to this point and find the process which those employing the terms have in mind.

It likewise follows that propositions such as "Ends and means cannot be divorced" are in one sense analytic.[12] Without reference to possible choice as a beginning of conduct, neither ends nor means can be identified. Given that reference, both are necessarily involved. Something may, of course, be independently "prized" or "wished for," but it cannot be "willed" or "chosen" without the initiating of conduct, hence a reference to means. Nor, again, can there be pursuit of a means without an end, since by definition if the means is pursued as "ultimate" it is itself the end and the distinction of means and end will be made afresh in its own analysis.

Means and ends in choice tend to be or to become systematized separately. Means are judged by their efficacy in achieving projected ends. With the development of the sciences the means in some first-order choices achieve a high degree of separateness. They become "purely technical" questions, and choice tends to pass over them as colorless, to deal with the ends. This refers, of course, to the means in first-order choice. For the process of first-order choice consists in initiating one course of means-end action where the projected terminus is the end to be achieved. We do not know too much about the means required in second-order choice. Here the alternatives are sets of first-order choices (or in traditional language, ethical principles), and the projected terminus is the actual selection or acts of will which constitute first-order choices. The means are our available resources—psychological, physical, and social—for "sticking to our principles" and finding out where they are applicable. The problem is complicated by the role of second-order choice, explored especially by the Freudians, as "rationalizations" rather than embedded principles for future action.

Ends tend to be systematized as a catalogue of "goods" or "values," intended to function as suggestions for first-order choices. The systematization of ends is therefore the very process of second-order choice. In any particular situation in which we wish to apply them we must

[12] In what sense such statements are intended to be empirically verifiable will be discussed below.

know some means before choice can take place. The first-order choice occurs when motion toward the end is initiated, regardless of whether it will in fact achieve it.

It is a commonplace that this systematization of ends separately from means has often led to their undue divorce from means and to the view that ethics is concerned solely with ends. This tendency was considerably strengthened by the way in which essence-philosophies ascribed fixed natures to existents, issuing in the doctrine of fixed ends or goals in nature. Current naturalistic discussions of the means-end relationship (for example, by John Dewey) have as a constant background the rejection of this doctrine. Such attacks upon the separation of means and ends are not merely pointing out their analytic or conceptual relationship described above. They intend to make empirical assertions about what goes on in men's lives. The factual implications of the naturalistic denial that means and end can be divorced, may be set forth as follows:

1. There is a tremendous variety of men's ends; theoretically, no activity or object would seem incapable of being an end; hence there are no fixed ends.

2. The ends of one group (or person) turn out on empirical investigation to be the means of another, and vice versa.

3. The ends of one group (or person) at one time are found sometimes to be the means of the same group (or person) at another time.

4. Any particular act that is a means in one respect may be an end in another respect.

5. An end in action (or reflection) may come to be regarded as a means in further action (or reflection), and vice versa. Similarly, an end in action (or reflection) may become regarded as a means in reflection (or action), and vice versa.

6. In the process of action and reflection new ends may arise (as well as new means), which may replace the previous ones even before they are achieved.

7. Ends have consequences themselves, and so point beyond, just as means have other consequences beside the end at which they are directed. Hence, reflective appraisal looks beyond both ends and means.

8. To hold to fixed values produces an inability to adapt oneself. The same is true of holding to fixed means without regard to increasing knowledge.

This naturalistic critique is intended to be a clarification, not a destruction, of the means-end relationship. It should not appear, as it sometimes does, that ends are not really ends because they are themselves evaluated by the worth of their consequences. The consequences may be examined simply in order to see whether they detract sufficiently to withhold that particular choice, just as the means may be examined to see whether they are too costly for that particular choice. The status as an end is not affected unless the *usual* consequences or *regularly available* means detract *sufficiently frequently and to such an extent* that this *type of choice* is retracted, or they become so attractive that a new goal emerges in an altered type of choice, so that the former end becomes subsidiary or may even thereafter be treated as a means. Thus, the test of an end is its functioning as an end, and when it ceases so to function in some person or group it has ceased to be an end.

Similarly, the naturalistic critique need not militate against the separate systematization of means and ends. It is one thing to ground the distinction by reference to individuals or groups in spatio-temporal contexts; it is another to destroy the scientific direction which the systematization of means and ends embodies. The procedure of starting with the ends and then adding or subtracting values affected in the means or in the consequences of the ends is an eminently reasonable one. That the starting points may be changed in the process does not challenge the need for starting points in a given context. In this fashion we are able to isolate phases of the events for separate study, although in prediction and planning action we must bring them together again. A statement of *my* ends is a hypothesis which you may test (or I myself may test if I can watch myself with sufficient objectivity) with regard to the set of choices I make in specified types of situation. Normatively, viewed by me (for whom the ends are the objects of second-order choice), the statement of my ends is a set of suggested termini in first-order choices. But both in your predictions about my reaction in particular cases, and in my planning my action in particular cases, attention must be paid to means and consequences before it will be settled whether the end is here and now to be actualized.

There is one objection to the above analysis of the means-end relationship in terms of the middles and projected ends of choices and their systematization. This is the fact that the means-end category is sometimes employed where the temporal reference disappears. For example, it is said that pleasure is the end of some actions, even though pleasure is concomitant with, not consequent to, these actions. This objection is, however, only apparent. The fundamental notion in the means-end relation emerges as causal rather than temporal. It is, however, concerned with practice, and so instead of implying merely "invariant relationship" it never loses the idea of control which is also predominant in the practical use of cause. Thus, actions which pleasure invariably accompanies may be regarded as causally productive of it, hence as means to it.

There is another sense in which pleasure in this example might be regarded as an end. It may be the terminus in the process of reflection on or justification of first-order choice and therefore be an end in a second-order choice. For example, you say that your justification for eating this food is that it has a chocolate flavor, and you want a chocolate flavor because it gives you pleasure. The process of justification thus terminates here in pleasure, which you have taken to be good, a stable end in many first-order choices. Nevertheless, we should hardly feel free to use the notion of "means" for whatever enters into the reckoning which culminates in the reflective choice of pleasure as the end, for the result might be that the "means" would turn out to be subsequent to the end, for example, where future pains are accepted in anticipation in the process of validating present pleasures.

It is probably better, therefore, to take the means-end relationship to be limited to the domain in which causality is applicable and the means to retain the idea of "instrumentality." Beyond that, different categories must be developed. These should be terms in which we can express the cost or price of embodying an end in choice—whether it be the cost of the means or of the consequences of choosing to act in that particular way. Terms serving such a purpose are: positive value, negative value, better, worse, and so forth. The categories suggested are not identical with the means-end relationship, but are categories in which both means and ends may be evaluated in broadened or altered contexts.[18]

We have thus seen that there is an interpretation of "a good" and "good for" in terms of the end-and-means phases of choice. This strengthens the initial interpretation of "good" by reference to choice. Its utility will become clearer if the remainder of the present terminology of ethics—better, best, bad and its degrees, right, wrong, ought, duty, and so forth—is given comparable interpretation by reference to phases of the act of choice or series of acts. The same should be done for

[18] In terms of such categories we can analyze questions like "Does the end justify the means?" This one is obviously in need of considerable analysis. Clearly some ends justify some means and not others. In general form, it is like asking "Is the object purchased worth the cost?"

the psychological notions of intention, motive, and purpose and for any other term that may be introduced. As suggested above, this need not be a terminology fixed for all time, but is to be judged by its efficacy in enabling us to systematize the realm of ethics. The ideal of such efforts would, of course, be the kind of strictly related terms which some philosophers have elaborated as pure systems.[14] At present such precise formulations seem to me to be premature in that they will not enable us to deal with the complex materials of ethics. It may, for example, even be advisable to give "bad" the independent interpretation of a rule of avoidance in choice rather than regard it as some purely mathematical function of "good."

II · VERIFICATION IN ETHICS

In theory the problem of verification in ethics should be no different from the same problem in any other field. Historically it has, however, been complicated by the belief that since the material of ethics consists of men's values it is somehow more accessible to men. We ought, accordingly, to be able to peer within ourselves and to read off our values. This assertion that we can discover our values by direct internal inspection rests upon the traditional dualism according to which matter is external and can be only indirectly known, whereas mind is our very being and so can be experienced. The view has had serious consequences upon social science. On the assumption that any man understands them, terms designating attitudes and values have been left without precise empirical analysis. Hence verification has been difficult and ambiguity rampant. For the naturalist, on the other hand, knowledge of the self, its values and activities, is on the same theoretical plane as knowledge of objects. The apparent difference arises only if we confuse experience as an event with ascribing some predicate to that event. Thus, the assertion "I want to help him" does not merely say that I am having some feeling but also attributes a definite character to the feeling. In such matters contemporary psychological theory, with its talk of unconscious desires, has made well known the fallibility of self-knowledge and the pervasiveness of "rationalization." Hence verification is required.

[14] For example, A. P. Brogan, "The Fundamental Value Universal," *Journal of Philosophy*, XVI (1919), 96–104; Felix Cohen, *Ethical Ideals and Legal Systems*, ch. iii; Albert Hofstadter and J. C. C. McKinsey, "On the Logic of Imperatives," *Philosophy of Science*, VI (October, 1939), 446–57.

In this part of our discussion we shall touch on problems of verification with respect to the following: assertions about instrumentalities, general and singular ethical statements, ethical statements involving logical relations.

Instrumentality-assertions have, of course, been conceded to be empirical by all ethical theories. No special points are involved in their verification. The statement that a certain means will in fact achieve a specified end is tested in ordinary experience or in one or another of the sciences. When complex instrumentalities are to be estimated in the social sciences (for example, whether a system of private ownership of land and industries or a system of public ownership will best provide general security) difficulties arise for two reasons—the complexity of the material and the introduction of questions of value. The latter refers not only to the values of the investigator but also to the fact that the estimation of instrumentalities involves at the same time an assessment of collateral values or disvalues to which the means will give rise. Hence, consideration of means and ends becomes intertwined. Careful analysis, the distinction of problems, and the elaboration of a standard of values alone provide a way of solving the problem.

The verification of ethical statements about "general values" or ends has taken a number of different forms in the naturalistic tradition. The Utilitarians, for example, reduced them to instrumentality-assertions: "*x* is good" meant "*x* on the whole achieves a maximum of pleasure for men." The fundamental value-statement "pleasure is the good" was not taken by them to be merely a co-ordinating definition of "the good." Sidgwick held to the statement on grounds of intuition, whereas J. S. Mill tried to treat it as empirical. Implicitly, he was aiming at the type of interpretation here offered and arguing that pleasure is the constant object of choice.[15] Once we take a value to be a choice of choices, as was suggested above, the mode of verification sought must lie in the types of choice that would ensue. A general statement that something is good means, therefore, that it is the rule of choice for a specified individual, a group, or all men or groups.

This is what is referred to both in ordinary life and in social psychol-

---

[15] In his argument that pleasure is good because all men aim at it, Mill implied that good meant object of preference. He then proposed to show that pleasure is in fact the constant object of preference. But in preparing for the test, he defined pleasure in such a way that being pleased was indistinguishable from preferring (*Utilitarianism*, ch. iv).

ogy when we speak of "holding a value." We judge a man's values by his acts, by the way he chooses between possible alternatives, in part by what he says, and especially by the way he reacts in unexpected situations. We may estimate our own values in the same fashion, reflecting on our reactions and feelings in diverse situations, the directions in which we readily choose or feel impelled to choose, the feelings of satisfaction or regret, joy or remorse, approval or guilt. In the more careful attitude-testing of social psychologists we find a procedure essentially no different, except that it is more calculated to take us off our guard, to reveal inconsistencies in value, and to give a more precise empirical meaning to general values. Thus has arisen, for example, the question whether there really are very general values at all. A student may approve of honesty in general and may manifest it in any matter in which money is concerned, but think nothing of taking assistance during an examination. Is this inconsistency on his part, or is the scope of a general value indeterminate? Which it is for a specified individual or group is a thoroughly empirical problem. Thus, in the extreme case, that of Kant, there seems to be no doubt that he was ready to identify truth-telling by very explicit and unambiguous marks and to follow it in any and every possible subsumption under it.[16] Any deviation on his part would have been an inconsistency. Most people would not devote themselves so completely to a single value, and a more complex hierarchy of values within more or less specified domains is the more common occurrence.

A statement about a group's values is, of course, really about the frequency and distribution of these values among its members and about its use of methods for inculcating a specified pattern. This can be tested in a simple statistical fashion, as we would test "Americans like ham and eggs for breakfast," or in a more complicated way when an interplay of such investigations is required. Thus the assertion "Americans take divorce to be an evil" would require to be tested not only in a study of attitudes on the subject but also by investigations such as: the way in which typical individuals behave in stress situations in the family; the statistical frequency of divorce; the lack of provision in our society for typical family life for children of divorced parents; the behavior of various types of groups toward divorced persons; the state laws governing freedom of divorce and the extent to which they are relaxed; attitudes—expressed in language and behavior—toward the remarriage of

[16] See his essay, *On a Supposed Right to Tell Lies from Benevolent Motives.*

divorced persons; publicity and notoriety attaching to divorce cases and to the lives of the much-remarried.

If we wish to study more minutely the process of verification in ethics, we ought to look not merely at the way in which we can test the holding of a general value by a group or individual—which implies a constancy in the trend of choices—but also at the process by which we verify the fact that a particular act of choice exemplifies or fails to exemplify the trend. For at such points the rule becomes confirmed or rejected.

Broadly speaking, we can observe the particular choice as it takes place, starting from a selective want emerging as a present preference and issuing in the direction of energies toward a particular end. Nevertheless, difficulties of interpretation sometimes occur. Suppose I want wine now and choose port; but suppose that upon sipping it I feel a strong aversion to drinking it and in fact do not. Does this mean that I was mistaken in thinking I wanted it then, or that my mood has changed? Does such a happening confirm or disconfirm the statement I might have made that port is good? Or is the most that we can do merely to discover that given the state of self s_1 at time t_1, I assert value v_1: given s_2 at t_2, I assert v_2, and so forth. Verification in ethics may be analogous to the appeal from Philip drunk to Philip sober, but there must be some constant Philip underlying the two states, or we shall simply say: given the imbibing of so many quarts, the judge condemns to death; given abstention for so many hours, he renders a verdict of acquittal.

The role of the constancy of self must not, however, be exaggerated. There is a constancy required in every experiment of any sort, which consists in those assumed facts about which there is agreement in the context of the experiment; for example, statements about perceived qualities. These statements may, however, be made the subject of experiment in a context in which something else is assumed. So it is with the constancy of self in ethical verification. It need never be a general constancy, a "metaphysical" self, an existent behind all bodily phenomena. Rather it is always some specific pattern of tendencies or values, assumed to remain constant throughout the period during which the verification concerning a single value is taking place. If questioned, it suffers the same fate as any hypothesis when it is scrutinized—it is independently tested in a context of fresh experiment with other assumptions, in this case of some other constancy of self. Thus, in the example given above my aversion to port at time t_2 renders it probable that I did not really want wine at time t_1 if the set of my relevant desires is assumed constant from t_1 to t_2 and if other factors may be assumed to have been equal; for example, that this port is a fair sample of the port I drink, or that I have not eaten or drunk in the interval, or that I am not sick. If circumstances did change, then of course it is left undetermined whether I did or did not want wine at t_1, and may be that I did. Now the task of establishing the constancy or change of relevant desires and circumstances consists in specifying them and gathering all available evidence: for example, whether I am usually fickle in my tastes, whether there was anything unusual taking place at the time (such as cumulative effect of past drinking), the relative frequency with which in the past a desire for wine issued in drinking, and so forth.

This pattern of interpreting the single event becomes clearer if we take a more extended process of choice manifesting the same difficulties. Mr. A. buys a philosophy book as the first step toward reading it, but does not get down to reading it, although he starts several times. Did this act of choice embody the fact that he holds philosophy as a value, that is, does it confirm or disconfirm the view that he values philosophy? Clearly there will be no adequate interpretation of the particular choice until we know how difficult the book was or how representative, whether Mr. A. is overworked at other tasks, whether he constantly buys philosophy books without reading them, whether he engages in philosophical discussion or turns aside every opportunity with an epigram, and so forth. Thus we shall determine objectively whether his value is buying philosophy books (and the rest pious sentiment), in which case the particular act of choice was completed, or really philosophizing, in which case the analysis of the particular will yield the factors which thwarted successful completion of what was then chosen.

The process is usually complex, and most results are tentative; but reflection will show that it is precisely such a process and no other that we employ in testing most of our judgments about our own characters or the characters of others. It is especially clear in reflection upon extreme changes in attitude. The confirmed bachelor, after being happily married, may decide that he had always really liked the opposite sex and point to actions he had hitherto incorrectly interpreted. The religious convert may desire to demonstrate an altered self and therefore point to factors which produced a rapid change. The ivory-tower poet who becomes socially conscious may have altered his values, which he would show by his attitude to his previous work, or he may have retained the values, but have come to realize that they were socially grounded and required a special type of attained social stability.

The cases most difficult of analysis are those in which a man confesses that a value v_1 previously held has given away to some contrary value v_2 and yet still insists on calling v_1 a mistake. His assertion would seem upon analysis to imply that there is some constant value (V), which seemed to him to yield or require v_1, which he came over a course of time to hold for its own sake and later discovered to be incompatible with V, which really required v_2 as an accompanying element. Thus, a man may abandon a profit system (v_1) for a socialist system (v_2), having genuinely hitherto approved of the first, whereas public security may be the constant value (V) with which he formerly associated v_1 and now associates v_2. The relation is not a simple one of means and ends. It is to be noted that the change of value, although it may on rare occasions take the form of a whirlwind substitution, would regularly seem to involve some constant value which acts as a pivot for the transformation. But the pivot of one change may itself be shifted when some fresh value has become stable enough to act as a pivot.

We have now seen roughly the way in which verification occurs when a man has been asserted correctly or mistakenly to hold a certain value, when there has been a change of value, and when a value formerly held was said to be mistaken. In all these the conception of the self implied is thoroughly empirical, that of a core of dominant relatively stable values or a pattern of choice. The breadth and continuity of the self is likewise to be empirically determined and may vary considerably from person to person. Thus the traditional attempt [17] to build up a whole good for a whole man by which he may check his present desires is merely formal, referring to the fact of a stable core of values at any one time by which others are tested. If it attempts to be material and invariably to cover all fields of a man's possible interest and the whole duration of his life, it runs the risk of being unwarranted generalization. If it threatens us with the bogey of a completely disintegrated self as the only alternative to its description of the unity of self, its picture is palpably false. We may readily grant (being far-sighted philosophers)

[17] For example, Sidgwick, *The Methods of Ethics*, 6th ed., Book III, ch. xiii, especially, pp. 381–83.

that we value a kind of self which lays its plans and guides its choice on a full-life basis, a self for whom "the same thing is always painful, and the same thing always pleasant, and not one thing at one time and another at another; he has, so to speak, nothing to repent of." [18] But this represents a definite preference, and quite other preferences do in fact occur. The period of life may be shortened in calculated comparison to a brief span of glory, as Achilles chose; or some may live for life's first half without in fact, as the moralist would like it, regretting their choice thereafter. Or again, some may in fact approach the type of a series of discrete states with a minimum of connection, and choose relatively for the moment. Differences of type are sometimes made manifest by the general attitude, after a large-scale change of values, toward the values abandoned. Some may repent of the past, others, treating it as a discrete and now detached portion of their lives, may think serenely, even benignly, upon their earlier folly. Still others may reckon the past to have been appropriate to its time of life and inexperience. We are obviously in a field in which insufficient empirical classification and study of forms has been carried on. From the naturalist's point of view the important thing is that in such a study we are dealing with ultimate values, that is, values functioning in those who hold them for the determination of other more special kinds of choice and frequently operating without being clearly recognized in spite of their pervasiveness, or perhaps just because of it and because they are less likely to alter. But in recognizing that they function as ultimate in the lives of specific individuals or groups, naturalist ethics does not give them an intuitive or transcendental status. Ultimate values can be explained by showing historically how they arose, replaced predecessors if any, and what were the determinants of this process. Ultimate values are simply intense or pervasive attitudes of men in a natural and social world functioning in a special way with relation to their other values. In the light of varying values—arising out of individual and social change—they may be accepted or rejected; in the light of growing understanding they may occasionally be susceptible of increasing control.

Our final problem in the analysis of verification is the interpretation to be given to apparently logical relations in ethical statements. Although frequently these are designated by logical terms, such as "contradiction" or "consistency"—as well as by metaphorical terms, such as

[18] Aristotle, *Nicomachean Ethics* 1166a 27 ff.

"coherence" or "harmony," "conflict" or "clash," and by more neutral terms, such as "compatibility"—the reference turns out to be for the most part to material relations the establishment of whose presence involves actual verification, not merely logical certification. This emerges most clearly in an analysis of the various conditions under which the term "contradiction" is employed in dealing with ethical material. It may, of course, be used in its logical sense, as when I say, "I value this x," and you reply, "It is not the case that you value this x." But apart from the logical relation of propositions, we find the word applied to the act of valuing and to the relations of objects of value (object including activity), or briefly speaking, values.

With respect to the act of valuing, it must be noted that to value and to disvalue—that is, to think good or choose as good and to think evil or reject as evil—are not contradictories. "I value this x" and "I disvalue this x," even if they refer to the same x at the same time in the same respect, are not contradictories; for x may be indifferent, that is, an object neither of value nor of disvalue. In fact, it may be questioned whether they need even be contraries. Although a man may not both do and not do x (when x is an action) and though he cannot, perhaps, wholeheartedly choose both to do and not to do x—for this would be akin to moving in two opposite directions at the same time—he may not merely waver in the sense of being undecided, but actually feel both drawn and repelled. It is the traditional predicament of Hamlet and of Catullus when he poured out his "Odi et amo." Modern psychology of the unconscious makes much of this phenomenon of ambivalence. Plato used it to prove that there are different parts of the soul which may aim in different directions,[19] finding a difference in the self when there was none in the object of desire and aversion.

If this is the case, valuing and disvaluing cannot simply be spoken of as contradictory acts.[20] Three sets of conditions, however, may be suggested which might lead to the employment of the term or analogous ones.

1. It might be known that a specified individual is of such a character that his inclinations are generally transformed into decisive choice, either for the most part or with reference to a special class of values. On

---

[19] Plato, *Republic* iv. 439–40.

[20] For the social counterpart of such ambivalence see Robert M. Lynd, *Knowledge for What?* pp. 60–62, where antithetical assumptions in American life are brought together.

the basis of this *knowledge of character* it might be said in his case, or in those domains, that valuing and disvaluing were opposed, contrary, or (a better term) incompatible. Likewise, for a group, either in general or in a specific domain, the same assertion could be given a rough statistical meaning.

2. It might be known, from the nature of a certain type of activity and the circumstances generally surrounding it or conditions required to bring it about, that there is little likelihood of ambivalence about it. On the basis of such *knowledge of the activity and its conditions* one might speak of valuing and disvaluing it as incompatible.

3. There might be an additional value presupposed or used implicitly as a standard of reference, whose realization will be hindered by both valuing and disvaluing. Thus, if I value wholehearted choice and ambivalence yields either no completed choice, or a deflection into fancy, or the suppression of one alternative which retards the decisiveness of the other choice, I may call the constituent acts of valuing and disvaluing contrary or incompatible. This is obviously a derived incompatibility, since what they are incompatible with is the achievement of wholehearted choice. On the other hand, if the regulative value were the creation of intense feeling, provoking self-searching, the simultaneous valuing and disvaluing of the same object would no doubt be reckoned simply as a co-operation of causes. On the basis of their *effect upon some implicit value's achievement,* acts of valuing and disvaluing may be deemed incompatible.

These three sets of conditions have been discussed with reference to the valuation and disvaluation of the same object by the same person. The analysis will likewise apply whether the subject of the acts be the same or different, whether the acts be all of valuing or all of disvaluing or some of the one and some of the other and whether the object be one in number, the same in form, or different in form. Likewise, the analysis should apply to groups, whether in a rough statistical sense or with reference to the organized activities of groups.[21] Thus, we may examine the general forms of "A values x" and "B values y," remembering that many substitutions can be made for A, B, x, y, and that "disvalue" in either statement can be substituted for "value." When it is known from

[21] The discussion may readily be extended to cover general acts of valuing if it be remembered that a general value judgment states a preference covering most or all occasions of relevant choice, with varying standards for the strictness of "most." Whether two such statements are contraries is readily apparent.

the existent character of A and B, or from the nature and conditions of x and y, or simply as a probability from examination of a series of cases of the same form that if either statement is true the other must be false, then, assuming that both may be false, the statements are of course contrary, and the acts of valuing concerned are incompatible. The third condition specified above would refer to the case in which both acts are not incompatible in this sense, but there is some implicit value z on the basis of which it is known that the existence of the acts of valuing of x by A and of y by B would prevent the actualization of z.

The third condition, it will be noted, goes beyond the others in being concerned, not with the possible coexistence of two or more acts of valuing, or holding of values, but with the effect upon the actualization of the value held. By actualization of a value is here meant, not the fact that something of that form is actually chosen or valued, but that the end chosen is actually attained or produced. It is, perhaps, attainment that most people have in mind when they speak of incompatible values. For, as we saw, choice involves reference to a beginning and an end of some determinate activity, and the end or outcome is what becomes systematized as a general value. "Value x is incompatible with value y" therefore would yield on analysis: "A values x," and "B values y," and "in specified circumstances the achievement of x by A and y by B cannot both occur." It must be remembered again that A and B may be the same or different, individual or group, and that some revisions in the precise mode of verification have to be made in the various cases. In general the analysis given for acts of holding a value will apply here. There is, of course, no correlation between the incompatibility of the acts of valuing and the incompatibility of the values, except when the former has been assigned on the third type of condition examined above. In the other cases, the compatibility of the acts of valuing is a necessary precondition for the incompatibility of the values, though the latter may be stated abstractly without the existence of the former. For if the two acts of valuing cannot occur together, there is no problem concerning the compatibility of two objects of value. In short, to judge values to be incompatible we must know, from the character of the actors or the nature of the objects or the circumstances in which the values would have to be achieved, that the values cannot be achieved together; or there must be reference to some implicit or recognized value whose achievement would be prevented by the joint achievement or attempt to achieve the values at issue which are derivatively called incompatible.

It follows that the incompatibility of specific values is relative to a system of natures, conditions, and sometimes other values. Hence only on the assumed constancy of such a system can the specific values be reckoned as stably incompatible. Close attention is therefore required when we are dealing with the values or aims of large opposing groups, to their conditions and to predictions concerning the duration of these conditions, the way in which these conditions will change, and whether and how the values involved will be altered. For values apparently compatible may turn out to be incompatible once we discover hitherto unrecognized consequences of their attempted actualization; and these very consequences may differ from age to age. A judgment of large-scale opposition of values, such as the Marxian theory of the irreconcilability of the aims of capital and labor, therefore involves a whole social science and complex historical analysis.

We have so far used predominantly the terms "compatible" and "incompatible," implicitly defining the former as the contradictory of the latter with reference to values and acts of valuing. "Consistent," taken in the literal sense of "standing together," would be a good synonym for "compatible" if it had not so definitely a logical usage. "Contrary" seems not unsuitable for some purposes we examined, and "contradictory" might even be used in those special cases in which the scene has been so carefully set that only two values monopolize the field, neither capable of realization without impeding the other. On the whole, however, it would be conducive to clarity to limit the terms which have a distinct logical flavor to the relations of propositions describing the values and system of conditions and to employ the remainder of the terms at present available for acts of valuing and values. Thus, acts of valuing might best be called "compatible" if they are "mutually tolerant," whereas values which we have referred to the actualization and coexistence of conduct might be called "coherent" if they "stick together" or "conflicting" if they "strike at one another" or "clash." A fuller analysis than that here begun will no doubt find more fruitful distinctions and, if necessary, enlarge the vocabulary sufficiently.

III · RELATION OF ETHICAL TO NONETHICAL SYSTEMS

The logical pattern of the possible relationship between an ethical and a nonethical system is, of course, the same as for any two systems. That is, terms of one and terms of the other system, each independently interpreted, are empirically correlated. If ethical terms are thus correlated with terms in another system, ethical statements might thereafter turn out to be deducible from statements in the nonethical system. We may illustrate by the complete connections which exist in the following somewhat Hobbesian theory. In this, the ethical expression "x is good" is taken to be correlated with the psychological expression "A desires x." And since feeling is declared to be a kind of interior movement, "A desires x" is eventually translated (with the aid of correlation statements) into the language of physics as "the complex of particles, A_1, A_2, A_3 is moving in a certain fashion with regard to x." This is therefore correlated with "x is good." The remaining terms of ethics being likewise translated, it would then be hoped that the generalizations of ethics could be deduced from physical laws. Thus "self-preservation is good" might be deducible from a physical law that certain movements (into which desire was ultimately translatable) would occur whenever certain other movements (into which self-preservation was resolved) occurred. This complete translation of terms and the complete deducibility of ethical from physical generalizations would constitute an ideally necessary connection—what has traditionally been called the complete "reduction" of ethics to physics.

The direction of such "reduction" is not limited a priori. Thus, even when ethical terms are translated into psychological ones, it is possible for the psychological to be translated into something other than physical terms. This sort of thing has actually happened in some evolutionary theories, where "x is good" is equated with the "biological" assertion "x has survival value for the group," and the latter is accompanied by the belief that evolution is the deity's special plan to make the universe culminate in man. Hence the ultimate translation of "x is good" would be "x fulfills the divine plan." But it could equally well have ended in a physical rather than a theological translation.

The traditional problem of "free will" versus "determinism" may itself be translated into the empirical question of the relation of ethics to nonethical systems. On this analysis, free will is equivalent to insistence on the "autonomy" of choice and the ethical system; determinism is equivalent to the belief in (or hope for) discoverable interrelations of ethical and nonethical systems. Complete or universal determinism postulates a complete "reduction"—usually to physical terms and laws.

The fact that ethics has not so been "reduced" is sometimes taken by nonnaturalistic philosophies to be evidence for "emergent qualities," "autonomous domains," or a dualism between the mental field, where ethics belongs, and the physical, where the physical sciences fall. A naturalistic approach is committed neither to such inferences nor to a complete determinism. The failure to discover the interrelations of ethics and nonethical domains has no more significance than the inability to "reduce" psychology to physiology or physiology to physics. For the relation of the sciences is an empirical matter, and there is no a priori reason to believe that complete "reduction" of any domain to another must be either impossible or inevitable. Natural events are rich enough and complex enough so that relatively irreducible phases are possible. Any assertion of ultimate results remains program, not metaphysical fact.

Nevertheless, the development of common experience and scientific knowledge has been sufficient to indicate that the act of choice is not utterly unrelated to other natural events occurring around it. A choice itself is an event in nature, complex indeed, but clearly grounded in the influences of physical, psychological, and social factors. There is no reason why the preconceptions of an idealist or a dualist philosophy should linger to bar the most intensive exploration of its relations. The field of ethics not only may be but is being constantly developed by the progress of all other sciences, especially the psychological and social studies.

Since any attempt to describe the interrelations of ethical and nonethical phenomena is bound to be sketchy or programmatic, I shall limit the discussion to brief comments on the empirical studies from which it seems to me ethics can most profit at present.

The first of these is the careful scrutiny (psychological and phenomenological) of the act of choosing or valuing. Ordinary language bears witness to possible differences within the act itself. There is wholehearted choice and halfhearted choice, and a whole possible scale of intensity. To study it one would have to focus attention on the way in which alternative rules and developed habits function in the act of choice. This might be done both introspectively and by observing the relative frequency of specific types of choice in regulated situations, or by any other device the scientific imagination may formulate. In fact, Aristotle began this study at some length in his ethics, when he distinguished the virtuous man from the continent man and the vicious from the incontinent. The continent and the incontinent have internal struggles in their choice, the former checking evil desires, the latter yielding to them against his better judgment; the virtuous man has no evil desires to fight against, whereas the vicious man takes pleasure in carrying out his evil desires and so has no pain, remorse, or struggle concerning them. In terms of such an investigation ordinary phrases like "strength of character" will find more precise empirical significance.

Again, within the evaluating act, on its reflective level, ordinary language reveals a differentiated series of degrees of approval and disapproval which certainly can be rendered more precise and may or may not be correlated with the previous differentiations in choice. Hartmann, for example, works such a rising scale out of the predicates employed by Aristotle in the *Nicomachean Ethics*. The predicates are: worthy of praise (ἐπαινετόν); beautiful (καλόν); worthy of honor (τιμητόν); lovable (φιλητόν); admirable (θαυμαστόν); superb (μακαριστόν).[22] It may well be the case that in scales of this sort different shades of emotion are attached to each predicate. Or perhaps in some instances there is also a differentiation in fields of subject matter. Such analysis will aid in the discovery of any consistent scales which may be implicitly employed and in the development of such scales as may be deemed desirable.

The second study is the discovery (historical and anthropological) of the varieties of values that have actually existed. This involves both description and conceptual refinement. It examines, for instance, the content of jealousy among present-day Eskimos, French, and Americans; and the persons to whom reverence is obligatory in various societies; and how the notion of honor differs in a knight quick to resent insult and a business man scrupulous in paying his debts. Inevitably the problem will arise why in each case differing manifestations are grouped together as exemplifying the same value and whether in fact they should be so grouped. Solutions to this problem will also provide empirical meaning to broad values. Sometimes the varying content will be found to have a psychological unity in the fact that there are different ways in which the same deep-seated impulse is expressed, as in the sexual drive. Sometimes the unity will lie in the fact that there are different ways of meeting a common social need, as in avoiding in-group conflict. Often the unity lies in the production of a similar effect; for example, the common ideal of justice may express merely the widespread desire for the removal of suffering at the hands of others. Often the common element will turn

[22] Hartmann, *Ethics* (English translation by Stanton Coit), II, 58–60.

out to be merely analogy, as when desire for prestige is treated as a form of acquisitiveness. In such cases the result may be the substitution of several motives for a single notion. This general study may also provide empirical criteria for the affirmation of identical elements in cultural diversity. For the student of ethics it will likewise suggest tentative patterns which may be applied with alterations to meet problems within another culture. In short, the task is not merely fact-gathering, to be performed by handmaiden sciences, but it entails philosophical analysis throughout.

The third study (involving all the sciences, from biology and physiology to economics, social psychology, and history) is the search for causal elements or necessary conditions of men's choice. The holding of a particular value or pattern of values by an individual or group is not simply a brute fact; it calls for causal explanation. Several factors point toward the possibility of success in such a study. There is the common core of conscious education of taste or preference in ourselves and others. There is a growing recognition that values are not innate traits or elements of character stamped in men by nature, but products in the growing child and still malleable adult of tremendous cultural and social pressures. Our insight into the force of tradition, the pervasive influence of economic factors, and the critical role of existent attitudes has grown tremendously. We thus realize that the fashioning of values is a task carried on in a society whether knowingly or in ignorance of what we are in effect doing. The observation around us of mass transformations in fundamental values has directed attention to the study of change. The large-scale investigation of causality in choice may perhaps be best carried out by examining historically what changes in values go along with other social changes and tracing more minutely their relations.

The naturalistic tradition in philosophy has constantly pointed to the need for causal examination of values and the relation of ethical to non-ethical phenomena. It has sought the aid of the prevailing sciences and in turn mapped programs for them. As the sciences grew, naturalism had concomitant phases. It interpreted values on a physical analogy as special movements of the particles or internal movements. Nineteenth-century naturalism was to a great extent biological, under Darwin's influence. Marxian materialism was an exception, and it marked the beginning of a fuller naturalism, which recognized the causal role of social factors.

The study of conditioning elements of men's values and the broad discovery that they lie to a great extent somewhere in the domain of human activity have revealed the possibility of the redirection of values. In spite of the shuddering of some poets and some philosophers, mankind at large would probably welcome a discovery that the milk of human kindness could be injected into the blood stream by means of a gland extract or even, as some novelistic psychology would have it, that men could shift their character-values with their climate. Although the problem is tremendously more complicated than these simple dreams, there is no reason to oppose the causal study of values on the ground of a special human spontaneity called "freedom of the will." There is plenty of room for spontaneity in human affairs, but it is an empirical phenomenon that falls within the context of men who are striving to achieve their values, to redirect some and preserve others. It is not an explanation of their doings. The mere assumption of freedom tends to make men leave the direction of change of values to chance. Freedom, in a naturalistic ethics, is to be found in the widest understanding that may be attained of the conditions and causes of choice, so that choice may be a function of knowledge.

What we have spoken of as the redirection of values is not, however, an appeal from the ethical to the nonethical. It is carried on within a set of values and involves altering some to preserve or enhance or achieve others. It occurs in social groups, as in our personal lives, when a conflict of values drives us to seek consistency by shifting some goals to make room for others, when we discover fresh goals emerging and estimate the interplay of means and ends. Redirection of values is not the mere occurrence of this process, but its conscious occurrence.

The stress of a naturalistic ethics emerges most clearly in the analysis of the redirection of social values. A naturalistic ethics does not consider the problem to be purely a matter of the individual's purification of his heart, whether on the principles of a specific theology or in some moral rearmament. It does not appeal to an unknown good to justify the evil that exists or to men's patience and resignation to enable them to endure. It does not urge that men's wickedness is a ground for their misfortunes. It does not turn ends into autonomous internal values restricted to consciousness and disregard means as mere technicalities. It does not commit itself to eternal values irrespective of their specific content and social consequences. On the contrary, it insists on the continuous testing of goals in the light of their social functioning, on the deep roots of values in the practices and institutions of a society, on the necessity of altering institutions and social forms as part of the process of achieving and re-directing values, on the need for a comprehensive view of the way in which values fit together, what causal props they have, what are to be the consequences of various means. In short, the naturalistic moral philoso-pher, estimating the values of his group or society, cannot stop short of fashioning a whole conception of good men functioning well in a good society.

5

A NATURAL HISTORY OF THE
AESTHETIC TRANSACTION [1]

Eliseo Vivas

I

A NATURALISTIC theory of aesthetics should recognize at the start that the distinct modes of human experience which analysis can discover today have emerged in the process of human development out of relatively less differentiated activities of men in nature. The gradual differentiation that has taken place is only a matter of degree, coming about slowly as psychological aptitudes develop under the pressure of biological and cultural exigencies. We seek, however, to analyze the structure of each mode of experience considered as distinct from the others. But this means isolating conceptually what is not completely distinct in reality, and this in turn imputes to the conceptual isolate a uniqueness and self-sufficiency which in reality no one mode of experience can claim. Our analysis, in search of that which is peculiar to each mode, is likely to overlook features shared by them all. This blinds us to the fact that the ordinary enterprises of living men are never "pure" activities, but are variously made up of the modes which we distinguish conceptually. There is, nevertheless, need for clear and distinct concepts, if we are to evaluate properly each mode as a rational enterprise and to distinguish the genuine from the false.

What, then, distinguishes the aesthetic from other modes of human experience? There are three other modes from which we must distinguish it—the moral or practical, the religious, and the scientific. Human activity is never purely one thing or the other, but it does tend to become one thing or the other, and to the extent to which it is human it is never anything else besides.

[1] This essay constitutes part of the work done during my tenure of a Guggenheim Fellowship in the year of 1939-40. Other work done during that year has already appeared elsewhere. For the opportunity to do this work I would like to express my gratitude to the John Simon Guggenheim Memorial Foundation and to its founder, Mrs. John Simon Guggenheim. American art and letters owe already a deep debt of gratitude to both.

Let us first see what constitutes a moral situation. For our purposes we need not look very closely into it; a quick glance will suffice. In a situation we call practical or moral an individual or a group faces alternative objects of choice or courses of conduct. This entails needs and objectives—entails, that is, a subjective element. It also entails an objective element: two or more objects or courses of conduct which elicit our interest. And the moral choice consists in selecting, in a specific situation, the object or course of conduct that is relatively most satisfactory to the specific need which prompts the choice. Relatively, because the satisfaction of one need may either block or further the satisfaction of other needs, and therefore a moral choice involves not only the inspection of the objects immediately before us but also considerations of consequences which ramify indefinitely beyond. Moral perplexities call for the use of the intelligence, thus involving cognitive activity. And they eventuate in resolutions which, to the extent to which they are successful, lead to enjoyments which have distinctive aesthetic elements. However, such aesthetic enjoyment, essential as it may be to complete the arc of experience, is not what distinguishes one mode from another. There are many interrelations between the moral and all the other modes of human activity; but they do not preclude the genuine differences we are attempting to disengage conceptually.

What constitutes the scientific or cognitive situation? When one asks himself questions regarding the source or mode of appearance of an object, or when he seeks to arrive at a generalized statement of its behavior, he has embarked upon a scientific enterprise. The statement which he seeks is one which, as we say, "expresses" the invariant connections the object of interest sustains with other objects, or with later phases of itself, in some clearly specifiable respect. These are formulated whenever possible in quantitative terms. And the process of scientific inquiry is an ever-expanding one, achieving as it proceeds formulations of ever-increasing generality. But whatever features it may have, for our purposes, what we need to note is that in the cognitive activity the object which initially instigated the inquiry serves only as a means to the discovery of a network of relationships which lead away from it, and which bind the object which prompted the inquiry to other objects which were not initially present. The object which gives rise to the cognitive enterprise is not itself of intrinsic interest. We select and are interested in only some of its aspects, and any other object of the same type, any other exhibiting the same external relationship, would do as well. By itself the object is merely an instrument, a means of exploring the behavior of all objects of which it is an instance with respect to specific conditions.

As in the case of the moral experience, the cognitive activity eventuates in the discovery of a pattern of relationships which may itself be contemplated aesthetically. This is, perhaps, always the reward of the scientist, that his activity reveals a structure worthy of intrinsic apprehension because it is essentially orderly and harmonious. Also, it may be that the motivating force back of the efforts of the scientist is often the anticipation of the aesthetic pleasure derived from the perception of the relationships he discovers. Indeed, accurate prediction may not at all be his subjective aim. The presence or absence of such subjective factors is irrelevant if our interest is to discover the distinguishing feature of the scientific enterprise. What distinguishes the scientific from other modes of activity is the fact that it is addressed to the exploration of transitive relationships verified in terms of predictions.

One does not enter a discussion of religion unaware of the hosts of prudent angels hovering at the edge of the problem, hesitating to rush in. But because it is obvious and innocuous, this much may be said without fear of much contradiction: The religious experience involves a predominantly affective relationship between a worshiper and an object; the worshiper addresses himself to this object because he discriminates it as a power or force which either sustains him or threatens him. This is what is left when we disengage the distinctively religious element from the moral and aesthetic accretions which implement it and help give it the dense and pervasive value it has for men. Depending upon the degree of intellectual development reached, the objects of worship are apprehended, either dramatically or abstractly. But in the latter case, to be religious, not merely philosophical, an object must be held in reverence and awe. The distinctive trait of the religious transaction is found in the communion between worshiper and Power, in which the former makes at least implicit acknowledgment of his status; but usually he either begs for new benefits, or expresses piety and gratitude for those already received, besides expressing his weakness and Its strength. Humility, gratitude, expectation, awe, fear, and love suffuse the act of communion, and these emotions have their source in a recognition—even though a vague and rudimentary one—of objective and hence verifiable factors in the world to which are imputed creative supremacy over the worshiper.

It will be noted that these modes of experience, the scientific, the moral, and the religious, have one thing in common: the object of interest in each one of these transactions is not an object of exclusive interest, holding our attention because in itself and by itself it is satisfactory to self-contained, *intransitive*, awareness. In a moral transaction we go from the object which initiates the act of moral reflection to an examination of the threats or promises which the object holds for other aspirations and needs. We transcend the object, in search of relationships to which it points, but does not embody in itself. We arrive at a decision regarding a course of conduct when we have seen its effect on other courses of conduct we wish to engage in. Again, in the scientific transaction we pass from the object or event which is at the center of investigation backward and forward to causes and consequences. Our interest, in other words, is in a complex of events, not embodied as meanings by the object from which investigation starts, but which lie beyond it. In the religious situation, again, the object is of interest in so far as we conceive of it as somehow connected with the success of our enterprises not only at the moment of religious reflection but also beyond it. In science, in morals, and in religion, in short, the object of the experience is, so to speak, a moment connected with a wider complex of moments in a transitive chain that goes on indefinitely. And I would suggest that it is here, in *the transitive* character of these three modes of experience, that we shall find what distinguishes them from the aesthetic mode. For in the aesthetic mode, in contrast, we look at the object in order to see it, listen to it in order to hear it, touch it or taste it in order to feel it; we fasten our perceptive attention on it, arrest it within it, in such a way that we do not wander from it, but rest within it attentively. As I have said elsewhere, "the aesthetic experience is an experience of rapt attention which involves the intransitive apprehension of an object's immanent meanings in their full presentational immediacy." [2]

That we can and often do enjoy this type of experience there is no doubt. That it is worth enjoying I shall attempt to argue later on. But there are two things that I do not believe can be proven first, that this is what has been meant by "the aesthetic experience"; for I know that the term "aesthetic" has denoted an incredible number of mutually incompatible modes of experience. Nor do I have the space to argue now that

[2] "A Definition of the Aesthetic Experience," *The Journal of Philosophy*, XXXIV (1937), 628–34.

the type of experience which I have selected for analysis is that which the term "aesthetic" should exclusively denote. In a study which pretended to exhaustiveness I would be under obligation to give the reasons why I have selected it and distinguished it from other modes of experience. But if in the meantime anyone should contest my usage, I shall answer that this is how I intend to use the term and that whether my usage is proper or not it points to a distinctive mode of experience which, under whatever name we give it, I am interested in analyzing.

II

The aesthetic experience is an experience of intransitive, rapt attention on any object which may elicit interest. Now, attention may address itself to what Prall calls "surface," so that one attends to color, or light, or sound, or movement only. Or it may concern itself with surface and with the meanings which the organization of surface elements embodies immanently. In either case, it seems to me, in disagreement with Prall, that it is proper to use the term "aesthetic" in connection with our response so long as our attention concentrates on the object and does not go outside it. But the wider use of the term "aesthetic" does not free us from the need to explain how we can behold objects intransitively which nevertheless embody all sorts of meanings and all sorts of values from all sorts of ranges of human experience without restriction. I take this to be the central problem of aesthetics and one which must be squarely faced, particularly by a writer who is convinced that if there is one thing which the aesthetic object positively does not do, when it fully lives up to its function as aesthetic, it is to point beyond itself referentially or serve as a mnemonic device. I hope that if this essay does no more, it at least makes a more or less successful beginning toward the solution of this problem. I shall attempt the elucidation by means of the notion of "immanent meaning," drawn from Dewey.[3] But it is only fair to notice that Dewey himself did not exploit it fully in his own *Art as Experience*.

In so far as this attempt is successful, this essay will go beyond an influential stream of contemporary theory that insists correctly that beauty has its locus in the form of a beautiful object, but cannot explain with adequacy how the form of a beautiful object may be charged with mean-

[3] John Dewey, "Meaning and Existence," *Journal of Philosophy*, XXV (1928), 352.

ings which elsewhere function referentially. Such meanings shall be called "immanent" or "reflexive." By means of the notion of "immanent meanings" I also hope to avoid the common error of supposing that we can find the distinguishing traits of the aesthetic object in it, considered by itself outside of the aesthetic experience. On the contrary, I shall argue that any object may function as an aesthetic object, though, of course, with varying degrees of adequacy.

Since it is essential to make these points as clear as possible, let me put the central issue in different words. Whether a transaction can be called aesthetic or not does not depend upon the kinds of meaning embodied by an object. Any kind of meaning or value whatsoever can be apprehended aesthetically, though cultural and physiological determinants exclude the possibility of some. What defines the transaction as aesthetic is the manner in which the aesthetic object, which is a complex of informed meanings for a given spectator, operates in the aesthetic experience. Our central problem, therefore, is this: to explain how meanings which function referentially when apprehended nonaesthetically, function immanently or reflexively when apprehended in the aesthetic transaction. At this point, however, two misunderstandings should be intercepted. The first is that while the object by itself does not carry its own distinguishing traits, neither does the subjective side, the experience, considered in its psychological aspect, abstracted from its stimulus. This is the error of psychologism.[4] It is the whole and complete transaction, involving an object and a subject, that is distinct from other transactions. The second possible misunderstanding refers to the functions performed by the diverse meanings informed in an aesthetic object. The aesthetic object may embody meanings of all sorts, but on the kind of meanings it embodies depend the intensity, duration, complexity and significance (or relative moral worth) of the aesthetic as compared with other aesthetic experiences or other experiences of any kind whatsoever. The distinction between trivial and great beauty is therefore not in jeopardy, and aesthetic theory must not only seek to explain how meanings can be embodied intransitively in an object but also in precisely what way the embodiment of certain types of meanings contribute towards the dimen-

---

[4] John Crowe Ransom, in his *The New Criticism*, New Directions, 1941, has exposed this error, in the case of I. A. Richards, in a manner that leaves us all deeply in his debt. See also my "Four Notes on I. A. Richards' Aesthetic Theory" for an analysis from a different point of view, *The Philosophical Review*, XLIV (1935), 354.

sion of greatness which some art exhibits as compared with others. And this it must attempt, not merely in poetry where it is comparatively easy to see but also in music.

Let us see how meanings become embodied immanently in objects. I once had to become acquainted for the first time with objects with which I have long been familiar. I had to learn how to use them. The process, especially in my earlier years, was not an easy one. Laboriously I learned their names, learned how to handle them, to distinguish them from one another. The process of getting acquainted with them consisted in the building up of an organized pattern of responses toward them which gradually became more complex. This pattern is made up of visual, motor, verbal, and all sorts of other responses and is accompanied by a feeling tone. This feeling tone, possessing a certain specificity as regards each object, unifies and cements the pattern, and it is present, to some degree, whenever for any reason the pattern comes into play. A pattern of responses of high complexity of co-ordination is possible because in the process of evolutionary development a nervous system, highly centralized, came into being. In humans these patterns of organized responses are aroused not only by the immediate sight of the objects which contributed to their coming into being but also by signs, chiefly verbal, which act as surrogates for the actual things themselves. Nor does the pattern of responses need to carry itself out in overt activity; it can be aroused implicitly in the body. When we perceive an object with which we are familiar, the attitudes and responses which previous experiences with it have instituted, are aroused, but need not deploy themselves overtly in full; we withhold them; we carry them out implicitly; somehow they become telescoped and stereotyped so that they are ready for full overt development, but they need not be developed overtly through and through. But this happens not only when we perceive the object but also when we "think" of it, which is to say, when any kind of stimulus acting as a surrogate for the object calls the pattern forth implicitly in us. This is, indeed, what thinking is.

On the basis of these suggestions we can see the difference between referential and immanent meaning. In a referential meaning an object—whether sign or symbol—serves as stimulus to call forth an organized succession of patterns of response; the stimulus evokes one pattern very quickly, and this in turn evokes another. In an immanent meaning an object or its symbol calls forth a pattern, but the pattern itself, instead of calling forth another, remains available and in exclusive dominance of the facilities—the nervous and motor system—which sustains it.

Not all apprehension of immanent meaning is distinctively aesthetic. And this calls for an important distinction, introduced and fully exploited by Mr. Dewey, between mere recognition and the vivid apprehension which constitutes aesthetic response. In recognition the response approaches the purely automatic and involves an insignificant temporal span and a minimum of effort and of feeling tone. But let an object arouse curiosity, and the time span becomes an important factor, effort changes recognition into intransitive alert attention, and feeling enters if interest is objective. The elicited pattern of responses is not stereotyped, and the object is seen freshly. This is the distinctively aesthetic response.[5]

Nothing has yet been said about emotion. Does it have no place in the aesthetic experience? I am afraid this is a question on which many writers on aesthetics find it difficult to think with clarity, not because it is complex or abstruse, but rather because somehow one tends to feel that the way one reacts to aesthetic objects is the proper way. There are several issues we must unravel; the first is whether in the aesthetic transaction emotion is always present, whether the aesthetic object always arouses it, and therefore whether we should include the emotion in our account of its distinctive traits. This question is first one of fact which cannot be settled in terms of one's own individual experience. Frequently, when the issue comes up it is settled with a decisive and final remark: "But *I* find, when I listen to music or read poetry, that I am prey of an uprush of emotion." The remark is interesting, and the information valuable, but not sufficient, because there are others who find the very opposite. It is a well-established fact that the emotion aroused by aesthetic objects varies very widely and sometimes is not even present.[6] In view of this fact, there is nothing we can do except to agree that whether the value of the aesthetic experience depends upon the presence or the absence of emotion, its character depends upon neither. Our definition of the aesthetic experience, therefore, will not include emotion as one of its traits.

But there is another reason why emotion does not enter into our definition, though the above reason is sufficient to exclude it, namely, that psy-

[5] Dewey, *Art as Experience*, New York, 1934, pp. 24, 52–53.
[6] See my "A Definition of the Aesthetic Experience," already cited, and the evidence therein referred to.

chology does not know anything about a *sui generis* aesthetic emotion. When emotion, then, is involved in the aesthetic response, it is ordinary emotion, the same garden variety of emotion that we find playing such a pervasive role everywhere else in the lives of men. In the cognitive, in the religious, in the moral experience, emotion is also found—and often in the same degree. Emotion, then, does not distinguish the aesthetic experience. Indeed, I incline to the belief that to the degree to which attention is focused on an object, and during the time when it is, to that extent and during that time emotion tends to disappear from our consciousness. At such times awareness is occupied solely with the object on which it is intent, and emotion is absent, because its presence involves, in part at least, awareness of internal processes as well as awareness of the objective situation which arouses and defines these processes. This is in actuality a question of degree; and it may be true, as is maintained by some authors, that "consciousness of ourselves . . . can probably never disappear. It is a matter of degree and focus." [7] I believe that sometimes it can disappear entirely, but must admit that states of sufficiently rapt attention on an object are rare and fleeting. But nearly anyone is able to approach that condition more or less. Our definition must be taken, therefore, as marking an ideal limit.

You may retort that while the emotion need not enter into our definition of the aesthetic experience, it cannot be left out of a reckoning of its value, since without emotion the experience is cold, is indeed an over-intellectualized experience. I am afraid that those who urge that the aesthetic experience has no value unless it is charged with emotion are right, but right only in so far as they are willing to limit the statement to themselves. If their interest is exclusively or overwhelmingly in their own emotional reactions, not in the objects present for apprehension, there is little to be said except that their interest is in their emotions, not in the object. But there are those who are interested in the object, and these people find objects, strangely as it may seem to some folk, enthrallingly interesting. To this extent, they find the experience valuable.

We should now be in a position to grasp more clearly what is distinctive in the aesthetic experience and how it is related to other modes of experience. Because the aesthetic experience involves the vivid apprehension of the immanent meanings of an object which is viewed intran-

---

[7] L. A. Reid, *A Study in Aesthetics*. New York, 1931, p. 80; also John R. Reid, *A Theory of Value*, New York (1938), p. 59.

sitively, it must be considered distinct from the cognitive in its narrower and proper sense. Aesthetic apprehension is clearly and distinctly *having*, not *knowing*. However, the foregoing account is intended to show not only how aesthetic enjoyment is distinct but also how its content is enriched by our previous cognitive and moral activities. Cognitive activity orders the world and clarifies its structure for us, enriching us with a vast fund of immanent meanings; without its aid, therefore, aesthetic perception would be thin in content and would approach the empty stare of an idiot; our moral and religious experiences charge the objects of our aesthetic experience with their significance and power. The quarrel, then, between those aestheticians who maintain that the aesthetic experience is a form of cognition and those that deny it would seem to be a verbal one. The former are right if the word "cognition" is used, not in its narrowest sense, as we have here used it, but in its widest sense, as synonymous with perception or awareness of any kind whatsoever. But note that mere attention, mere awareness, makes no assertions, does not involve itself in analysis; it just possessses its object. On the other hand knowledge is transitive and expectative: it goes from the object that starts it on its quest to other objects, and at its best it anticipates exactly on the basis of what has been examined, conditions not yet realized. If in spite of these considerations anyone should like to use the term in its widest sense, we must acquiesce. But we must also mark that the distinction we have sought to draw between an experience of intransitive attention and one which is transitive is a factual distinction and one of kind, not obliterated if we use the word "knowledge" to denote both kinds of experience. And if this is the case, we have now the problem on our hands of contriving a new terminology capable of preserving this distinction.

III

It was said above that any object can enter into an aesthetic transaction, but this is not altogether true; for men find it impossible to contemplate aesthetically an object which outrages them morally or which violates accepted truths. Nor does it follow that because objects are aesthetically available any object can enter as easily as any other into an aesthetic transaction. But even if it were the case, it is not true that any object can show itself capable of sustaining aesthetic attention as well as any other.

The question therefore arises, what factors determine the acceptance of art? There are two classes of factors, the objective and the subjective, which account for the success or adequacy of an aesthetic experience. The division is not a perfect one, because objective traits are determined by subjective factors and vice versa, since in all perception, but particularly in the aesthetic *trans-action*, the mind and the environment both are active creative factors in determining both the experienced object and the experiencing of that object. Therefore, the characters of an object to which power of sustaining intransitive attention can be ascribed are objective relatively, not absolutely; they are objective for a subject, and this in turn does not always make it easy, in the actual conduct of the analytic enterprise, to determine whether the standpoint for which a given objective trait obtains is one which can be occupied by one or by more than one perceiver. But we are not interested in idiosyncratic experiences; we are solely interested in objects which can enter into public usage, and our analysis of their traits must therefore be carried on in terms of "a normal aesthetic perceiver" for whom the objects under analysis are aesthetic objects. Before we can discuss the aesthetic object, we are therefore faced with the necessity of defining "a normal aesthetic perceiver." I despair, however, of doing it well enough to get it by the logician on guard. Men of former ages were much to be envied, for they seem to have known with an unshakable conviction what generic "man" is. Our age is obsessed with the sense of the variability of human nature and baffled by the problem of distinguishing the traits which all men share from those which are the accidents of transient cultures and local climates. Yet without a human norm discussions of value are almost certain to fall into prattling soliloquy.

The subjective conditions of an aesthetic experience need not be expatiated on at length. They consist of those factors, already referred to in passing, of physical and psychic health and energy which are essential to the free play of interest in the things and events of the world for their own inherent sake. Freedom from anxiety, leisure, no less than a cultivated habit of concentrated attention, are essential if we are to grasp fully the immanent meanings of the object before us and not wander off from them into relaxed trains of irrelevant revery. Nor can we perceive an object intransitively unless the object is approached with prior knowledge of its character and function. Without such knowledge, it would lack significance; it would act as an irritant to a scientific enterprise rather than be the repository of an act of intransitive contemplation. Again, only those can see or hear what is before them who have been trained to do so, since perceiving is a business which requires a large investment of capital and of training. These are old platitudes on which it is not necessary to waste any more time.

Two kinds of factors determine the power of an aesthetic object to call forth intransitive attention: one formal, and the other material. Of the former, the most general and the most difficult to isolate is that quality which is sometimes called "freshness" and sometimes "liveliness." This is a factor which could also have been discussed above under the head "subjective factors," for bad habits of perception and released stock responses will transform the freshest and most uniquely distinctive object into a rubber-stamp image for a lazy or hasty mind. Familiarity kills interest because it calls into play purely habitual responses which have a predominately automatic character and therefore partake only feebly, if at all, of a conscious nature. This familiarity, however, can have its source, not in the perceiver's habits, but in the object's own characters, in that the mind by which it was constructed had moved along hardened grooves, and therefore was only able to embody stereotyped immanent meanings which lack the power of shocking us into awareness.

How do objects call forth fresh perception? An explanation of how this is possible would involve us in a thorough discussion of the psychology of perception.[8] Here all we need to do is to try to state the most general principle, which is this: objects which are mere rubber-stamp duplicates of stock objects of usual experience are not likely to elicit fresh attention from man. For a normal perceiver, however defined, there are forms and meanings which he has assimilated and to which a ready and facile reaction is possible. To call forth fresh perception, certain innovations and variations are required—variations which may need to be subtle or gross, depending upon the degree of encrusted habits of response they must plow up. Fresh aesthetic perception therefore operates between two extremes: the utterly familiar and the utterly new. The familiar defeats the activity, because it stimulates a patterned response, which, tending toward the automatic, hardly rises to the status of the conscious. And the new defeats aesthetic attention because it forces on us a scientific inquiry. Its newness makes it a puzzle which in-

[8] John Dewey, *Art as Experience, passim;* also Stephen C. Pepper, *Aesthetic Quality; a Contextualist Theory of Beauty,* New York, 1938, *passim.*

vites resolution; we must classify it, discover its function, get acquainted with its structure, and this is the very opposite of intransitive contemplation. But there is more, because even if we did not engage in this scientific reconnaissance of the object and were to contemplate it for its own sake, it would fail to embody for us any immanent meanings. To the extent to which it failed, the experience would be thin and fleeting. Whatever tends to push a thing out of the utterly familiar prototype to which it belongs, yet does not tend to render it utterly unique, tends thereby to lift it into the status of aesthetic object.[9]

In order to find out what accounts for the intransitivity of our perceptive act, we must study the organization of the object. This is, however, more obviously displayed by objects of art than by natural ones, because art is purposely constructed to arouse a distinctively aesthetic response. We must therefore turn to art. In turning to art, however, it would be a sorry error to forget that its power, great as it is, is not a distinct property of it, possessed exclusively by itself. In this essay I have sought to show what are the natural sources from which sophisticated art experience develops. These sources are "natural" in two senses of this ambiguous word. They do not involve "trans-natural" or "supernatural" factors; they are amenable to scientific inquiry by means of those techniques of investigation and analysis employed in all the sciences. But they are also natural in that they are native in the ordinary experience of all men, even of those who have failed to achieve a high level of artistic sophistication. It is because they are natural in this latter sense that they can be developed and refined into those modes of response which enter into our commerce with the highest products of artistic creation.

If we turn to art in search for the factors which make the intransitive response possible, we shall find that *unity* is the most outstanding and most conspicuous of these. It is so fundamental a trait that its importance has long been recognized. Anything whatever can arouse aesthetic attention, but from the instantaneous perception of an object to the sustained and intrinsically self-renewing perception of which art is the stimulus there is a vast difference, and that difference must be traced to the fact

[9] A great many devices are used by the artist to achieve this end, and a study of them is the study of the history of the development of form in the various arts, traditions, and schools. Many generalized statements of these are possible. See, for instance, Dewitt Parker, *The Analysis of Art*, New Haven, 1926, chs. ii–iii. Compare with Pepper, *Aesthetic Quality*, chs. i–viii.

that the art object is an organization. The organization may be loose or tight, the elements which make it up may embody a more or less challenging complex of immanent meanings. Again, the elements which are organized into a unified whole may be homogeneous or heterogeneous. But this, at least, we can say with assurance, that there is no art object unless its maker has succeeded in organizing its elements into a unified whole. This is by no means the whole story, but it is the first chapter, without which the story could not be told coherently.

Although the importance of unity has seldom been overlooked, its significance has not always been adequately explained. The reason for this failure is that all too frequently aesthetic analysis of the object is carried on without reference to the subjective process in terms of which that object attains aesthetic status. In the light of the preceding discussion, it becomes clear that the function of unity lies in the fact that it determines the intransitivity of the experience; it fastens attention within the object and retains it within its boundaries, temporally and spatially. Unity guarantees the fluid transition of attention from one organic component of the object to another, and back again, through the various other components, to the starting point; it excludes shocks from the outside which might interrupt concentration; it guarantees the centripetal flow of perception. But we must conceive of aesthetic unity, not as "logical" unity, or as mathematical, or as one purely of composition, considered by itself in abstraction from that which is composed; aesthetic unity is achieved by a tight relationship, an intimate going-together which binds the parts into a single, self-contained object of experience in which every part carries its own meaning, a meaning which is homogeneous with the whole and literally an inextricable part of it. Through this interdependence the whole controls the specific value of each element at the same time that each element controls the whole. When skill has been spent in the construction, the embodied meaning achieves an intense vividness and specificity which objects of recognition cannot possibly claim.

Can we explain how such large numbers of elements, which when considered separately are so heterogeneous, come to combine and reinforce one another in the production of a single homogeneous effect? It is not difficult to do so if we bear in mind the full import of the statement that the unity of the object is a qualitative affair, in the sense that the combination of the unified elements is felt—or perhaps it might be more accurate to say, the falling apart of the elements when unity is lacking is felt—because they all contribute to the total embodied character which gives the object its uniqueness for perception. In aesthetic perception the object has a distinctive, unique, and therefore untranslatable quality: the specific quality of loveliness, or horror, or pathos, or tenderness that it possesses—the desolation of an abandoned mining town, the solid reality of Cézanne's apples on a table, the bitter desolation of blind Lear. The distinctive, unique quality is possible because the responses aroused by the object are harmonious with one another. But "harmony" need not be a term of incantation before which analysis is suspended. It refers to the fact that the responses aroused by any one element do not interfere with those aroused by the rest, but all of them, each gaining in amplitude by co-operation with the others, successfully exclude stimuli coming from outside the object which would call forth interfering responses. Of course, a modicum of conflict is essential to interest, but I imagine that, as is true of garlic, a small amount goes a long way.

Hence the importance of the time span in the perception of any aesthetic object, on which Dewey so rightly insists; and hence the role played by rhythm, which is the ordered motion of elements. For without rhythm there can be no unity; without it the response of one element would fall out of the pattern of ordered motion of the rest. Since these are pure conjectures, it is prudent not to carry them any farther. But even if they lack all value, that lack cannot impugn what we have said about the phenomena they try to account for. Unity is a combination of elements by virtue of which the object which they constitute achieves a distinctive, unique, monadic character for aesthetic perception. Without this character the object cannot give rise to an intransitive experience, and without the intransitivity the experience lacks its peculiar intrinsic value and sustained intensity.

The intransitivity of the attention depends on the unity of the perceived object, but the unity is a unity of a very large number of elements, and this variety is no less essential to the amplitude and prolongation of the experience than is the unity, for attention would soon lapse into indifference without the renewal of variety. As perception focuses successively on one after another of the elements present to attention, it is refreshed, and interest is shocked and renewed by the change. The devices employed to bring about a sustained act of attention, to keep it fresh, and to fortify it when it weakens are many, and they are studied by the analyst in terms of categories appropriate for each medium.

If what has been said about the aesthetic object is found acceptable, we must quarrel with those theories which attempt to distinguish *in the object, in the experience,* that which it expresses from that which does the expressing. For, as we have seen, in an aesthetic object we cannot find mute elements; they are all in themselves meaningful or expressive. Of course, this is an ideal limit. But it is to ideal objects that we have been referring all along. Outside the aesthetic experience, then, we may be able to discriminate within the complex of meanings embodied by the physical object certain orders; we can speak of the "expressiveness" of the medium, considered in abstraction from the moral and religious values and from the truths it may embody. But we shall find, if we consider the matter, that what we are actually distinguishing, if we are speaking of an aesthetic object—which is to say, of an object *in* the aesthetic experience—is not meanings from vehicle, but some meanings from others. Some of these, if considered by themselves, are referential, while others are by themselves utterly dumb. But in the aesthetic object, the former lose their transcendence and become reflexive or immanent, and the latter take on values that by themselves they could never carry. To contemplate an object aesthetically is to contemplate an objective expressive act, and only in analysis can that objective expressive act reveal its machinery. But in analysis objects do not function aesthetically. It is true that for analysis these meanings will be found to be embodied in a physical instrument which determines them; as scientists we shall seek to understand the interrelationships that may exist between vehicle and meanings. But in the aesthetic experience we are not concerned with making the distinctions that as scientists we seek to explore. Have the same painter paint, as we say, ineptly, "the same picture" in oils and in water colors. The physical vehicles which embody the meanings of both pictures—the mediums—being different, there will be two pictures for aesthetic contemplation, not the same picture in two mediums. The fact that we are interested in technique does not gainsay this, for when our interest is aesthetic, not the interest of a craftsman curious about the devices used by the artist for achieving his effects, it will be an interest in embodied meanings.

One reason why the import of these remarks is sometimes overlooked is that writers of works on aesthetics conceive of the aesthetic experience in terms of their predominantly analytic approach to the aesthetic object. Another is undoubtedly the failure to recognize the exclusive role that immanent meaning plays in the aesthetic transaction. Both these factors, I fear, are exhibited in Mr. Greene's monumental and exhaustive treatment of aesthetics. In this excellent book, in which the problems of aesthetics are treated from an idealistic point of view, we find the assertion that art is "the expression, *via* artistic form, of intelligible artistic content." [10] The use of such a phrase indicates that Mr. Greene conceives of the medium as an instrumental vehicle whose function, besides merely to please, is to carry, in art that is really worthy of the name, a referential rather than an immanent complex of meanings. This in turn is the reason why pure art is said to be expressive of emotive-conative content, though no explanation of how that expression takes place is offered. The second factor is to be discovered when Mr. Greene reveals what he himself experiences when he responds aesthetically to an object. An example of this is found on page 269, where, discussing types of artistic content, Mr. Greene points out that "the chief content of the work of art consists of the artist's interpretation of certain universals . . . as this interpretation has been expressed by him *via* artistic form in an artistic medium." He is careful to indicate quite clearly that these universals are "normally not apprehended abstractly either by the creative artist or the observer of his work, but are apprehended as embodied in the medium; and he is also careful to make clear the danger of forsaking the object altogether. But the medium, which on our interpretation is itself fully meaningful, is for him, in spite of his care, only a means through which the spectator is referred to something not present immanently in it. The object is thus a referential sign, not a significant symbol, or, in other words, it is a mnemonic device, that leads back and forth from itself to "that wider human experience . . . and that wider reality . . . to which the work of art itself directly or indirectly refers them."

It is not my intention to assert that this is not a genuine account of a type of experience and that it has no value. Both are readily granted. The passage is quoted solely as an illustration of how our aesthetic experience, such as it is, determines our conception of the aesthetic object. Clearly, Mr. Greene's experience with art, with its center of gravity in

[10] Theodore Meyer Greene, *The Arts and the Art of Criticism*, Princeton, N.J., 1940, p. 11. See also p. 443 *et passim*.

the referential aspect of the art object, is not a pure aesthetic experience, but is cognitive in orientation. It is therefore not surprising that his understanding of the relation of content to form in the object in the experience should be defective. Note, however, that a more adequate conception of the aesthetic transaction does not deny the essential and important point that Mr. Greene is trying to assert, for the wider human experience and the sense of wider reality that are for him so important, play, according to our theory, a rather large role in the pure aesthetic experience, since they both determine the specificity of the immanent meanings present to attention.

These strictures are leveled against the expression theory as it is commonly interpreted, because, while it has done yeoman service in its various versions as a means of understanding certain aspects of aesthetic phenomena, it brings with it a plague of theoretical difficulties which are quite specious. For instance, the expression theory has difficulty in dealing adequately with music. What does music express? Since the distinction between the expressive vehicle and that which it expresses is basic to the theory, it cannot suffice to say that music expresses itself. It must therefore express something else. But what? Emotion, of course. But surely music does not express emotion literally, that is, does not press emotion out of itself. But what, then, do we mean by the phrase? Do we mean that music "arouses" emotion? It is, I am afraid, what some writers take it to mean. But unfortunately this is simply a hasty generalization, for as we saw, music does not always arouse emotions. There is no denying, of course, that music acts as a stimulus and always arouses in us complex organic reactions. But these do not always become emotions. And some trained listeners find that the presence of emotion in their experience seriously interferes with their interest, which is in the musical composition itself. Some of these listeners go so far as to report that they never allow themselves to fall into habits of emotional response. Music, therefore, cannot be said always to arouse emotion, though perhaps it does so always in some auditors and at times in all.

Nor does music express emotion in the way in which men or brutes express it. Living things express emotion in that they act outwardly in a way that we correlate from experience with inward felt reactions; an actor can express an emotion by simulating the outward countenance of those who feel it, whether he feels it himself or not. This is obviously not the same sense in which the expression theory can be interpreted when applied to music, since there is no pictorial representation, in the literal sense of these words, of the outward manifestations of the emotion in the musical pattern. The phrase must therefore be taken in some other sense. Now we often say of a garden that it is gay or of a landscape that it is desolate or sad. Is this the meaning in which we should take the phrase "music expresses emotion?" But we shall find when we look into this statement that we do not mean that the landscape is actually sad or grieving. What it means, I suspect, is that it embodies a specific objective character, as objective a character as its spread or its color, and that for some reason we call this objective character by *a word borrowed from the language of the emotions.*[11]

It is this that we mean if we are interested in music as an object of aesthetic perception. When I say, however, that the music embodies meanings I do not intend to say that the music is one thing and its meanings are another. Rather do I imply that the music is meaningful through and through for aesthetic perception and that the meaning perceived is musical meaning. This does not detract from its value, for if a thing has value when it arouses interest, music has value for those who are interested in it. Nor need we doubt that in those equipped to listen to it objectively it arouses an intense, all-absorbing interest, which it satisfies completely. But a thing may arouse all sorts of interests, and the interest music seems to have for some auditors is in the emotional debauchery to which it leads them. I know of no reason why we should object to anyone's using music as an emotional stimulant. Instruments are, after all, neutral within limits set by the stuff out of which they are made, by their construction, and by the ingenuity of those who use them. It would be a piece of unwarranted dogmatism to argue that music should be listened to only for the sake of the musical meanings it embodies. But it is an equally unwarranted piece of dogmatism in those interested in

[11] Of course the question remains, "Why do we associate objective traits of inanimate things with inward states of animate beings?" This is a question on which, at present, so far as I can find out, almost any explanation would have as much right to attention as any other, since we do not seem to have any empirical evidence on which to base a verifiable hypothesis. I incline to agree with Carroll C. Pratt's discussion of the problem in his *The Meaning of Music*, New York (1931), Part II, sections 9 ff. But in her recent *Philosophy in a New Key*, Cambridge (1942) Miss Langer argues against Pratt in a way that must be taken into account. This essay was written in the Spring of 1940. Were it to be written over today, the discussion would have to be modified to take into account Miss Langer's position. The results, however, in this connection, would be essentially the same as those here reached.

music as an emotional stimulant to argue that theirs is the only or the highest value music can yield.

IV

Denial of the validity of the distinction between expressive vehicle and expressed meaning as usually made within the act of aesthetic attention does not imply denial of its validity as a tool for analysis, when its need is basic. For one of the tasks of criticism is that of comparing objects as expressive vehicles in order to discover which lead to a successful aesthetic experience and which fail to do so. But such comparisons could not be made unless the critic were able to make objective discriminations and to indicate to which of the object's constituents is to be traced the failure or the success of the experience.

Success or failure in an aesthetic experience, when it can be traced to the object, depends primarily, as we saw, on the organization of meanings which its maker is able to achieve. But it also depends on the intrinsic value of the meanings embodied. And this broad distinction leads to two general categories of criticism. When the organization itself leaves nothing to be desired, we refer to the object as "perfect"; but when the meanings embodied are satisfactory we refer to the object as "significant." And several questions arise regarding the relationship between perfection and significance in the work of art.

We are speaking, of course, of the effects which objects have on the "normal" spectator. We must conceive of him as a product of his culture and endowed with the capacity to engage in aesthetic experience. Such a person, if the picture we have of him is that of an actual human being and not a purely conceptual formulation of an ideal type, has a multitude of interests, practical, scientific, and religious, as well as aesthetic. Some of these are dominant at one time, others at other times. But unless his personality is badly split, these interests interpenetrate each other, sometimes furthering and sometimes blocking each other more or less, but achieving in the process of living some measure of conviviality and interfusion. So close is that interfusion in a personality which is not abnormally split that it is impossible to rearrange or to destroy some interests without affecting others; and in an act of response to external stimuli their interplay and concerted presence may always be counted on.

Our aesthetic experience is pure if it is intransitive; but the responses which enter into an intransitive experience are the normal responses of a complete human animal, responses which touch a large number of fields of interest. The aesthetic act may then be an autonomous act. And it is this characteristic which makes our response a "disinterested" one. The response is disinterested in the sense that *during the time it takes place* no interest demands a transitive satisfaction outside the object that arouses it. But it is not autonomous in the sense that interests whose source is to be found in extra-aesthetic human experience do not enter as factors determining the specificity of the meanings embodied immanently by the object which brings forth the perceptive act.

The basic error of certain modern aesthetic theories consists in the implicit and, it would seem, often utterly unconscious assumption of an aesthetic spectator who, like "the economic" man, is devoid of all interests except one. This is the reverse and compensatory error of the theory already criticized above, which conceives of the art object as a mnemonic device recalling a wider experience or reality not immanently embodied in it. As errors, there is no choice between these two types of doctrine; but in justice to the theory we are now to criticize it must be said that it has helped us arrive at our clear knowledge of the distinctively aesthetic. Its central defect is that it takes as reality a purely conceptualistic oversimplification of the aesthetic spectator and leads hence to a conception of art which is only a shadowy picture of the robust aesthetic experience enjoyed in the actual world. The denial of the legitimate presence of moral meanings in the aesthetic experience current in some contemporary theories, the anaemic character of art for art's sake, the assertion of the purity of art, the enactment of the intrinsic value of art into an absolute value, these notions and other doctrines and attitudes draw what specious justification they have from the implicit assumption of an "aesthetic man," devoid of any other interest whatever. The normal spectator of whom I am speaking is not Clive Bell's aesthetic man. He is a man capable of enjoying an intransitive experience, but not a man devoid of other interests. He is Unamuno's man of flesh and blood, an existential man, a moral and intellectual, a political as well as an aesthetic animal. Such a man cannot prevent all his interests from entering as determining factors in his reactions to all objects, the aesthetic included. But he is often able to behold objects intransitively.

When such a man's dominant interests and accepted values, whether intellectual or moral, are disappointed or outraged by art, the object which is the cause of the outrage is judged defective. On the other hand, when they are satisfied, the object is deemed by him to possess a dimension that a purely aesthetic object utterly lacks. These should be truisms, but are not, as is evident from much contemporary criticism. Great art, then, is art charged with meanings which are tied up with a complex and intricate network of responses in the perceiving organism, meanings belonging to a multitude of ranges of experience, to the moral, the religious, the intellectual, and also the purely sensual.

But the relation between cognitive or moral values and beauty is not as simple as the above remarks would seem to indicate. And since the problem is, as we said above, one of the central problems of contemporary aesthetics, we must try to throw more light on it. It could be argued that if moral or intellectual value is an essential ingredient in great art, we cannot call great the art of the past, when it involves, as it often does, intellectual conceptions which we have long ago discarded or values that we no longer espouse. The problem, in just this form, has obsessed I. A. Richards, who has sought to understand how contemporary unbelievers can still read religious poetry in high seriousness. Some time ago I proposed an answer to this problem, which now seems to me too simple. I suggested [12] that we are able to read with seriousness art embodying beliefs which we do not hold only at a tremendous discount, for we read it seriously only when we find "beyond the superficial doctrinal commitments of a poet, deeper beliefs on which we can focus our attention after extracting them from the poet's explicit commitments." And this, except for the phrasing, is true enough. But it overlooks other factors operating in our reaction. And of these the chief seems to be the intense interest which art can arouse because of the relative isolation and autonomy of the experience during the time it is taking place. This is what I. A. Richards's suspension of belief amounts to. The defect of Richards's phrase is that it records the fact, but does not explain why or how our beliefs can be suspended. Now, we suspend belief during the aesthetic experience because the object before us, being an organization of coherent and mutually self-sustaining immanent meanings capable of being apprehended intransitively, shuts out successfully the possibility of comparing and testing its beliefs with ours. But our beliefs operate indirectly, for as we have already seen, it is only in

[12] In "The Use of Art," *The Journal of Philosophy*, XXI (July, 1938), 409.

terms of our experience, moral and intellectual, that objects can possess for us immanent meanings. Mr. Greene's wider experience and reality are efficient determinants of what is before us, but all there is before us in our most successful aesthetic experiences is a unique or individual object. To the extent to which the experience is carried to a successful aesthetic climax, this indirect role is the only one that our beliefs can play. And as long, therefore, as the artist stays within the realm of what is for us the possible and does not violate our sense of reality or our moral sense, he can and does often engage our serious attention. But note that when he does so we must credit his success to his skill as much as we must credit it to his power as thinker or to his moral sensibility. For it is to that skill that we must trace his ability to keep us within his home grounds, so to speak, thinking in his terms and seeing the world as he sees it. The sense of reality—or of intellectual depth or of moral insight —that is so frequent an accompaniment of our adequate aesthetic experiences, is therefore no more than "a sense," deriving from our submission to the conditions of the artist's world. Properly speaking it consists in participation, not in knowledge. We share the artist's world, his bias, and his views. But they are not questioned by us, or challenged. We live through his bafflements and perplexities and with him arrive at his decisions, never questioning them, as we should if we were to accept them as knowledge, in terms of criteria external to them. "Knowledge" implies judgment, comparisons of propositions with facts external to them and with a large body of other previously established propositions. It calls for a transitive experience in which we go beyond the object and incorporate the knowledge now being acquired into a system of already accepted knowledge. This is not what happens in the aesthetic experience. When we respond aesthetically, we do not judge, we submit and accept, compelled to do so by the skill of the artist, who, having caught our interest, retains it within his object by deploying for our attention an interrelated pattern of self-sustaining meanings centripetally organized. The aesthetic experience is not an experience of truth. It is just an experience of pure attention. But being intense and vivid, it becomes the standard by which we measure ordinary experience, which is in comparison felt to be less real. Hence our ascription of superior reality to it. Superior reality it may have, but in the sense here suggested. But the truth the object may contain is the ordinary garden variety of truth, empirical truth, the only truth there is.

We must not infer from this, however, that pure or abstract art, free though it is from moral or intellectual meanings, cannot be deeply moving and may not therefore be called "significant" or great in a legitimate sense of this ambiguous word. Against that inference stands the evidence of those who love music, and that evidence is overwhelming. Music, even though devoid of moral meanings, is "significant," and those who know how to listen report experiences which, while they are ineffable in their total quality, seem nevertheless to have something in them akin to experiences the depth of which is usually ascribed only to objects which embody moral meanings.

An explanation of how this is possible may seem to be out of the reach of a writer who takes the position on emotions above stated, and there is no question that for him the challenge of the question is crucial. If in terms of this theory I have made some sort of a beginning toward the explanation required, I hope that I may be forgiven the confidence with which I have put it forward. Ordinarily we speak of "ideas" when the response involves as its predominant constituent a complex of verbal and perhaps some vague pictorial elements. But this is a restriction due to the fact that the instrument of communication is chiefly verbal and that the eye plays such an important role in our behavior. However, it should be remembered that gestures of face, arms, hands, shoulders, or the whole body are, especially in some cultures, integral and important constituents of "language." This should show that any type of body response can become an idea. The painter "thinks" in ideas which may be entirely free from verbal constituents, and this is even more true of the musician, since in his case the constituent of his responses is further from ordinary experience than that of the painter. When sounds which enjoy a modicum of organization assault the organism through the ear and arouse responses which deploy themselves implicitly within us and achieve within us, because of the subjective organization of the sounds, reflexive cross reference, we have "significant" sounds, we have what listeners call musical ideas. The significance of these sequences is immanent in the sense that our responses to them do not arouse other response patterns. There is, however, one complication worthy of note: in some auditors organized sound stimuli arouse response patterns which include visual images. But this is not always the case. And when it does happen, the visual imagery is part of the content of the musical idea. Since organized sound stimuli are intrinsically interesting, they are intrinsically valuable. This is the case even when the response is a predominately auditory one and even when the feeling-tone which accompanies it is not the dominant factor of interest. The value of pure music depends upon our interest in it, and our interest in turn depends upon the existence of patterns of response capable of being called forth by the sound stimuli. Again, music is significant if we value it, but the depth we attribute to it depends not only on its objective complexity but upon the complexity of responses with which we listen to it.

The word "significance" in this explanation may cause difficulty, since it is inherently ambiguous. Therefore it is advisable to remark in the interest of clarity that meanings which point beyond themselves, referentially or, when they are immanent, to themselves, reflexively, are significant because the terminal object to which they point, referentially or reflexively, is an object of interest, that is, a valuable object. "Signification," used to denote a semeiotic relation, cannot be separated from, even if it may and should be distinguished from, "significance," which is the term used to denote the value aspect of a signification relation. There is, therefore, good ground for the ambiguity to which the terms "meaning" and "significance" usually commit us, since the pointing transactions into which we enter when we think or reflect disclose terminally interesting objects.

6

THE UNNATURAL

Herbert W. Schneider

OF what use is the concept of nature? Two traditional uses (I mean, of course, good uses) are readily distinguished, and I propose neither to call them into question nor to expound them. But there is a third, which, though it has a long tradition, is today in ill-repute, especially among naturalists; it is this use which appears to me especially worth saving. In connection with each of the three uses I shall be concerned with two special problems: (1) Has "nature" a plural? (2) What is excluded as unnatural?

According to one meaning the term "nature" denotes the totality of existence. All things are natural in so far as they exist, have existed, or may be expected to exist. The unnatural things are things imagined to exist—ghosts and spirits, unicorns and dragons—or things imagined— utopias, round squares, imaginary numbers, and all eternal objects or things conceived. The mind in act is natural, but the mind has objects beyond nature. The mind is in this sense free to examine nature from beyond, to pursue naturally unnatural ends, to love or to hate what exists, and in general to be "free" of nature so far as its objects and interests are concerned. There is nothing unnatural in such a being, in an existence that can embrace the nonexistent, since the evidence that it does so is a part of natural knowledge. To know universals is not unnatural, but whether universals have a natural existence is, of course, an ancient problem which this concept of nature does not settle one way or the other. Science and art exist in nature or they do not exist at all. Similarly, history is not unnatural, for the processes of history are continuous with the patterns of growth and decay. Any existence is historical, for there is a history even of nature. Human history is a special case of a natural history. The concept of nature, according to this usage, does not imply any particular theory of the structure of existence or of totality. Nature may be merely a collective name for atomic existences, it may be an organic structure, or it may be a more or less unified collection of more or less related processes. Whatever the totality of existence proves to be, there is obviously no point in conceiving of more than one totality. By definition nature is singular and all-inclusive. Unnatural things do not exist.

Another concept of nature excludes man and his works from nature. Nature is man's home, mother, habitat, or environment. Man grows up in nature, but when he comes to maturity he ceases to be what the Germans still call a *Naturmensch* and fashions by art a home of his own out of the raw materials of nature. He never gets completely out of nature, but his works and his culture are in a significant sense his own, because he can assume responsibility for them. In this sense nature, including human nature, is distinguished from art, culture, history, and the human pursuit of human happiness. This approach to nature, too, implies no particular theory of nature, but it is anthropocentric, interpreting nature in terms of its relation to human experience and history. Nature is external to man and to his values, not in the sense that man is external to nature, for he is not, but in the sense that nature is his workshop. It gives him room, tools, and opportunity for art. Man as creature is natural; as artificer he goes beyond nature. Here again the term "nature" is used in the singular, less for the purpose of designating a real unity, than as a collective term to designate the infinite conditions of art and of man's pursuit of happiness.

Both these concepts of nature, nature as existence and nature as human environment, are primarily collective and denotative. Their purpose is not analytical. Analysis takes place within the context of nature. The things to be analyzed are *res naturae*. I turn now to a more analytical use of the term, to *natura rerum*. Using any vague term, such as Lucretius's *res*, for any existence or process, we now seek within these affairs, circumstances, events for something that may be called their nature. There is an important difference between *res naturae* and *natura rerum*. The correlative of the term "nature" according to this latter use is neither the nonexistent nor the human, but the accidental or adventitious. "Unnatural" here means what is external to the normal structure or occurrence of a thing. When a thing is interpreted as *res naturae*, there are clearly no unnatural aspects of the thing; but if there is a nature in things, we may well look among things also for the unnatural. Taking this third approach, we find it more difficult to explain why there is a singular *natura* in the plurality *rerum*, and we are obliged to state with reasonable definiteness what there is in things besides their nature. How do unnatural things happen? By "the unnatural" I mean, to begin with, the nonnatural. I am seeking a descriptive account of the distinction between the natural and the nonnatural aspects of things. Having determined this, I shall subsequently raise the question of the normative use of the distinction and discuss the unnatural as a criterion for value judgments.

As the term "nature" is used in this connotative, analytical sense, there is no evident reason why all things should have one nature. There may be a specific nature for each thing, and in fact "natures," in the plural, were for centuries the objects of science. But in Lucretius and in the basic purpose of any inquiry *de natura rerum* nature (*physis*) is essentially singular. For natural knowledge is an inquiry into the working interrelations of things, and though there be many specific types of workings and many individual differences, the search for the nature in things is a search for their dynamic continuity. Mechanisms are things co-operating toward a result. A mechanism is a teleological structure. A machine that is a machine for nothing in particular is not in the full sense a machine. To regard all natural mechanisms as one vast machine implies the discovery of a world product or of some identifiable end to which all things contribute. Failing this discovery or faith, the search for mechanism is really a search for the structure of "mechanisms" (plural). Particular processes eventuate in particular things or circumstances, but in their working they may exhibit common principles and forces.

A natural or mechanical process is something more than a series of events causally connected; it has an individuality or functional structure. Something is achieved; the events lead to an eventuality. There must be cumulative changes, intelligible culminations, identifiable directions, in short, individual structures, if processes are to be called in any significant sense natural. There must be evident beginnings and endings, there must be literally "something doing," otherwise the search for nature in things is vain. But any natural process, for example, erosion, combustion, digestion, decay, perception, is by nature continuous with other processes, intelligible not in isolation, but as a function in a more complicated pattern of motion and change, such as the formation of a river valley, the radiation of heat and light, the sensitivity, growth, and decay of an organism. Nature, or *physis*, is not merely the particular generation or genesis of a particular, but the continuity among such individual processes. Nature is the common source of diversified products. The term "nature" is here not merely a collective term. For to discover nature in things means precisely to discover dynamic connection among things in action. Hence the existence of *natura rerum* implies (1) that events are not merely atomic, (2) that mechanisms can be discovered among them, one by one, and that therefore there is no need for believing either in the mechanical unity of all things or in absolute chance, (3) that the degree to which things act naturally is the measure of their continuity.

Having found that things work together, philosophers are readily tempted to infer that things exist in unity—that nature does not exist in things, but things in nature. This inference has guided much of philosophic thinking since Lucretius. Resisting this temptation, and returning from Spinoza to Lucretius, I am nevertheless keeping nature in the singular for the reason mentioned. Nature, even when denoting the relativity among processes, not an absolute process, is essentially singular. There is only one nature in things, because nature exists, not within particulars, but among them. Things are natural in so far as they work, and working implies a mechanical continuum. To conceive a particular nature for each process is, therefore, to misconceive the aim of the search for nature in things. Nature is singular precisely because it is relative to a number of things.

Nature is primarily a category of creation. Nature is the mother of mothers. The analogy of the mother is, however, misleading in one respect, for it is often assumed that as the egg or child leave the parent body, so natural creatures can literally leave their creator and become literally external to what they now look upon as an alien world. Nature is more like a matrix than a mother, more like a soil to a plant than a mother to a child. To be uprooted is to be unnatural.

Nature conceived in these terms seems to me to have the same place in naturalistic philosophy that "reality" has in idealism. Just as reality is, according to idealism, the reality in and of appearances, not an unconditional absolute, so nature is not an absolute or self-contained process, but a relativity, continuity, or co-operation among processes. Nature is neither in things nor external to them, but of them. It is normative. The real is the genuine. Similarly, "to be true to one's nature" is not a foolish phrase, though it is redundant. To be one's natural self is to be true, healthy, sound, reliable.

I know that this conception of nature will be regarded as excessively naïve. Have I never heard of the modern criticism of Aristotelian ontology? Are not these natural norms simply the medieval essences, which have long ago ceased to be natural? I am consciously reverting to this ancient ontology, because I think I see the blunders of its corrupted, medieval guise and the folly of its modern repudiation. I think this ontology steers a course midway between the idea of substance and the idea of specific essences. Processes are plural, but are bound together by the nature (not natures, not substance) that is in them. They fit together somewhat; they work together in some measure. There is some fitness in most things—not in each thing severally, but in things relative to each other. By fitting together, things disclose nature. It is not true that each thing has a nature all its own or that all things fit together. Nature is measured by the productivity of things. Nature is the principle of fertility in things. If "actuality" meant in English what *Wirklichkeit* ought to mean in German and *energeia* meant to Aristotle, nature might appropriately be called actuality. Natural things are active not merely in the sense that they have effects but also in the sense that they have products. Productivity is always co-operative, involving the co-action (I wish I could say "coercion") of several things or processes. Natural power is neither pure potentiality nor perfect form; neither internal nor external relatedness.

Nature is a norm, but neither a statistical norm nor an ideal. The "real" is commonly identified either with the ideal or with the actual, and there seems to be no third alternative. It seems to me that the natural lies between the ideal and the actual. The empiricist or actuarial conception of nature as a norm lies, in a sense, between the ideal and the actual. But such a norm, based on expectancy and probability, is what I mean by a statistical norm; it is inadequate for a theory of nature, whether or not it be adequate for a theory of causality. "Natural" means more than probable. For example, both an ideal love and an unnatural love may be statistically exceptional, but they are not instances on the same scale and may bear no direct relation either to each other or to average love. Natural love is not average love but normal, healthy love. There is something artificial about both sexless and homosexual love. The statistical status of these artificial kinds of love may be quite different in Plato's culture and in ours, and the moral evaluation of them may be different, too. But it seems to me that it is possible to define their unnatural character without examining either their statistical or their moral status, just as it is possible to identify a normal or healthy organism without calculating averages. A normal automobile is a working machine, no matter how many wrecked cars there are to influence the average. To discover how a machine works is a thoroughly empirical problem, but not merely statistical. It is a problem in dynamics. Examination of an automobile will reveal which is front and which is back, and in which direction the machine is "headed." Mechanical analysis generates norms; it does not presuppose them. Similarly, the idea of health, which guides the physiologist as well as the physician, develops empirically from a study of the operation of organisms. The meaning of health is determined by the organism investigated, not by the investigator. False conceptions of health can be proved false. In general, natural norms are empirically verifiable, provided, of course, that the "working" of a mechanism is understood to be the object of inquiry.

That is natural which works. I realize that such a conception of nature will be regarded as a crude, pragmatic naturalism and that it shares the strengths and weaknesses of pragmatic method. The vagueness and plainness of my use of the term "working" makes the theory liable to a variety of caricatures. But in spite of this danger I prefer it to the idealist's identification of the real with the ideal, to the orthodox naturalist's belief that all things are equally natural, and to the orthodox empiricist's belief that the probable is natural.

There is only one order of nature, but there are many ways of being out of order. The unnatural is essentially pluralistic, and it would seem futile at the outset to find a single trait that would do justice to it. Knowledge of the unnatural comes primarily neither by definition nor by analysis, but by observation. How a machine works is known by analysis; but that it is not working can usually be felt or perceived. Failures advertise themselves to a man of practical experience; but practical experience does not necessarily lead to mechanical knowledge. The unnatural is perceived; the natural must be understood. Accidents we have with us always, but the knowledge of nature or of "the works" in things comes only with science. Among the most common signs of unnaturalness in things are accident, irrelevance, artificiality, arbitrariness, futility, monstrosity, inappropriateness, destructiveness, and disease. None of these will serve as an adequate synonym or definition of the unnatural, but each of them contributes something to its identification. To illustrate will be, under these circumstances, the most natural procedure for our inquiry, though we shall probably be obliged to end our illustrations without arriving at a clear idea of the unnatural.

We begin with the accidental and the irrelevant. In the context of logic, in which the scholastics developed their doctrines of nature and essence, the nonnatural was the dispensable, the unnecessary. Any trait which a given thing could have or not have without changing its nature was called accidental to it. Translating this distinction into the context of mechanism the accidental would be the nonfunctional, the useless, or the futile. Wherever there is mechanical design, there is the possibility of parts that contribute nothing. Such parts are foreign or unnatural to the machine. In physiology an organ that serves no known use is only by courtesy called an organ; on the supposition that it once served a use, it is usually called vestigial. There is good evidence, however, that there are now useless parts of the body; such "parts" are not participants and may therefore appropriately be regarded as external to "human nature." In so far as we have reason to believe that there are things without use, that is, things not involved in any given processes, we may say that those things are unnatural relative to those processes. Absolutely useless things would be difficult to imagine. But more important than the question whether absolutely futile beings exist, is the fact of relative uselessness or irrelevance. Things are more or less directly involved in any given process; relative to this process there is always a large field of the more or less irrelevant. In other words, there is some discontinuity among mechanisms; they are more or less useless to each other. There is positive evidence that many things are futile, in the sense of failing to achieve the natural ends of their kind. The unnatural in this sense measures the degree to which there is relative independence among mechanisms.

Not only the useless, or idle, is unnatural, but there are unnatural, inappropriate uses which things may serve. To hammer a nail with a screw driver is an unnatural use of a screw driver. It *can* serve this purpose, but does so only in the absence of a more appropriate instrument. It is not naturally a hammer. Though most things have many uses, they do not serve all of them equally well. Here again, naturalness and unnaturalness are matters of degree. Propriety, decency, appropriateness in conduct and art and their opposites have some foundation in nature, though no doubt most standards in these matters are conventional. To use men as guinea pigs or as cannon fodder seems an inappropriate use for men, considering their nature. But this raises one of the most difficult and polemic questions in our whole subject—the question of human nature. Is the human being designed to function as a rational animal or as a beast of prey? Who can tell with certainty? Some there are who claim that man has no nature whatsoever, but this, too, is a rash judgment. So long as human beings exhibit so great a variety of norms it seems impossible to say with confidence what man is by nature. But there is nothing anomalous about this predicament in our anlysis. The knowledge of nature in general, we said, is experimental, and the evidence is not all in. Why should not our knowledge of human nature be still in its infancy? Meanwhile, we are relatively familiar with human failure and futility. We know more about what is unnatural for man than what is natural. It is easier to determine some of the things that are inappropriate for man than to determine what is appropriate for him. There is no reason to assume that man has any single natural function or that he is designed for any special task. A complicated, flexible mechanism like man can probably do many things well; in fact his *eudaimonia*, or essential functions, may change from time to time. There is no reason to suppose that human nature, or nature in general, is fixed or determinate. Nothing need be assumed in this inquiry, for it is possible that nothing may come of it. Men and other things could conceivably exist without nature, though practical knowledge of them would then be impossible. For, to use William James's familiar distinction, we may have abundant "acquaintance knowledge" of unnatural human behavior without gaining an understanding of or "knowledge about" the natural. Failure to hit a mark implies a mark, to be sure, but not the ability to aim well at it or the knowledge of how to hit it. And natural or practical knowledge, in the complete sense, means not merely definition of nature or "knowledge *that*," but analysis, or "knowing *how*." Hence the perception of inappropriateness, impropriety, awkwardness are signs pointing in the direction in which to look for their opposites, but do not imply that the positive knowledge is *ipso facto* contained in the negative, any more than being in pain implies knowledge of being in health.

Another form of abnormality in things besides the two described so far (uselessness and inappropriateness) is disease, or deformity. If the state of nature is a working state of organized and healthy productivity, it follows that any form of corruption is unnatural. Of course, the disease or corruption of one process may in turn be productive in some other process. The decay of flesh is food for plants. Death and decay are regarded as natural processes in so far as they are an essential part of life cycles. But sheer destruction, defeat, and frustration are unnatural. A forest fire, for example, is an accident or unnatural end in the life of a forest if it merely destroys the life that was in process without contributing to anything. If it was the means of clearing a tract for cultivation, or if it facilitated the erosion of a hillside or in some other tangible way led to a tangible result (whether good or bad for man or forest), what seemed a mere accident that befell the forest turns out to be natural from some other point of view. Of course, any event has causes and consequences, but a causal chain is not necessarily a natural process. A forest fire may kill a hawk, whose death spares the life of a mouse in an adjacent field, which as a consequence is able to have its litter of young before it falls prey to an owl, which but for the forest fire might have found some other mouse, and so forth. This is a causal chain, but not a natural process. We would ordinarily describe it as a series of accidents. It is a natural process for owls to use mice as food, but to become prey is an unnatural end for a mouse. To be burned in a forest fire is even less natural for a hawk than to be eaten by a hawk is for a mouse. A forest fire is more of an accident for a forest tree than to be cut for lumber. It is unnatural for a forest acorn to be eaten by a domesticated pig, though not unheard of, whereas it is natural for domesticated corn to be so consumed. The conflicting interests of bird and mouse, or animal and vegetable need not blind us, as it does them, to the understanding of the mechanism of struggle. Eating and being eaten are natural processes, co-operation in things. I trust I need not explain that by co-operation I do not mean peaceful co-operation or stoic reasonableness in nature. It is natural for certain organisms to have certain parasites. The host and the parasite, though the utility is unilateral, are factors, though antipathetic factors, in a biological pattern or process to which both their lives belong. Even though the parasite is a diseased rather than a healthy condition of its host, it is a natural disease. Apples, in my part of the country, are naturally wormy; whereas at Amherst, I am told, a worm in an apple is an accident. Other diseases are more incidental to the life of a particular organism, and most organisms endure from time to time what we call accidents. There are degrees of naturalness between the evidently unnatural accident and the evidently natural parasite. All may be equally pernicious or fatal to the organism. Here the statistical factor seems to be the measure of naturalness. Parasites are simply perennial pests, regular diseases. But there is a sense in which no matter how frequently a man might suffer injury from auto accidents, these injuries would be unnatural, whereas the ailments of old age are natural. Even if carelessness in driving were, as we say, second nature to a man, he would still be running nature merely a close second. To repeat, the normal processes are distinguished from accidental sequences neither by mere statistical calculation nor by reference to human or good uses, but naturalistically, that is, by insight into a mechanism that works cumulatively toward an end-product or result. Interference with such a process is unnatural in the sense of being contranatural—a positive obstruction, not mere irrelevance or inefficiency.

We are now prepared to discuss naturalistic theory of value. If the natural and the unnatural types of being have been correctly distinguished here, it follows that nature is neither a perfectly indifferent order nor a single integrated process, but a selective, directive continuity among processes. The presence of the unnatural is a constant reminder that normally things are neither indifferent nor alien to each other. There are natural affinities and natural enemies, not for nature as a whole, but relative to any given process.

All values and disvalues, both the natural and the unnatural, are relative to the nature of a particular process. But, to repeat, the nature of a process is not to be found in isolation, but in a network of machinery or processes. Consequently, in the analysis of natural values means are related not only to ends but also to each other. This is another way of saying that there are few means which are means to only one end. Though ends be ever so diversified, they have a common matrix of means, in so far as they are natural. This interrelatedness of means is in one way a nuisance for art, and value theory would be much simpler if every end had its own special means. But in another way art would be artless were means so neatly segregated by nature. The network of means makes it possible to go in many directions from any given point and thus provides many opportunities at the same time that it poses problems for art. Or, to change the figure slightly, the structure of the chessboard makes the game both possible and difficult; then, too, easier games can be played on the same board, or it can be used in other ways without playing any game whatsoever. Similarly, the dynamic relatedness of natural means is not so determinate as to make only one pursuit of one end practical, nor is it so indeterminate as to enable any means to serve any end. There is enough "accident" in things to encourage gambling and enough mechanism to make planning possible. Were the nature of things either what Lucretius explained it to be or what Spinoza proved it must be, it would not be a propitious field for values, least of all for human values. But as it is, it could be worse.

Any process is a selective agent. Some things are of value to it, others injure it, others are neutral. Its nature is not its good, nor is the unnatural necessarily its evil. But nature is a criterion or proving ground to which its values can be referred. Given an acorn growing according to nature, certain kinds of soil are good for it, certain animals dangerous, certain degrees of frost fatal, and so forth. Any natural process is thus a locus of natural values. Whatever is unnatural to it may be neutral or may be evil, but it cannot be of value to it as a natural process. Anything, like lubrication, that contributes to the natural functioning of a mechanism is naturally good for it. The final cause or end product of the mechanism or process, I would not call its natural good, but its purpose, aim, or meaning. Health is a natural good of the body, not because the body's aim or interest is health, but because it needs health to do its work. Whatever contributes toward making a normal acorn into a normal oak is good for the growth of an acorn. Similarly, there are natural evils for an acorn. And as for artificial or unnatural uses which an acorn may serve, these generate artificial sets of values and evils. What can be said for an acorn as a value-center can be said of a magnet and its field, as well as of man and human affairs. There are natural values for man, and unnatural. In fact, the chief point of this tedious analysis is to show that man is not so unnatural as he thinks he is in having both natural and unnatural values. So far as nature goes, man is like any other value-center. But so far as man goes, he has built up an exceptionally large body of values which have only an indirect, if any, relation to nature.

There may be little sense in reviving the design argument without the universal designer and without general determinism, since the design argument has been used chiefly to buttress these old faiths. Nevertheless, there is homely truth in it. It is important to know what things fit together and which are incompatible. There are affinities in things, and, though they explain nothing, they are the subject matter of all explanations. To ignore design in things is one of the most serious forms of *ignoratio elenchi;* not because the *natura rerum* is the aim of all things, but because knowledge naturally is of designs or patterns. The mind participates in nature in so far as it works on workings. To understand things in operation it operates on them, to be sure, but it must be guided by the norms of operation. To know nature is more than a knowledge of efficient causes and less than a knowledge of final causes; it is to know the interrelation of the efficient and the final. It is knowledge of relativity. It does not pretend to say why all things fit together or what they should serve. But it can tell what things can do as a matter of fact.

A design argument that admits plurality of functions and relativity of processes is naturalistic. Obversely, the naturalism that committed itself to faith in a single process or universal evolution was either a half-hearted naturalism, living half by faith in providence, or a dogmatic monism, pretending to have discovered more mechanism than it could prove. Empirically, naturalism should be relativistic, since it must discover *natura in medias res.* Any belief in the absolute structure or universal organism is an *obiter dictum* of science, a confession of a not unreasonable faith.

Similarly, any attempt to make nature the ultimate value for man or to preach naturalism as a gospel is unnatural to the spirit of natural knowledge, for it places it in the pulpit among more professional and confident preachers. Naturalism is a discovery of particular values, not a philosophy of value; it betrays its own nature when it preaches the unity of *ens* and *bonum.* Naturalism is a search for the sources and forms of power, but it has no obligation, either logical or moral, to become a love of power. To understand how things work together is a good beginning for moral science, but not the essence of it.

Naturalistic norms for human life are in no sense categorical imperatives. There is no reason why man *should* seek his nature, if he chooses not to do so. Unnatural values are good for unnatural ends. I wish to point out, however, that those who, like Santayana, consciously turn their backs on nature, and then find their purely spiritual goods to be naturally powerless, have the natural reward for their escape. The indifference of some men to nature and the indifference of nature to man are neither of them in the nature of things.

7

THE HISTORY OF PHILOSOPHY

George Boas

PHILOSOPHERS who study the history of their subject will normally ask two questions: (1) how is the philosophy of a given individual related to that of his predecessors, contemporaries, and successors; (2) has the development of philosophy followed any determinable course? Thus, in discussing the former question one may ask what, for instance, Descartes owed to the scholastics; how far were his ideas novel; how did he react to the objections of Gassendi, Hobbes, Henry More; what did he contribute to the philosophies of Malebranche, Spinoza, Bossuet; how closely did Rameau adhere to his musical theories; did Racine utilize his theory of the passions? In discussing the second question one may invent such a formula as Hegel's, or Lewes's, or even Jouffroy's, later expressed by William James. When one surveys the field, one sees that the latter type of question has proved more seductive than the former, probably because the very exercise of the philosophical profession habituates one to the search for generalizations, so that investigations of the former type of question do not seem "profound" enough to be satisfactory.

It might not appear at first sight as if the two types of investigation were independent, for if one is to write the history of philosophy, would it not seem appropriate first of all to know the histories of the separate philosophies? Having determined the latter, one could then move on to generalize them into a schematic account of the former. But as a matter of fact one can acquire the materials for a general history of philosophy with very little information about the fortunes of the particular philosophies which might be thought to make it up. One has simply to outline what is known as the philosophical position of each philosopher—here an assumption enters to the effect that each philosopher has a philosophical position—and observe its logical relationship to that of the other philosophers. Whether every philosopher has a philosophical position will perhaps be clarified below, but in practice his philosophical position turns out to be a set of ideas which the Germans would call *Kerngedanken*, with the result that his opinions as a whole become divided into the *Kern* and the *Hülse*. The latter do not appear in the histories.

The history of philosophy thus turns into a history of the *Kernge-danken* and is written in terms of essences which, as Hegel correctly saw, belong more properly to a realm in which history has no place. It is a realm in which the eternal, rather than the temporal, is at home, in which logical patterns may be outlined, but not the birth and decay of ideas as psychological and biological events. In such histories one finds philosophical schools—Platonism, Aristotelianism, Stoicism, Epicurean-ism, Scholasticism, English Empiricism, and so forth. Their authors raise such problems as "What is the 'real' meaning of Platonism?" or "Was Berkeley 'really' an empiricist or a Platonist?" The use of such a word as "really" indicates that there is some ground for doubt, which ground is frequently the apparent inconsistency in a writer's various ideas. When one finds that a writer has maintained two contradictory ideas, one may conclude (1) that the contradiction is verbal, not real; (2) that since he must have maintained one of them earlier than the other, his later views were his "mature" views and hence his "real" views; (3) that his earlier views were his "real" views, since he framed them in the full vigor of his youth; (4) that he was not aware of the inconsistency and "really" intended to affirm that idea, which is consistent with his *Kerngedanke*, otherwise determined; (5) that regardless of whether he was aware of the contradiction or not, that set of ideas which can be fitted into a logi-cal pattern with other sets of ideas is his "real" philosophy; (6) that he was aware of the inconsistency, but for reasons of malice or for other reasons preferred to say nothing about it. There are doubtless other con-clusions, but these six will do as illustrations.

Such disputes have arisen in the case of Plato, Aristotle, Saint Augus-tine, Kant, Schelling, and, in our own day, Royce and James. The case of Royce is especially interesting. It will be recalled that in his later writings he began to call what he had earlier called "the Absolute" by the name of "the Community." He was apparently unaware of the fact that he had radically changed his views, feeling that he had rather changed his terminology and thus enlarged the implications of his earlier position. But his readers did not all agree. Theologians, who had been glad to identify the Absolute with God, felt uneasy about identifying "the Community" with God, in spite of Royce's assurance that Saint Paul was on his side. Miss Calkins, whose Self-psychology was of course in disagreement with Royce's view that the Self was not a datum, but an achievement, but who admired much that he wrote, maintained also that the Community and the Absolute could not be the same. Whether they can or not does not, happily, concern us here; what does concern us is whether the problem of which Royce was the real Royce and whether there were two is one which cannot be prejudged. Our answer is that the question arises only if one assumes beforehand that it is normal for a man not to change his mind, but to be consistent from youth to old age, and if one assumes in addition that philosophizing is an activity like geometrical deduction. Both of these assumptions seem to the writer of this article to be contrary to fact.

That one feels it necessary to reconcile or reduce a man's various ideas may also arise from a theory that in certain "ages" certain ideas were in vogue and that when an author living in, for instance, an "ethical period" writes about metaphysics, his real interest is ethical and not metaphysical. His ethical writings express his *Kerngedanken*, and his metaphysical writings express his *Hülsegedanken*. The most famous application of this technique in our own times is to be found in Windelband. He defined the history of philosophy, it will be remembered, as "the process in which European humanity has embodied in scientific conceptions its views of the world and its judgments of life." [1] It was characteristically enough *die europäische Menschheit*, not the men who engaged in this process. If Mankind can have views of the world and judgments of life, one might expect that they would always be the same in content, since, however much men may come and go, Mankind endures. Indeed, Windelband emphasizes a certain lack of progress when he considers the difference between philosophy and science.

While in other sciences, a quiet building up of knowledge is the rule, as soon as they have once gained a sure methodical footing after their rhapsodical beginnings—a rule which is interrupted only from time to time by a sudden new beginning,—in philosophy the reverse is true. There it is the exception that successors gratefully develop what has been already achieved, and each of the great systems of philosophy begins to solve its newly formulated problem *ab ovo*, as if the other systems had scarcely existed.[2]

Are we reading too much into this if we say that individual philosophers each incarnate, according to this statement, over individual European mankind in their meditations? A negative answer would seem justified when one sees how Windelband interprets philosophers as expressive of certain ages. Thus he says,

[1] *A History of Philosophy*, tr. by J. H. Tufts, p. 9.   [2] *Ibid.*

The Academy and Lyceum were . . . injured in their working by the two schools which . . . owed their great success to the fact that they formulated the tendency of the time toward the practical wisdom of life with the clearness and impressiveness of one-sidedness: namely, the *Stoic* and the *Epicurean*.[3]

This use of the term *der Zug der Zeit*, or *die Richtung der Zeit*, may be innocent enough, but in this case one of the few means we have of knowing what "the tendency of the times" was is precisely that which it is held to have caused. Windelband here argues as if there were an ethical period which caused men to have ethical interests. But if the men in question had not written on ethics, what would have become of the ethical period? The methodological question thus becomes, "Is there a tendency of a time which orients the philosophical meditation of that time, or is the tendency of a time itself in part determined by the philosophical meditation of that time?" We say "in part" to permit nonphilosophical interests to play their role.

The disjunction is not easily resolved. For if one makes a radical distinction between philosophical and nonphilosophical thinking, the tendency of the time may itself be identified with the nonphilosophical thinking and the assertion that the tendency of a time orients the philosophy of that time means that nonphilosophical thinking is the cause or determiner of philosophical. Windelband does make such a distinction and indeed seems to believe that nonphilosophical thinking, at least that part of it which is science, determines as a kind of cause the intellectual life of mankind.[4] But this must have been a slip of the pen, for it is manifestly false. What Windelband usually says is that human interests during certain periods—otherwise undistinguished—turn toward ethics; at other periods they turn toward religion; at others, toward natural science. Thus, to use an example of our own, at the present time in America there seem to be two prevailing interests in philosophic circles—if one can judge from the journals and from the association meetings—philosophy of science and of aesthetics. But the philosophy of science is, perhaps, the more widespread of the two. Are we then to say that this is a scientific period and to write the history of contemporary philosophy as the effect of the scientific interests of this period? Are we to argue that natural science has such prestige that philosophy strives to adopt its technique and discards all problems which cannot be solved by that technique?

[3] *Ibid.*, p. 159.   [4] *Ibid.*, p. 3, first sentence.

Such may very well be the attitude of future historians of our time. The volume for which this essay is written would not be as it is if the prestige of the natural sciences were not very great, nor would the one vague word "naturalism" be the only one discoverable to cover the general temper of its contents. After all, this is but one manifestation of contemporary philosophy, and there are doubtless as many nonnaturalists in America as naturalists. What makes this period a "scientific" period is not the general acceptance of science as fundamental metaphysically, but the persistent criticism of the results and procedures of science. Just when the contemporary period began should be determined by one who believes in periods, but it is reasonable to maintain that most of us today are more critical of natural science than the contemporaries of Herbert Spencer were. Thus, when we discuss "the philosophy of science," we are more likely to write papers, for instance, on the methodological assumptions of Einstein or Heisenberg, either attacking them or defending them, than to accept them and attempt a deduction of their implications for epistemology, ontology, cosmology, and the other traditional branches of philosophy. In other words, this may be called a scientific period in that some of us are now more aware than our predecessors were of the philosophical problems implicated in science.

But at the same time the present is a period when scientists appear to be peculiarly aware of philosophy. Not only are our Einsteins, Eddingtons, and Millikans announcing their views on God, freedom, and immortality, but they are also critically scrutinizing the technique of experimentation, the use of definition, meaning, the foundations of scientific truth, and the like. One would be hard put to it to tell whether Bridgman's *Logic of Modern Physics* or the introduction of Campbell's *Physics, the Elements* are science or philosophy. Nor would it be worth one's while to make the effort. Yet the fusion of the two interests, the scientific and the philosophical, is certainly a characteristic of our time. It is not, however, the differentia of our time, for from the days of Aristotle, if not earlier, scientists have had philosophical preoccupations. The Hippocratic Corpus, the works of Theophrastus and Sextus Empiricus, are good examples from ancient times; Burtt's *Metaphysical Foundations of Modern Science* is sufficient for modern times. Medieval science is so notoriously philosophical that no proofs are needed to make out a case as far as it is concerned.

What this period will be called will depend in all probability upon the interests of the historian. To have periods requires the discovery of pervasive traits; these traits must be different from the traits of preceding and succeeding periods. Since every period will, like our own time, be similar to and different from other periods, the historian given to periods will have to emphasize differences and obscure similarities. But each period will also manifest an inner diversity of conflicting philosophical interests. There are alive today, and teaching, Kantians, post-Kantians, right- and left-wing Hegelians, large numbers of Thomists, logical positivists, critical realists, neorealists, pragmatists, and many others. Each of these groups breaks up into smaller groups, as the symposiums they publish eloquently demonstrate. One has only to take a period or a movement at random and the same thing will appear: the Encyclopedists, the British Empiricists, the Cambridge Platonists, the Seventeenth-Century Rationalists, the Italian Renaissance, the Thirteenth Century, the Patristics, the neo-Platonists, the Peripatetics, the Academicians. The diversity within these groups and periods is as impressive as the unity. But the historians have been more interested in unity than in diversity, and since a common trait can always be found for any group of entities, their interest in unity has always been satisfied.[5]

But groups such as we have indicated differ in their attitude toward certain philosophic problems. Are there not certain periods when specific problems are in the air, upon whose importance most people are agreed, though they may differ about the correct solution of them?

It cannot be denied that—since problems are in general observed deviations from the rule—they cannot arise until a rule has been formulated. Thus, so long as it was believed that organic chemistry was radically different from inorganic, the problem of artificially synthesizing organic compounds could not arise; similarly, after the distinction between the two chemistries was broken down, the problem of synthesizing all organic compounds which it was of any interest to synthesize was bound to arise. Again, whether the American Indian was a man or an anthropoid ape is a question which could not arise before 1492 and the question of the date of our visual qualities until 1675.[6] But this simply means that

[5] See C. S. Peirce, "The Order of Nature," in *Chance, Love and Logic,* ed. by Morris A. Cohen, New York, 1925, p. 112. The common property which Peirce proved to exist was a negative one, the lack of that which distinguishes all other things. May not this type of property be that which constitutes periods?

[6] See A. O. Lovejoy's interesting comment on this in his *Revolt against Dualism,* Chicago and New York, 1930, p. 19. He points out how Lord Bacon had formulated the conjecture that there might be a temporal lag between the start of "the

the conditions which give rise to philosophic problems vary from time to time and that some of them become more or less pressing as time goes on. It has, for instance, been maintained that the concentration of people in Athens in the fifth century B.C. was responsible for the Sophistic movement, entailing, as it did, the necessity of learning the arts of urban living. This may be true or false, but if true, it does not mean that there was an urban period of philosophy; it means that philosophers who lived in urban centers—and it is they of whom we have the records—were interested in the problems which urban life entailed. But the following philosophers, to the best of our knowledge, were contemporaries of Protagoras: Zeno the Eleatic, Melissus, Empedocles, Anaxagoras, some Pythagoreans, Democritus, and even Socrates. Yet according to Windelband, Empedocles, Anaxagoras, Zeno, and the early Pythagoreans are put in the "cosmological period"; Protagoras and Socrates, in the "anthropological period"; Democritus in the "systematic period," and these periods are arranged in chronological order. What the periods turn into is problems and what Windelband does is to forget chronology, except as it applies on a grand scale, and to group men according to what he conceives to be their major interests. The rise of these interests may be plausibly explained in a variety of ways, and theoretically these ways can be dated. Thus if every philosopher living between 500 B.C. and 399 B.C. lived in an urban center and studied the same problems, and if their predecessors lived in nonurban *milieux*, and if these problems were not studied before 500 B.C.—or let us say 480, to give the philosophers time to grow up—then it may make sense to speak of an urban period, the problems of which were conditioned by urban life.

We must, however, never lose sight of the fact that problems continue to be discussed long after they cease to be stylish. For ideas, like instruments, acquire a kind of beauty when their utility is lost. If this were not so, it would be difficult to justify the history of ideas. Thus, although one may explain the rise of an idea by causes anterior to or contemporaneous with it, its survival requires no explanation beyond the principle of what one might call "conceptual inertia." This term is not used in a pejorative sense; after all, we can think only with the ideas we possess

---

images or rays of the heavenly bodies" and their arrival "to us." But he rejected the hypothesis. Roger Bacon for dialectical reasons—*nulla virtus finita agit in instanti* (Bacon, *op. cit.*, ed. by N. H. Bridges, London, 1900, II, 69)—argues to the finite velocity of light, but he concludes that it does not occur *in tempore sensibili et perceptibili a visu, sed insensibili.*

or have acquired, and we know that the habitual use of certain terms, like the habitual performance of certain acts, becomes second nature. Our second nature being as compulsive as our first, we can seldom achieve that eminence of self-scrutiny and self-criticism which is needed to survey our behavior as if it belonged to someone else. Consequently, though we may deprecate the use of "periods" in historiography, we must not do so because the ideas of one period survive into others. We must, nevertheless, note this survival.

If it is noted and taken seriously, it will be seen that at any date a number of different ideas exist and frequently conflict and that out of that conflict may arise many of the problems which are said to be characteristic of the age. For instance, the Platonic theory of ideas, as Professor Cherniss has suggested, was probably formulated to reconcile a group of paradoxical ethical, epistemological, and ontological doctrines which had been developed at the end of the fifth century.[7] The problem presented by the relativity of standards, Plato thought, could best be solved by positing the subsistence of an ideal standard. So in our youth the conflict between the traditional "idealism" of the schools and the platform of the six new realists stimulated a long series of articles, replies, attacks, and rejoinders which ceased—if they have ceased—only when the six realists began to emphasize their disagreements with one another and to develop special interests: value-theory, cosmology, psychology, journalism, and so forth. It has sometimes been maintained that our age is peculiarly chaotic and that in other ages, at any rate in one age—the thirteenth century—men were more united in their views, less given to originality, more desirous of conformity. But such a point of view has no justification in fact, for, though we cannot here take up twenty-five hundred years of philosophy year by year and country by country, we can indicate that even in the thirteenth century there was conflict over the doctrine of the twofold truth, over the primacy of the intellect, over the problem of individuality.[8] To defend one's own views and to attack an opponent's have always been fertile stimuli to philosophy and one cannot correctly trace the course of philosophic history unless one knows precisely what the conflict was at a given time. For though there are certain "persistent problems of philosophy," such as the relation of

[7] Harold Cherniss, "The Philosophical Economy of the Theory of Ideas," *American Journal of Philology*, LVII (October, 1936), p. 445.

[8] I purposely exemplify my thesis by the three problems selected by Windelband.

universals and particulars, verification, immortality, freedom of the will, yet they do not always mean the same thing.

Every problem in philosophy has an emotional aura which we shall call its "significance." The significance of freedom of the will to an Epicurean was identical with that of determinism to a Stoic. They disagreed because in the one camp they thought that peace of mind could be achieved by freedom; in the other, by determinism. To a Christian freedom of the will was likely to be argued on religious grounds; evidence was to be sought in Biblical texts, not in the feelings which a believer in it would have on this earth. To a man of the nineteenth century the problem became psychological strictly—or at least often was psychological—and one who believed in freedom had to combat the scientific doctrine of universal causation. It would be absurd to ask whether the psychological, the ethical, the religious, or the scientific problem is the real problem. The problem changed both its meaning and its significance as time went on.

Moreover, at any given time some of the persistent problems are more interesting than at other times. Freedom is still a subject of dispute, except in certain Roman Catholic circles, but one sees no more papers on it in the philosophical journals. The historian of philosophy must, therefore, raise the question why people grow tired of discussing certain questions, for boredom explains much of what happens to the history of an idea.

But as soon as this is admitted, one sees that the fundamental question to be asked is psychological: exactly what is the role of abstract ideas in human life? How are they formed; what makes them seem true; have they any causal efficacy in conduct, or are they epiphenomena; if they have causal efficacy, is it limited and, if so, by what and under what circumstances; if they are epiphenomena, whence do they derive their apparent relevancy to the world of fact; what, too, are their real causes, conscious or unconscious; is all thought "rationalization" and, if so, of what psychic powers—economic or errotic appetites; why do some abstract ideas, like those of "unity," "eternality," "activity," "order," have pleasant and unpleasant connotations? These are but a few of the questions which a historian cannot avoid if he is to treat his subject matter naturalistically. He asks himself not only what changes have human ideas suffered but also why do ideas change?

When such questions are raised, the field is no longer that of the history of philosophy, but that of the history of philosophies. The search will not be for underlying unities and occult harmonies, but for the "strife of systems," for nuances of meaning which a given symbol may have, for the growth of an obscure thought into something of major importance. As an example of the last, consider the distinction made by Empedocles between the elements and the two powers of love and strife. Is this not the earliest recognition of what later became inert matter and immaterial force? Would there not seem to be here a dim prescience of the principle which was made explicit only at a later date that nothing changes "of its own accord," that stability is the rule and change the problem and that all changes are to be explained by reference to an agent, or efficient cause? There is, of course, nothing so precise as this in the language of Empedocles. Yet that he felt the need of metaphors to describe composition and decomposition, that he was not content to speak of elements uniting and breaking apart, but must speak of "all uniting in one *through Love*," "each borne in different directions *by the repulsion of Strife*," [9] signifies an unwillingness on his part to accept change as inherent *in rerum natura*. To trace the history of what is simply an image in Empedocles through Anaxagoras and Aristotle until it emerges not only as a methodological principle in natural science but as a mold into which even nonscientific thought is poured is surely a necessary part of his history of philosophies. There is no saying a priori why this type of explanation should have had so great a fortune. One can simply trace its history and see how profoundly it modified our conceptions of the universe, custom being all that is required to explain its self-evidence. That it is not an inevitable way of thinking is shown by the fact that mathematics makes no use of it and that, *pace* Meyerson, as natural science tends to become mathematical, it tends to accept change, not as a puzzle, but as something quite normal.

There is another type of problem which historians of philosophy have been too ready to overlook. Words like "nature," "soul," "idea," "the reason" have been used over a period of years by a variety of philosophers, and it has sometimes been assumed that where the same word was used, the same idea was symbolized. The importance of philosophical semantics has been clearly shown by the work of Professor Lovejoy, who has examined fruitfully the shifts in meaning which such concepts as "pragmatism," "romanticism," and "nature" have undergone. Some-

[9] Burnet's translation; see fragm. 17 (Diels).

times a single author will swing from one shade of meaning to another, apparently unconscious of his ambiguity. Sometimes a critic will object to an author's argument because his use of a term differs from the critic's. Sometimes two people believe that they are in agreement when they are merely using the same verbal symbols, as when a post-Kantian idealist thinks that he is carrying on the tradition of Plato. One of the most ambiguous terms in occidental philosophy is the word *One*, with its derivatives. It is both descriptive and eulogistic. Eulogistically, it may be both ethical and aesthetic; descriptively, it may refer to substance, function, origin, goal, or any combination of them. Yet how many historians of philosophy ever stop to distinguish the different monisms? How many can tell us when philosophers first began to use "the One" in a eulogistic sense? Who has discussed the possible conditions under which some men forgot about "the One" or even, like William James in a famous passage, expressed their dislike of it? How many have ever questioned the plausibility of seeking for an occult unity before recording the opinions of the various types of monists?

The strife of systems has been elaborated into a metaphysical principle.[10] Of all metaphysical principles, it would seem to be the most persistently exemplified in history. But we need not commit ourselves to accepting it as an ontological characteristic if we are willing to admit the emotional satisfaction "the One" and similar abstractions gives the human race. There is scarcely a philosophic term, however rarefied its connotation—"Being," for instance—which has not stimulated lyric expression in some philosopher. Now most of the classic problems in philosophy are formulated in such terms. The problems of the one and the many, of materialism versus idealism, of the eternal and the temporal, and the like, are all couched in language which would appear at first sight to be descriptive, but which upon examination turns out to be normative. When they are answered, the philosopher who has answered them has not only discovered a hitherto unknown truth, but has been made happy or unhappy. To discover in what sense the world is eternal is also to discover in what sense it is noble, if we are in the Platonic tradition. Men who have not been aware of the "principle of creative duality" have usually divided the universe into two worlds, one of which has been called "reality" and the other "appearance." Also they have

---

[10] I refer, of course, to W. H. Sheldon's somewhat neglected *Strife of Systems and Productive Duality*, Cambridge, 1918.

almost invariably thought the former better than the latter. Yet it might be possible that the reverse would be true; experience shows us only too often a beautiful mask shielding a foul reality, and proverbial wisdom cautions us not to be misled by such. Yet Schopenhauer is usually held to be the first occidental to imagine such a possibility; a pessimism so deep as to maintain that the very nature of reality is evil is not recorded in histories before his time. However unusual Schopenhauer's point of view, it shows us that men need not equate the real with the good. It also shows us, however, that even Schopenhauer was incapable of avoiding a value-judgment of reality.

To write a history of philosophy without taking such influences into account is to falsify it. But in order to take them into account, one must know more psychology than is at the disposal of the usual historian. We have nothing but the most questionable evidence in support of the theories which attempt to explain them. Does a man seek unity in philosophy when his practical life is disunified? That he does might seem reasonable to certain psychologists, but we have no way of knowing what forces drove most of our philosophers to their conclusions. Do we know why Parmenides preferred unity to multiplicity? Even if we did have the evidence in his case, we should not necessarily have it in the case of his disciples. For two men may be in complete agreement for quite different reasons; the driving force in the case of the disciple being sometimes his devotion to his master. This will seem trivial, perhaps even satirical, to some readers; yet if one is to explain the persistence of ideas, one must not hesitate to include those causes which actually operate, however they may be tinged with absurdity. And the desire to defend one's master—as well as the desire to refute him—is a real cause of his philosophy's survival.

One might also advance with some justice the thesis that one's philosophy is not the satisfaction of unfulfilled desires, but the idealization of one's desires, whether fulfilled or not. Thus it has been maintained that a people's gods are an idealization of their lives, belligerent people having belligerent gods, pastoral people worshiping good shepherds; and so forth. According to such a theory James was a pluralist because of his variety of interests, his incapacity for sticking to one occupation. Was he not artist, physician, psychologist, philosopher in succession? But here, again, the story has too many gaps; we simply do not know enough about the lives of our philosophers to say how completely their systems articulated them. Yet we can say that no adequate history of philosophy is possible until we have such information.

The emotional satifaction of ideas is not, of course, the whole story. There have been moments in the history of philosophy when change has been produced by processes of inference. Such a moment occurred when Democritus built up his atomism from the macroscopic atom of Parmenides, and when Berkeley deduced the subjectivity of the primary qualities and Hume the meaninglessness of "personal identity." These men apparently saw new implications in the systems of their predecessors and brought them into the light of day. Fichte's suppression of the things-in-themselves, Spinoza's parallelism, Hegel's dialectical process, may all be examples of this. It is customary in fact to write the history of philosophy as if it consisted in nothing but such activity, each philosopher reflecting upon the thoughts of his predecessor and inferring new truths from them or detecting unsuspected weaknesses in them—more frequently the latter than the former. Thus Aristotle is described as "bridging the gap" between Plato's two worlds and Plotinus as "reconciling" Platonism and Aristotelianism. That many philosophers do read and meditate on the writings of their predecessors is, of course, undeniable. But that their meditations consist predominantly in inferences seems highly dubious, unless the process of inference be interpreted in a wide sense. Pure logic has no orienting principle within it. Of two equally possible inferences, there is no a priori certainty which will be made. One must first have some notion of what one wants to prove and then see whether the premises permit it. The selection of the *demonstrandum* is not logical to a greater degree than it is psychological. Thus Schopenhauer's feeling that he had gone back to Kant may have been unjustified, but his philosophy is just as much a logical derivative of Kant's as Fichte's is. One of the fundamental differences between these two post-Kantians is not the logical source of their systems, but something that is extralogical, namely, their evaluation of unsatisfied desire. To Fichte it seemed a good, to Schopenhauer an evil. To the former an endless search was inherently better than one which terminated in acquisition. Both agreed that acquisition was impossible. To take another example; how explain except psychologically Berkeley's failure to push his reasoning to the point attained by Hume? Was it due to a lack of reasoning ability on Berkeley's part? Was he stupider than Hume? It must be admitted that few philosophers have been as intelligent, as shrewd as Hume, but nevertheless Berkeley was scarcely credulous. Does he not clearly set forth the goal of his reasoning in his *Three Dialogues?* When he has reached the goal, he sees no point in going further.

There can be discovered in every philosopher a kind of proto-philosophy, consisting of those assertions, sometimes consistent, sometimes not, which he takes for granted. The writer of this paper has begun a collection of such assertions in Aristotle. They include such statements as: "It is better to act than to be acted upon"; "Nature does nothing in vain"; "The world must not be governed badly." Many of them appear repeatedly as the premises of arguments. It is safe to say that they were self-evident to Aristotle, and they thus reveal in a startling fashion the guiding principles of his reasoning. But self-evident assertions are not inherently self-evident: many of them have been successfully questioned, and in geometry their contraries have been fully asserted. Is there not a possibility that a historian could discover why certain formulas at times seemed to evoke no challenge, no doubt of their truth, whereas at other times they appear not only untrue but also absurd? To Aristotle motion in the sublunary world was "unnatural"; if everything occurred "in accordance with nature," no motion would be possible. For motion is always the process of actualization, and in the "real" world all is actual. Local motion, being the search for natural position, can characterize only those things which have been dislodged from their natural position, and the force which has dislodged them is "unnatural" and connotes "violence." That reality was in a state of permanent stability could have aroused no doubt in Aristotle's mind, if for no other reason than that his fellow philosophers had been saying so for at least three hundred years. That he saw motion going on all about him was no more evidence of its reality than the sight of arrows flying was evidence to Zeno that they moved. So today we lean on tabletops without falling through and listen to physicists who tell us that tabletops are largely empty space. Evidence for the nature of reality was not to be acquired from sensory perception. Consequently, for Aristotle things, if left to themselves, would return to their natural position and there come to rest. In the superlunary world a kind of motion did occur—circular motion, the eternal and noble pattern of all motion, almost a Platonic ideal, which went nowhere. As a result of all this, what later became the first law of motion would have been a complex anomaly to Aristotle. Things unimpeded, to begin with, would not move at all; moved in a straight line, they would come to rest with the expiration of the force and the line must be finite in extent. Here, then, is a perfect example of a primary idea of modern physics that would have been a problem, in fact an impossibility, for ancient physics. Yet the Law of Inertia seems to us today as clear and indubitable as the dynamics of natural position seemed to Aristotle.

The question why the self-evident becomes the problematic is surely one which the historian of philosophy cannot avoid. Yet very few have attempted to answer it or even exhibited much awareness of it. Meyerson is an outstanding exception; his weakness was to maintain that the one self-evident truth which he was willing to admit having been accepted by all thinkers was an a priori pattern of thinking. Consequently there was one proto-philosophy for all men, and hence no history of it. But to avoid dispute over this, we can examine fundamental opinions which we know to have been accepted after having been for some time considered false. One has only to think of the methodological principle already mentioned, that sense-perception gives no evidence of reality. There is no doubt that "the Greeks" were at times empirically minded, but the empirically minded Greeks, outside the field of medicine, have not survived. The Greeks who occupy most space in our histories of philosophy had no hesitation in denying the evidence of the senses. Consequently, qualities, change, and many relations had to be denied "real" existence. The discrepancy between the intelligible and sensible worlds was always attributed to the frailties of sensation, not to weakness of intellect. That the changing world of qualities presented problems which the reason could not handle might have been used as antirationalistic propaganda, as indeed it was by certain skeptics. But the dominant thinkers in Greece preferred not to criticize the reason; they retained the reason unscathed and criticized perception.

The emergence of perception into respectability is certainly one of the most interesting histories to trace. Only an extremist would maintain that its findings are not subject to intellectual refinement. But the kind of refinement which an empiricist of today would practice is quite different from that practiced by Aristotle. For the modern empiricist would have a proto-philosophy, and one of its postulates would be the reality of change and quality. I do not say that all modern philosophers are empiricists or that the kind of empiricism found in such a science as physics is identical with that found in economics. I maintain merely that it would not seem bizarre today to find a philosopher absorbing such experience as change and quality into his system with no more profound reason than that they are experiences.

The works of writers such as Meyerson in France, and in this country Burtt and Randall, give us evidence of proto-philosophies which are taken for granted because they seem like common sense, self-evident truths, or necessary assumptions. They are, perhaps, mental habits more than anything else, which individuals absorb from their reading and conversation. It is only when one has lost a habit that one realizes its true character; until that time one's second nature seems as deep as one's first. Ought it not to be possible to study the processes by which such habits are acquired and lost? How did it happen, for instance, that "the Infinite" came to take on a eulogistic connotation? How did it happen that variety rather than unity became a goal? How did the genetic or historical attitude of mind become established? When questions of this type are studied, one has a history which goes beyond the verbal form of problems into the state of mind which orients their solution.

But beside the self-evident principles which direct our thinking, and hence must figure in any complete history of philosophy, there is the history of the problems of philosophy. Writers who derive from Hegel suggest that there was no epistemology in pre-Socratic philosophy, pre-Socratic philosophy being primarily "cosmological." Accepting this as true, the question might be raised why epistemology became a problem later than cosmology did. Again, the ancients concerned themselves very little with aesthetics. What is there besides the *Hippias Major*—in itself trivial enough, even as satire—on the subject of beauty in pre-Plotinian thought? The answer given by Hegelians to the question why new problems arise is of course no more of an answer than "the Will of God"; but at least it suggests the relative novelty of certain problems. The answer given by that form of neo-Hegelianism known as dialectical materialism is more *terre à terre;* but it is so overburdened with metaphysical baggage that it is not worth much more than its source.[11] What is needed is a theory of the obsolescence of abstract ideas. Any theory which maintains that ideas die when they are proved false overlooks at least two things: (1) the inertia which keeps old ideas going long after they have

---

[11] Its theory of rationalization appears to be too narrow even to Marxians. Even to Engels, for that matter, if we may believe his famous letter to Bloch. But if that letter is taken seriously, what becomes of the economic basis of abstract ideas? A theory is not of much account if it is to be used only against one's opponents.

been proved false; (2) the stimulation to disproof. Miss Stimson's study of the reception of Copernicanism illustrates the former; it could be supported by a dozen other investigations, if one wished to make them, into the fortunes of the theory of sensible species, phlogisticism, biological evolutionism, relativistic physics. The latter problem could be studied only by a psychologist. At present it is safe to say that we know next to nothing of why ideas become (or are) unsatisfactory to people. It is not enough to say that the major cause is their disharmony with acquired knowledge, for human beings have shown an uncanny ingenuity in retaining ideas which contradict other ideas of which they are fond. Readers of the history of philosophy know that this has even gone to the extent of believing in two kinds of truth, one for one set of ideas, one for another. There is, of course, a deeply rooted conservatism, which makes every new idea suspect, so that the battle of ideas is frequently fought on the level of prejudice. But no one can explain Galileo's interest in testing Aristotle's dynamics as the simple desire for something new. In fact we shall never know exactly why he had such an interest. But we can assume that, like other innovators, he was not afraid of novelty, which meant that he was not so convinced of the truth of generally accepted ideas as automatically to believe false anything that contradicted them. That attitude was characteristic of many of his contemporaries, and if such a term as "the Renaissance" can still be used, its justification lies, perhaps, in this similarity of attitude. For when one thinks that in a single century the following novelties were introduced; the discovery of many Greek and Latin classics, the introduction of a new architecture, the opera, printing, the new astronomy, the discovery of the Western hemisphere, and the Reformation, one can see that an attitude friendly to innovation could find some encouragement. One needs no *Zeitgeist* in a transcendental sense to explain this. There need be no *Geist* expressing itself in these various adventurous ways. Each novelty came about as the result of a long series of preparatory essays. The history of each can be traced with more or less certitude and has been so traced. If there was any *Geist* common to the development of the opera and that of exploration, it was a *Geist* which found equal satisfaction in errors of literary history and of geography. It tried both to revive what it erroneously believed to be the dramas of Aeschylus and also to find an economical route to the Indies. There is no need to invoke anything more recondite than the human appetite for news and the human desire to follow the styler in order to explain much of what occurred in cultural history of that time.

But, as everyone knows, the friendliness to novelty was not unopposed. It took some time for the new astronomy to be published and circulated. Printing was still considered vulgar by certain lords well into the sixteenth century. The Reformation succeeded largely because of political backing; in countries like France, where such backing was not available, it failed—and that in spite of economic disadvantage. Even today, the phrase "the spirit of the Renaissance" is used with contempt by certain writers who profess a predilection for the thirteenth century. If there was a *Geist* issuing from the brushes of Leonardo, the pen of Ficino, and the telescope of Galileo, there was also an opposing *Geist*, and neither one in isolation suffices to explain what actually happened. What goes by the name of *Geist* is concretely certain turns of speech and certain problems that became popular at a certain time. But it must never be forgotten that they were popular only in a limited *milieu*.

The interests of human beings, whether philosophical or not, are stratified. A cross section of a modern community would resemble a cross section of the earth, running from the cultural pre-Cambrian to very recent formations. It would be too painful to illustrate this metaphor, for even dates are considered to be pejorative. But we can see the same stratification of ideas in a single philosopher. In Bergson, whom I choose because of his reputation for innovation, one can see traces of the pre-Socratics in his insistence that there is resemblance between the instrument and the object of knowledge; of Plato, in his dislike of matter; of Aristotle, in his theory of the reason as a dissecting and classifying device; of Plotinus (via Schelling via Ravaisson), in his theory of degenerative creation; of Kant, in his "pragmatism"; of Schelling, in his *élan vital*, oscillating between stability and motion, determination and spontaneity; of Maive de Birau via Ravaisson, in his theory of habit; of Boutroux, in his acceptance of indeterminism. It is doubtful whether Bergson would have denied this. Nor need any of his admirers feel that to admit it would lessen his greatness. For when one reads Bergson—not as a classic, but as a contemporary—one is struck by his power of saying things which may have been old-fashioned in isolation, but whose synthesis seemed new and invigorating. Moreover, in spite of his "anti-intellectualism," in practice he has been as intellectualistic as Hegel, putting everything in its place, leaving nothing unclassified. One could draw up two columns—one, of things showing maximum mobility; one, of things showing maximum stability. Everything in the world would be in them. There is thus in Bergson a recapitulation of the history of philosophy so obvious that few readers conscious of their subject's past can read him with the serious interest his influence shows he deserves.

If this is true of both philosophers and periods, the history of philosophy would, perhaps, be more fruitfully studied if the subject were first analyzed into problems, ideas, basic metaphors, presuppositions, and if their several histories were studied. In that case certain traditions are untangled which change their denotations as well as their connotations during the course of years. One can trace their several histories with a certain degree of accuracy, always allowing for the inevitable errors of anachronistic interpretation. Though one has no such grandiose result as a general history of an all-pervasive interest, yet one has a useful and illuminating understanding of the human mind in so far as it is seen in the satisfaction of one of its major interests. When these have been studied, we can then bind them together and call them a history of philosophy.

Professor Lovejoy's *Great Chain of Being* is the history of a metaphysical problem which arose overtly in a metaphor of Plato's. The development of that metaphor into a philosophical problem, the attempted solution of the subordinate problems involved in the main problem, the emotional associations of the terms employed to state them, and the supposed implications of the various solutions carried the historian, before he terminated his study, into a field apparently remote from metaphysics —that is, biology. It would not appear at first sight as if the transformation of species had anything to hope for or fear from the metaphor that God's lack of jealousy made the realization of all potencies inevitable. Yet "the principle of plenitude" was one of the earliest justifications for evolutionism. For in order for the human mind to become receptive to evolutionism, its emotional set had to be altered. When, for instance, it was seen that evolution would explain both the present diversity of creatures and Noah's obligation to carry on the Ark breeding stock of all the creatures that roamed the earth, men who wished to retain the Bible were more willing to accept the new doctrine. When it was believed that evolution contradicted what Huxley called "the Miltonic Hypothesis," men who wished to retain the Bible were less willing to accept it. The resistance to a new doctrine, though partly caused by its novelty, is also partly caused by its relation to other doctrines which are cherished by the people to whom it is addressed. Clearly this appears at present in the scorn which dialectical materialists express toward any bit of historiography which gives psychical causes as *verae causae*. Yet when they are accused of being too narrowly materialistic, they immediately produce Engels's letter to Bloch, which has been already referred to. That type of dogmatism is common to us all. We must believe something in order to live, even if our beliefs are merely verbalizations of our habits. Inevitably we test new ideas by their congruence with those we already possess, when we are aware of their congruence. That we are not always aware of it needs no proof. But certainly a large part of the history of philosophical ideas must be occupied with clarifying their supposed congruence or incongruence with ideas already accepted. Those of us who have read the philosophies of the past know how right Cicero was when he said that nothing was so absurd that no one would take it seriously and nothing so profound that no one would think it absurd. But the test of absurdity is precisely the philosophical question which the historian of philosophy must first analyze.

When he begins his analysis, he immediately encounters the question raised in the beginning of this paper: What is the role of abstract ideas in human life? And it is that question which no one has as yet answered satisfactorily.

What we do know about the history of philosophy can be summed up in the following words, according to the opinion of the writer of this paper.

1. There is no single subject matter which may be called "philosophy" and of which the history may be written. Philosophers have from Thales on been interested in a variety of subject matters, but some of them have come to have no relation to what is now called philosophy. Their methods of inquiry have varied as much as their interests. One can, of course, and one should note the rise and fall of these methods and interests.

2. Very few, if any, philosophers have ever had a system of philosophy in the sense that geometry is a system. Many have had a small group of leading ideas which they think they develop deductively, but upon examination every system turns out to be, from the point of view of subject matter, a group of interests determined by historical accident, and from the point of view of method, a mixture of deduction and non-

deduction. Theoretically there is no obstacle to the discovery of the motivating causes of their meditations; practically there are many obstacles—ignorance of biographical data which are essential, ignorance of the psychology of thinking, ignorance of the emotional associations of certain symbols used in their works. Until this ignorance has been eliminated—and in the case of certain philosophers (the pre-Socratics, for instance) it cannot be eliminated—no history even of philosophical problems can be complete.

3. Philosophical ideas, like nonphilosophical, cannot be separated from the total intellectual life of a period. To make such a separation is to run the risk of serious falsification of the meaning of the problems involved and of the methods used to solve them. The reasons why an idea arises, as well as the reasons why it ceases to interest people, frequently do lie in nonphilosophical domains.

The result appears to be that histories of various philosophical ideas, taken singly, would be more fruitful than a history which would attempt to synthesize all of them into a general history of philosophy. The general histories so far written appear to be based upon the selection of certain problems and ideas as important and upon too narrow an interpretation of the causes of philosophical change. The selection of ideas must be based upon certain a priori considerations—such as the "superiority" of monisms to pluralisms, of originality to traditionalism, of the anticipation of one's own ideas or those current in one's own time, of what seems true, or plausible, to the historian. Thus, much of the text in the histories of philosophy which we already possess is occupied in pointing out the unintelligence of our predecessors—of arguing instead of recording. We have no need for simple expositions of other men's ideas, except in certain cases in which their authors are peculiarly obscure, but we need a critical untangling of the twisted threads of discourse, the discovery of ambiguities, the clarification of both denotations and connotations which have not been understood.

8

THE MATERIALS OF
HISTORICAL KNOWLEDGE

Edward W. Strong

All time processes are histories, but man only is the writer of them, so that historical comprehension becomes the significant trait of human history.—F. J. E. WOODBRIDGE.[1]

THE historian of man is for the most part concerned, and rightly so, with documents and artifacts as the materials from which to reconstruct the historical past. If he elects to study and to write the political, the religious, the scientific, or any other specific history of a particular time and place, the materials of his study will be selected for their relevance to the task in hand. This does not exempt him from considering material conditions related to what men have done or have been able to do. Conditions of geography, food supply, raw materials, disease, and human endurance are physical factors in places and times of human history. One or more of them may be a limit or a challenge to what men did and thought, which must be taken into account by a historian if he is to explain what happened. References of this kind made by a historian in the course of his work or, as with Huntington and Toynbee, in the search for correlations between what men have done and the physical circumstances of their performance, treat material conditions as subject matter of historical description and hypothesis.

A naturalistic examination of historical study might take as topic the relevance of scientific knowledge of material conditions to historians' interpretations of human histories. In this essay an initial notice of this topic leads into an inquiry which asks how, as historians, we have knowledge of the past and how, with respect to our temporal careers, historical knowledge contributes to our comprehension of our own history. The two questions are envisaged primarily as having to do with procedures and results of historical work. The argument throughout rests upon considerations of what the historian has to work with (the materials) and his orientation of inquiry as bearing upon what might be

[1] *The Purpose of History*, p. 57.

done methodologically to further the contribution of historical knowledge to historical understanding.

A study of human affairs involves ideas about men as agents having needs, abilities, and purposes. These ideas are in part derived from a reading of history and are shaped in a student's mind by what he finds recorded; but our ideas about human nature past and present are shaped also by contemporary scientific knowledge. What we accept as a true description of man's learning process and his place in nature has consequences for what is acceptable or unacceptable in historians' interpretations. In so far as the historian writing today has shaped his ideas of human nature in conformity with scientific knowledge, there are claims and suppositions made by earlier historians in their interpretations of human history that must be modified or rejected. When mythological beliefs about man and nature give way to verified propositions about the processes and structures of things, this is not only a further event in intellectual history but also knowledge about the conditions of that history.

The field of historical studies is a distinct domain of knowledge, but not a domain isolated from knowledge-results of contemporary science. The results affect judgments to be made about past happenings in human history. Yet one may admit this connection and still contend that there is little or nothing in common between historical method and method in the sciences. In disputing this extreme contention, an argument for the relevance of scientific knowledge to the reconstruction and interpretation of the past must recognize differences of method and result in historical work in contrast to the work of physical scientists. The historian cannot experiment. He is not able to verify his propositions by direct confrontation of the happenings asserted by them. He has not been able, in reconstructing continuities, to formulate causal laws for the prediction of future occurrences. These are commonplace differences between historical study and natural science.

Since the last half of the nineteenth century the idea of a historical science, or science of history, has had considerable currency with historians. The questions whether and in what sense history is a science (whether referring to the attitude of the historian, his techniques of investigation, or his written history) have been fraught with controversy and disputed, with conflicting answers, among historians, social scientists, and philosophers. Attempts to answer the general question "What is history?" have resulted in widely different definitions given to history and different arguments and conclusions. At one extreme it has been asserted that history is "nothing but the facts" or the telling of what happened just as it happened. At the other, it has been held that a synthesis of facts depends upon a system of philosophical reasons. Between these extremes, the dispute over whether history is a science or an art is a kind of middle battleground. The main engagement has centered upon problems of historical knowledge: partiality versus impartiality of the historian; subjectivity versus objectivity of subject matter; historical truth in contrast to scientific truth; the particular and unique nature of historical events in contrast to the abstract and common nature of scientific objects. It is not the intention of this paper to ajudicate old quarrels. It is rather to contribute an analysis of historical knowledge leading to constructive suggestions based on ways of working its materials.

Statements in written history are made to convey knowledge of past happenings. We will maintain that in history, as in science, no statement is a knowledge-statement unless the procedure by which it is confirmed or confirmable can be specified. When a procedure of confirmation is not specifiable for a statement purporting to describe or to explain what happened, such a statement will be called a speculative supposition. For example, if no procedure of confirmation is specifiable for statements which Hegel makes about the world-historical spirit, these statements are speculative suppositions, not knowledge-statements. Knowledge-statements in history are statements of facts and of relations of facts. The facts are not the once-actual happenings in the past. These happenings are the unobservable referents of statements made about them. Nor are the facts the materials which the historian studies. Fact-statements are established by a critical study of documents and artifacts which stand (when so studied) in the relation of evidence supporting these statements. Historical evidence is indirect in being a sign and account of a referent which can never be confronted directly as an empirical verification of the fact-statement. Fact-statements are thus more or less likely inferences from available evidential materials. Many such statements are so well established that they may be regarded as practically certain.

Connections between fact-statements are made in judgments about the relations of events. The usual kind of relation-statement made in narrative history is that of the continuity of events. The materials studied not only support inferences about particular happenings but may also support judgments about their sequences. These happenings are the referents of the historian's fact-statements; but referents that have ceased to be and will never be again a matter of direct observation are not tests of statements. The fact, and evidence of the fact, established by the historian working with documents is asserted in his statement of the happening. His written history consists of reconstructed events (the *historical* or *historian's* past). The referent of fact-statements and relation-statements asserting events is the once-actual happening (the *perished* past). Obviously, the historian is unable to verify his statement, presented as the reconstructed event, by correspondence with the original happening. Within the limits of our discussion thus far, it would appear that, apart from the materials which afford the historian his evidence for the reconstruction of the past, history is not an empirical inquiry. Although the historian is able to specify what he believes any observer would have seen if he had been present at the time and place of a particular happening, the inference about the happening is not verifiable by it.

The foregoing conclusion seems inescapable in view of the nature of the time process of actions that have ceased to be, leaving only remains, products, and records of their occurrence. What we have not so far brought out, but now intend to argue, is that the reconstruction of the perished past in its representation, the historian's past, relies on a rule of empirical equivalence, the analogue in history of the rule of empirical reference in science. In physical science, propositions about existence are grounded in specifications of data of observation. The procedure of verification specified for a proposition establishes the empirical meaning of the proposition. The truth or falsity of propositions that are empirically meaningful is established when the referent of the proposition is directly observed (or is asserted as probable on the basis of inference) as a test of the assertion made about it. The empirical condition for the verification of a proposition is stated by the rule of empirical reference, namely, that if a proposition is to be regarded as a candidate for verification, its referent must be capable of direct observation or of inference from observed occurrences.

We have pointed out why the rule of empirical reference cannot be employed in statements about the perished past. Nevertheless, the reconstruction of continuities in narrative history involves a rule of empirical equivalence. The rule is formulated to handle the following kind of problem. The reconstruction of events (the historian's past) is also the reconstruction of the continuities of events. In actual occurrence, a sequence of happenings is a time process in which earlier and later happenings take place. Each sequence or succession of process involves the persistence of a continuant; for example, a man's body performing a sequence of actions may be said to be such a continuant. In historical representation, processes no less than single happenings and situations have to be reconstructed. The linkage of successive events presented by the historian is his account of their continuity. Beginnings or origins and endings or consequences have their meaning in such linkages. The linkage itself is not an origin or cause of the events which are arrayed in sequence.

If continuity, in this respect, is the historian's sequential tying together of events, how are we to decide between knowledge-statements and speculative suppositions about continuities? The spirit of an age or of a people, race soul, the dialectic of reason or of material movement, the momentum of events, the sway of tradition, the career of a nation —if any of these is presented as a continuity, is there any rule for demarcating rationalization and metaphysical suppositions from hypotheses which have an initial empirical probability in their favor? The answer to this kind of question is formulated in the rule of empirical equivalence. The referent of a statement of continuity is some continuant time process of successive happenings. The rule of empirical equivalence requires that a statement of continuity must have a continuant specifiable in empirical description if it is to qualify as a knowledge-statement (that is, as an empirically probable hypothesis). The application of the rule arises in the course of reconstructing events. The historian cannot confront a continuant of the perished past, the time process which has come to an ending; yet this continuant is the referent of the continuity of events related in his history. He can defend, however, the likelihood of his relation-statement of continuity by pointing out, as a matter of direct observation, an empirical equivalent in processes now going on. The empirical description of these now-actual processes is the equivalent of the perished continuant. It is appealed to when problems arise with respect to the empirical probability of the referent of statements of continuity asserted by the historian in his reconstruction of the historical past. The use of the rule involves no assumption that history repeats itself.

I · THE MATERIALS OF HISTORICAL RECONSTRUCTION

The particular events reconstructed by the historian have their evidence in source materials. The facts that support the reconstruction are arrived at from the critical study of these materials. Now a chronological array of events could be made from a random selection to be arranged in sequence according to time of occurrence. The result would be a succession of particular events without regard for any relation between them except the time relation of being before, contemporaneous, and after. Chronology is not itself a continuity of events. Events are sequentially reconstructed with regard to individuals and groups and with respect to situations and means of communication. A series of events, for example, is presented as the actions and affairs engaged in by Thomas Jefferson during his presidency. The continuant agent in these actions and affairs is the particular man. Further continuants are specified with reference to Congress, the Supreme Court, state governments, and other individuals, groups, and institutions. Agencies as well as agents, associations of men as well as individuals, and configurations of practice as well as individuals in action are continuant time processes. Beginnings, ongoings, and endings are located with reference to a continuant.

When the continuant referred to has come to an end in the past, the historian relies on the rule of empirical equivalence in a general application, an application so familiar and unquestioned that a statement of it seems almost needless. If a historian is examining a coin, utensil, tool, garment, building, or other physical article similar in kind to these, he takes the existence of the article to be a sign of human production. It is a fact of direct observation that the shaping of things into artifacts is a work of man, and not of natural processes apart from man. The record in documents of actions and production engaged in by men long since dead is not questioned so long as these conform to abilities that men could be expected to have from what is now known of the limits of human capacities and powers. It is "common sense" to assume the continuant Thomas Jefferson as a biological, psychological, and social unity of process identified by naming him. Most of the continuities of narrative history are these commonplace identifications. Yet even on this commonplace level there are problems which require critical application of the rule of empirical equivalence. Not only are reports about extraordinary experiences of men subject to scrutiny with respect to the credulity and credibility of the reporters. They are also subject to appraisals based on known conditions of human behavior. For example, what is described as the seizure and transport of a prophet is for later medical knowledge the case-history of an epileptic.

The special application of the rule of empirical equivalence is in the reconstruction of continuities which the historian presents as movements, trends, directions, and courses of history. Speculative suppositions have passed as knowledge-statements when neither the historian nor his reader have inquired what constituted an empirical equivalent of a past continuant asserted by the historian as a continuity of events. It is not argued here that speculative suppositions have no place in historical interpretation, only that it is a condition *sine qua non* of clear ideas in history to be able to distinguish between them and knowledge-statements. Unless the historian can specify the empirical equivalent of a past continuant (the referent of his statement of continuity), the continuity by which he arrays events is a rationalization, not a probable reason. The idea of the universal progress of mankind (or of the "reason of mankind") is a rationalization in so far as no empirical equivalent can be established for this continuant asserted for the entire course of history. Continuities such as the rise of nationalism, the trend of imperialism, or the persistent influence of the American frontier are generalizations of specific continuities. It is only when these specific processes have empirical equivalents that the generalized continuities have a status of empirically probable hypotheses in the historian's representation. This does not mean that a continuant once persistent must still persist as a condition enabling a historian to make a knowledge-statement of continuity. What it does mean is that a historian who had no way of directly knowing a process equivalent to a past continuant would have no empirical limitation for assertions of continuity. The empirical equivalent is not a repetition of what happened in the past, but an observed condition of present happenings which is predicated hypothetically of past performance and production.

The force of the rule of empirical equivalence becomes evident when one turns to the kind of history written by Spengler in *The Decline of the West.* The organization of events as manifestations of the culture spirit of an "organic" society is a speculative supposition of a master continuity for each delineated culture. There is no equivalent (life-process of a total society) in processes under observation establishing an empirical probability for the referent asserted in Spengler's reconstruction of continuities. The sequential relation of events as manifestation of an inherent spirit is a metaphysical assumption, not an hypothesis having an initial likelihood. The rule applies not only to historical interpretations but also to the probation of documentary testimony of the kind epitomized by eyewitness reports of the devil. The empirical equivalent for the understanding of these reported experiences leads us to probability judgments of hysterical and pathological conditions known empirically to be connected with experiences of the kind reported.

Where a continuant beginning in the past has not come to an end before a present time of inquiry and reconstruction, present characteristics afford unique signs and clews to what preceded. This class of continuant is material for historical reconstruction as present (presented) evidence for past occurrences. To designate existent relations and practices whose characteristics are consequent upon and continuous with antecedent formation and performance we will use the term "continuant past." The continuant past is in the present of the person who notes the relation of what is being done as a sign of what has been done. Endings of continuants remove, and beginnings of continuants add, materials available to historians writing at different "presents."

A second class of materials is made up of remains and survivals—the documents and artifacts, both those which have chanced to survive and those which have been deliberately conserved. All such remains and survivals will be designated as the materials of the "conserved past." The pyramids in Egypt and the works of Plato are instances of the conserved past. In both instances there has been a persistence of physical things: in the former the stones shaped into a structure, and in the latter the manuscripts and copies of the original production. The worship connected with the pyramids and the civilization which existed when Plato wrote came to an end. They are not strands of our continuant past. The only way in which the materials of the conserved past are continuous with the lives of men now living is through their utilization and appreciation of them. Our activities of conservation, utilization, and appreciation are themselves later and further continuants, subject to termination in the future.

Artifacts of the conserved past were, at an earlier time, happenings interconnected with other happenings in processes of being made and used. From physical remains and from documentary records the historian reconstructs events in their interconnections. The more a historian works toward a reconstruction transcending limited and specific continuities, the more the rule of empirical equivalence becomes essential if he is concerned to make knowledge-statements. Lacking the materials of the conserved and continuant pasts-in-the-present, only general conditions of the perished past could be formulated. The empirical equivalent of a past process does not supply the historian with the material from which to establish facts for the representation of particular events. It cannot establish the existence of a particular happening at a particular time and place. But when the historian asserts some generalized relation-statement as a judgment of continuity, the rule of empirical equivalence is applied as a test of the likelihood or probability of the referent.

Past productions of men, materials presented in the form of records and artifacts, enable the historian to reconstruct what happened. The material comes dated, or is datable by internal signs and by connections with dated products. It is worth noting that the traditional division between prehistory and history coincides with the division between bodies of undated and those of dated materials. As men begin to date their products and as account is kept of sequence of happenings, time assignments are preserved in the objects and stories of the past. These assignments convey the "when" essential to narrational sequence. The beginning of a "historical" period coincides with the human concern to preserve a story of happenings and to bring it to the knowledge of men to come. The working distinction between prehistory and history is here determined by the amount and kind of material available to later historians for the writing of history. A history of history may, although it need not, begin its account with the earliest genealogies and chronicles and may sift folk-story, epic, and mythology for beginnings of the story of things past.

To see how equivalence applies to reconstructing chronological order for undated materials, let us first note the procedure employed in geological dating. A series of layers is no obvious time scheme. Observed physical processes, however, support a hypothesis of the successive formation of layers. The further measuring of rate yields a calculation of the time required for the formation of a stratum. Strata lying in the order of formation may now be read as a geological calendar, and this calendar may in turn be used to date the ages of fossils and to reconstruct sequence of development.

The dating procedure of an archaeologist engaged in excavating the layered remains of a long-established site of human habitation is partially like that of a geologist. In the absence of date marks on artifacts, sequence of production is inferred from levels of deposition. The span of time represented by a level is reconstructed by study of the artifacts and hypotheses about progress of work based on known time spans of production which are assumed to be comparable. Since retrogression in productive ability in arts and techniques cannot be ruled out in advance, sequence cannot be supposed simply by taking the better executed production as necessarily of later date than the one that is more crudely done. Although the archaeologist, unlike the geologist, cannot assume fixed rates of process, he will find in human materials marks convertible into time reckonings.

In historical studies of anthropological materials, it has been assumed that fundamental inventions occur but once and in one locality, and thenceforth spread to other groups. The assumption has an initial probability if it can be proved that during the period of recorded history fundamental inventions have had a single origin and that all subsequent appearances are derivative. To the extent that this has not been established as a historical equivalent, the assumption of a single production remains a speculative supposition. The equivalents drawn from historical knowledge are further supplemented by taking into account the physical conditions of dissemination. The rule of empirical equivalence requires that, under the conditions of topography and with the means of travel available, the means of communication would have sufficed to carry a practice or device to outlying areas. The rule is here a check on working directly from an assumption of a single origin and subsequent diffusion to rationalizing arguments which arrange sequences in support of the theory. In dealing with bridging hypotheses tying undated materials in relations of temporal sequence, probability is proportional to equivalents supplied by historical and physical knowledge. The test of these hypotheses is their workability in giving a consistent and adequate organization of data.

We have a second class of hypotheses when we propose to take a contemporary correlation between the constitution and the behavior of a social group as an equivalent for the reconstruction of past relations and processes. Here hypotheses are verified positively or negatively by the weight of evidence afforded by the materials of conserved and continuant pasts. An hypothesis of this kind is used to see if it holds for the past as it does for the present situation taken as a possible empirical equivalent. The use of holding hypotheses will be taken up in the discussion of the method of configurational organization.

II · THE ORIENTATION OF THE HISTORIAN

We have previously spoken of facts as being established by critical study of materials. This way of speaking calls attention to the difference between the documents and artifacts examined by the historian and the results of his critical work. The historian studies his materials to arrive at facts or, more precisely, at statements of facts about past happenings. The reliability of reports with respect to their authorship and of placing and dating information is a kind of skilled detective work. The weighting to be given facts as evidence is partly dependent upon the results of this work. Beyond this, evidence is a question of relevance. Questions of relevance arise in the making of judgments, that is, as the historian infers fact-statements from materials and judges the connections of these statements to each other in making relation-statements. The relevance of facts to a relation of them depends upon judgments about the support given to a relation-statement by the facts. Fact-statements derived by critical inferences from the materials are not arbitrary, since the sources will support some statements and not others. Relation-statements, when well supported by a set of fact-statements, have the status of complex facts or, in respect to the historian's representation, the status of a complex event made up of subevents. The historian, like the scientist, usually has some query which constitutes his hypothesis or preliminary judgment leading to inquiry. The relevance of the hypothesis is eventually decided by the amount and kind of confirmation supplied by fact-statements; but in the selection of materials and direction of inquiry, relevance was initially instituted by the hypothesis.

An initial context of meaning is subsequently modified and revised in the course of inquiry.

A single fact-statement is insignificant as a statement of an event. Single fact-statements acquire historical significance when the connection of events is asserted in relation-statements. Relevance has to do with initial and subsequent judgments of connections between relation-statements and fact-statements. From all the materials with which a historian might work, certain materials are turned to and critically studied for fact-statements relevant to the specific inquiry which the historian is concerned to make and to the specific history he is concerned to write. The historian does not infer isolated fact-statements from the records he works with, but accepts their connected accounts of what happened subject to critical assessments of reliability.

Although we have spoken of particular fact-statements as though each might be made to assert a particular event, the assertion of a particular event may be a representation dependent upon a set of fact-statements marshaled to support the assertion. Each of the fact-statements may be in turn a critical summation of several sources in the materials. What is to be done further with fact-statements is partially decided in view of clews and suggestions forthcoming in the work already performed. Context of relevance, or meaning, for further study and redirection of inquiry occur to the historian in the course of work. Relevance is inseparable from procedures of inferring and judging in working from source materials to relation-statements, and from relation-statements to source materials. The procedures are not "subjective" constructions of the historical past, nor are they dependent upon "the ability to see causal dependencies" in the perished past, an ability possessed by no man. Mandelbaum's [2] assertion that there are "determinate interconnections which are rooted in the events themselves" is legitimate for historians' judgments about past happenings by the rule of empirical

[2] *The Problem of Historical Knowledge,* New York, 1938, p. 271. Mandelbaum maintains "that the relevance of one fact to another depends upon a causal connection between the events asserted by the facts" (p. 214). In his theory of historical knowledge, we are asked to choose between one or the other of two mutually exclusive alternatives. Relevance is either a "subjective" construction of the historian's mind, or a correspondence between the connection of facts and a causal relation of past happenings. We have argued that judgments of causality rest upon empirical equivalence. The events of the historical past are reconstructed by the historian and are represented by him as the relations of happenings in the perished past. The linkage of continuity between reconstructed events cannot be tested by correspondence to a continuant time process that has ceased to exist.

equivalence, but not by a theory of correspondence between statements and their referents in the perished past.

The past of completed action, we have so far maintained, is the referent of the historical past reconstructed by the historian from the materials of the conserved and continuant pasts-in-the-present. The continuant past directly engages the historian not only as present configuration and practice affording sign-clews of what preceded but also as the existential condition of his own interests in and comprehension of the past. The determinate condition and setting of a historian with respect to his judgment and comprehension of the past will be designated by the term "perspective." Both conserved and continuant pasts are interpreted (1) by the perspective of the historian and (2) by the perspective of temporal reference.

The perspective of the historian, his orientation to the materials with which he works, is within a cultural context. This is brought out admirably by Charles A. Beard in *The Discussion of Human Affairs*. Every work of historical inquiry and history writing involves the person, the time, the place, the purpose, the preliminary interests and ideas, and the underlying assumptions of the historian. The historian does not stand disengaged from his own social conditioning and embodied acquirements. Even the canons of impartial scholarship have their origins and developments (see Shotwell's *An Introduction to the History of History*). Although the historian cannot stand outside perspectival context, he can be critical of the situation in which he begins and carries on his work. He may, like Gibbon, select a field of materials for historical study that is remote in time from the interests and attachments of his own day, thereby hoping to avoid partiality in his interpretations. Yet the fact that the history was thought worth the effort, the principles of selection invoked, and the judgments made upon what is of primary and what of secondary importance in the representation of the past will testify to time, place, and purpose of the historian and will implicate criteria of selection and emphasis in the treatment of economic, political, religious, and other practices and institutions.

The perspective of temporal reference is implicated in every judgment in which the contemporary or the present is demarcated from the past. The meaning of the term "present" is itself contextual or situational. The judgment of presentness made by a historian is based on a persistence of characteristics specified in contrast to characteristics that come before or after those designated. We continue to speak of the seventeenth century as the beginning of the period of modern philosophy so long as the characteristics of our contemporary inquiry are similar to those of the earlier time. Only when the characteristics have become so altered that men are impressed by differences rather than by similarities will our "modern" be designated by another term in relegating it to a past of that which is no longer continuant in character.

When, in the lapse of time, historians of some future day demarcate those centuries of our "modern" to be an age between the "middle" and themselves, the chronological revision will be the expression of an altered perspective. Some historians have been victimized by their devices of temporal perspective into thinking of a classical or of a medieval "spirit of the age" as though the men of those past times were historically conscious of being at the beginning or in the middle of the chronological order—an order representing the perspective of the historian who framed it to demarcate the characteristics of his time from those that came before. The modern, present, or contemporary is the time of living men. Every time is a modern time for those who live in it. The characterization of ideas, arts, and institutions as medieval is retrospective and could only occur through the incidence of characteristics reorientating men to a new comprehension of a preceding time.

Chronology is the scheme of time locations for events and processes to be related in order of coexistence and succession. The use of the term "present" as co-ordinate with a fixed interval of time, whether a minute or a century, is an arbitrary usage. The dates to be covered by a historical account depend upon the continuants referred to in the historian's reconstruction. An age is the time of a man's life, of a social group, of an institution's development throughout a number of phases, of specific military or political happenings, of a school of art, of scientific discoveries, and so forth. The perspective of temporal reference is constituted in the historian's consciousness and comprehension of a set of characteristics in contrast to others coming before and after. The historian of philosophy who speaks of Descartes's thought as modern must today admit many differences between the characteristics of philosophical thinking then and now. Eventually, if not now, a termination must be designated for *this* period of the modern, just as a termination has been designated in naming periods ancient and medieval.

Consequences subsequent to earlier happenings lead to re-examinations of prior meanings and interpretations. There is no absolute standpoint in this succession of temporal perspectives in which the work of preceding historians becomes subject matter for further judgments. The meaning of the World War of 1914–1918 is an indefinitely expanding meaning, as there are later and further consequences and a succession of changing perspectives upon this period. Even a cursory examination of histories concerned with the French Revolution reveals alterations of judgment with changes of temporal perspective.

The perspective of temporal reference is not only from the present but also upon the present when men become concerned with contemporary affairs with respect to persistence and change of institutions. The inadequacy of narrative histories to provide an understanding of how changes are correlated with relations and processes of a society follows, to a considerable extent, from the aim and method of historians in their reconstruction and interpretation of the past. Unhappily, this inadequacy has been regarded as a desideratum of a so-called scientific history which aims to describe what happened just as it happened, on the assumption that this is the full and only task of reputable historiography. Anything more than this is suspect as a philosophy of history or is regarded as the task of the social sciences leading to results achieved by a comparative method.[3] There are, indeed, good reasons for dispensing with the moralizing of didactic historians and for rejecting the shibboleth that history repeats itself. Methods of historical criticism refined in the nineteenth century are incumbent upon competent historians in their profession today. There is, nevertheless, a task devolving upon historians which is inseparable from their perspectival role of communicating histories to present and future readers. The task is defined in answer to a question: To what ends and for what purposes are these histories being written?

If we begin with the histories of Herodotus and Thucydides and follow a course of reading through Roman historians, medieval chroniclers, and the historians of the modern world, only the very general interest of preserving the story of men's deeds for present and future readers is common to all. They convey information, instruction, and entertainment and contain innumerable illustrations and exemplifications of human characteristics. When we look beyond all these common traits to the perspectives of historians and the perspectives of their temporal references, the question why history is written has widely diver-

---

[3] F. M. Fling, *The Writing of History*, New Haven, 1920, p. 17. "The historian is interested in quality, individuality, uniqueness; the sociologist in quantity, in generalization, in repetition."

gent answers varying with men's conceptions of their reason for being. Fate, fortune, or providence are not explanatory concepts entertained by a modern historian in bringing home the significance of the events he relates.

The modern conviction that history is to be written as a development of specific time processes in desirable or undesirable directions (that is, as concerned with specific judgments of progress) has two corollaries. In the first place, there is a span of time up to the present moment of study during which the men about whom the historians are writing were themselves imbued with beliefs in and about progress. These "modern" men believed in themselves as makers of their history from their living present toward the future to be shaped by their efforts and the efforts of their successors. Some of them, indeed, mistakenly believed that there was a force of universal progress which insured an unremitting and indefinite improvement. The historian who writes of this portion of the past has continuant evidence of it, in addition to conserved materials, and is himself conditioned by it. In the second place, if the historian is to write history in the belief that he is writing for men who will today and henceforth be shaping the course of events, this serves to define for him the significance of understanding the present by the study of the past. For the present to be understood is *this* present of men who are makers of history toward fulfillment or frustration of their desires.

The historian is writing for the times of men. It may be that the contribution he can make to an understanding of the present by the reconstruction and interpretation of the past has its main purpose and possible performance in providing orientation. The possibility, however, that a method of organizing facts might lead to a knowledge of the *modus operandi* of happenings is not to be dismissed from consideration if some procedure is specifiable which could have this result. If such a procedure can be suggested, historians should be the first to welcome its trial as pertinent to their purpose as history makers in the double sense of representation and instrumentation.

III · NARRATIVE AND COMPARATIVE ORGANIZATION

Organization of events by both continuities and comparisons would appear to be requisite to an understanding of the present in which we live. Teggart, in his *Theory of History*, has shown that the divorce of the comparative studies of the social sciences from the studies of continuities has unfortunate consequences for both fields of study. The divorce tends to limit historical reconstruction to unique sequences of unique events and to limit social studies to generalizations classifying phenomena rather than functioning as hypotheses in the interpretation of past happenings. A procedure which might successfully overcome this divorce would be to conjoin the reconstruction of events with an account of continuant configurations. This conjunction opens a further and possibly highly fruitful application of the rule of empirical equivalance.

In studying the present and the past with regard to sets of relations (configurations) holding for processes, we must be on guard against a reductive fallacy. The actions of men and the interactions of groups are only metaphysically to be likened to mechanical motions or to organic processes. Compulsion exercised by one group of men upon another is not a pressure calculable in the same way as that of a gas in a confining chamber. An organic analogy, for example, treating individuals as cells in the life of the social body, is no less misleading than is the mechanical analogy when used to explain social behavior. The subjects of historical-social studies are men engaged with modes, situations, and conditions of their organized behaviors; and these organized behaviors are configurations persisting and changing in time processes. Wherever we take up the study of men, we can hypothesize by the rule of empirical equivalence that they lived in associations, by formulas, and within structural limits which together made up their contemporary system of social life.

A comparative study seeking no more than a classification of societal characteristics will not in itself promote historical understanding. How persistence and change of configurations over a course of time have taken place is not explained by placing classifications of similarities and differences in series. To connect them by an assumed continuant, for example, Comte's progress of mind in each of the three stages, is a speculative rationalization. If our referent in the perished past is a continuant configuration, we will necessarily be concerned with the reconstruction of continuities as part of the task of explanation. The following proposal of a procedure of configurational organization is not a radical departure from practices in history and the social sciences. It is an endeavor to make explicit the possibilities of these practices when methodically instituted and joined together. The social sciences do not limit themselves to comparative organizations of their data, but they engage also in historical reconstructions along lines of development in their special fields. And historians consider parallel cases and make comparative judgments. The specialization of fields of study, valuable up to a point, is beyond that obstructive to a joint study of events and configurations as an historical problem of the *modus operandi* of men's organized behaviors.

One neglect of a too-narrow specialization is the failure to make systematic use of the knowledge-results of contemporary social sciences, using these conclusions as hypotheses for the reconstruction of continuants. Historians employ the rule of empirical equivalence in its general or "common sense" application, but do not methodically extend it to encompass the bearing of knowledge in economies, social psychology, and politics upon the reconstruction of the perished past. Although there are conflicting schools of thought in each of the social sciences, each contains a body of propositions which has been well established. Earlier theories of an original, unchangeable human nature, of prior imperative drives which dictate the forms of social organization and practice, and of immanent, pervasive forces acting propulsively through a society in directing its course of development are rejected to be replaced by hypotheses which accord with the results of observation and experiment. These hypotheses are the best-grounded empirical equivalents for reconstructing movements and forces in the past.

Even in a narrative history organized to do no more than to relate sequences of particular events, to neglect the knowledge-results and grounded hypotheses of contemporary sciences involves a double peril. Either the historian makes factual description his ideal and prunes his history to a statement of happenings shorn of interpretation, or, in going beyond this to write of movements and forces, he introduces speculative suppositions around which to organize his narrative. This division into a monograph for facts and a theme for interpretation follows from the method recommended by Shotwell and by Langlois and Seignobos. Shotwell divides the work of the historian into two steps. The first he calls scientific. The historian works over his materials by techniques of internal and external criticism. He is "scientific" in approaching and conducting his task with objectivity and impartiality. If we use the term "scholarship" for careful and thorough criticism, the term "scientific" characterizes the attitude of the historian. It does not characterize the results of his work, since no body of fact-statements is in itself a science. Having ascertained the facts, the historian passes to the second step, that of their organization and narration. This is characterized as an attempt to present a synthesized whole—an integrated and unified depiction of sequences of events. Historical synthesis calls for the exercise of historical imagination and the rational art of the historian.

The method of organizing universal narrative history has not differed from that of the more limited histories. It is more "philosophic" in that it has greater scope of speculative supposition, which assumes a master theme or continuity for stages, worlds, civilizations, ages, or periods. Thus Hegel's dialectical striving of the World-Historical Spirit is presented as the theme of Reason's progress toward freedom within political and other institutions and with oriental, classical, and Germanic worlds as stages of universal progress. Hegel's theory of history, like Augustine's, served to rationalize the historian's interests and beliefs. The past is represented as an illustration of the main theme. This method of linking present and past institutions by an immanent principle, even if the principle had some likelihood by the rule of empirical equivalence, would not provide a correlation of present configurations with those in the past.

A method of comparative organization that would yield historical knowledge obliges us to rely upon the rule of empirical equivalence; that is, to make reconstructions of past configurations depend upon hypotheses themselves derived from a direct knowledge of interrelations and continuance. If social scientists were unable to establish relations which hold for observed processes, the attempt to arrive at comparative results in history would be baulked at the beginning. We would have no initially probable hypotheses for the reconstruction of past processes.

The study of continuance is concerned with the persistence of relations and the sequence of actions within one or another configuration. The correlating of continuant configurations does not require a linkage of continuity between them. The sets of holding relations may or may not be continuous with the configuration directly studied by social scientists which provide the historian with his hypotheses. The study of marches in the formation of military and trading centers, the study of types of natural and social challenges with respect to the responses made by groups of men, or the study of relations between economic configurations and political developments can be undertaken without presupposing a continuity of the several instances correlated with each other. Yet it would be essential to reconstruct the continuity of happenings for each of the continuant configurations and for two reasons. In the first place, the hypotheses employed afford no detailed knowledge of past happenings and their specific sequences. Fact-statements and the support they give to relation-statements are decisive to the qualification, modification, confirmation, or rejection of an hypothesis proposed as an empirical equivalent. The hypothesis provides a leading question for the work of inquiry, but it does not construct the facts which stand in the relation of evidence for or against it. The only way of establishing how long and how stably any set of relations has held for happenings is by a continuity reconstruction. In the second place, if time process is neglected by a comparative study, the "what" but not the "how" of persistence and change will be formulated. The results of the inquiry will be similar to Comte's social statics. Speculative supposition is then called upon to account for a "dynamics" of forces.

To say that a set of relations holds for activities, productions, behaviors, and performances of men over a period of time is a statement of a determined configuration, not of determining forces. The agents engaged in and productive of human affairs are men acting with, within, by, for, and through social configurations. Their habits, interests, aims, beliefs, ideas, needs, and practices can be studied with respect to modes of social existence in various group associations; and the alignment and conflict of groups can be further studied with respect to actions and interactions. A total system formulated from subconfigurations of groups and institutions and with respect to patterns of action and interaction is the determined condition of happenings; but the system does not compel a course of action to follow a predetermined development to an inescapable consequence. So far as the system of relations holds for activities over a course of time, the nature and direction of processes within the system are determined. Predictions can be made with respect to consequences working out within the system, but all such predictions are premised on the holding of the system. They are of the following hypothetical form; if the system continues to hold, then a trend of process working toward certain kinds of consequences can be expected to continue and to eventuate in the consequences. But if the relations are altered, the total configuration no longer holds in the same way and a different likelihood of occurrence replaced that which preceded. In so far as men desire to avoid the predicted consequences and are successful in taking action to alter the configurations within which these consequences have a likelihood of happening, description of and prediction by means of configurations are pragmatically useful for the making of history from present to future. A knowledge of configuration of action in the past has instrumental value for individuals and groups able to turn this knowledge to their use and purpose.

The method of configurational organization depends upon knowledge of empirically equivalent hypotheses for the reconstruction of past relationships. A possible objection to even trying the method might be that it fails to explain the occurrence and influence of great men in history. Occurrence of such individuals is not explicable if by this one means "predictable"; but a great man, no less than a group of men, is subject to study within a determinate configuration. This is not to argue that men who have had great influence through their ideas or have been effective by means of their command of actions were socially predetermined to express their thoughts and decisions. Men's actions are inescapably conditioned by the set of relations within which they live and through which they act, but the perished past cannot act as a cause determining their behavior. There is a continuant past in the present which marks the beginning of every man's life, that is, an ongoing persistence of institutions and practices independent of his will within which he acquires habits, interests, purposes, and historical comprehension. In this acquisition arises an internal determination which, though marked by characteristic social limits and compulsions, may be productive of novel results.

A continuant configuration is not presentable as a causal explanation of happenings except indirectly as the set of relations holding for operative agents and agencies. Although configurations are not laws of history, a general, descriptive formula is not precluded; for example, Marx's dialectic of changes within a societal system leading to its revolutionary disruption. But to regard dialectic as a cause of changes or as a law governing them converts a descriptive formulation into a metaphysical prescription. The inevitability of a course of happenings is argued from a logic of history illicitly treated as a causal necessity. Since men are productive agents, it is proper to describe their actions in terms of efficient causation. At the same time, men's actions are qualitied and conditioned by the continuant configurations of social existence within which, individually and in groups, they acquire and employ means for ends which they come to prefer. Configurations persist and develop in the retentions and transmission characteristic of human behavior. All behavior that is definitively an affair of human history is socially conditioned. This generalization is not, in itself, very helpful for historical reconstruction. We need to find out how men have behaved within determinate societies with respect to economy, political and military actions, religious practices, moral customs, legal procedures, and work in sciences and arts. Yet the generalization does at least serve as a leading principle for the method of configurational organization when we come to employ an empirical equivalent as an hypothesis for historical reconstruction.

By way of illustration, let us take the problem of reconstructing connections between men's modes of social existence and their ways and types of thinking. The social conditioning of behavior—a generalized principle resting on confirmations in a number of specialized fields of study—leads to a trial of hypotheses that are initially probable because based upon results of direct investigation. Such hypotheses for historical inquiry might be instituted in the following way. Where studies of human behavior have shown that individuals' ways of thinking and acting are concommitant with membership and position in economic-social configurations, it is hypothesized that thought and actions in the past are correlatable in a comparable manner. The trial of hypotheses is made by a study of historical materials along the lines proposed by the hypotheses to establish confirmation or nonconfirmation by fact-statements. If an hypothesis holds (or in so far as it holds), human behavior will be describable by habit-patterns of response to situations and symbols and by the kinds of defenses, justifications, rationalizations, and valuations made by an individual in common with others of his group. In so far as an individual is shown to have viewed and responded to situations in socially determined ways, his thought and action are formulable as a correlation of individual and group. The position of the group or class with regard to institutions and instrumentalities defines the mode of social existence of individuals within the group. A historian might thus set himself the problem of determining whether (and how) a mode of social existence is connected with a typical way of thought and whether (and how) a way of thought functions as an expression of class position.

As the example would indicate, what is proposed is systematic use of hypotheses in historical inquiry which cuts across a traditional separation between historical and scientific knowledge. Interrelations of work between social scientists and historians would follow from this use. An empirical equivalent is a scientifically grounded hypothesis for the work of historical reconstruction. A concluding judgment with respect to description and explanation of past happenings by one or another hypothesis is consequent upon the investigation of historical materials. When it is recognized that not only those who are by profession historians but also workers in anthropology and other fields concerned with the study of men are engaged in historical inquiry, the trial of hypotheses is not reserved for any one specialty. Advances to be made by means of combined investigations, a situation now commonplace in the physical and life sciences, are worthy of serious consideration in the study and teaching of history and the social sciences. A conjunction of method is the most feasible liaison between specialties. The rule of empirical equivalence and method of configurational organization look to a closer concord between various fields in which historical work is undertaken.

IV · HISTORICAL UNDERSTANDING

To contribute to the sum of knowledge about the past remains the aim of historical study and history writing. The present essay has taken seriously the attendant claim made by many historians that knowledge about the past contributes to an understanding of the present in which we live. Because the historian is concerned with knowledge, he is concerned with reliable and relevant fact-statements. Judgments, supported by fact-statements, reconstruct historical pasts which represent not only what men did but also how and why they acted. The representations afford insight and commentary upon men now taking the sun. Understanding of the past thus orientates us to an appreciation of our historical present and by representing continuities in which the present is the latest situation engenders expectations about the immediate future. Our question is whether historical reconstruction might not accomplish considerably more than this by a method which would result in knowledge which would provide a basis of prediction as guidance for action. The pragmatic question has been dismissed by many writers on method among the historians. With respect to the method laid down for narrative organization, the dismissal has followed as a matter of course. But rejection argued from the incompetence of a method to reach results instrumental for the further making of history does not dispose of the question if there is a workable procedure for attaining these results. Method is decisive to what can or cannot be done in the organization of subject matter, not some prior philosophical theory about the "real" nature of history. Even if the theories of historiographers (for example, Rickert, Windelband, Langlois, and Seignobos) were not written to canonize the limitations of the historical methods they regard as essential, it is worth noting that their effect is to rationalize the results. If something more can be done with the materials of historical reconstruction by a method of configurational organization, to protest that this is not historical method or historical understanding would show more fondness for philosophical theory than for historical knowledge.

The limitations that historians have accepted for themselves and for historical understanding are well exemplified in the handbook written by Langlois and Seignobos, *Introduction to the Study of History*. This work asserts that "history enables us to understand the present in so far as it explains the origins of the existing state of things." [4] Unless an origin, however, is a cause persisting throughout the continuity in which it is discriminated as a beginning, no later or terminal situation noncontiguous with it is explained. Langlois and Seignobos represent an origin as an event causally connected with the next event in a series. [5] The present state is "explained" as an effect of the preceding cause in a series of events. This exclusive reliance on organization by a series of unique events leads to a logical but nonetheless disconcerting conclusion about the understanding of the present provided by a historical understanding of the past.

The evolution of the civilized societies has within the last hundred years been accelerated to such a degree that for the understanding of their present

---

[4] *Introduction to the Study of History*, New York, 1912, p. 319.
[5] *Ibid.*, p. 292. "The whole history of events is a chain of obviously and incontrovertibly connected incidents, each one of which is the determining cause of another. The lance-thrust of Montgomery is the cause of the death of Henry II; this death is the cause of the accession to power of the Guises, which again is the cause of the rising of the Protestants."

form the history of these last hundred years is more important than that of the ten preceding centuries. As an explanation of the present, history would almost reduce to the study of the contemporary period.[6]

Why not, indeed, go one step farther and assert that it does reduce to a study of the contemporary period and bring the contemporary down to current events? If each particular event is the determining cause of the next in the series, there is no advantage, for an understanding of the present, in an indefinite regress into the past, but only in knowing the cause contiguous with and now affecting what is happening. How that cause in turn is an effect of the next removed cause is an affair of past and completed action not now effecting anything. The argument for the "indirect utility" of history not only excludes the study of anything but the contemporary period, but is, furthermore, fallacious in treating origins as causal explanation of the present situation. Langlois and Seignobos summarily reject the idea that any direct utility results from historical understanding. "It is an obsolete illusion to suppose that history supplies information of practical utility in the conduct of life (*Historia magistra vitae*) lessons directly profitable to individuals and people . . ."[7]

The chief merit accorded to historical understanding is that it is an aid to intellectual culture in the four following ways: (1) it is hygienic for the mind as a cure for credulity; (2) it promotes understanding of and tolerance for a variety of usages; (3) it cures us of a morbid dread of change; (4) it keeps us from biological analogies. If these are the total sum of values realized by the operations of analysis and synthesis, the result is meager support for the claims of historical understanding.

Considerably more in the way of a positive contribution is attributed to written history by Nevins. In the beginning of the first chapter of *The Gateway to History*, entitled "In Defense of History," he extols the usefulness and worth of the historian's work. "It enables communities to grasp their relationship with the past, and to chart on general lines their immediate forward course." A narrative history brings its account of past happenings up to a contemporary situation in relating sequences of events. In Nevins's phrase, a "sense of continuity" is conveyed by the sequential relation. That is to say, the representation of a line of events in which the present happening is located as the latest in

<hr/>

[6] *Ibid.*, p. 320.   [7] *Ibid.*, p. 319.

a series suggests the direction or trend into the future. But if this is the "relationship with the past" established by a narrative organization of events, how does it enable communities "to chart on general lines their immediate forward course?" The series of events making up the line or continuity of events is not a causal determination for the further continuance of a line of happenings. Moreover, if continuities are unique sequences of unique events, how is prediction (charting) of the immediate forward course of a community established on *general* lines? Does "general" mean generalized from particular continuities, or general as limited to no precise import and being no more than a rather loose expectation?

Nevins's account of method leaves the question unanswered as to how the historian who has aroused expectation has enabled communities to predict their forward course. His narrative "grasp" of a relationship of the present with the past is the strand of happenings—the reconstruction of a sequence of events. To have an understanding of a general line, it would be requisite to reconstruct a set of relations holding for processes. On the hypothesis that the continuant configuration which has been holding will continue to hold, prediction can be made as a probability judgment. Without such organization, expectation is summary opinion and more or less shrewd guesswork.

The assertion that the study of the past enables us to understand the present has three possible supports with respect to organization. The assertion rests on organization by continuity, on comparative classifications and correlations, or on a method in which sequences of events are reconstructed jointly with a reconstruction of sets of relations holding for processes. We have called the last of these the method of configurational organization. To assert its feasibility as a procedure implicates a definition of history which cuts across the traditional separation between historical and comparative studies to be found in the definitions of Windelband, Rickert, and Troeltsch. For these historiographers history is concerned with unique, unrepeatable, individual wholes which cannot be studied by methods of abstraction, comparison, and generalization employed in the social sciences. Written history is a concrete and intuitive representation—an individual, reconstructed whole of events representing a unique, individual whole of the once-actual happenings. Yet how do these men know that the once-actual happenings were parts of unique wholes? If we are not willing to rest the answer upon empirical equivalence (that is, to rest the meaning of the referent upon a whole that can be observed and described as its empirical equivalent), what is the alternative? Are we to say, with Lord Balfour, that there is always an artist to be reckoned with in the writing of history and mean thereby not only literary style but also a wholeness constructed for events?

It is not fallacious for Baur to speak of the historian's sympathetic insight and for Troeltsch to commend the historian's power of intuitive representation. The insights and intuitions result from working with the materials of historical reconstruction and from ability to ask fruitful questions. Intuition, however, never tests itself or comes within sight of the perished past. The historian's "eye" for the past, which "sees" what happened in presenting a "view" of it, would be a miraculous gift if taken literally. Although historical judgments have their support in fact-statements, no matter who has uttered the judgments, no assemblage of fact-statements is a substitute for perspicacity. There is always a historian to be reckoned with in the interpretations of history.

There is some justification for defining history as "a science of reasoning." Yet though knowledge of the perished past is indirect, to call such knowledge and its method of study "subjective" is a misleading way of speaking. A historical statement is subjective in the sense that its referent is not an object open to direct observation. One may further say that the procedure of "historical analysis" is an "intellectual operation." Granting this, we are not forced to accept the conclusion of Langlois and Seignobos: "From the very nature of its materials history is necessarily a subjective science." [8] The conclusion appears plausible when emphasis is laid upon the "subjective impressions" by which the historian imagines past happenings and when institutions are referred to as "mental habits." Yet a corrective of this subjectivism, interestingly enough, is stated by Langlois and Seignobos themselves.

"The realities of the past are things which we do not observe and which we can only know in virtue of their resemblance to the realities of the present. In order to realize the conditions under which past events happened, we must observe the humanity of today and look for conditions under which analogous events happen now. History thus becomes an application of the descriptive sciences which deal with humanity, descriptive psychology, sociology or social science; but all these sciences

[8] *Ibid.*, p. 217.

are still but imperfectly established, and their defects retard the establishment of a science of history." [9]

The use of the terms "resemblance," "application," and "analogous"
in the foregoing quotation could be translated into the rule of empirical
equivalence and the method of configurational organization without doing violence to the statement. Langlois and Seignobos do not proceed to
this methodological position, and the reason lies in their separation of
historical work into analytical operation devoid of hypotheses and synthetic operations subsequently introduced. "The facts as furnished by
criticism are isolated and scattered; in order to organize them into a
structure it is necessary to imagine and group them in accordance with
their resemblance to facts of the present day, an operation which also
depends on the use of analogies." [10] There is no need here to criticize
the assumption of isolated facts. Beard has presented a strong case for
the contextual setting of historical inferences (*The Discussion of Human Affairs.*) What is very much to the point is the meaning of "organization by resemblance and analogies." It appears to be a judgment of
equivalence between happenings directly observed and past events asserted by fact-statements; and, furthermore, it seems to admit judgments about configurations of observed processes as empirical equivalents of continuant configurations in the past. Granted that we have to
"imagine" the happenings reported in documents, the empirical equivalents used as hypotheses of historical reconstruction are not subjective.

The historian who works with empirical equivalents will not be
likely to make the mistake of designating evolution, development, or
continuity as a science of history. Some historians have held that a science of history (in result, not simply in the sense of method) is instituted
in the idea of evolutionary development. Thus, Bury (*Inaugural Address*) asserts the primary importance of "the great transforming conception" of evolution. "It has brought history into line with other
sciences and, potentially at least, has delivered her from the ethical and
political encumbrances which continued to impede her after the introduction of scientific methods." For Bury the idea of progress is a scientific principle—an entering "into closer relations with the sciences
which deal objectively with the facts of the universe." Unity of theme
in an idea of the universal progress of mankind is far from a scientific
principle. Either the development of mankind is just a general way of

[9] *Ibid.*, p. 224.   [10] *Ibid.*, p. 317.

referring to every narrative history as being concerned with the reconstruction and representation of continuities with no underlying assumption, or the historian to start with assumes that there has been some great, unbroken process of social development tying specific continuities together. The latter is a speculative supposition or metaphysical hypothesis.

It was stated earlier in this essay that it was not our purpose to argue for the exclusion of metaphysical suppositions from historical interpretation. Our intention was rather to bring forward a rule for discriminating between speculative suppositions and knowledge-statements as a condition of making our ideas clear in the field of historical reconstruction and representation. Where historical representation rests on a speculative supposition, it is important for historical understanding to realize that a historian is employing a basic assumption and to bring it out into the open. If organization is made by speculative assumption for which there is no empirical equivalent, interpretation based on the assumption is a matter, not of knowledge, but of rationalization. History as knowledge is not thereby limited to complex facts, the judgments of relation-statements supported by fact-statements inferred from the materials of historical reconstruction. The historian can, without leaving the grounds of knowledge, attempt to reconstruct and to represent continuities within continuant configurations, using available, confirmed results in other sciences as empirically equivalent hypotheses for this work.

The method of configurational organization promises results in history which would reinforce the assertion that historical understanding of the present may be acquired by knowledge of the past. The constructive aims of this essay have been to formulate a rule for discriminating between speculative suppositions and knowledge-statement and to present a method of configurational organization grounded in the materials of human history. The results of such a method are not decided in advance of trial; but if the trial is successful, the results should prove well worth the work.

9

NATURALISM AND THE SOCIOLOGICAL ANALYSIS OF KNOWLEDGE

Thelma Z. Lavine

THE philosophy of John Dewey constitutes the vanguard of twentieth century naturalism. For him the significance of naturalism lies chiefly in the principle of continuity.

To me human affairs, associative and personal, are projections, continuations, complications, of the nature which exists in the physical and pre-human world. There is no gulf, no two spheres of existence, no "bifurcation" . . . to anyone who takes seriously the notion of thorough-going continuity . . .

The term "naturalistic" has many meanings. As it is here employed it means, on one side, that there is no breach of continuity between operations of inquiry and biological operations and physical operations. "Continuity," on the other side, means that rational operations *grow out of* organic activities, without being identical with that from which they emerge.

The primary postulate of a naturalistic theory of logic is continuity of the lower (less complex) and the higher (more complex) activities and forms. The idea of continuity is not self-explanatory. But its meaning excludes complete rupture on one side and mere repetition of identities on the other; it precludes reduction of the "higher" to the "lower" just as it precludes complete breaks and gaps. The growth and development of any living organism from seed to maturity illustrates the meaning of continuity.

Metaphor is inadequate, however, to convey the position of contemporary "thoroughgoing" naturalism. To affirm the "growth" of the "higher" out of the "lower," to deny "gulfs," "gaps," or "breaks," is to speak the language of the seer, not that of common sense or of science. Yet it is only in metaphor that the continuity of things can be apprehended. To common sense, things are discrete. The juke box, sulfanilamide, the inspiring morale of the Soviet army, midweek choir practice —gaps, gulfs, and breaks pervade the world of the common man. Nor can the principle of existential continuity be saved by an appeal to science, on the ground that although to common sense things may appear discrete, science reveals them to be in reality continuous. The latter argument may take either or both of two different forms: physical reductionism and panevolutionism. Physical reductionism consists in the assertion that science progressively "reduces" differences in kind to simpler sets of entities and eventually to complex forms of a single set of entities, namely, the entities of physics. The principle of continuity may be formulated on this view as a methodological postulate for the special sciences: All phenomena must be reduced either to the entities of physical science or to entities which themselves have been reduced to the entities of physical science. This argument is based on a familiar misapprehension of the nature of scientific "reduction"; scientific reduction is not an operation of dissection upon three-dimensional solid objects, but the correlation of carefully selected characteristics of specially isolated phenomena. Reduction relates the terms of one analysis to the terms of another analysis. Panevolutionism, the alternative attempt to obtain scientific status for the principle of existential continuity, claims as its prototype the biological theory of evolution. By a simple process of imaginative generalization it views the totality of existence as one mighty, continuous, evolutionary process; the "topmost flower" of human culture has its roots, so the argument runs, in the primeval mud. As a special scientific technique and a general method of analysis of the genetic interrelations among biological species, the whole weight of the biological theory of evolution falls against such an intuitive generalization of itself. Metaphysical genetics has neither biological nor any other scientific authentication. Thus the continuity of things cannot be conveyed by common sense or by scientific periphrasis, but only poetically; and the temper of naturalism in the twentieth century is not poetic—at least, not on the level on which principles are formulated.

If naturalism is to be interpreted in terms of a principle or postulate of continuity, the postulate does not concern a continuity of existence, such as Professor Dewey suggests, but of analysis. To postulate the continuity of analysis is to demand, if one is a naturalist, that the investigation into all problems in all subject matters employ the methods of the special sciences or methods which may be incorporated by the special sciences. The naturalistic principle may be stated as the resolution to pursue inquiry into any set of phenomena by means of methods which administer the checks of intelligent experiential verification in accordance with the contemporary criteria of objectivity. The significance of this principle does not lie in the advocation of empirical method, but in the conception of the regions where that method is to be employed. That scientific analysis must not be restricted in any quarter, that its extension to any field, to any special set of phenomena, must not be curtailed—this is the nerve of the naturalistic principle. "Continuity" of analysis can thus mean only that all analysis must be scientific analysis. Continuity between the "lower" and the "higher," between the "physical" and the "human," between the "biological" and the "logical" signifies that the mode of inquiry into each of these territories must be experiential. The denial of "breaks," "gaps," and "bifurcation" becomes, on re-interpretation, the repudiation of the exclusion of scientific analysis from certain spheres, in favor of some form of analysis deemed more fitting. The "growth" of "rational operations" "out of" "organic activities" of which they are "complications" and the analogy with the development of an organism call attention to the corollary that in the interests of simplicity and economy, as well as of control, integrating interrelations must be established among the various special analyses.

The history of philosophical naturalism is not a series of qualifying elaborations of a particular group of tenets. Naturalism has no essential tenets beyond the principle of continuity of analysis. In the history of thought the naturalist is he who promotes and achieves the extension of the methods of science into those regions from which they are conventionally excluded, or to which their applicability has not been adequately demonstrated. A point of view is not naturalistic by virtue of concurring in empirical investigation when the scientific treatment of the given problem is so well accredited that only the mystics venture protest. Since the naturalistic postulate requires unrestricted extension of experiential inquiry, "half-hearted naturalism" (Professor Dewey's term) is readily identifiable in any age: extolling the consolidated achievements of empirical studies, it is engaged in protecting currently threatened phenomena against the encroachments of scientific investigation. By the same token the history of naturalism is marked by the progressive inroads of the special sciences into regions previously held to be inviolable.

The fortunes of the naturalistic principle in the twentieth century approximate a catalogue of the writings of John Dewey. In basic accord with the reading of the postulate of continuity offered by the present discussion, he concludes his *Logic: the Theory of Inquiry:* "Since scientific methods simply exhibit free intelligence operating in the best manner available at a given time, the cultural waste, confusion and distortion that results from the failure to use these methods, in all fields in connection with all problems, is incalculable."

It is the objective of the present essay to promote the operating of such free intelligence in a field from which it has been almost universally excluded. The argument is in behalf of an unrestricted sociological analysis of knowledge.

I

Representative critics of the sociology of knowledge sustain a marked convergence of views, which is singular in contrast to the disparity of their positions in other connections. They are agreed that the sociological analysis of the elements of cognition be restrained from extension to "reason" or to the "logical schema of proof" or to "validity." The terms of this restriction vary insignificantly.

1. Von Schelting concludes his attack [1] upon *Ideology and Utopia* with these compensatory remarks:

> Fortunately, Mannheim's epistemological inconsistency does not hinder him in dealing with concrete cases of ideologies and utopias, or with ideological and utopian elements in certain conceptions, and in practice he often successfully applies these notions to those conceptions and ideas to which they really are applicable (unrestrictedly or in large measure). . . . The *whole* spiritual sphere, in past and modern social life, *can* be considered in its purely *factual* aspect (without regard to its normative intrinsic values and objective validity) and *insofar* as it is the "expression" or "product" of social structures . . . or *insofar* as it fulfills a "function" in social reality . . . The nonsense first begins when one believes that factual origin and social factors as such . . . in any way affect the values of ideas and conceptions thus originated, and especially the theoretic value—which is to say, the truth—of cognitive achievements.[2]

With Von Schelting the restriction of sociological analysis is offered in the form of an aspect theory of knowledge, bolstered by the philosophically familiar device of the "insofar": the "purely factual" aspect of the spiritual sphere may be subjected to sociological analysis "insofar"

[1] Review of *Ideologie und Utopie*, by Karl Mannheim (Bonn, 1930), *American Sociological Review*, I (1936), 664–74.
[2] *Ibid.*, 674.

as it may be "factually" related to the elements of sociological analysis; the aspect of cognition which consists in objective validity and theoretic value is exempted from sociological analysis.

2. Mandelbaum repairs the dikes of historical realism against the rise of historical relativism [3] by a distinction between statements and judgments, and again between judgments of fact and judgments of value; these distinctions in turn rest upon the "genetic fallacy" argument and a radical distinction between act and content, and they entail the correspondence theory of truth.

Now the investigation of these determining valuational factors provides an interesting field for that which Mannheim and Scheler have called the sociology of knowledge, for it is certain that judgments concerning the desirability of particular forms of historical inquiry, and even judgments concerning the desirability of historical inquiry as such, are in part determined by the sociological conditions under which the individual lives. Yet this fact in no wise justifies the historical relativist in his claims. For it is one thing to say that a particular historical work would never have been written except for certain valuations, and it is quite another to contend that these valuational factors determine the content of the historical work itself.[4]

3. Professor Lovejoy, the stanch defender of critical realism throughout the vicissitudes of scientific and philosophical thought in the twentieth century, formulates the defense against sociology of knowledge in terms of a distinction between a nonrational and a rational component of knowledge—the rational component being fortified by a theory of a minimal set of universal epistemological conditions, the contents of which may be presumed to have been made familiar in the course of the quelling of the revolt against dualism.

The spokesmen of this sort of sociological relativism, in short, patently give *some* place to common criteria of factual truth and legitimacy in inference, which their theory, in its extreme interpretation, would exclude. They do not . . . really believe . . . that their own thesis . . . ought to be accepted only by persons of a particular status or position.[5]

Professor Lovejoy's stand is especially striking in view of his well-known attack upon those epistemological theories of perception which

[3] Maurice Mandelbaum, *The Problem of Historical Knowledge; an Answer to Relativism*, New York, 1938.
[4] *Ibid.*, pp. 193–94.
[5] Arthur O. Lovejoy, "Reflections on the History of Ideas," *Journal of the History of Ideas*, I (1940), 18.

exempt perceptual phenomena from analysis in terms of physiology, optics, the velocity of light, and so forth. These he regards as "transmissive" theories, that is, as theories which admit the function of these phenomena, but deny that their influence consists in anything but the immaculate transmission of the *cognoscendum* as it is in itself. Professor Lovejoy has, apparently, no quarrel with a "transmissive" theory with regard to the influence of social phenomena upon knowledge.

4. In the joint opposition to the sociological analysis of cognition Professor Lovejoy has at last found a common bond with a pragmatist. Professor C. I. Lewis holds that there are two general types of analysis of mind, the *ratio essendi* (causal analysis) and the *ratio cognoscendi* (evidential analysis). Each type of method is Thomistically limited in its sphere of application:

> The causal or "cosmic" explanation of science and common sense, runs from cause to effect, from hypostatized thing to observable evidence. The analysis and verification of knowledge runs from effect to cause, from evidence to the thing evidenced. . . . Epistemological investigation is, naturally, by way of the *ratio cognoscendi:* that is its peculiar task. Those "theories of knowledge" which reverse the direction of explanation and give a causal, natural-scientific account, merely substitute a more or less uncritical and psychological methodology, based upon dubious assumptions, for their proper business.[6]

Sociological analysis of cognitive validity, then, constitutes confusion or heresy.

5. The schematism of the logical empiricist C. W. Morris is apparently employed in an article [7] by Gerard de Gré, with the purpose of effecting a similar theoretical immunity from sociological analysis of a special class of cognitive phenomena. Let us say, suggests Mr. de Gré, that statements are analyzable into their relations to things, to other statements, and to the people who are concerned with them, respectively. Then the sociology of knowledge, having as its objective the analysis of the relation between thought and thinkers, must be obviously misguided in attempting to extend sociological analysis to the categories of "things" and "other statements," which, quite plainly to Mr. de Gré, have no connection whatsoever with the social, or pragmatic, category,

[6] C. I. Lewis, *Mind and the World-Order*, New York, 1929, pp. 425–26.
[7] "The Sociology of Knowledge and the Problem of Truth," *Journal of the History of Ideas*, II (1941), 110–15.

the less so since they connote, respectively, the sphere of material and formal validity.

6. In fundamental accord with the preceding argument is Hans Speier's simpler dualism of theory and practice.[8]

The theories which claim that ideas are socially determined regard thinking as instrumental to action. The relation between ideas and social reality is therefore constituted in the medium of needs. . . . Theoretical reasoning [as distinguished from "technical" and "promotive" modes of thinking] has no immediate and no necessarily intended relationship to change which is to be brought about by human agents. The specific truth contained in cognition cannot be identified with or reduced to anything in the practical sphere. . . . The need that is pertinent to theoretical reasoning is the desire to know.[9]

Thus theoretical reasoning is by scholastic definition the satisfaction of the need for contemplation, which, presumably, is to be taken as an ultimate, insusceptible of the analysis of positive science.

7. In Professor Sabine's presidential address of 1938 [10] he is concerned to find a basis for the unity of natural and social sciences; in connection with this interest, the presumptions of the sociology of knowledge receive his attention. Professor Sabine distinguishes between beliefs, which "may possibly be explained by whatever principles can be adduced to explain human behavior," and propositions; "and the logical operations by which propositions are validated can never, without confusion, be identified with the mental or social conditions that make human beings believe them." The nature of the logical operations, upon which sociological analysis has no rightful claim, is further elucidated by the concept of a set of interscientific "canons of validity," which provides both for the unity of all possible science and for the desired restriction of sociological analysis. So far Professor Sabine maintains the conventional dogmatism concerning sociological analysis of the forms of validity. In conclusion he rests his case with an appeal to philosophic proportion, an appeal somewhat tempered by his plain-spoken acknowledgment of the importance of investigating the relations between knowledge and social phenomena:

---

[8] "The Social Determination of Ideas," *Social Research*, V (1938), 182–205.
[9] *Ibid.*, pp. 183–87.
[10] George H. Sabine, "Logical and Social Studies," the presidential address to the eastern division of the American Philosophical Association, December, 1938; cf. *Philosophical Review*, XLVIII (1939), 155–76.

The investigation—psychological, sociological, and historical—of this relationship between knowledge and practice, between science and the social matrices in which science is conceived and from which it is born, is of the utmost interest and importance. That it will be actively prosecuted in the future, as it has begun to be in the recent past, is a foregone conclusion and also a thing to be desired. . . . *Yet in the interest of philosophic proportion and scientific caution* it is worth insisting that conclusions touching matters of this sort, insofar as they have any historical or sociological foundation, depend upon the same principles of validity that guarantee the results of all other conclusions whatsoever.[11]

8. Not only does a distinction between "substantive" and "logical" find favor with Professor Talcott Parsons, but he is particularly concerned to exempt still another aspect of cognition from sociological analysis: cognition of "the non-empirical field." Durkheim's attempt to indicate the possibility and significance of a social factor in certain "basic" categories, Parsons characterizes as "the fundamental philosophical difficulty of trying to derive the source of empirical knowledge from empiricist considerations." His own view of the source of knowledge consists in the recognition of empirical reality, determined by an absolute logical schema of proof, and the "systems of symbolic representations of sacred entities the "reality" underlying which lies in the non-empirical aspects of the universe." His position thus "leaves room for an epistemology of a genuine realist nature, but involving non-empirical elements which are also non-sociological." [12] Sociological analysis is restricted from trespassing not only upon the true but also upon the holy.

9. Robert K. Merton's frequently cited article, "The Sociology of Knowledge," [13] enjoys the conventional innocence of a bibliographical account. Although it is not incumbent upon him to engage in argument, he does not hesitate to make clear his stand. If sociology of knowledge is pervaded by a cliché, *Seinsverbundenheit des Wissens* (the existential conditioning of knowledge), Merton replies in kind, affirming that "it becomes increasingly apparent that the social genesis of thought has no necessary bearing on its validity or falsity." [14] A modicum of variety is afforded by his view that sociological analysis has in fact greater possi-

---

[11] *Ibid.*, p. 175. Italics added.
[12] The quotations in this paragraph are from Talcott Parsons, *The Structure of Social Action*, New York, 1937, pp. 431–48.
[13] *Isis*, XXVII (1937), 493.   [14] *Ibid.*

bilities for application when it is restrained from treating matters of validity. Under these limitations, Merton holds, it can be extended to the physical sciences, the validity of which has achieved a status which would seem to render its sociological examination unthinkable.

So general and so complacent an opposition to the sociological analysis of validity gives one pause. Obviously it is unaffected by the partisan philosophical and methodological differences of its members. Bitter age-old battles and shrill modern schisms give way to the potency of a deeper-lying issue: whether or not man's cognitive endeavors should be studied by the methods of the special sciences, and especially by those of the social sciences. That "logic," or "reason," or "objectivity," or even "philosophic proportion" demands a negative stand on this issue is thus the basis of one of the mightiest theoretical coalitions in the history of occidental thought.

Some may regard the pervasiveness of accord on this issue as one of the surest indications of the presence of truth. Must it not be that the issue locates some fundamental cleavage in the nature of the universe, or in knowledge, or in the human sphere? But acceptance of such fundamentality would be premature, so long as "validity" and "objectivity" and the great coalescent group and its "logic" have not been subjected to analysis.

II

However jealous for the integrity of valid knowledge are the arguments of the opposition against sociological analysis, "logical" analysis of validity is always acceptable and has, in fact, become institutionalized as one of the major divisions of philosophy. The distinctions which characteristically emerge in "as such" (the term is Mannheim's) discussions of logical and methodological matters are not likely, however, to be of marked service to the particular science in its hour of methodological need. This section will concern itself with some clarifications concerning validity which are drawn with reference to the peculiar requirements of the present problem of the sociology of knowledge. The function of this section within the discussion is to establish the meaning and the legitimacy of sociological analysis of cognitive validity.

The distinction which is of first importance in connection with this special problem appears nowhere in the literature of the opposition. It is the distinction between "the validity" of a specific proposition, or of a cognitive element in the widest sense, and the standard, or norm, or ideal, of validity in terms of which validation takes place, and which alone bestows meaningfulness upon any predication of "validity."

To speak of "the validity" of a cognitive element, whether statement, proposition, concept, idea, schema, or theory, is to indulge in a commonly sanctioned ellipsis which is for most purposes innocuous. Failure to apprehend this ellipticity, however, may result in gratuitous confusion as to the interests of the sociology of knowledge in validity. It is imperative to distinguish the following: the norm which establishes criteria and determines the procedure of validation; the validating act; and the resultant established validity of a specific proposition. The restraint of sociological analysis from extension to the norms which formulate criteria and establish the procedure of validation is significant, although misguided; the same restriction in connection with the validation act itself misses its mark. For, given a clear articulation of the definitions and criteria which constitute the validity norms of a specific set of phenomena, the validating of the specific proposition is of such slight interest to the sociologist of knowledge as not to warrant any restrictive rules. The sociologist of knowledge may be quite content that within the group of accredited sciences in most cases the actual validation act be considered on the "logical" level. The reason for this is not that the act is affirmed a priori to have no social significance. The pursuance or nonpursuance of the act of validation with regard to a specific claim is, for example, of the greatest sociological significance. However, with the developing articulateness and precision of scientific method, the act of validation, channelized in terms of carefully constructed criteria and formalized techniques, approaches, as to a limit, a state of automatism.

These distinctions may be made concrete. The construction of the concept of time by relativity physics rests upon the setting and synchronizing of clocks at distant places:

It is a fundamental postulate that the adjustment of the clocks is to be accomplished by signal lights. The synchronization of the clocks is now simple enough. We merely demand that light signals sent from the master clock at intervals of one second arrive at any distant clock at intervals of one second as measured by it, and we change the rate of the distant clock until it measures these intervals as one second. After its rate has been adjusted, the distant clock is to be so *set* that when a light signal is despatched from the master clock at its indicated zero of time the time of arrival recorded at the distant clock shall be such that the distance of the clock from the master clock, divided by the time of arrival, shall give the velocity of light, assumed already known. This operation involves a measurement of the distance of the distant clock, so that in spreading the time coordinates over space the measurement of space is involved by definition, and the measurement of time is not a self-contained thing.[15]

Similarly, in Otto Klineberg's celebrated study of the intelligence of "national" and "racial" groups in Europe, it is not the details of his use of the standardized Pinter-Patterson series of nonlanguage performance tests or his application of the standard criteria of Nordic, Alpine, and Mediterranean types which interests the sociologist of knowledge, but the significance of the refinement of the central norm of "representative" samples of racial and national groups.

Such are the validity norms in which sociological analysis is interested. On this view "aberrations" in the validation act are more fruitful ground for psychological than for sociological investigation. In fact, what may be construed as a social aberration in connection with a case of validating (for example, as an important group construed the establishment of guilt in the Sacco-Vanzetti trial) will in most instances be more significantly regarded as the positive functioning of a further set of criteria, that is, as the functioning of an additional validity norm. From these considerations it will follow that "the validity" of a given proposition, as the end-product of the validation procedure, is not an object of interest to the sociologist of knowledge. The "truth" or "falsity" of a proposition is only the product of a formalized validation process; it is the determining norm which is the object of sociological interest.

These distinctions are obscured by the characteristic assertion that "the social genesis of thought has no necessary bearing on its validity or falsity." But sociology of knowledge does *not* dispute "the truth of cognitive achievements"; its concern is with the norms which establish both the criteria of the object (for example, its location among current categorial divisions or special subframes of reference) and the formal procedure of its validation, that is, its discrimination and identification.

The next requisite clarification concerning "validity" is somewhat expedited by this first set of distinctions. The sociological "attack" upon "objective validity" has been charged (notably, by Von Schelting and Mandelbaum) with circularity, on the ground that its own thesis

[15] P. W. Bridgman, *The Logic of Modern Physics,* New York, 1928, pp. 73–74.

must "assume the possibility" of "objective validity" in order to state its case.

"Objective validity" has significance within the present context in two senses: as a special type of validity norm and as a possible predication, in terms of this norm, of given cognitive elements. As has been indicated above, the latter sense is of minor concern. The focus of interest is upon the *norm of objective validity*, rather than upon the consequent objective validity of certain selected propositions. Objective validity is a historical norm which has undergone historical modifications in the service of the special sciences. Its constant function, however, has been the maintenance of standards of discrimination for the objects of attention and for their interconnections. The obligations of the sociology of knowledge with regard to this general norm are discharged by recognition of the norm and by its thorough socio-historical analysis.

There remains the interesting task of ascertaining the basis of the charge of circularity. The arguments of the opposition rely chiefly upon repeated cheerful discoveries that the sociologist of knowledge must acknowledge the objective validity of scientific facts. The force of this *coup* is not turned aside by the above distinction between "the objective validity" of specific facts and the determining objective validity norm. The functioning of a validity norm *is* perceived by the opposition. In fact, the opposition rest their case on an objective validity norm: the philosophical correspondence theory of truth. This is the occasion for Von Schelting's triumph:

But we have not yet exhausted the implications of Mannheim's theory. It also implies [*sic*] . . . the "traditional" concept of truth! For there would obviously be no meaning at all in basing the value of social conceptions upon their rôle in the social process, unless it is presupposed that this very rôle can be ascertained in a way that necessarily carries conviction, on the basis of historical facts, and by the means of logic. . . . This presupposition carries the assertion that there is a possibility of objective cognition of historical facts and their relationships. Mannheim himself explicitly declares that it is impossible to ascertain the contribution to historical development of every "utopia," every "socio-historical conception.[16]

The basis of the charge of circularity is now revealed. Any objection to the correspondence theory of truth which relies upon objectively

[16] *American Sociological Review*, I (1936), 668.

valid knowledge for its demonstration thereby relies upon the correspondence theory as the presupposition of objective validity. Sociological analysis of the objective-validity norm is, so far, no more than a special case of this type of vicious circularity. But it entails an aggravated viciousness: the attempt to delineate a social factor in the regions restricted by traditional tenets for the solitude of pure reality.

Definition of the term "validity norm" need no longer be delayed. The term "norm" appears frequently in diverse contexts in the literature of sociology and has made its way into the opposition literature concerning the sociology of knowledge. The sociological analysis of knowledge requires initially a general category of relatively autonomous meaningful cognitive elements. The further discrimination of the cognitive element as concept, proposition, statement, sign, or meaning is not relevant to this problem. The theoretical importance of this category lies in the fact that all cognitive elements have the function of determining order within human experience. This legislation of order has no connections with any specific epistemological doctrine concerning the nature of that which is ordered. By an easy extension of sociological and ethical usage, it is possible to regard the elements which command and sustain the structure or order of experience as the norms of cognition. Then the classes of cognitive elements and of cognitive norms are coextensive.

Historically, the normative function of one class of cognitive elements has been neglected. These are the cognitive elements which have the initial function of rendering determinate and meaningful some segment of experience. They are thus the primary instruments of order. In view of their gestalt-determining function, they may be regarded as presentational norms.

Identification of presentational norm is a requisite for comparative anthropology, which has laid bare the realist error of assuming that there is a class of crucial experiential "facts" which are universally perceived. The realist who finds it necessary to account for cases in which such facts are *not* "perceived," commonly bases his explanation on the phenomena of "focus of attention" or "selectivity"—phenomena which a realist focus of attention will, of course, regard as requiring no analysis.

Muzafer Sherif relates an instructive instance of the absence of any presentational norm to correspond with our "year":

. . . there are people in the world who do not keep track of the years. Thus Kober gives us a concrete case . . . : "The California Indian did not record the passage of long intervals of time. No one knew his own age . . ." If we commence our study of such a people with a study of their whole culture, and grasp the concepts they use and the classifications they possess in common . . . we shall . . . avoid the stupidity of including in our tests such an item as "How old are you?" which comes as an alternative item for "five-year-old intelligence" in the Stanford revision of the Binet test.[17]

The genesis of a presentational norm is carefully treated by Sherif in his well-known study of the formation of a frame of reference for the judgment of "distance" in the perception of an unstructured autokinetic effect, both by the individual and by the group.

What has obscured the normative instrumentality of this class of cognitive elements has been the universal acknowledgment of the function of another class of cognitive elements as rules, or principles, determining validity. The cognitive elements which have achieved the status of explicit rules or principles have varied with the eras and with the interests of specific inquiries.

But the quarrel which the sociology of knowledge has with this situation does not concern the selection of any particular cognitive elements as rules or principles. It is that the increasing sophistication of the special sciences with regard to the status of their formalized legislation for inquiry still remains provincial. For there has been little sophisticated treatment of the class of cognitive elements which render meaningful the innumerable "facts" of scientific and commonsense experience —facts whose validity is not currently called into question by the special interests of a given inquiry or by a crucial nonscientific situation. The fine flower of a self-conscious positivism is insupportably rooted in a sterile and unexamined realism of large areas of scientific and common-sense definition. All cognitive elements, not merely those which contingently engage our attention, are norms of the order of our experience.

The sociology of knowledge is concerned to subject to socio-historical analysis the several types of norm which are operative in the construction of objectively valid knowledge; the regulative, or directional norm, which establishes basic categorial distinctions; the validity norm, which legislates the criteria of concrete types of phenomena and the require-

17 Muzafer Sherif, *The Psychology of Social Norms*, New York, 1936, p. 8.

ments involved in their verification; the procedural norm, which establishes for certain modes of inquiry general methods of identification, measurement, corroboration, and so forth; the presentational norm, which provides for the recognition as a meaningful structure of that which is experienced; the objectivity norm, which legislates for all the special sciences the general principles of the precise discrimination of the object of interest.

A normative schema has, for the sociology of knowledge, the dual advantages of demanding an account of the situation generating the norm and an account of the cognitive function of the norm itself. For the concept of norm (disengaged from transcendentalism) entails the notions of responsiveness to a state of affairs requiring control, and legislation of a specific type of order. Order, as the characteristic cognitive function, is seen by this schema as significant only with respect to an answer to the question "Order for what, in response to what?" The objective of the sociology of knowledge is the systematic analysis of the types of distinctively social responsiveness of cognitive order, as established by the class of cognitive norms.

The concept of normative legislation throws light upon the tenacity of the absolutism maintained by those opposing this newest naturalistic advance, the sociology of knowledge. However divergently that absolutism has been formulated, its logical basis is the significant argument that relativism entails the logical paradox of relativizing its own arguments unless absolute provision is made for the legitimacy of its conceptions. Thus the various overlapping restrictions placed upon sociological analysis of cognition by the strange bedfellows noted above mark the general boundaries of the absolute which they hold essential to the logical integrity of knowledge. Some principles, they say, must be kept independent of social relativization if an infinite regress upon relata is to be avoided.

Unless the core of soundness of this logical ground of objection is unwaveringly apprehended, no defense of the sociology of knowledge can maintain itself. No alternative defense on other grounds can be made adequate in its stead. Such an unhappy defense is attempted by C. Wright Mills in a courageous article advancing the cause of sociology of knowledge. His argument (on this score) is foredoomed, because it cannot meet the only sound objections and just demands which the opposition can muster. In response to their demands for an absolute upon which social relativism might logically depend, Dr. Mills makes the unpardonable offer of a probability:

These anti-relationistic arguments . . . assume the existence of an absolute truth having no connection with inquiry; and they are significant only from an absolutist viewpoint. The imputations of the sociologist of knowledge may be tested with reference to the verificatory model generalized, e.g., by Peirce and Dewey. Their truthfulness is then in terms of this model. Granted that this model is no *absolute* guaranty, it seems the most probable we have at present.[18]

It is not the aim of the present discussion to exploit the delights of dilemma. The concept of the normative function of cognitive elements provides the absolute logical foundation demanded of social relativism. The absolute function of the norm makes possible the compatibility of a logical absolute with a thoroughgoing, unrestricted sociological relativization. For the ordering of experience is absolute from the standpoint of the persons who are engaged in the establishment of that order. This fact holds regardless of whether order is established by means of presentational norms alone or, more reliably, by reference to appropriate validity norms. This fact holds also in the face of conscious recognition that the norm employed cannot furnish more than the probability, relative to the data at hand, of the predication ventured; since the legislation of meanings, procedures, and verifications is taken as absolute in the establishment of any probability judgment. This fact holds again despite the developmental nature of thought, since no degree of awareness of the possibilities of the fertility of scientific imagination or of increase in exactitude can challenge the absolutism of the specific cognitive norm requisite to grasping the meaning of a given situation. The normative function of *any cognitive element* constitutes a functional absolute.[19]

The demands for an absolute have been supplied from the heart of the cognitive situation itself. This arrangement will not be acceptable to those who conceive of the norm, its function and its implications, as necessarily nonnaturalistic, as being, that is, by nature insusceptible of scientific analysis. But from the standpoint of the present discussion the

[18] "Methodological Consequences of the Sociology of Knowledge," *American Journal of Sociology*, XLVI (1940), 323.

[19] I am indebted to Professor Margaret Dey, of Vassar College, for the suggestion of this term and for her sympathetic criticism of the entire essay.

logical issue between the naturalistic promotion of the sociology of knowledge and its absolutistic opponents has been settled by the identification of an internal cognitive absolute.

This view of the internal cognitive absolute, consisting in the normative function of all cognitive elements, facilitates the account of the social responsiveness of the order which they institute. And the independence of the norm is not endangered by its social analyzability, since the independence which this discussion has established for the norm is a functional independence, not an analytic ultimacy.

There remains the task of determining the criterion of cognitive value on the part of the cognitive norms themselves. The problem must be articulated, and thus limited, by the commitments of the preceding discussion. The criterion of cognitive value must be such as to take notice of the types of demand to which specific norms are responsive. The interests of this essay have confined examination of the types of demand upon the cognitive norm to three: the establishment of structure within the historical and institutional segmentation of experience, which in turn entails both the responsiveness to empirical reality and (thirdly) the responsiveness to the social state of affairs. Each of these demand types is itself susceptible of division into subtypes, and there are many additional possibilities for demand-types, depending upon the interests of analysis. The only criterion that suggests itself as being at once sufficiently broad to cover this complexity of reference and sufficiently familiar in methodological contexts to seem appropriate is that of adequacy. The principal disadvantage of this term is its association with the limited conception of the demands upon adequacy which is characteristic of pragmatism. The adequacy of a cognitive norm is thus conditional upon the fulfillment of many requirements. It will be noted that the analysis of adequacy is undertaken only with respect to the "responsiveness" aspect of the norm, not to its normative function, which is logical and absolute, insusceptible, while it is sustained, of degrees, emendations, or demands.

There are two misapprehensions of some interest upon which this notion of adequacy as the criterion of cognitive value has bearing. One is the opposition's concern, expressed chiefly by Von Schelting and De Gré, with the presumption of the sociology of knowledge in offering, or in threatening to offer, "truth-value judgments" or "sociological truth concepts." It cannot be denied that there is ground for this concern, most conspicuously in the bold indiscretions of ideology and utopia. Were anyone to maintain seriously that truth is determined exclusively by social phenomena, he would be ridiculous, but no more ridiculous than were he to maintain some more time-honored naïve monism. The mutually exhaustive truisms that truth is determined by mental laws, that truth is determined by independent existence, that truth is determined by society have their correlates in the three types of demand upon cognitive adequacy which have been discriminated above. In contrast to a monism, a demand type has greater sharpness and meaningfulness, precisely because its scope does not exhaust all possible meanings. Thus, it is the specificity of interaction and adjustment of separate demands, mental, existential, and social, which furnishes the key to the understanding of concrete cognitive adequacy. However, the opposition's point is taken, not against a social monism, but against the view that truth is responsive to social demands. In this fashion is betrayed the traditional hypostatization of normative function and the curtailment of positive science which has been examined above.

The second misapprehension is the logical criticism of Mannheim's attempt to establish a particular social group as the criterion (not as the exclusive determinant) of cognitive adequacy. But if the adequacy of a cognitive norm is conditional in part upon its responsiveness to concrete social demands, then it must be granted that the sociologist of knowledge is in a position, through his historical study of cognition, to point out the optimum social conditions for the development of specific types of interest and inquiry.

Then Mannheim's suggestion of a *sozialfreischwebende Intelligenz* as constituting such an optimum condition for the contemporary development of political theory, need raise no question beyond the factual question of its specific soundness.

The meanings of "validity" and "objectivity" have been explored. The compatibility of a naturalistically unrestricted sociological analysis with an absolute cognitive function has been ascertained. There remains a view of the concrete contributions of the sociology of knowledge as a special science. And, finally, some suggestions must be made toward an explanation of the vast and astonishing opposition to the naturalistic extension of the methods of the social sciences to the entire field of knowledge.

III

A naturalist is not one who knowingly substitutes dialectic for empirical inquiry. The sole aim of the present essay has been to remove the alleged logical difficulties which confront the postulate of continuity in connection with the sociology of knowledge. Some implications of the argument remain, however, to be drawn.

Neither a priori confirmation nor a priori repudiation of any specific mode of social responsiveness of cognitive elements is tenable. No logical argument can legitimately reduce the complexity of social responsiveness or render it malleable to treatment by dogma. Society contains many groups and many interests, and these are themselves the products of a historical process. What may be the historical concretion of social, political, or economic demands upon a specific cognitive norm constitutes an empirical problem of varying complexity.

Recognition of the experimental character of social analysis of cognition must be supplemented by the granting of free reign to the development and employment of directional principles. Narrowness in the conception of the possibilities in types of social responsiveness has no logical or methodological grounds. Fortunately, however, advocation of a properly expanded conception of the sociological analysis of knowledge need not descend into mere pious exhortation to increased research—that hallmark of methodology in newly established inquiries. For there already exists a promisingly heterogeneous group of directional principles for the sociology of knowledge, on the basis of which research has made confirmational progress.

Already employed with some degree of success are the following directional norms: the principle of cultural uniqueness, entailing the demonstrable uniqueness of cognition as a culturally responsive phenomenon; the principle of the historical and social continuity between primitive and contemporary forms of thought; the concept of religion as a symbolic formulation of social structure; the concept that the variant of established religion consists in responsiveness to a specific social demand; the principle of the multiple responsiveness, intellectual, social, and political, of technological innovation; the concept of technological innovation as responsiveness to the concrete historical stage of class conflict; the concept that objective political thought is ideally responsive to a particular social class at a particular historical stage of the class conflict; the concept that the fundamental characteristics of thought are responsive to an alternating fixed polarity of epochal social qualities; the concept that canons of logic, basic categories, criteria, and procedures developed historically in connection with the special sciences are responsive to a multiplicity of social demands.

Products of related scientific interests are: the abundant researches into the social responsiveness of language types; the concept of speech itself as the response to a set of concrete evolutionary social demands; the Gestalt principle concerning perception, fructified by the concept of the social responsiveness of specific types of gestalts as the "norms" or "frames of reference" of perceptual knowledge. These are some of the current approaches to the sociological analysis of cognition. The advantages and limitations of each has in most cases yet to be experimentally determined.

Of greater importance is the determination of interrelations among these types of approach, so that the findings concerning social responsiveness on one approach may be related to the findings of another approach either causally or by some predictable mode of correlation. *Rapprochement* between any two types of approach, in the form of a joint directional principle and method, must also, presumably, wait upon the *Zeitgeist* of the social sciences.

The sociology of knowledge will one day systematize all cognitive elements in relation to their social responsiveness. When this occurs, large areas of literary criticism, philosophy, history, psychology, sociology, economics, mathematics, physics, astronomy, and biology will need to be rewritten. For a knowledge of the social responsiveness of the cognitive elements involved cannot fail to revise the conception of their concrete sequence, correlation, and causation, as well as to bring new understanding of the significance of individual norms.

Promotion of the sociology of knowledge is not subsumable under the general heading of anti-intellectualism. The sensational exposé of social determinants of knowledge is not the goal of sociological analysis. That this should be considered as its prime objective, however, is highly significant as characterizing the thought of the opposition. For the presence of so-called "extratheoretical factors" in cognition implies the anti-intellectualistic conclusion that all thought is illusion and all action irrational only on the premise that rationality entails unconditional general immunity from scientific analysis.

Only one legitimate concession need be made to the requirement of a cognitive absolute: the concept of the ultimacy of normative function. The immunization of cognitive elements from positive analysis in any further sense must be viewed either on logical grounds, as a gratuitously involved conception of the requirements of a logical absolute, or on non-logical grounds, as a specific interest in the qualitative uniqueness of a concrete set of cognitive elements.

The modern version of cognitive "purity" which entails, among other remedial measures, the desocialization of scientific meanings by means of exclusively operational definitions, shares with the more venerable versions of purity a disregard of the socio-historical medium. Now, it may readily be granted that the objectivity norm of the special sciences has increasingly refined the means of discriminating between personal idiosyncrasy or "community-centrism" and the phenomenon under examination. But what is thereby achieved is not the desocialization of the concepts employed, but a rigorous account of criteria and modes of procedure—both of which entail the functioning of validity norms susceptible of sociological analysis.

In fact, there is no more promising source of increased discriminatory power for the objectivity norm than the sociology of knowledge. For it brings to self-consciousness the social demands to which scientific methodologies respond. This process of refinement of the objectivity norm is not the simple problem of safeguarding against cultural "infiltrations" or distortions. Beyond "community-centrism," there are the centrisms which constitute the norms of the science and its role within the institutional structure of the society which sustains it. Which centrisms become formulated as self-conscious scientific principles, and which are the targets of the discrimination rules of the objectivity norm, is itself a problem determined by a series of socio-historically responsive cognitive norms.

The attempt to circumvent the cultural, socio-linguistic, or historical responsiveness of cognition by an operational theory of meaning results most successfully in an operational transcription of the forms of procedure established by validity norms. Apart, however, from the directional function of the historically responsive regulative and validity norms, there could be no carefully channelized formal procedure to receive the benefit of operational restatement. Nor could there be "proper" scientific meanings to come to the rescue of rival operational definitions of the "same" scientific terms. Operationism at best is a transcription of established formulae; and at worst, an attempt to direct inquiry.

Cognitive purity at the expense of the extension of the special sciences is untenable, whether it is urged in behalf of a loftier, more "intelligible" realm or in behalf of the events which take place in scientific laboratories. The sociology of knowledge repudiates such cavalier treatment of historical phenomena. Cognitive norms are historical facts, to be noted and, if possible, explained. To attempt to explain them in part by the categories of the social sciences is not to bring on "intellectual chaos." For the norms which sustain and guide thought and action are not created by sociological analysis. Neither can they be destroyed by its fiat. It is a fact of the universe that all cognitive elements are socially responsive—a fact which a new inquiry within the social sciences elects to investigate.

Changes in scientific conceptions have always been a source of embarrassment to the theories which hold that the cognitive absolute consists in something more than historical normative function. The sociological analysis of cognition is able to throw some light upon the phenomenon of change. Sociological analysis never decides the fate of a norm. But sociological analysis of knowledge can in most cases clarify the fate which has befallen a norm or still lies before it. Cognitive adequacy consists, in part, of a response to social demands. The survival value of a cognitive norm is insofar determined by the durability of the concrete social demands to which it responds. Under what circumstances will new social demands eventuate in changed norms? Conversely, under what circumstances will new methodological demands remain unheeded, due to the persistence of the social demands of the norm? These are problems which the sociology of knowledge may be expected to solve.[20] The social responsiveness of no cognitive norm

---

[20] The analysis of social dynamics is a separate inquiry. To equate the determining of causal laws of social structure and change (i.e., the determining of interrelations among the demands on the cognitive norm) with the analysis of the response of the cognitive norm to social demands is to fall into an insidious sociologistic version of the epistemic fallacy, which attributes exclusive truth to the analysis of knowledge. Theories which undertake to formulate the laws of social structure and change are, of course, highly responsive to social demands. It may be of the greatest importance to the self-consciousness of a rational society that the sociology of knowledge reveals the nature of this responsiveness on the part of these crucial theories. But the sociological analysis of social theories must not be conceived as solving the problems which those theories address, i.e., the problems of social causal-

endures unchanged from the time of its inception. However, responsiveness to the more permanent social forms may be presumed to have a proportionately high survival value.

Social situations make their own demands upon inquiry. The demands of a localized or inchoate social disruption may result only in academic dispute and a sense of intellectual conflict and frustration. And a violent social upheaval may destroy many of the cognitive norms and correlated institutions which were responsive to the old social order. This is the significance of the "intellectual chaos" envisioned by the opponents of the sociology of knowledge: it is the threat of social revolution. But the cognitive norm cannot be immunized from the potentiality of change by any "logical" devices providing exemption from sociological analysis. For intellectual chaos is the final socio-historic response of cognition: it is the response to the complete overthrow of a social order. Muzafer Sherif writes:

People cannot eat and drink norms. The norms cannot give life, if nothing else is left in life. But friction may increase to such a pitch that the whole superstructure of norms collapses. . . . We find many illustrations of this as we look at the history of revolutions. The end result is not chaos, but the formation of a new superstructure of norms.

Finally, a word on the implications of theory for practice. The tracing of these implications constitutes an interesting problem for the social scientist: the examination of the effect of knowledge of social responsiveness upon scientific practice.

In innumerable interstices within each field of knowledge there occurs the functioning of cognitive norms worthy of sociological analysis: the selection of certain criteria, the repudiation of others; the decision as to the level of abstraction beyond which analysis is restricted; the conception of what constitutes verification of hypotheses within the field; the disputes concerning the adequacy of entrenched directional principles.

Disputing factions may see the ground of their contention in a new light, as incompatibility of social affiliation, rather than as an ultimate divergence of categories or methods. Intellectual stagnation in a partic-

---

ity. On the contrary, the sociology of knowledge must implement itself with the methods and the findings of the inquiry into social dynamics in order to treat the problem of cognitive survival-value.

ular quarter may be enlightened, if not fructified, by the revelation that its frame of reference is incommensurable with those of other inquiries because it alone continues to be responsive to social demands which are no longer made.[21] And what of the physical sciences, the model upon which epistemological theories are traditionally constructed? What of that Jehovian source of diurnal logico-cabalistic guarantees of similar scientific good fortune? The success of the physical sciences may be due to the social demands which have been made upon them—social demands which may never be duplicated.

Whether the result of such knowledge will be the entrenchment of the *status quo* and its conflicts or the abandonment of certain cognitive norms is determinable by the total social situation which affects the institutions and the personalities involved. Insight into this social situation thus belies opponent Merton's assertion that Mannheim's use of the term "opponent" indicates the inapplicability of his thought to the analysis of science. In science, as distinct from politics, Merton holds, the only "opponent" is ignorance, or the resistance of nature.

But on the assumption that "valid" knowledge is, by definition, devoid of social responsiveness, the discovery that certain cognitive norms are, in fact, socially responsive, will not be conceived to create any problems for the social scientist. The instances of social responsiveness will be regarded as rare departures from the objectivity norm of each specific inquiry. The only problem will be to determine the causes of this departure and to eradicate any vestiges of the identified social responsiveness. Thus, to the inadequacy of its judgment concerning the requirements of a cognitive absolute the opposition to the sociology of knowledge adds the ineptness of proposing to treat social conflicts by methods of theoretical fiat.

The implications which this projected sociological study of knowledge has for naturalism and for the principle of continuity of analysis may now be reviewed. The principle of continuity—the nerve of the naturalistic position—demands that the investigation into all problems in all subject matters employ the methods of the special sciences. Interpreted in terms of the schematism offered above, the principle of continuity is a regulative, or directional, norm for inquiry. The naturalistic

[21] Thus the sociology of knowledge functions, not as some of its opponents fear, to promote the uniqueness of all cognitive endeavors, but to clarify some of the problems which must be treated in any conception of scientific intertranslatability.

principle has the dual character of all cognitive elements. In its normative function it is a functional absolute, an unconditioned "principle" which legislates conditions, stipulates requirements. As the institution of a particular species of order, it is a response to the set of historical demands—of cognitive structure, of independent existential reality, and of society—whose specific interaction constitutes the complex demand for the order which the norm establishes.

The order which is established by the principle of continuity is that of scientific method. This fact must not be assumed to confer upon the naturalistic principle a status different from that of other cognitive norms. Surely the growth of the fields of history of science, social anthropology, and social psychology, which subject to systematic analysis various types of scientific responsiveness, have already cast the gravest suspicion upon the notion of an unconditioned scientific method. Yet an independent scientific method remains the "magic helper" of the greater part of philosophical and methodological literature. "Pickwickianisms," that is, explicit equivocations and simple reaffirmations of ancient philosophical faiths follow immediately upon any publicized increase of insight into social and historical processes. They have a single objective: to construe the methods of the sciences as intrinsically unrelated to such processes.

If the view of the special sciences as socio-historic phenomena has not yet achieved acceptance, it has, however, gained a fairly broad dissemination. But philosophical positions, with the single exception of the political philosophies, have received neither publicity nor acceptance as socio-historic phenomena. In the institutions of higher learning, to hold a philosophical position is to select from the several possibilities the set of tenets which seems best suited to the purposes of dialectical strategy. To engage in philosophical dispute is primarily to attempt to identify in the concrete opposing system the stock series of difficulties and failures to which that type of system is traditionally known to be prey. To write a history of philosophy is to isolate in a pure and uncompounded state, as one would isolate a chemical substance, the tenets crucial, respectively, to the philosophies on a selected list, chronologically arranged, and perhaps discreetly labeled as to weaknesses, "influences," and contrarieties. A given philosophical position thus considered "as such," "logically," "on its own level" is an instance of a special type of cognitive norm. Without a knowledge of the historical demands which call into being and sustain the concrete norm and an awareness of the role of the norm in the new socio-historic situation of which it becomes an element, the analysis, evaluation, and historical study of philosophical positions must remain scholastic.

Only when the materials and techniques for such a rewriting of the history of philosophy are developed will the seriousness and dignity of philosophy be truly apprehended, by professional philosophers as well as by their recalcitrant students and by the cynical lay public. The present argument in behalf of naturalism is therefore not a defense of a "logical" position happily endowed with mysterious powers for solving some basic problems of Western civilization. An adequate account of naturalistic philosophy cannot now be written. It will appear when interest in the formulation of its tenets ceases to be the exclusive interest. There must be a thorough analysis of the demands which gave being to those tenets at a certain stage in history. There must be a study of the forces which produced changes in the conception of those tenets and can account both for the periods of strength and of oblivion of naturalism. And there must be an examination of the significance of naturalism as a factor in the socio-historic situations in which it has been present.

The tenacity of the opposition to an unrestricted sociology of knowledge and, more generally, to the naturalistic principle, must thus in the end be analyzed on grounds other than the logical ones which have been offered above. Such an analysis falls within the field of sociology of knowledge and cannot be attempted within the scope of the present discussion. Certain elementary observations may, however, be made. The univocal opposition to the extension *quam maximum* of a concrete scientific method must sustain examination in terms of the advantages which such restrictions may be conceived to give the opposition. These advantages may be presumed to be of two general types. First, the preservation from challenge or disruption of those cognitive norms which are responsive to the social demands of the group to which the opposition belong or with which they choose to affiliate themselves. Second, the preclusion of the occupational disadvantages deriving from a revision of many phases of their line of endeavor which would require a species of imaginative insight, a locus of information, and a technical skill which they do not possess. In turn, the desire of the naturalist that the special sciences be advanced without compromise in any connection indicates a dominating devotion to development and progress which may, upon analysis, be revealed as responsive to the social demands of the groups in greatest need of social change.

It follows that in the contemporary historical situation the present discussion can do no more. It has met the opposition on logical grounds. It has presented the possibility of a naturalistically unrestricted socio-logical analysis of all cognitive norms, providing for a rigorous cognitive absolute without compromise of either logical or scientific integrity. The general development of sociology of knowledge, especially in con-junction with other modes of inquiry, may be expected to constitute a far more serious strain upon the staying powers of the opposition than can discussions, such as the present one, upon the logical and method-ological level. Too simplistic a conception of the issues involved cannot fail to produce in the sociologist of knowledge and in the sympathetic naturalist a sense of futility and discouragement. On the broader view, they will perform their chosen tasks and commit the conflict into the hands of the socio-historic future.

I0

LOGIC WITHOUT ONTOLOGY

Ernest Nagel

THE fact that the world we inhabit exhibits periodicities and regularities has been frequently celebrated by poets, philosophers, and men of affairs. That frost will destroy a fruit crop, that a convex lens will concentrate the heat of the sun, or that populations tend to increase toward a fixed maximum, are typical of the uniformities discoverable in innumerable sectors of the physical and social environment; and however we may formulate such uniformities, no philosophy which construes them as anything else than discoveries will conform with the long experience of mankind. Every form of naturalism, to whatever extent it may emphasize the impermanence of many of these regularities or note the selective human activities involved in discovering them, will recognize them as basic features of the world; and even when it attempts to account for them, it will do so only by exhibiting a more pervasive, if more subtle, pattern in the behavior of bodies.

Nevertheless, no demonstrable ground has yet been found which can guarantee that such regularities will continue indefinitely or that the propositions asserting them are necessary. If, as many philosophers have maintained, the proper objects of scientific knowledge are principles capable of a priori validation, both the history of science and the analysis of its methods supply ample evidence to show that no science of nature has ever achieved what is thus proclaimed as its true objective. There are, indeed, relatively few practicing scientists today who place any credence in arguments claiming to prove that any principle about an identifiable subject matter is at once logically necessary and empirical in content.

No such general agreement can be found, even among lifelong students of the subject, concerning the status of various logical and mathematical principles constantly employed in responsible inquiries. Indeed, it is difficult to ascertain which natural structures, if any, such propositions express; and it is often no less difficult to exhibit clearly and without self-deception the grounds upon which they are acknowledged. In any event, many of the sharp divisions between professed naturalists are centered around the different interpretations which they assign to principles as familiar as the so-called "laws of thought," the basic assumptions of arithmetic or the axioms of geometry. Thus, one classical form of naturalism maintains, for example, that the principle of noncontradiction is a necessary truth which is descriptive of the limiting structure of everything both actual and possible; another form of naturalism holds this principle to be a contingent, but highly reliable, conclusion based on an empirical study of nature; and a third type of naturalism takes this principle to be void of factual content and an arbitrary specification for the construction of symbolic systems. Analogous differences among naturalists occur in their interpretation of more complicated and recondite mathematical notions.

Such disagreements among those professing naturalism is not a source of embarassment to them, since naturalism is not a tightly integrated system of philosophy; perhaps the sole bond uniting all varieties of naturalists is that temper of mind which seeks to understand the flux of events in terms of the behaviors of identifiable bodies. Nevertheless, a naturalistic philosophy must be consistent with its own assumptions. If it professes to accept the methods employed by the various empirical sciences for obtaining knowledge about the world, it cannot with consistency claim to have a priori insight into the most pervasive structure of things. If it aims to give a coherent and adequate account of the various principles employed in acquiring scientific knowledge, it cannot maintain that all of them are empirical generalizations when some are not subject to experimental refutation. And if it admits that logical principles have a recognizable function in certain contexts (namely, in inquiry), it cannot consistently hold those principles to be completely arbitrary simply on the ground that they are void of factual content when considered apart from those contexts.

No one seriously doubts that logic and mathematics are used in specific contexts in identifiable ways, however difficult it may be to ascertain those ways in any detail. Does it not therefore seem reasonable to attempt to understand the significance of logico-mathematical concepts and principles in terms of the operations associated with them in those contexts and to reject interpretations of their "ultimate meaning" which appear gratuitous and irrelevant in the light of such an analysis? Such, at any rate, is the point of view of the present essay. In what follows, the difficulties and futilities of some nonoperational interpretations of logical principles will first be noted; the limitations of certain naturalistic but narrowly empirical approaches to logic will then be discussed; and finally, an operational interpretation of a small number of logical and mathematical notions will be sketched. However, and this is perhaps the common fate of essays such as the present one, no more than the outline of an argument will be found in the sequel. The present essay contributes no unfamiliar analyses. Its sole objective is to make plausible the view that the role of the logico-mathematical disciplines in inquiry can be clarified without requiring the invention of a hypostatic subject matter for them; and to suggest that a naturalism free from speculative vagaries and committed to a thoroughgoing operational standpoint expresses the temper of modern mathematico-experimental science.

I

1. Among the principles which Aristotle believed "hold good for everything that is" and therefore belong to the science of being qua being, he counted certain axioms of logic. These principles, according to him, were to be asserted as necessary truths and were not to be maintained as hypotheses, since "a principle which every one must have who knows anything about being is not a hypothesis." One such principle is that "the same attribute cannot at the same time belong and not belong to the same subject in the same respect."

Aristotle's formulation of the principle contains the qualification "in the same respect." This qualification is important, for it makes possible the defense of the principle against all objections. For suppose one were to deny the principle on the ground that an object, a penny for example, is both sensibly circular in shape and sensibly noncircular. The standard reply to this alleged counterexample is that the penny is circular when viewed from a direction perpendicular to its face and noncircular when viewed from a direction inclined to the face, and that since the different shapes do not occur "in the same respect" the principle has not been invalidated. But if one were now to ask for an unequivocal specification, antecedent to applying the principle, of a definite "same respect" with regard to the penny, so that the principle might then be subjected to a clear-cut test, a skillful defender of the principle as an ontological truth would refuse to supply the desired stipulation. For he would recognize that if a "respect" is first specified, it is always possible to find within that respect a way of apparently violating the principle.

For example, suppose a "same respect" is specified as viewing the penny from a direction perpendicular to its face. The penny will, nevertheless, subtend an angle of thirty degrees and also an angle of sixty degrees. To this, the obvious and proper retort is: "But not at the same distance from the face of the penny." Nevertheless, the principle is saved only by a new restriction upon what is to be understood by "the same respect"; the defender of the principle has altered his *initial* specification of what is the *same* respect. It is, of course, possible, when an attribute is suitably specified, to discover a set of conditions under which a thing does not both have and not have that attribute. The crucial point is that in specifying both the attribute and the conditions, *the principle is employed as a criterion* for deciding whether the specification of the attribute is suitable and whether those conditions are in fact sufficiently determinate. Because of the manner in which the qualification "the same respect" is used, the principle cannot be put to a genuine test, since no proposed case for testing the principle will be judged as admissible which violates the principle to be tested. In brief, conformity to the principle is the condition for a respect being "the same respect."[1]

Analogous comments are relevant for the phrases "same attribute," "belong," and "not belong," which are contained in Aristotle's formulation of the principle. For example, how is one to tell in a disputed instance of the principle whether an attribute is "the same" or not? If someone were to maintain that a penny has a diameter of $1\frac{1}{16}$ of an inch and also a diameter of $1\frac{2}{16}$ of an inch, he would be told that the assertion is impossible, because even though the attributes are not "the same," in predicating the former one implicitly excludes the latter; and he would, perhaps, be asked whether the measurements were carefully made, whether the same system of units was really employed, and so forth. In

---

[1] The point at issue involves noting the difference between the following two statements: "However an attribute is selected, it is possible to find a respect such that a given attribute does not at the same time belong and not belong to a given subject in that respect," and "It is possible to find a respect such that, however an attribute is selected, the given attribute does not at the same time belong and not belong to a given subject in that respect." The hypothetical defender of the principle can successfully maintain the first, though not the second, because he undertakes to specify the "sameness" of respects only after he has selected an attribute —that is, after the principle is used to determine a respect, which will thus automatically satisfy the principle.

short, since the assertion in effect maintains "the same attribute" to belong and also not to belong to the same subject, it is absurd. But let us press the question why, if the penny has the first of these attributes, it cannot have the other. The impossibility is not simply an empirical one, which rests on inductive arguments; for if it were, the supposition would not be absurd, contrary to the hypothesis, that an unexpected observation may one day discover the penny's diameter to have both dimensions. The impossibility arises from the fact that we use the expressions "length of $1\frac{1}{16}$ inches" and "length of $1\frac{2}{16}$ inches" in such a way—in part because of the manner in which they may have been defined in relation to one another—that each formulates a different outcome of measurement. We may be sure that no penny will ever turn up with a diameter having both dimensions, because what it means for the diameter to have one of the attributes of dimension is specified in terms of the absence of the other attribute. The principle of contradiction is impregnable against attack, because the "sameness" and the "difference" of attributes are specified in terms of the conformity of attributes to the principle.

Accordingly, the interpretation of the principle as an ontological truth neglects its function as a norm or regulative principle for introducing distinctions and for instituting appropriate linguistic usage. To maintain that the principle is descriptive of the structure of antecedently determinate "facts" or "attributes" is to convert the outcome of employing the principle into a condition of its employment. The Aristotelian view is thus a gratuitous and irrelevant interpretation of one function of this logical law.

2. More recent advocates of an ontological interpretation of logical principles argue their claim in terms of the conception of logical relations as invariants of all possible worlds—a conception also sponsored by Leibnitz. "Pure logic and pure mathematics," according to an influential proponent of this view, "aims at being true in all possible worlds, not only in this higgledy-piggledy job-lot of a world in which chance has imprisoned us." Reason, according to this interpretation, is an investigation into the very heart and immutable essence of all things actual and possible: "Mathematics takes us into the region of absolute necessity, to which not only the actual world but every possible world must conform." As another version puts it, logic is the most general of all the sciences: "Rules of logic are the rules of operation or trans-

formation according to which all possible objects, physical, psycho-logical, neutral, or complexes can be combined. Thus, logic is an ex-ploration of the field of most general abstract possibility." According to this view, then, logical principles are "principles of being," as well as "principles of inference"; they formulate the most general nature of things, they are universally applicable, and they express the limiting and necessary structure of all existence.

Two issues raised by these brief citations from contemporary litera-ture require comment.

a) When logical principles are asserted to hold for "all possible worlds," what is to be understood by the adjective "possible"? The crux of the matter lies in ascertaining whether "possible worlds" can be specified without using the principles of logic as the *exclusive* means of specification. For if a "possible world" is one whose sole identifiable trait is its conformity to the principles of logic, the view under con-sideration asserts no more than this: the subject matter of logical prin-ciples is whatever conforms to them. In that case no "possible world" could fail to satisfy the principles of logic, since anything which failed to do so would not, by hypothesis, be a possible world.

The point involved is so fundamental that it is desirable to illustrate it in another way. Consider any abstract set of postulates *E*, for example, Hilbert's postulates for Euclidean geometry, contained the *uninter-preted* terms *P, L,* and *N.* It is clearly not significant to ask whether *E* is true as long as these terms have this character. But physical experi-ments become relevant for deciding the truth or falsity of *E* if, for example, *L* is used to denote the paths of light-rays, *P* the intersections of two such paths, and *N* the surfaces determined in another way by any two intersecting paths. Nevertheless, an experimental inquiry can be undertaken only if the paths of light-rays can be identified in some manner *other* than by the sole requirement that light-rays are things satisfying the formal demands contained in *E.* For if a different method for identifying light-rays did not exist, it would not be possible to as-certain whether a particular physical configuration is such a path with-out first establishing that the configuration conforms to the implicit specifications of *E*—that is, without first ascertaining the truth of *E* for that configuration. Accordingly, since by definition nothing could be a path of a light-ray which did not satisfy *E,* the question whether *E* is true of all paths of light-rays would not be a matter to be settled by experiment.[2] It is evident, therefore, that if the question of the truth of a set of principles is to be a factual or experimental issue, their subject matter must be identifiable in terms of some other characteristic than that it satisfies those principles.

Let us apply these considerations to the formula: "Not both *P* and non-*P*." If it is simply a formula in some uninterpreted symbolic system, the question whether the formula is true in "all possible worlds" cannot arise. On the other hand, if its constituent symbols are interpreted in some manner, great care must be used in deriving further conclusions from the fact that on one such interpretation the formula expresses a "necessary truth." Thus, suppose that the letter "*p*" is taken to denote any "proposition" and that the other expressions in the formula are assigned their usual meanings; the formula will then express the principle of noncontradiction. But either there is some way of identifying propositions other than by the criterion that anything is a proposition which satisfies the formula, or there is not. On the first alternative, the assertion that the formula holds for all propositions will be a statement strictly analogous to general hypotheses in the empirical sciences; the evidence for the assertion, considerable though it may be, will be only partially complete, and in any case there will be no reason to regard the formula as expressing a necessary truth. On the second alternative, the assertion will be an implicit definition of what a proposition is; the principle of noncontradiction will be a necessary truth, since nothing could be a proposition which does not conform to it.[3]

The view that logic is the science of all possible worlds thus suffers from a fundamental ambiguity. If the only way of identifying a "possible world" is on the basis of its conformity to the canons of logic, logic is indeed the science of all possible worlds. But the view is then no more than a misleading formulation of the fact that logical principles are

---

[2] Of course, the question whether *a particular physical configuration* is the path of a light-ray (that is, whether it satisfies *E*) would remain an experimental issue.

[3] This discussion is obviously oversimplified. Thus, if the formula is a logical consequence of some set of axioms which are used as implicit definitions for propositions, then the principle of noncontradiction will be a necessary truth even though it now falls under the first of the above two alternatives. However, the point of the discussion is not affected by the neglect of such complications. In the present essay the word "proposition" is used loosely, and is frequently employed interchangeably with the word "statement." It is, of course, important in many contexts to distinguish between a proposition and a statement, since the former is often taken to be the "meaning" of the latter. However, the issues under discussion are fairly neutral with respect to the different views which are current concerning what propositions are so that no serious confusions need arise from the loose use of the word.

employed as stipulations or postulates, which define what we understand by the consistency of discourse.

b) The second point requiring comment bears on the view that logical principles express the limiting and necessary structures of all things. If the domain of application of logical principles is identified on the basis of the actual use to which those principles are put, this view cannot be construed literally. For it is not things and their actual relations which are said to be logically consistent or inconsistent with one another, but propositions or statements about them; and it is to the latter that principles such as the principle of noncontradiction are relevant. No one will hesitate to acknowledge that "The table on which I am now writing is brown" and "The table on which I am now writing is white" are mutually inconsistent statements. But this inconsistency cannot, according to the view under discussion, be predicated of two "facts," "states of affairs," or "objects"; for if there were such facts the view would be self-refuting. Accordingly, inconsistency is something which can be located only in discourse, among statements, not among things in general. And if so much is admitted, an obvious dialectic requires that consistency be localized in a similar domain, in discourse and among statements.

But dialectic aside and bearing in mind only the identifiable functions of logical principles, there is no obvious warrant for the claim that the latter are the rules in accordance with which all possible objects can be transformed or combined. Certainly they are not rules of operation upon things in any familiar or literal sense of "transformation of things"—unless, indeed, the things said to be transformed and combined are elements of discourse, constellations of signs of varying degrees of complexity. The "pervasive traits" and "limiting structures" of all "possible worlds" which logic is alleged to formulate thus appear to be traits of discourse when it has been ordered in a certain way. The interpretation of logical principles as ontological invariants seems therefore, on closer view, to be an extraneous ornamentation upon the functions they actually exercise. But the regulative role of logical principles, suggested by the foregoing discussion, will be exhibited more clearly in the sequel.

II

Empirically minded naturalists, convinced that propositions concerning matters of fact must be supported by sensory observation, but convinced also that logical principles have factual content, have not had an easy time in accounting for the apparent universality and necessity of these principles. The interpretation of logical principles widely accepted by both traditional and contemporary empiricists is that they are hypotheses about traits of minds and things, based on inductive arguments from experience.

I readily admit [Mill declared] that these three general propositions [the Laws of Thought] are universally true of all phenomena. I also admit that if there are any inherent necessities of thought, these are such. . . . Whether the three so-called Fundamental Laws are laws of our thoughts by the native structure of the mind, or merely because we perceive them to be universally true of observed phenomena, I will not positively decide: but they are laws of our thoughts now, and invincibly so.

More recent writers concerned with defending an empirical philosophy, though they may reject Mill's psychological atomism and sensationalism, frequently do not differ from him on the view that logical principles are inductive truths. The following is a sufficiently forthright contemporary statement of this conception.

Logical validity is grounded on *natural* fact. . . . When we are in doubt as to the logical validity of an argument, there is only one test. If the class of such arguments gives us materially true conclusions from materially true premises, it is valid, if not, it is invalid. . . . The crucial question which this frankly empirical approach to logic must face is whether it can explain the formal characters of logical inference. The experimental hypothesis attempts the explanation by showing that those inferential procedures which have brought knowledge in the past exhibit a certain invariant *order* whose metaphysical correlate is to be sought in the *serial* characters of existence. . . . The laws of logic . . . cannot be disproved, but they may become inapplicable and meaningless. We can say nothing about the *probability* of this being so, but we can just conceive of the possibility that the so-called *apriori* laws of logic may not enable us to organize our experience. That is why they are not formal or empty. That is why they tell us something about the *actual* world. That is why we can say that every additional application of logic to existence is an experimental verification of its invariance.

However attractive such an interpretation of logical principles may appear to a consistent empirical naturalism—to a philosophy which appreciates the limitations natural structures place upon our thought and action, but which nevertheless finds no warrant for the assertion that a priori knowledge of such structures is possible—there are insuperable difficulties involved in it. These difficulties arise in the main because those who profess such an interpretation misconceive the character of empirical or scientific method.

1. Little need be said in refutation of the view that logical principles formulate the "inherent necessities of thought" and are generalized descriptions of the operations of minds. Surely the actual occurrence in the same person of beliefs in logically incompatible propositions makes nonsense of the claim that the principle of noncontradiction expresses a universal fact of psychology. Moreover, if logical principles were true descriptions of anthropological behavior, they would be contingent truths, refutable on evidence drawn from the observation of human behavior; but in that case, the necessity which is so generally attributed to logical principles, however much this may be disguised by calling their contradictories "unbelievable," would be left unexplained.

2. The view under consideration maintains that the validity of a type of inference sanctioned by logic can be established only by presenting empirical evidence to show that an inference of that form always leads from materially true premises to materially true conclusions. It must be admitted, of course, that a valid inference is often defined as one which invariably yields true conclusions from true premises. But it by no means follows that an inference ever is or can be established as valid in the manner proposed. Suppose, for example, "*A*" and "If *A* then *B*" are asserted as true statements (the expression "if . . . then" being used in some one of the customary ways), so that the conclusion that "*B*" is true may be drawn in accordance with the familiar rule of *ponendo ponens*. Let us now imagine that as a matter of fact "*B*" is false and that we are therefore urged by someone to abandon the rule as a universal logical principle. Would not such a suggestion be dismissed as grotesque and as resting upon some misunderstanding? Would we not retort that in the case supposed "*A*" or "If *A* then *B*" must have been asserted as true mistakenly or that if this is no mistake then the assertion of the falsity of "*B*" must be an error? Would we not, in any event, maintain that statements of the form: "If *A* and (if *A* then *B*) then *B*" are necessarily true, since not to acknowledge them as such is to run counter to the established usage of the expressions "and" and "if . . . then"?

Proponents of the view under discussion often declare that in interpreting logical principles as empirical hypotheses they are offering a justification for logic in terms of the procedures and standards of adequacy employed in the most advanced natural sciences. It is worth noting, therefore, that not a single instance can be cited from the history of science which would support the conception that the validity of logical principles is ever established by the suggested method. Is it not significant that whenever consequences derived from premises believed to be true are in disagreement with the facts of experimental observation, it is not the logical principles in accordance with which those consequences were drawn that are rejected as experimentally unwarranted? Indeed, it is not apparent how the suggested method for establishing the validity of logical principles could operate in any typical inquiry. For the truth of most premises employed in the sciences cannot be established except on the basis of an investigation of the consequences which are drawn from them—drawn in accordance with and with the help of logical principles. For example, the principles of Newtonian mechanics, which constitute part of the premises in many physical inquiries, cannot be established as adequate to their subject matter unless it is first discovered what these principles imply. This will be even more obvious if we note that these premises employ such complex notions as differential coefficients, real numbers, and point masses; the premises cannot be construed as "descriptions" of matters of fact accessible to a direct observation, that is, as statements whose truth or falsity may be settled prior to examining their logical consequences. The proposed method for establishing the validity of arguments is thus clearly not a feasible one, since no experimental control can be instituted for determining the alleged material truth of logical principles.

It follows that no "metaphysical correlate" to logical principles need be sought in the "serial character of existence." And if logical principles do not function as contingent hypotheses about matters of fact, if they are not to be established inductively on the ground of their conformity to "certain structural and functional invariants of nature," there is no clear sense in which "every additional application of logic to existence is an experimental verification of its invariance." Logical principles are compatible with any order which the flux of events may exhibit; they could not be in disagreement with anything which inquiry may disclose, and if they should ever require revision, the grounds for such alterations must lie elsewhere than in the subject matter of the natural sciences. To be sure, should the cosmos become a chaos to the extent of making the continued existence of reflective thought impossible, the use of logical principles would thereby also become impossible. But as the above discussion indicates, the continued employment of those principles is not contingent upon the invariance of structures other than those which sustain the continuance of reflective inquiry.

3. In spite of its profession of allegiance to scientific methods as the canonical techniques of competent inquiry, the empiricistic interpretation of logic is based upon an inadequate conception of what is involved in those methods. Indeed, even when, as has already been noted, those subscribing to this interpretation explicitly reject Mill's psychological atomism, they do not always successfully free themselves from his oversimple views on the formation of scientific concepts. Two closely related points require brief discussion in this connection: the narrow criterion of meaningful discourse which is explicitly or tacitly assumed by many empirical naturalists; and the inadequate conception which they hold of the role of symbolic constructions in the conduct of inquiry.

a) It has often been maintained that the theoretical sciences deem to be ultimately meaningful only the statements which either formulate directly observable relations of qualities and things or can be translated without remainder into statements that do so. According to another version of this thesis, every meaningful statement must consist of terms which either denote simple, directly experienceable qualities and relations or are compounded out of terms denoting such simples. Even false hypotheses, so it has been urged on occasion, are meaningful only because they formulate the structure of some actual observable situation—a structure which happens to be wrongly attributed to a given situation. Since the familiar logical and mathematical principles seem so obviously significant, and since in their usual formulation they are ostensibly about the relations which properties of things bear to one another, the interpretation of these principles as empirical hypotheses is sometimes deduced as a corollary from this general view.

Little need be said to show the inadequacy of the suggested criterion of meaning. If it were applied consistently, most of the theories employed in the various positive sciences would have to be dismissed as in fact meaningless; and indeed, those who have accepted the criterion have been consistent enough to exclude almost all general statements as not expressing "genuine propositions." For in the first place, to the extent that theoretical propositions have the form of unrestricted universals, they do not formulate the explicit outcome of any actual series of direct observations. And in the second place, many theoretical statements contain terms (such as "point-particle," "light-wave," "electron," "gene," and the like) which denote nothing that can be directly observed and cannot be construed as being explicitly definable with the help of only such terms as do so. Moreover, there is surely no evidence for the claim that for every false hypothesis there is a situation for which it is true.[4] It is clear that underlying the suggested criterion of meaningful discourse is an ill-concealed reproductive psychology of abstraction and that in any case those who employ it cannot do justice to the actual procedures of the sciences.

A naturalism which is based on modern scientific methods cannot afford to propose illiberal restrictions upon inquiry. It must recognize that no formula can be constructed which will express once for all "*the meaning*" of any portion of scientific discourse. Instead of attempting to construct such formulae, it must turn seriously to the analysis of specific uses and functions of specific systems of expressions in specific contexts. It will have to note that statements in scientific discourse always occur as elements in a system of symbols and operations, and it will therefore attempt to understand the significance of statements in terms of the complicated uses to which they are subject. It will, accordingly, not assume dogmatically that the directly observed qualities and relations of the explicit subject matter of a science must constitute the sole and ultimate reference of every significant complex of its symbols. It will surely recognize that according to standard scientific procedure evidence taken from sensory observation must be relevant to propositions alleged to be about matters of fact: such propositions must entail consequences, obtained by logical operations in determinate ways, which can be experimentally tested when the appropriate circumstances occur. It will thus accept the pragmatic maxim that there is no difference between the objects of beliefs and conceptions where there is no possible difference in observable behavior. But it will not, therefore, insist that all significant statements must be descriptive of what can be directly

---

[4] For example, within the framework of the Newtonian analysis of motion, an indefinite number of false hypotheses for gravitational attraction can be constructed, since a false theory of gravitation is obtained if the exponent "2" in Newton's formula is replaced by a different numeral. Are these different theories to be dismissed as meaningless because there do not happen to exist an infinity of situations for which these theories are true?

observed. And it will remain sensitive to the possibility that even statements about the explicit subject matter of a science may involve a reference to the operations (overt and symbolic) performed in inquiries into that subject matter.

b) Nowhere is the systematic undervaluation of the constructive function of thought in inquiry more glaring than in the widespread neglect of the role played by symbolic manipulations in scientific procedure. The more comprehensive and integrated a theoretical system is, the more obvious does the need for such manipulations appear. For especially in the theories of modern science symbols usually occur which refer to nothing that can be directly experienced; and the significance for matters of direct experience of the conceptual constructions which enter into those theories cannot be made explicit except with the help of extensive symbolic transformations. Accordingly, no statement detached from the symbolic system to which it is integral can be evaluated for its empirical validity; and no isolated concept can be judged as warranted on the basis of the essentially irrelevant criterion of pictorial suggestiveness. But since calculation or symbolic manipulation thus acquires an indispensable though intermediary role in inquiry, the need for reliable techniques of constructing and expanding symbolic systems becomes progressively more pressing; the institution of an entire department of investigation devoted to the formal study of symbolic systems is the practically inevitable consequence.

It is a common and tempting assumption that in performing a chain of calculations one is at the same time tracing out the existential connections between things, so that the formal pattern of symbolic transformations reproduces in some manner the structure of the subject matter under investigation. However, the specific mode in which theories are constructed and bodies of knowledge are integrated is only partially determined by experimental findings. Various norms or ideals —such as the desire for a certain degree of precision, for intellectual economy and notational convenience, or for a certain type of comprehensiveness—also control the direction of inquiry and the articulation of theories. Many symbolic constructions and operations are therefore indices of the standards regulating the course of systematic investigations, and are not merely indications of the expected conclusions of experiment or of the intrinsic relations between phases of subject matter. A myopic concern with the sensory warrants for scientific findings—such as often characterizes traditional empiricism—easily leads to neglect of this aspect of systematic scientific formulations; the traits of discourse are then identified as traits of subject matter,[5] and principles whose function it is to institute a desired order into inquiry are not distinguished from statements about the explicit subject matter of inquiry. When the identification is made, the construction of symbolic systems (including the use of hypotheses) is in effect viewed as an inessential scaffolding for attaining some form of intuitive knowledge. When the distinction is not made, logical principles are in effect deprived of their identifiable functions.

III

The preceding discussion has, in the main, been negative. There remains the task of making explicit the suggestions it contains concerning an alternative interpretation of some logical and mathematical notions. Nothing like a systematic account of logic and mathematics can be attempted, and only a small number of logical principles and mathematical terms will be briefly examined. But even such an examination may exhibit the fruitfulness of an operational analysis of formal concepts and may make plausible the view that the content of the formal disciplines has a regulative function in inquiry.

1. Although logic is one of the oldest intellectual disciplines, considerable difference of opinion exists as to the scope of logical theory and as to which concepts and principles properly belong to logic. The present discussion will be confined to such admittedly formal principles as the so-called laws of thought and other "necessary truths" and to principles of inference such as the principle of *ponendo ponens*. The discussion will be facilitated if at the outset two senses are distinguished in which logical principles are commonly asserted: as principles which are

[5] An example of such a transference is found in the claim that, because the consistency of a set of formal postulates is established by exhibiting a group of related objects—a so-called "concrete model"—satisfying those postulates, logical traits (such as consistency) must represent pervasive ontological or empirical invariants. In point of fact, however, not only can some postulate sets be established without recourse to empirical facts in the indicated manner; most postulate systems cannot be shown to be consistent by genuinely empirical methods. But what is perhaps more to the point, this argument for identifying logical with existential properties fails to observe that consistency is demanded of symbolic systems as part of an ideal for the organization of statements and is not a trait subsisting in nature independently of symbolic formulations.

explicitly about symbolism or language; and as necessary truths whose ostensible subject matter is usually some nonlinguistic realm.[6]

a) The three laws of thought are employed in the first sense in cases something like the following. Suppose that in a bit of reasoned discourse the term "animal" occurs several times. The argument will clearly be a cogent one only if in each of its occurrences the word retains a fixed "meaning"—that is, only if it is used as a name for the same kind of object. The requirement that in a given context a term must continue to be used in essentially the same manner, is expressed as the principle of identity. Analogously, the principle of noncontradiction requires that in a given context a term must not be applied to a given thing and also denied to it; and the principle of excluded middle is formulated in a corresponding way.

When stated in this manner, these principles are obviously *prescriptive* for the use of language, and as such are not *descriptive* of actual usage. They specify minimal conditions for discourse without confusion, for they state at least some of the requirements for a precise language. Everyday language, and to some extent even the specialized languages of the sciences, are vague in some measure, so that they do not entirely conform to the requirement set by these principles.[7] Although fairly effective communication is nevertheless possible in connection with many pursuits, situations do arise in which a greater precision in the use of language is required. The laws of thought thus formulate an ideal to be achieved—an ideal which is capable of being attained at least approximately—and they indicate the direction in which the maximum of desired precision may be obtained.

Few will deny that the laws of thought as here formulated have a regulative function. Nevertheless, the admission is often qualified by the claim that if the ideal these laws formulate is a reasonable one, not an arbitrary norm, there must be an objective ground—a "structural invariant"—which lends them authority. Moreover, it is sometimes urged that this ideal must be a necessary and inescapable one, since otherwise a genuine alternative to it would be possible; however, com-

---

[6] This distinction roughly corresponds to the difference noted in much current literature between "meta-logical" statements and statements in the "object-language" of a science.

[7] Thus if the term "red" is vague, there is a class of colors concerning which it is indeterminate whether the term applies to them or not, so that the principle of excluded middle fails in this case.

munication would be impossible if language were so employed as to conform, for example, to the denial of the principle of identity. But this latter argument for the intrinsic necessity of these principles is surely circular. For if by "communication" is understood processes similar to those in which we are familiarly engaged when talking, writing, or carrying on research—processes which illustrate the use of symbols in at least partial conformity to the laws of thought—communication would indeed be impossible were the requirements set by these laws satisfied in no degree; but communication would not be possible simply because these laws are analytic of what is understood by the word "communication." Whatever might be the human needs which communication satisfies, the desire to communicate and the desire to enforce the ideal specified by the laws are directed toward the same end. It must, nevertheless, be acknowledged that the ideal of precision in using language is not an arbitrary one. It is not arbitrary, because communication and inquiry are directed to the achievement of certain objectives, and these objectives are best attained when language is employed in a manner approximating as closely as possible the norms expressed by the laws of thought. The assertion that this is so requires support by empirical evidence—evidence which it is possible to produce. But the available evidence is drawn from the study of the behavior of men engaged in inquiry; it does not come from a consideration of structural invariants found in other domains.

The three laws of thought are, however, not the only principles of logic explicitly dealing with symbolism, and some consideration must now be given to that important class of principles known as rules of inference—of which the rule of *ponendo ponens* is, perhaps, the most familiar. The first point to note in connection with such principles is that it is possible to specify accurately what rules govern the valid inferences in a language, only when the "meanings" of certain terms in that language are precise—that is, when terms like "and," "or," and "if—then" are used in determinate ways. In fact, however, the ordinary usage of such terms is vague and unclear. Everyday language, in the main, is employed according to routine habits which are fixed and stable over a narrow range, but which are indeterminate in many crucial cases; accordingly, inferences are drawn and sanctioned on the basis of crude intuitive considerations as to what is "really meant" by the terms involved.[8] The explicit formulation of canons of inference serves to clarify vague intent; and what is, perhaps, less commonly recognized, such formulations help to fix usages when they have previously been unsettled: they serve as proposals for modifying old usages and instituting new ones.

The various modern systems of formal logic must, accordingly, be viewed, not as accounts of the "true nature" of an antecedently identifiable relation of "implication," but as alternative proposals for specifying usages and for performing inferences. The adoption of a system such as is found in Whitehead and Russell's *Principia Mathematica* is in effect the adoption of a set of regulative principles for developing more inclusive and determinate habits for using language than are illustrated in everyday discourse. No known recent system of formal logic is or can be just a faithful transcription of those inferential canons which are embodied in common discourse, though in the construction of these systems hints may be taken from current usage; for the entire *raison d'être* for such systems is the need for precision and inclusiveness where common discourse is vague and incomplete, even if as a consequence their adoption as regulative principles involves a modification of our inferential habits.

The question naturally arises whether the conventions which explicitly formulated rules of inference institute are entirely arbitrary —whether, in other words, the adoption of one set of regulative principles for reconstructing linguistic behavior is as "justifiable" as the adoption of a different set. The issue raised does not refer to the construction of various abstract "uninterpreted" symbolic calculi, for which diverging rules of "inference" or "transformation" may be developed; for it is usually admitted that the arbitrariness of such abstract systems can be limited only by the formal requirements of symbolic construction. The issue refers to the ground upon which one system of

---

[8] For example, everyone who has an elementary knowledge of English would agree that the rule of *ponendo ponens* is a correct canon of inference. On the other hand, a person unsophisticated by training in formal logic and not committed to one of the modern logical systems, may hesitate to accept the rule that a statement of the form "Either A or B" is a consequence of "A," where "A" and "B" are any statements; and he will probably seriously doubt the correctness of the rule that "If A then (if B then C)" follows from "If A and B, then C," where "A," "B," and "C" are any statements. The hesitation and the doubt must be attributed to the fact that "or," "and," and "if—then" are frequently used ambiguously and have fairly clear and determinate meanings only in relatively few contexts.

regulative principles is to be preferred to another system, when such principles are to be employed in the conduct of scientific inquiry. But this manner of putting the question suggests its own answer. If everyday language requires completion and reorganization for the sake of attaining the ends of inquiry, the "justification" for a proposed set of regulative principles will not be arbitrary and can be given only in terms of the adequacy of the proposed changes as means or instruments for attaining the envisaged ends. Thus, if inquiry is directed toward achieving a system of physics which will be coherent, comprehensive, and economical in its use of certain types of assumption and operation, one set of canons for inference will be preferable to another if the former leads to a closer approximation to this goal than does the latter. The choice between alternative systems of regulative principles will then not be arbitrary and will have an objective basis; the choice will not, however, be grounded on the allegedly greater inherent necessity of one system of logic over another, but on the relatively greater adequacy of one of them as an instrument for achieving a certain systematization of knowledge.[9]

It is needless to dwell further on the function of rules of inference: their primary role is to guide the development of discourse in a certain direction, namely, in the deduction of the consequences of sets of statements; they thereby contribute to making the use of language more determinate and precise and to attaining the goals of specific inquiries. It must be admitted, however, that it is frequently difficult to exhibit adequate evidence for the superior efficacy of one type of inferential system over another, especially when the specific goals of inquiry are themselves vague and are conceived, in part at least, in aesthetic terms.[10] The point to be stressed is that however great this difficulty may be, it can be resolved only by considering the specific functions of such logical principles in determinate contexts of inquiry; it cannot be resolved by investigating the causal factors which lead men to adopt those principles or by a genetic account of inferential habits.

For example, the view has been advanced that certain simple forms of

[9] Something more will be said on this point below. These remarks should not, however, be taken to mean that all habits of inference, and in particular language itself, have been instituted on the basis of a deliberate convention. How language first arose and how some of our common modes of inference actually came into being, are questions of fact about which there is in general little reliable information and concerning which everyone seems to be equally in the dark.

[10] For example, when a theory is required to be "simple" and "elegant."

inference are generated by physiological mechanisms sharing a common
character with mechanisms present in the subject matter of inquiry in
which those inferences are used; and it is sometimes said that a theory
of logic is "naturalistic" only if it holds that rational operations "grow
out of" the more pervasive biological and physical ones. It may be safely
assumed that there are causes and physical conditions for habits of
inference, even when we happen to be ignorant of them. It is not evident, however, especially since habits of inference may change though
the subject matter in connection with which they are employed does
not, that the mechanism underlying a specific habit of inference is identical with the mechanism involved in that subject matter. And it is even
less evident how, even if this were the case, the causal account would
enable us to evaluate inferential principles, since the cogency of such an
account is established only with the help of those principles. Suggestions for inferential canons may indeed be obtained from observations
of natural processes; but the fact that a principle may have been suggested in this way does not explain its normative function. Again, the
known facts about the earth's history make it most reasonable to assume
that the higher and more complex activities of men did not always exist
and that they have been developed out of more primitive ones; and it
would certainly be a matter of great interest to learn just how this has
come about. However, in the present state of our knowledge a genetic
account of logical operations is at best a highly speculative and dubious
one; and what is more to the point, even if a well-supported genetic
account were available, it would contribute little or nothing to an understanding of the present functioning of logical principles or to the explanation of the grounds of their authority. In the absence of a detailed
knowledge of the past, the reaffirmation of the historical and structural
continuity of our rational behavior with the activities of other organisms
is an act of piety; it does not increase the clarifying force of an experimentally orientated naturalism.[11]

b) Logical principles are also asserted as necessary truths which do
not refer to linguistic subject matter. Thus, "Everything is identical
with itself" and "If A then A" (where "A" is any statement) are formu-

[11] These comments should not be construed as a rejection of some form of "the
principle of continuity" as a fruitful guide and norm in inquiry. Nor should they
be taken as denying that the study of simpler and more basic biological behavior
may provide an illuminating context and essential clews for the understanding of
the "higher" functions. These remarks are included simply as a protest against frequent abuses of a useful postulate of procedure.

lations of the principle of identity; "Nothing has and also lacks a given property" and "It is not the case that A and not-A" (where "A" is any statement) are formulations of the principle of noncontradiction; while "If A and (if A then B), then B," and "If (if A then B) then (if not-B then not-A)" (where "A" and "B" are any statements) are examples of other principles usually regarded as necessary. These principles are ostensibly about things, their attributes and their relations, not about symbols for them; they are held to be necessary truths, because their denials are self-contradictory.

The first point to note about these logical laws is that if they are asserted as necessary truths, they are asserted to be such in some more or less precisely formulated language, whether in the crudely precise language of everyday use or in some more exact artificial symbolic system. And it is not difficult to show that although their subject matter is not the language of which they are parts, they occur in that language because of the habits of usage or the tacit or explicit rules which govern that language. For example, if the characterizations "true" and "false" are employed in the customary manner, no statement can properly (that is, without contravening that usage) be characterized as both true and false; and if the word "not" is so used in connection with acts of affirming and denying statements that a false statement is rejected as not true, the principle of noncontradiction is instituted as a necessary truth. More generally, if a precise usage is fixed for a number of expressions in a symbolic system, statements constructed out of some of these expressions will usually occur such that to deny them is to misuse those expressions. Accordingly, the laws which are regarded as necessary in a given language may be viewed as implicit definitions of the ways in which certain recurrent expressions are to be used or as consequences of other postulates for such usages. No language is so utterly flexible in its formal structure that no limits exist as to the way expressions in it can be combined and used. The necessary statements of a language help to specify what these limits are. But to the extent to which ordinary language is not precise, which statements in it are necessary cannot be determined exactly. The so-called systems of "pure logic" do not suffer from this fault; they can therefore be used as norms for instituting a more precise employment of language in situations in which such precision is essential for the task at hand. Indeed, as is well known, one result of such instituted precision is to facilitate the process of deriving consequences from premises and to supply dependable means for checking inferences.

This function of logical laws—to serve as instruments for establishing connections between statements which are usually not themselves logically necessary—is too familiar to require more than passing mention. A point worth observing, however, is that the necessary laws of logic can be reformulated so as to become principles of inference, having as their explicit subject matter the relations of expressions in a symbolic system. For it can be shown that a given language may be so reconstructed that it no longer will contain necessary truths—without thereby affecting the original possibilities for deducing statements which are not necessary—provided that corresponding to the necessary truths initially in the language appropriate rules of inference are introduced. The cost of such a reconstruction may be prohibitive in terms of the inconveniences and complexities which arise from it.[12] Nevertheless, the theoretical possibility of making it helps to show that the function of necessary truths is to regulate and control the process of deduction. It follows that the previous comments on rules of inference apply with equal force to laws expressing necessary connections.

A few final remarks concerning the grounds for accepting logical laws must be made. The main stress which is to be made in this connection is that any "justification" of such laws can be given only in terms of the adequacy of the language in which they are part to the specific tasks for which that language is employed. This point can be enforced by recalling that in the empirical sciences it is not possible to perform experiments which would subject isolated statements to a crucial test, since every experiment actually tests a vaguely delimited system of theoretical and factual assumptions involved in the experiment and the statement. Analogously, it is not feasible to "justify" a law of logic by confronting it with specific observational data; the belief that it is pos-

---

[12] For example, the necessary truth "if (if A then B), then (if not-B then not-A)" could be eliminated from our language, provided that we introduce the rule that a statement of the form "if not-B then not-A" is deducible from a statement of the form "if A then B." On the other hand, it is usually assumed that when "A," "B," "C," "D" are any statements, they may be combined to form the new statements "if A then B," "if C then D," and "if (if A then B), then (if C then D)"; accordingly, since "not-A" and "not-B" are statements, "if (if A then B), then (if not-B then not-A)" must be accepted as a statement on the basis of the stipulation just mentioned. Hence, if the occurrence of such necessary truths is to be prevented, more complicated rules must be introduced for combining statements to form new ones.

sible to do so is part of the heritage of traditional empiricism. On the other hand, since logical laws are implicit laws for specifying the structure of a language, and since their explicit function is to link systematically statements to which data of observation are relevant, logical laws may be evaluated on the basis of their effectiveness in yielding systems of a desired kind. Thus, it has recently been suggested that in order to develop the theory of subatomic phenomena in a manner conforming both to experimental evidence and to certain ideals of economy and elegance, a "logic" different from those normally employed may have to be instituted.[18] The suggestion is still in a speculative stage, and it is interesting only as a possibility. Nevertheless, it calls attention to the fact in a striking way that under the pressure of factual observation and norms of convenience familiar language habits may come to be revised; and it indicates that the acceptance of logical principles as canonical need be neither on arbitrary grounds nor on grounds of their allegedly inherent authority, but on the ground that they effectively achieve certain postulated ends.

It must be emphasized, however, that this way of justifying logical principles has nothing in common with the view which construes them as descriptive of an intrinsic and pervasive structure of things. It has been argued that just as in geometry there are intrinsically different kinds of surface and each kind imposes "certain limits on the range of alternative co-ordinate systems which can be used to map it out," so "the objective structure of the system of fact imposes some limitation on the alternative systems of language or symbolism which are capable of representing it." The conclusion drawn from this argument by analogy is that propositions which would describe this structure "would almost inevitably take the form of propositions which formulate certain very abstract and general and widespread linguistic usages"; and since logical principles do "formulate" these usages, there can be only one genuinely valid logic, only one absolute system of necessary truths. But even if one accepts the questionable analogy which underlies the argument, elementary considerations of scientific procedure must lead one to reject the conception of *"the* objective structure of *the* system of fact" capable of being known without the mediation of any selective symbolic

[18] See Garrett Birkhoff and John von Neumann, "The Logic of Quantum Mechanics," in *Annals of Mathematics*, XXXVII (1936), 823–43. The proposed logical system involves abandoning certain rules of inference which seem truistic both to "common sense" and to those accustomed to the system of *Principia Mathematica.*

system. The study of scientific inquiry requires us to admit that structures cannot be known independently of activities of symbolization; that structures considered for investigation are selected on the basis of special problems; that the various structures discovered are not, according to the best evidence, all parts of one coherent pattern; and that the precise manner in which our theories are formulated is controlled by specifically human postulates no less than by experimental findings. The attempt to justify logical principles in terms of their supposed conformity to an absolute structure of facts thus completely overlooks their actual function of formulating and regulating the pursuit of human ideals. If the preceding discussion has any merit, however, the reasonable view is that the relative success of a system of logic in doing these things is the sole identifiable and objective basis for measuring its worth.

2. Mathematics is almost universally proclaimed as the organon par excellence of modern science. But while its usefulness in empirical research is acknowledged, its statements and terms are still commonly believed to describe structures and entities which are either not embodied in the flux of events or when embodied are only imperfectly exhibited to human organs. The aim of the following brief discussion of the uses of two simple mathematical ideas in measurement is to suggest that from the point of view of the function of mathematics in inquiry such an interpretation is gratuitous.

a) The familiar distinction between "pure" and "applied" mathematics is one of the most enlightening and fruitful contributions of modern logical research. It has called attention to the need for adjudicating issues of experimental fact in a manner different from that of issues of formal logic; it has helped to break the paralyzing grip of dogmatic rationalism upon scientific minds; and it has stimulated the application of novel mathematical systems to the study of natural phenomena. Nevertheless, the distinction has precipitated new problems, especially when it was shown to the satisfaction of many students that the propositions of pure mathematics are logically necessary. For if this is the character of such propositions, what is their relevance to laboratory procedures and why do physicists still insist upon empirical evidence for many propositions which apparently can be established by logical means alone?

Consider, for example, the proposition of arithmetic that $7 + 5 = 12$. On the basis of the reconstruction of arithmetic contained in Whitehead and Russell's *Principia Mathematica* and elsewhere, this is a truth of logic, for whose validity observation and experiment are irrelevant. A view such as that of J. S. Mill, according to which the proposition is an inductive generalization from experience, cannot therefore be correct. On the other hand, no physicist will accept the proposition that five gallons of alcohol added to seven gallons of alcohol equals twelve gallons of the liquid as a necessary truth, and painstaking measurements are undertaken before such propositions are incorporated into the body of our knowledge. But at the same time, every physicist employs arithmetical truths in performing measurements of volume as well as in calculating with his experimentally obtained readings, as if these truths were indeed not subject to experimental control. Is the physicist simply inconsistent? Is Mill's view of arithmetic right after all—that arithmetic is an experimental science? Or is the physicist concerned with the magnitudes of certain inaccessible "real volumes" of his liquids, to which the volumes he actually measures are only approximations, the relations between the "real volumes" being logically necessary?

Such questions can be resolved if the process of measurement is examined in some detail; no more than a bare outline of an adequate answer can be indicated here. Physical measurement of a property (such as volume) is possible only if a set of standard measures are first instituted. Such standards are constructed on the basis of certain stipulations as to what shall be understood by a unit, and by the equality and physical sum of two objects with respect to the property. For reasons not necessary to discuss, these stipulations are so devised that they coincide with formal assumptions sufficient to develop a considerable portion of arithmetic. Accordingly, the physicist takes for granted a formal science of arithmetic, but uses it as a system of postulates for constructing physical standards of measurement. Since the question whether certain physical relations between a given set of bodies satisfy these postulates is a matter for experimental determination, the physicist is not inconsistent when, on the one hand, he accepts a statement such as was cited above only on the basis of experimental evidence and, on the other hand, he performs his calculations in accordance with the formal rules of arithmetic. Mill is therefore wrong in believing that the propositions of "pure" arithmetic are empirical truths; but he is right in holding that statements which formulate various quantitative relations between properties of physical objects—statements which frequently have the same appearance as those of formal arithmetic—are inductive generalizations from experience. The Frege-Russell view that arithmetical truths are necessary is a tenable interpretation of formal arithmetic; but it involves a fatal oversimplification of the situation when it is taken to mean that in the context of empirical inquiry—even in such simple operations as that of counting—all the expressions contained in statements of quantitative relations are definable exclusively in terms of purely logical notions. And in any event, it is the overtly identifiable properties of things that are measured by laboratory procedures, not some hypostatic attributes of which the necessary propositions of pure arithmetic are descriptions.

The point which deserves special stress is that in measurement the formulas of arithmetic are norms for isolating certain properties and relations of bodies and for instituting further operations upon them. Properties do not have an intrinsic magnitude independent of measurement; and if statements of quantitative relations are to be physically significant, definite stipulations must first be made concerning the conditions under which properties of objects are to be associated with determinate numerical measures. The experimenter's specific difficulty lies, not in performing numerical calculations, but in isolating properties and finding operations that may be performed upon them which will exhibit such relations with respect to one another that the formal calculations will be relevant to what he observes. Accordingly, in specifying standard units and multiples and submultiples of unit quantities, the experimenter will take pains to construct them in such a way that the results of the operations performed upon them will tally with the conclusions of numerical computations. In a word, the experimenter employs arithmetical postulates as regulative principles for the construction of physical scales of magnitude. This becomes even more evident when the notion of "experimental error" and the rationale for the introduction of the so-called "real number" continuum into measurement are examined. It is a common but superficial view that an experimental error is a deviation from an intrinsically "true" or "real" value of a magnitude, which by some misfortune eludes our grasp. The "true" value of a magnitude is in fact *defined* in terms of the actual values obtained by measurement, so that it is not an inaccessible, occult determination of physical properties; but what is more to the point, the notion of a "true" value is introduced for the sake of facilitating the quantitative comparison of properties and the consistent use of systems of calculation. To the extent that the actual materials investigated do not directly conform to the formal demands of measurement, complicated and roundabout methods are required for handling those materials in the desired manner. The techniques associated with the use of the real number system in measurement supply such methods; but the need for those techniques only enforces the view that pure arithmetic functions as a system of regulative principles in inquiry.

b) The use of the real-number system and its associated techniques in empirical inquiry has often been a serious obstacle in the way of accepting a thoroughgoing experimental naturalism. One example taken from this use will now be considered to illustrate the thesis of this essay.

It is difficult to interpret expressions which assign real-number values to the magnitudes of physical properties as signifying empirically identifiable traits in the explicit subject matter of physics. For example, a real number is commonly defined as the limit of an infinite sequence of rational numbers. But since the phrase "velocity of a body" is ordinarily employed to refer to the rate of change of place of a body over finite distances, the phrase "the instantaneous velocity of Mars," when strictly interpreted, must be taken to refer to the limiting value of an infinite sequence of velocities, taken over an infinite sequence of overlapping distances which converge to a point. In using real-number expressions to denote the instantaneous velocity of Mars at a given time, we are therefore predicating something of Mars which on the basis of the ordinary use of the term "velocity" it could not possibly have. The expression "the instantaneous velocity of Mars" thus seems to denote nothing in the heavens. Nonetheless, it would be rank folly to throw out the expression as "meaningless."

Consider an example analogous to, but technically simpler than, the expression "the instantaneous velocity of Mars." Suppose we are told that the distance between two given marks or "points" is equal to $\sqrt{2}$ feet. How is this statement to be construed? In performing an actual measurement of a distance, instruments are employed (for example, a yardstick) which are calibrated either by comparing them with a standard set of calibrations or by performing certain fundamental calibrations upon them. In either case, the calibrations are the end-products of procedures which must terminate after a finite number of steps; and it will, perhaps, be evident that the only numbers required for making the calibrations are the rational ones. But since $\sqrt{2}$ is not a rational number, there will be no calibration on the measuring rod to correspond to it. Accordingly, no measurement, no matter how refined, can ever establish the given distance to be $\sqrt{2}$ feet; for every measurement we may make (which will consist of comparing a standard rod with the given points) will yield a rational number, never an irrational one. More generally, experimental measurement does not require the use of irrational numbers. What then, if anything, do statements containing reference to such numbers signify?

One type of objection to the above argument is worth considering. After all, it may be said, we can determine whether the given distance has the indicated irrational magnitude by comparing it with the diagonal of a square with sides one foot long; for it is well-known that the diagonal of such a square will be exactly $\sqrt{2}$ feet long. And accordingly, the objection may continue, by generalizing this procedure it could be shown that the signs for irrational numbers do signify empirically identifiable traits in the subject matter of physics.

The force of this objection depends on two crucial assumptions: that we do possess an instrument, a square body, with whose diagonal a comparison may be instituted; and that a system of measures has already been established for the diagonal of this square. It will be evident that the validity of the first assumption rests on our ability to identify certain configurations in the physical world as conforming to the requirements of Euclidean geometry. In particular, certain physical surfaces must first be shown to be Euclidean planes, certain edges of physical objects must be exhibited to possess the properties required of Euclidean straight lines, and certain corners of bodies must be established as satisfying the stipulations for Euclidean right angles. In brief, the assumption depends upon the existence of an adequate warrant for a complicated physical theory. But since this theory happens to be one which cannot be adequately warranted without measurement and since the measurements required involve the use of irrational numbers as magnitudes of length, the initial difficulty concerning the empirical identification of distances having such magnitudes has only been postponed, not resolved.

The second of the above assumptions raises equally serious questions. For it in fact begs the entire issue as to what is signified in natural subject matter by the signs for irrational numbers when the latter are taken as measures of distances. It might be said in reply to this, however, that the magnitude of the diagonal of a square is equal to $\sqrt{2}$ feet as a matter of convention or stipulation, so that the empirical denotation of the critical phrase can in fact be unambiguously identified. But this reply is only a make-shift and will not stand examination. An adequate theory of measurement must make consistent the use of irrational numbers (whose denotation we shall for a moment suppose to have been fixed by an explicit convention such as the one just proposed) with the use of rational numbers, when the latter are employed in the customary manner in connection with calibrated measuring rods. Now it is a well-known arithmetical truth that a rational number can always be found which will approximate as closely as we wish a given irrational one; for example, in extracting the arithmetical square root of a number we obtain a sequence of such rational approximations. Accordingly, if the diagonal of the assumed square body were measured with a calibrated rod, the value which would be obtained for its magnitude would always be a rational number—no matter how small the subdivisions on the rod may be or how subtly the experiment is conducted. Consequently, if the magnitude of the diagonal is given the value of $\sqrt{2}$ feet on the basis of an unqualified convention and if the diagonal is measured with a calibrated rod in the usual way, incompatible results are obtained: the diagonal will have a magnitude which is both a rational and an irrational multiple of a unit of length. The difficulty is thus not resolved by fiat.

Nevertheless, although the objections considered do not resolve the problem, they do suggest an approach to a solution. For it will be evident from the above discussion that the irrational numbers come to be used as magnitudes of physical distances in terms of calculations, whose relevance depends upon the acceptance of a comprehensive physical theory together with the various conventions involved in formulating and employing it. We must therefore recall in outline some relevant operations involved in the use of irrational numbers in physical measurement.

Let us first make clear under what conditions we would reject the statement that the distance between two given marks is $\sqrt{2}$ feet. We would reject it if, when one end of the measuring rod is brought into coincidence with one of the marks, the other mark falls between two calibrations on the rod such that $\sqrt{2}$ does not lie between the two rational numbers corresponding to these calibrations. For example, if the rod is calibrated to tenths of a foot, the statement would be rejected if the second point were to fall into the interval between 1.3 and 1.4 feet. On the other hand, the statement would normally be accepted if the mark in question were to fall into an interval on the rod such that the irrational number lies between the two rational numbers corresponding to the boundaries of the interval. For example, the statement would be accepted if the point were to fall into the interval between 1.4 and 1.5 feet. But the magnitude of the interval between two successive calibrations on an instrument (that is, the sensitivity of the instrument), is in general a function of the state of experimental technology as well as of the specific objectives for which measurement is undertaken. As these techniques and objectives change so that finer discriminations become possible or desirable, different numerical values would have to be assigned for the magnitude of a physical distance if rational numbers were exclusively used in measurement. Moreover, without irrational numbers the purely mathematical operations required for developing and expanding physical theories would either be entirely impossible or be very much hampered and restricted.

On the other hand, suppose that we wish to formulate the results of experimental measurement in such a way that even when the sensitivity of our instruments is increased, this formulation will be consistent with the individual readings obtained in a series of actual measurements, each one yielding a rational number; suppose that in order to make the operations of mathematics more general and powerful their field is enlarged by the adjunction of new mathematical elements to the rational numbers; suppose, furthermore, that we wish to construct our physical theories in such a way that in their explicit formulation all reference is suppressed, in the interest of economy and generality, to the specific instruments required to test them. Under these assumptions the rationale for employing irrational numbers to specify the magnitudes of physical properties is clear. Rational numbers may suffice for stating the outcome of each single experimental determination of a magnitude; but if these individual determinations are required to be related as partial tests in a comprehensive, systematic inquiry, the irrational numbers become excellent and practically indispensable means for indicating in a compact way the values obtained in an indefinite series of experimental determinations. On the one hand, therefore, there are good reasons for rejecting the view that statements nominally about irrational magnitudes literally signify hypostatic properties which are empirically inaccessible; on the other hand, such statements have a definite function in systematically organized investigations and may be used to denote the predicted and identifiable results of a series of individual experiments conducted in certain ways. Far from being "meaningless," expressions nominally referring to irrational magnitudes are important links in a far-flung theoretical-experimental inquiry.

If this brief analysis is at all adequate to the facts it discusses, a twofold conclusion may be asserted: there is no simple relation between expressions like "$\sqrt{2}$" and the "objects" they signify; and such expressions help to organize the conduct of empirical investigations in the interest of achieving certain specific ends. A discussion of the conditions for the significant use of language in terms of an initial assumption that signs and their "objects" are related by a simple correspondence, can easily mislead us to look for those "objects" where they cannot possibly be found. This is especially the case in the theoretical sciences of nature; for the signs they employ do not, in general, serve as mere labels for the experienced properties of their ostensible subject matter, but frequently function as means for integrating inquiry by indicating how different experimental data may be brought into mutual relation. Thus, even when they occur as parts of statements which characterize a given subject matter, signs often do not signify "objects" already identified *in* the explicit subject matter, but serve rather as indices of modes of conducting inquiries *into* that subject matter.

That this is so will surprise only those who take language out of the context of overt operations of reflective thought. It is not unreasonable to maintain that every language, however much one may try to purify it of such elements, will inevitably contain expressions whose adequate understanding requires a consideration of the aims and activities of those who use that language as much as it involves a reference to the ostensible subject matter of that language. The conception of language as a mirror of existence, in the sense that the articulation of adequate discourse must have a structure identical with the order and connection of things, must therefore be judged as an oversimplified account of the relations between language and its subject matter. Ever since Duhem wrote on the subject, it has become a commonplace to observe that statements in the sciences are systematically connected and that only systems of beliefs can be put to a definitive test. It is not yet a common-place that isolated portions of discourse possess significance only in terms of their place and function in a system of language habits. Language is the instrument for expressing the structures of things and processes; but not all its parts are symbols for elements in those things and processes, and not all its parts can be understood without reference to the norms and objectives which control the construction and the use of that instrument.

II

A NATURALISTIC VIEW OF MIND

Yervant H. Krikorian

MIND has been the subject of much reflection, and many different conceptions of it have been proposed. As soul it has been pictured as a fugitive in the natural world, its home being supposed to lie in a transcendental world. As an Absolute it has been thought to be all-knowing and all-powerful. As an epiphenomenon it has been regarded as a shadowy "something" that has no effect in the world. In the face of this confusing variety of views one feels the necessity of a critical approach to mind. Such an approach requires a guiding procedure or method. The most fruitful procedure is the experimental method. This method is accessible to all, is self-correcting, indefinitely progressive, yet never claims finality.

For naturalism as a philosophy the universal applicability of the experimental method is a basic belief. But many have rejected this belief. Mystics with their private intuitions, idealists with their primacy of spirit, dualists with their bifurcation of nature, all believe that certain facts are beyond the reach of experimental confirmation. Objections to thoroughgoing experimentalism have been especially common in the study of mind. Professor Hocking gives typical expression to this attitude when he asserts that the "mind with which natural science can deal is but a Near-mind." [1] For him the nature of mind eludes scientific, experimental psychology; he therefore suggests a metaphysical psychology as "the only satisfactory science of the mind." [2] But are the facts of mind the cul-de-sac of experimentalism? Is mind so elusive, so transcendent, that objective methods are not applicable to it? The naturalist as experimentalist must either admit defeat before these claims or must proceed with the belief that mental phenomena, like all other phenomena, can be understood by means of the experimental method.

This analysis of mind will be guided by still another basic belief that is characteristic of naturalism, namely, that nature is the whole of reality.

[1] "Mind and Near-Mind," *Proceedings of the Sixth International Congress of Philosophy*, Cambridge [Mass.], 1926, p. 209.
[2] *Ibid.*, p. 215.

This belief has numerous interpretations. In the present context "nature" means what empirical science finds it to be and what a completed empirical science would find it to be. Empirically nature includes physical objects and living beings, inclusive of human beings and their ideals. One need neither argue, to show the simplicity of nature, that differences in nature are nothing but differences in complexity of structure nor assert, to emphasize the qualitative variety of nature, that there are unbridgeable gaps. Everything that we know presents in its natural setting structural connections and qualitative differences. Moreover, the importance of the naturalist's belief that nature is the whole of reality lies not only in what it affirms but also in what it denies. It denies what a philosopher like J. Maritain maintains: "There is a spiritual, metaphysical order superior to external nature . . . above all the mechanism and laws of the material world." [3] This order "is no part of this universe . . . it rises above the created world, the sensible, and the supra-sensible." [4] And beyond this order there is also the order of grace, and "this is entirely supernatural." [5] The naturalist turns away from these supernatural worlds. For him there is no supernature, no transcendental world. Beyond nature there is more nature. It is true that nature as completed science is an unattainable ideal and therefore in a sense transcendent; but this unattainable ideal is indefinitely approachable and has no supernatural implications. In relation to the study of mind the belief that nature is the whole of reality implies that mind should be examined as a natural phenomenon among other natural phenomena. It has its origin, growth, and decay within the physical, biological, and social setting. It is in this setting that mind will be examined. First the matrix of mind, which is life, will be considered, and then the specific type of behavior that mind is.

I

To understand mind, one must first consider the matrix in which it functions. This matrix is life. The matrix of life, in turn, is physical. Disembodied life never comes within our knowledge. Structurally living beings are physico-chemical systems. They reveal no new peculiar entities; they are composed of elements the chemist is familiar with.

[3] *The Degrees of Knowledge*, London, 1937, p. 316.
[4] *Ibid.*   [5] *Ibid.*, p. 317.

The exact proportions and the specific relations of these elements in living organisms present complex problems to the biochemists; yet these problems are like any other unsolved problems of the exact sciences. Also, functionally living beings have their roots in the physical world. Growth, movement, the circulation of the blood and other functions have a physical basis.

The nature of the physical world needs no detailed analysis here. It is a manifold of spatio-temporal entities with certain specific dimensions, related to one another in such a way that, given their present condition, one can predict their future and reconstruct their past. This picture of the world has been traditionally called mechanism. Mechanism in its strict sense is explanation in terms of the laws of mechanics. As Broad writes, it is "a necessary condition of a mechanical explanation that the laws employed shall be those of Mechanics; i.e., Newton's three laws of motion or some substitute for them." [6] Helmholtz provides us with a good illustration of mechanism in his famous lecture "On the Conservation of Energy," where he would explain all phenomena in terms of motions of discrete material particles subject to the action of attracting and repelling central points, forces whose magnitudes are functions of the distance between the particles. Mechanism in current thought, however, has acquired a wider meaning and application. An electrical theory, for example, is, in the wider meaning of the term, a mechanistic explanation, though it is not explanation in terms of the laws of mechanics. Similarly, chemistry, though mechanistic in its explanation, is not mechanistic in the strict sense of the word. Particularly when biologists, psychologists, and historians argue for the applicability of mechanism to their various fields, they hardly maintain that the phenomena of life, mind, and history can be explained by the laws of mechanics. Mechanism in its wider meaning may be identified with causal explanation, where the relations employed are nonteleological causal relations, that is to say, invariant correlations, and where the entities employed are physico-chemical entities. There are, thus, different types of mechanism. Some are strict and some are mild. The differences depend upon the entities and the relations involved. Strict mechanism is simple in its structure; it tries to explain in terms of a single kind of entity and a single kind of law. Milder types of mechanism em-

---

[6] "Mechanical Explanation and Its Alternatives," *Proceedings of the Aristotelian Society*, 1918–1919, p. 89.

ploy different kinds of physico-chemical entities and more than one kind of law. What is important is the fact that life must be interpreted and defined within the medium of mechanism, whether strict or mild.

Yet because life is within the medium of mechanism, it does not follow that it can be defined in terms of mechanism. The mechanist, impressed by the pervasiveness and effectiveness of the physico-chemical, claims that life is nothing but mechanism and therefore needs no new categories to define it. As J. Loeb writes, in answer to the question whether life is amenable to physico-chemical analysis,

> In spite of the gulf which separates us today from such an aim I believe that it is attainable. As long as a life phenomenon has not yet found a physico-chemical explanation it usually appears inexplicable. If the veil is once lifted we are always surprised that we did not guess from the first what was behind it.[7]

The issue is an empirical one; and empirically there are different modes of action—some are mechanical, others are teleological. To be more precise, all events may have a mechanical aspect, and yet some events may also have a purposive aspect. In the realm of life, for example, we find adaptation, intelligence, functional action. It is, of course, possible to entertain the belief that actions that are not mechanical are mere appearances and that they must be reduced to mechanism, but here one is playing the favorite game of nonempirical philosophers by calling mere appearance whatever does not fit one's ideal. It is true that one must have ideals not only in practical life but also in one's attempt to understand nature. Experimentalism does not mean that we can understand nature merely by gathering facts, but rather by interpreting them after they are gathered. Mechanism is one form of interpretation; purpose is another. It may be that the two are not incompatible —that certain objects are both mechanical and purposive. Living beings are through and through physico-chemical, yet there is no mechanical definition of life. Life is a purposive behavior, and our task will be so to define life that it may dwell in the world of mechanism and be of it, yet without being turned into mechanism or without mechanism being turned into it.

If the definition of life as a certain type of purposive behavior makes mechanism in biology impossible, it makes vitalism no less so. Vitalists,

[7] *The Mechanistic Conception of Life*, Chicago, 1912, p. 26.

in their attempt to do justice to the purposive aspect of life, introduce an unbridgeable break between mechanism and purpose. Living beings are asserted to be more than mechanism, and this "more" is believed to be a nonperceptible, nonmechanical entity or agent, such as entelechy, *élan vital*, or anima. Vitalists offer an array of arguments against mechanism, and at the same time consider them favorable to vitalism. The form, the growth, the action, the evolution of the organism all need, they say, a nonphysical agency for their explanation.

That biological phenomena are very complex and that many problems have not yet been clarified are facts the experimental biologist would be the first to accept; but he would reject the claim that the unsolved problems cannot be approached and eventually solved by experimental procedure. Rejecting this view, Driesch claims that morphogenetic systems are "harmonious-equipotential systems" and that this fact cannot be explained by physico-chemical or machine concepts, but by the introduction of an independent agency. Similarly, Bergson claims, in the special sense in which he uses the word "finality," that finality would be established should it be proven that "life may manufacture the like apparatus, by unlike means, on divergent lines of evolution." [8] Such facts or alleged facts are experimental issues. The obscure problems raised by Driesch and Bergson are gradually finding experimentally intelligible explanation. But even should one give the vitalists a sympathetic ear, what really is being offered? An unverifiable agency, one that is neither a "substance," an "attribute," nor a "quantity," but something endowed with miraculous knowledge prior to any experience. This agency is supposed to solve the obscure problems of biology. "It is my firm conviction," Driesch writes, "that we cannot avoid the admission of vitalistic autonomic agents, possessing no experience, i.e., no 'secondary' faculties, and yet endowed with *specific* knowing and willing." [9] This firm conviction only verbally solves the difficulties of biology; actually clarifies none.

Vitalists are certainly right to demand teleological concepts in the realm of biology, but teleology does not necessarily involve a chasm between matter and life, between mechanism and purpose. What one may essentially object to in the vitalists is their limited view of the material world. Spinoza comes much nearer the truth when he says:

[8] *Creative Evolution*, tr. by Arthur Mitchell, New York, 1911, p. 54.
[9] H. Driesch, *Science and Philosophy of the Organism*, London, 1908, II, 143.

No one has thus far determined what the body can do merely by the laws of nature, insofar as nature is considered merely as corporeal or extended, and what it cannot do, save when determined by the mind. For no one has yet had a sufficiently accurate knowledge of the construction of the human body as to be able to explain all its functions; nor need I be silent concerning many things which are observed in brutes which far surpass human sagacity . . . all of which sufficiently shows that the body can do many things by the laws of its nature alone at which the mind is amazed.[10]

Finally, the definition of life as purposive behavior within the medium of mechanism makes panpsychism untenable. The panpsychist, to overcome the conflict between mechanism and purpose, claims that every point in the universe is alive and conscious. For him there is no non-living, nonpurposive reality. The belief is that on deeper scrutiny the world of mechanism, the world of rigid uniformity, dissolves into a world of free and purposive beings. As Ward puts it, "The panpsychist . . . maintains . . . that there are no things wholly inert, devoid of all internal springs of action, and only mechanically related to each other"; [11] and he subscribes to this philosophy. Royce argues for a similar view. He says, "My hypothesis is that in case of Nature in general, as in case of the particular portions of Nature known as our fellowmen, we are dealing with phenomenal signs of a vast conscious process." [12] From this point of view when "you deal with Nature, you deal with a vast realm of finite consciousness of which your own is at once a part and an example." [13] The fundamental assumption of the panpsychist is that uniformity and mechanism are incompatible with freedom and purpose. The general claim is that the world is either subject to mechanism, and if so, is dead and purposeless, or that it is a realm of teleology, and therefore free and living.

But life as we empirically find it is local, derivative, and precarious, depending on a complex physico-chemical organization and vanishing with the disintegration of this. To assert that the physical and the chemical elements which compose the system are alive is either to enlarge the meaning of life beyond utility or to make an assertion that is not empirically supported. Panpsychists rightly insist on the principle of continuity, but this continuity is from matter to mind, rather than from

[10] *Ethics* III, 2.
[11] *Realm of Ends,* Cambridge [Eng.], 1911, p. 62.
[12] *The World and the Individual,* New York, 1900–1901, II, 226.
[13] *Ibid.*

mind to matter. Of course, if material organization can at a certain level show adaptive behavior and at another level thinking behavior, one must modify certain traditional views of matter; but it would still be true that life and mind are derivative, organizational concepts.

To establish their claim panpsychists frequently resort to epistemological arguments. Starting with the belief that mind is primary in knowledge, they maintain that known objects must ultimately be mental. But at the end of this argument, where does one find himself if not in the natural world of naturalism, where one uses water for quenching thirst, stones for building houses, iron and steel for constructing bridges? To affirm that all inert things are alive is, to say the least, to create an embarrassing world. Since the panpsychist's analysis of the cognitive situation leads to such an extreme conclusion, it seems reasonable that some other analysis should be attempted. Here again one may doubt the major premise—that mechanism and purpose are incompatible. It may be that what we need is distinction between these two concepts rather than disjunction. An object may be a model of mechanism, yet at the same time exhibit purpose. The possibility of this belief will now be considered.

Life is purposive behavior within the medium of mechanism. What makes this conception difficult to believe is the failure to distinguish between the discrete properties and the organizational properties of an object. It is true that in certain cases objects are so simple that they do not involve duality. The length of an object is the sum of the units of measurement which compose it, and, again, the weight of an object is the sum of the units of weight contained in it. These might be called additive organizations. But there are many organizations which are not merely additive. Could one say that because an object exhibits no curvature when examined discretely, that is, point by point, it exhibits no curvature when examined organizationally? One would face similar difficulties should one attempt to define a molecule as nothing but the sum of its atoms, a song as nothing but the sum of its notes, or a social group as nothing but the sum of its members. It is experience that must show what organizations are additive and what organizations are non-additive. And if one overcomes his natural prejudice against explaining the characteristics of organization in terms of additive concepts, there is nothing strange when it is suggested that within the medium of mechanism purpose may be exhibited.

Purpose is a property which belongs to organization, but the idea of purpose is not identical with the idea of organization. Such identification is a source of confusion. Latta, for example, writes, "We find purpose in things in proportion as we find in them systematic unity and that a thing has a purpose in so far as it is a unity of conditions in a system." [14] Bosanquet similarly asserts that if purpose is to retain a meaning, "it must abandon the whole analogy of finite contrivance and selection and must fall back on the characteristics of value which, apart from sequence in time from selected purposes, attach to the nature of totality which is perfection." [15] Hoernlé expresses the same view: "When we ask what character in natural objects exhibits purposiveness the answer must surely be that it is organization." [16] There are many organizations or unities where it is hardly legitimate to apply the concept of purpose. A triangle is a certain unity or organization of lines, yet triangles as triangles are not purposive. Similarly, molecules are organizations of atoms, but molecules as such have no purpose. Purpose is a property of organizations which exhibit a specific type of result. What type of result is purposive?

From the empirical point of view the purpose of an object is to be discovered in the observed or anticipated results of that object. The purpose of a saw, for example, is to cut; the purpose of a musical instrument is to produce pleasant sound; the purpose of a motor car is to transport. In biology, the function or purpose of the eye is to see; the function of the heart to propel the blood; the purpose of living beings to maintain themselves. On the human level of action, the purpose of a physician is to cure illness; the purpose of a teacher to instruct students; the purpose of a lawyer to defend his clients. Although in all these cases the objects have an infinite number of other results, only some of the results are considered purposive. In each case we could say that the purpose of an object or action is the biased result toward which the action moves. This conception of purpose is wider than the usual one. The idea of purpose is not being limited to actions where the biased or propensive result is anticipated. In the case of tools or instruments purpose is external; the bias is imposed on them. In the case of merely organic beings purpose is internal, but there is hardly the anticipatory

14 "Purpose," *Proceedings of the Aristotelian Society*, London, 1907–8, p. 27.
15 *The Principle of Individuality and Value*, London, 1912, pp. 126–27.
16 *Studies in Contemporary Metaphysics*, New York, 1920, p. 160.

or the ideational element. Only on the human level does purpose find its full meaning, for here the bias is anticipatory.

Purpose, as has been suggested, has two aspects—ends and means. This distinction between two aspects of purposive action is evident in human behavior. We desire certain things as ends and select others as means. For indefinite ends we usually have an indefinite number of means, but as ends become definite the means become definite. The same distinction is often made by psychologists in their description of animal behavior. Chimpanzees, for example, use sticks or other objects to achieve their ends. Rats, similarly, select means to reach their goal; of two paths leading to food, they choose the shorter.

The confusion in discussions of mechanism and purpose is frequently due to the fact that an object may belong to both mechanism and purpose. Material instruments provide us with an illustration of this dual membership. At every point they are mechanical. A tool, a musical instrument, and a machine are made of nothing but material entities. No philosopher has as yet raised the question whether or not tools, musical instruments, or machines are observable in the way that some have doubted that life or mind is observable; and no one has felt it necessary to introduce vitalistic entities, such as the entelechy or the *élan vital*, to explain the working of a machine. Yet material instruments have purpose; a watch indicates time, a violin produces pleasant sound. What is even more significant, these material instruments are grouped together, not because of similarity of structure, which they need not possess, but because of the purposive function which is common to them. A sundial, an hourglass, a watch are classified, despite mechanical differences, as timepieces; or, again, a violin, a flute, a trombone are grouped together as musical instruments. The definition of timepieces or musical instruments is not in terms of mechanical structure, but in terms of function. Material instruments thus belong to both mechanism and purpose. Material instruments are purposive, however, in relation to other purposes. Their purpose, therefore, is an external one; their selectivity, their means and end activity, depends on human purpose.

Living beings, not unlike material instruments, are physico-chemical systems, yet they are purposive in the sense that their behavior is biased toward a result. Whatever their mechanical structure, or however devoid of other biases, any being is a living being if it is biased toward self-maintenance. I do not wish to imply that self-maintenance is the only bias of living beings. It is, however, their most general trait. From the amoeba to man, living beings tend for the most part toward self-maintenance. What, then, is self-maintenance? Maintenance of one's fortune or property is quite intelligible, as one can easily distinguish between the maintainer and the maintained. In self-maintenance, however, the two being, as it were, identical, the analysis is more complex.

The fruitful procedure would be to regard self-maintenance as a type of behavior. The living organism as a system of energy acts within an environment. Any response to environment releases energy and brings expenditure and disequilibrium. The organism acts in a way that tends to maintain its equilibrium, which is adaptation. As D. M. S. Watson writes, "Perhaps the most striking of all phenomena of life is the power which all animals and plants possess of so regulating their functioning, and when necessary their morphology, that their life is continued in equilibrium with the conditions under which they find themselves." [17]

In this behavior the environment need not be interpreted in teleological terms; nor need the fitness of the environment be considered as purposive in origin. Frequently the environment is not conducive to life. The conditions of the environment should be taken as independent of the organism; they should be taken as conditions which the organism must take account of. Nor should the structural basis of adaptive behavior be construed in the Lamarckian or the Darwinian sense that every structure in an animal has a definite use. There are many useless structures. Even in cases where structures have specific utility, it does not follow that their origin is purposive; they might have arisen casually. What is significant is the fact that within the given environment and with the given structure the behavior is adaptive, self-maintaining.

Yet the notion of self-maintenance as adaptation, as the tendency to maintain equilibrium, should not be oversimplified. Self-maintenance is sometimes interpreted as merely the attempt to restore a prior condition. As Rignano puts it, "Every organism is a physiological system in a stationary condition and tends to preserve this condition or to restore it as soon as it is disturbed by any variation." [18] That in self-maintaining

[17] "Adaptation," Report of the *British Association for the Advancement of Science*, 1929, p. 89.
[18] *Psychology of Reasoning*, tr. by Winifred A. Hall, New York, 1923, p. 6.

behavior there is relative restoration of the previous state of the organism need not be denied, but what is more significant is the fact that in this behavior an integrated relation is established between the organism and the environment. As a matter of fact, the organism is in process of growth or decay, and it is at these different stages of the organic processes that adaptation is being maintained.

II

Life has been defined as purposeful behavior in the medium of mechanism. This purpose was said to be self-maintenance. There has been no reference to higher or lower forms of life; to distinguish between these forms it is necessary to introduce a new concept, mind.

The naturalistic approach to mind is the experimental approach. This means that mind must be analyzed as behavior, since behavior is the only aspect of mind which is open to experimental examination. Yet not every type of behavior or response is mental. For example, the physical reaction in crystallization, or the chemical reaction in oxidation, or the reflex response of an organism is not a mental response. Mind is a specific type of response. Provisionally, mind may be defined as response to the meanings of stimuli. This is not response to the bare or immediate stimulus, but to what the stimulus stands for, that is, its possible consequences. In more functional terms, therefore, mind may be defined as control of behavior by anticipation. Though this type of behavior finds its fullest expression on the human level, there are degrees of it on the level of the "lower" animals. Mind as anticipatory response has primarily three different dimensions.

First, mind as anticipatory response is the use of means for ends. Here mind is intelligence or cognition.

Second, mind as anticipatory response is pursuit of ends as ends-in-view. Here mind is interest or conation.

Third, mind as anticipatory response is knowledge of mind, either one's own or another's. Here mind is consciousness.

These dimensions of mind will be considered in the order given.

We begin with the first dimension of mind. Cognition has always been considered the most distinctive trait of mind. It is through cognition that more skillful and more resourceful adaptation is possible.

Mind as cognition is, first of all, a response that is directed toward what the stimulus represents or means. The notion of meaning in the present discussion is psychological, rather than exclusively logical. Whether the logical notion of meaning may be reduced to the psychological need not concern us. Behaviorally, response to the stimulus as symbol is response to what the stimulus stands for, what it represents in terms of consequences. For example, one who is buying a hat does not see hats merely in their qualitative immediacy, that is, as patches of blue, brown, and green, but as objects to be worn. Or, again, a chess-player does not respond to the objects on a chess board as mere objects, but as pawns or knights or bishops with certain future consequences in the moves. Or a mathematician in his manipulation of mathematical figures does not respond to them solely in their immediacy, but as symbols related to one another in certain ways. The response to meaning has different levels. On one level of mind the response is to the meaning of an object as perceptual experience. One responds to a bright object as something that burns. On another level of mind the response is to the meaning of an object as linguistic symbol. One responds to the word "fire" as a symbol for something that burns. Linguistic symbols draw attention to the potential consequences of a stimulus without being that stimulus. On a still higher level of mind the response is to the meaning of an object as part of a system. The meaning of fire for the physicist involves a system of physical ideas. Some philosophers, in defining mind as a system, indicate an important phase of mind.

Mind as cognition is, secondly, prospective or futuristic, in the sense that future consequences of stimuli function as present stimuli, controlling behavior. Response to meaning is primarily readiness to act in relation to some expected result of the situation. In this respect mental behavior is fundamentally different from reflex action. In reflex action there is a certain automatic pattern—a specific stimulus causes a specific response irrespective of environmental or organic conditions. Accidental swallowing starts a series of actions that follow each other in a set way. Mind as cognition, unlike automatic action, is prospective; the response is not merely to what is immediately given but also to what is expected. On the level of integrated reflexes, as Professor Holt argues, there is recession of the stimulus. "As the number of component reflexes involved in response increases the immediate stimulus itself recedes further and further from view as the significant factor." [19] And what is

[19] *The Freudian Wish*, New York, 1915, pp. 76–77.

significant is the anticipated result. It is primarily this phase of behavior that marks mind as intelligence. For example, a physicist in his experimental work is guided by future results involved in his experiments; and a physician in making a prescription is controlled by the expected consequences of his medicine. The futuristic reference of mind, however, need not be interpreted primarily in introspective terms. Anticipatory response is a type of behavior, and this behavior is observable. When a person is told that a guest is about to come, he can be seen to be getting ready to welcome him. Anticipatory response may have its introspective aspect, yet introspection itself, as will be shown, may be behavioristically described. Nor need one make a mystery of the potentiality in the future reference of mind. The future possible consequences were previously experienced as actual consequences of the same kind of stimulus and were recorded in the neuromuscular system as a "neurogram." Thus having been conditioned to the stimulus, they are ready to be set off by it when it is met again. Potentiality, if it is to be a *vera causa*, has got to be something here and now; something that is not a mere potentiality.[20]

Mind as cognition, finally, is suppositional. By supposition is meant readiness to act in relation to some expected result. For example, one who hears and supposes that the stock in which he owns shares is falling is set to do everything to avoid the loss: he verifies the news by telephoning his broker, and, if the news is really adverse, tells him to sell at once. There are degrees of supposition. When one daydreams, plays games, or watches dramas, the supposition may be characterized as an "as if" attitude. For the child the doll is "as if" a baby; for the tennis player the opponent is "as if" an enemy; for the audience the actor is "as if" a real character. Where decisions must be made, or transactions completed, or final action taken, the suppositions become full-fledged beliefs, irretrievable commitments. For one who is crossing a street, the coming car is a real danger to be avoided. The supposition here is not an "as if" attitude, but real and final. In still other cases, where decisions are not immediately necessary, suppositions are similarly readiness to act. An intense partisan is ready to act for the aims of his party; an industrialist, for the preservation of the capitalistic system; and a pious person, for the tenets of his religion. Supposition also may take the form

[20] E. H. Holt, *Animal Drive and the Learning Process*, New York, 1931, ch. xviii.

of doubt; it is then vacillation. One who is in doubt about the truth of a statement hesitates to act. In its extreme form doubt may paralyze conduct; in its moderate form it may goad one to reconstruct his beliefs. Finally, the suppositional aspect of anticipatory response defines truth and error. When the expected result is fulfilled, the supposition is shown to be true; when it is not fulfilled, the supposition is shown to be erroneous. Anticipatory response as supposition is always on trial. What is expected, even if one is absolutely certain, may not occur.

In the analysis of mind as cognition, the response has been shown to be meaningful, futuristic, and suppositional. An examination of some of the familiar modes of cognition—*perception, memory,* and *thought*—should make clearer the nature of mind as cognition.

Let us begin with perception. When perceiving an object, for example, an apple, one says it is edible. The response is to more than what is immediately given; it is to future results which function as present stimuli. The perceptive behavior is regulated by this expectation. One sees the apple not merely as a present object, but as something which can be picked up and eaten. Expecting the apple to be luscious, one will pick it up; expecting it to be tasteless, one will let it alone. Similarly, one responds to fire as to something that will burn. As Professor Dewey writes, "To *perceive* is to acknowledge unattained possibilities; it is to refer the present to consequences, apparition to issue, and thereby to behave in deference to the *connection* of events. As an attitude, perception or awareness is predictive expectancy." [21] On the biological level, as distinguished from the mental, the response in case of the apple would be to actual edibility; on the mental level the response would be to potential edibility. Of course, edibility is not necessarily the only meaning of an apple. Under certain conditions some of its other qualities may be chosen, as, for instance, its hardness, its economic value, its pleasing appearance. The meanings one can give to an object are indefinite in number. This does not mean that the perceptual object is nothing but a grouping of universals, but rather that the application of one meaning to an object does not exhaust its other possible meanings. Moreover, one need not create the insoluble paradox whether the mind in perception sees the "real" or the "illusory" object. There is no intrinsic difference in the perception of real or illusory objects; both have their natu-

[21] *Experience and Nature*, Chicago, 1912, p. 182.

ral conditions and natural consequences. Whether the perceived object is real or illusory is determined in terms of the fulfillment or failure of one's expectation.

Now, as to memory. Memory is a term of wide meaning. For the present no distinction will be made between terms like "memory," "recollection," "remembering," and so forth. It is sufficient to determine what one means when one says, "I remember this or that," "My memory on that issue is clear (or fails me)," "Our memories seem to disagree." In all these cases what is important is the fact that memory judgments refer to objects or situations in the past. Yet the reference is not to the past as a whole; the past to which memory refers is the individual's own past. "Memory requires," James writes, "more than mere dating of a fact in the past. It must be dated in *my* past." [22] But even the individual's own past is not in every sense the object of memory; it is only when one says "I remember so and so" that the distinctive features of memory appear. Memory as described is primarily a mode of anticipatory behavior. Memory is "reëxcitation of responses uniquely correlated with certain events in the past history of the organism." [23] The original, or remembered, responses, as perceptions or ideas, now stored in the nervous system as neural patterns, were anticipatory; therefore their revival is anticipatory. The present memory may not fully coincide with the original responses; yet with all its modifications or new nuances it follows a pattern of behavioral expectations. And as in the case of perceptual judgments, the truth or falsity of memory judgments is determined by fulfillment or failure of expectations as related to hypotheses. And, again, the truth of an isolated memory is always a particular truth and has all the limitations which such truths possess. The more complete or more universal knowledge of the past is attained by connecting discrete memory judgments, by enlarging and enriching their significance, and, finally, by verifying inclusive hypotheses. One other point should be mentioned. To the naturalistic account of memory the objection is sometimes raised that memory is independent of the traces of the past responses stored in the nervous system. Bergson particularly argues that memory is purely immaterial and has no physiological counterpart. [24] He bases his assertion on the contention that in

[22] *Principles of Psychology*, New York, 1890, I, 650.
[23] R. B. Perry, *General Theory of Value*, New York, 1926, p. 341.
[24] *Matter and Memory*, tr. by Nancy Margaret Paul and W. Scott Palmer, London, 1911.

certain kinds of aphasia forgetting is never really final. But because certain lesions do not destroy memory, it does not follow that additional lesions would not destroy it. To a stimulus more than one response is made, and each response has its own physiological pattern. A chair, for example, evokes visual, kinesthetic, and auditory responses. When the brain, cord, vocal organs, or any other organ connected with any of the motor acts is injured or destroyed, that particular pattern cannot function, and "loss of memory" occurs. But since there are other sets connected with this same object which are not injured, the individual is able to respond to it by any of these and is therefore able to "remember" it.

Finally, thought must be considered. There are different kinds of thought: associative thought, casual thought, "day-dreaming," and so forth. For the present, thought will be considered as reasoning or problem solving. Reasoning, in its preliminary stage, is an anticipatory schema, a frame to be filled in. When problems are easy, the original schema is simple; when problems are difficult, the original schema is modified, or may even be superseded. The specific ideas that fill the schema are also anticipatory. Ideas are anticipated operations and their consequences in relation to some situation. In behavioral terms, to have an idea is to be ready to respond in a specific way to a stimulus; to reason is to rehearse various anticipatory responses in relation to a problem. The difference, therefore, between reasoning and actual manipulation is that in the former case the operations are preseen and are only possible ones. When one says that one has an idea as to how a certain machine will work, one anticipates the series of operations which one would actually perform were one running the machine. As one's ideas develop, they become more and more general in their application and abstract in their nature. Gradually ideas freed from specific applications are related to one another, and operations are performed by symbols. But in this whole development of ideas anticipatory operations are basic. Inference, or the if-then relation, conceived of as causal or strictly implicative, is a chain of complex expectations. Here, again, the physiological basis of reasoning should not be ignored. Thought, ideas, meanings are asserted by some to be psychic entities, psychic wholes, independent of body. McDougall demands a psychic entity to do the relating, to perform the activity of reasoning.[25] But why postulate an unverifiable psychic entity for this activity? As Lloyd Morgan puts it, "May not

[25] *Body and Mind*, London, 1913, p. 311.

the relating activity, so-called, be just as reasonably assigned to the physiological process in the cortex and the organization as a whole as to the correlated psychological process, hypostatized as a psychic entity?" [26]

The functional character of mind as cognition should be kept clear. Mind as cognition is primarily intelligence, an instrument in the living process, though knowledge in itself may become an interest. Mind as anticipatory response enlarges the temporal scope of behavior. The animal response is more or less limited to the immediate present; the human response, on the other hand, through perception, memory, and thought, surveys the past, present, and future. And this survey is experimental. Thinking is an imaginary experiment. In this experiment possible consequences are manipulated without exposing one to the finality of actuality. Thus, on the human level adaptation is transformed to adaptability. Lower organisms frequently attain adequate adaptation, but this adaptation is fixed. Human beings, on the other hand, are characterized by their adventurousness: they imagine new environments and new methods. This transformation is both their strength and their weakness, making possible, on the one hand, the conquest of nature and the creation of civilization, but on the other, confusing life with a multitude of expectations.

III

We pass now to the second dimension of mind, mind as conation, will, or pursuit of ends. Organic life is primarily an urge or drive. On the mental level drives become anticipatory and ends become ends-in-view.

The first thing to be noted is that mind as conation is a biased anticipatory response. Mere anticipation is readiness to act toward a possible result, but it implies no demand to secure this result; on the other hand, biased anticipation signifies the disposition to bring it about. As Professor Perry puts it, "To expect an event signifies only a disposition to act *on* it; while to be interested in an event signifies a disposition to act *for* it, or to provide an occasion for acting on it." [27] If I merely anticipate that my friend will offer me a cigarette, my nervous system is in readiness to receive it, but if I wish my friend to offer me a cigarette, the readiness to receive it is in agreement with my wish to smoke.

[26] *Instinct and Experience*, London, p. 280.
[27] *General Theory of Value*, New York, 1926, p. 318.

Mind as conative anticipatory response is primarily this biased prospective response.

Mind as biased anticipatory response takes different forms. To begin with, it may be positive or negative. This polarity of response has often been called appetite and aversion, pleasure and pain, good and evil, joy and sorrow.[28] Mind as positive anticipatory response demands the presence of a result; as negative anticipatory response it demands less of a result. Moreover, mind as biased anticipatory response may be specific or general. This is to say that biological appetites may become specific desires. Hunger, for example, may be satisfied with anything that is edible; but it may demand some specific food. Again, affection may be attached indifferently to any creature; but it may also be attached to some one individual. As Royce liked to argue, love is not love unless it has succeeded in making its object irreplaceable. Mind as biased anticipatory response is also general. Sympathy for one's neighbor may be extended to the nation, and even to humanity. Just as Royce argued for the love of the specific, Plato argued for the love of the universal. Finally, mind as anticipatory response may be real or imaginary. I may wish to have actual wealth or imaginary wealth. If I wish actual wealth, I take steps that may secure it; if I wish imaginary wealth, I merely imagine myself in possession of the wealth.

It is in the discussion of conation that vitalistic or mentalistic concepts are often felt to be necessary. For example, McDougall, after defining value as that which excites our conative tendencies, says, "Hence consciousness of value, like consciousness of meaning, is a mode of consciousness which has no counterpart in the physical sphere; value . . . is a purely psychical fact." [29] But for a naturalist the analysis of conation does not demand "purely psychical facts." Conation, whether it be instinctive or cognitive, has a bodily basis. Conative action as behavior is open to investigation; as a matter of fact one frequently observes the interests of others more clearly than they do themselves.

The second thing to note about mind as conation is that it is cognitive. The bias on the human level is anticipatory. It is the human prerogative to know the ends that are followed. The cognitive element in relation

[28] Objection might be raised that joy and sorrow are not anticipatory. Yet both in their content—in the enjoyment of music, for example, anticipated notes are ingredients—and in their general tendency to prolong or to shorten the given experience they are anticipatory.
[29] *Body and Mind*, London, 1923, p. 329.

to conation, however, has two different meanings which should be distinguished.

Cognition in relation to conation may mean that ends, my own as well as those of others, may be the objects of judgment. For example, when one says human beings love freedom, this statement may be taken as a judgment about what human beings love. Or when I say that I love freedom the judgment would be about what I love. Formally, these judgments do not differ from other forms of matter-of-fact judgments, except that the facts involved are wishes, desires, and ends. Empirical studies of political, ethical, religious and similar activities are greatly concerned with judgments of this type. As factual judgments their claims may be true or false. There is nothing subjective or relativistic about these judgments in the derogatory sense.

Cognition in relation to conation may also mean that the object of cognition is an object of bias or desire. In this case the function of judgment is to mediate bias, and the anticipated objects are ingredients of bias—they are demanded or rejected. This type of judgment might be called conative judgment. The cognitive structure of conative judgments is similar to the structure of other types of judgment. Both the factual statement "Freedom will soon come to human beings" and the conative statement "I hope freedom will soon come to human beings" are suppositional in their nature. The claim of the first judgment, as well as of the second, may be true or false; though in the first case one may merely expect a certain result, while in the second, anxiously wait for the expected result. The content of conative judgment may be any object whatsoever. Temporally, it may be events of the past, the present, or the future; spatially, it may be objects that are near or far; existentially, it may be objects that are real or imaginary. As any object or event may become the cognitive object of conation, increase of knowledge tends to widen the area of one's likes and dislikes. The consequences of this fact are both harmful and beneficial—harmful in the spread of deceptive propaganda; beneficial in the dissemination of enlightened information. It is, of course, equally true that conative attitudes affect the nature of our cognition. Our feelings toward individuals, groups, and situations have consequences relevant to their factual aspects. As bias is mediated by judgments, they become on the reflective level more and more complex and more expressive of human desires. Poetry, for instance, expresses human yearnings more deeply, and at

the same time it is a new object of enjoyment. But in arguing that conation as anticipatory response has a cognitive element we are not trying
to offer a rival type of cognition to the usual descriptive, observable cognition. According to Royce, "The world of appreciation is . . . the
deeper reality. Its rival, the world of description, is the result of an
essentially human and finite outlook." [30] There is no need for this sharp
dualism. Conation or appreciation is not a different or superior type of
cognition, but rather, on the mental level it has an object toward which
a biased attitude is taken.

We have been arguing that on the human level conation is cognitive
and that this cognition brings new modifications to behavior, yet the
cognitive element in conation has been denied by some. The mechanistic psychologist denies the cognitive element in conation on the ground
that conation for him is merely a chain of reflex actions. But the mechanist forgets the facts of organization and integration. As the reflex activities integrate and the immediate stimuli recede, anticipatory response
becomes an ingredient of conative behavior. Analytically all organic
behavior may be reduced to reflex actions and, if one likes, to physical
and chemical actions; but this fact in no way refutes the novelties involved in organized reflex actions. In maintaining that mind as conation
is anticipatory there is no intention of introducing a break into the
continuity of nature, but rather of emphasizing the novelties involved
in this continuity. Similarly, some psychoanalysts, on different grounds,
depreciate or deny the cognitive element in conation. Because in emotional adaptation human beings sometimes resort to falsification of the
facts to others as well as to themselves, it is not true that they always do
so. Should the latter statement be true, then the psychoanalysts' own
theory would have no logical basis for acceptance. The psychoanalytic
theories have been useful in breaking down our rationalized and senti-
mentalized interpretations of human nature, but these dramatic claims
have not always been so helpful in giving an empirical account of human behavior. The objection is to what they deny rather than to what
in the main they affirm. And, again, because human ends are determined
by biological needs, it does not follow that on a certain level of integration of the nervous system there are no genuinely cognitive elements
in desires. Though it is true that on the mental level conation cannot
exist without cognition, it may exist without awareness of itself. I may,

30 *The Spirit of Modern Philosophy*, Boston, 1892, p. 411.

for example, wish to buy an object when the object of desire is known, but I may not be aware, at the moment, of the desire itself.

The third thing to be observed is that mind as conation is comparative or preferential. Mind as preferential response is concerned with judgments of "better" or "worse," "best" or "worst." By preferential judgment I do not merely mean that preferences may be objects of judgment and thus may be true or false, but also that some of the anticipated consequences are preferred to others, that there is a personal bias, a motor-affective response toward some results rather than toward others. It is with this sense of preferential judgment that we are concerned.

Frequently it is believed that the naturalistic account of preference is inadequate, that the ideas of "better," "higher," or "best" demand a supernaturalistic, or at least a nonnaturalistic explanation. In this way, it is supposed, the stature of man, as well as the status of "ultimate values," is saved. Professor Urban, for example, giving expression to the idealistic tradition, maintains that "ultimate values, e.g., the good, the beautiful, and the true . . . cannot be apprehended by such general propositions as form the material of natural science, more specifically in this case biological or psychological science." [81] Instead, he argues that these values have their inner validity and have to be directly acknowledged. Professor Niebuhr, representing the theological tradition, argues that the ideal choices and values of the human spirit cannot be bound within the natural world. "The naturalist sees human freedom as little more than of *homo faber*." [82] It is in "divine transcendence the human spirit finds a home in which it can understand its stature of freedom"; [83] yet he asserts that human beings are incapable of this transcendence. Man is thus "in the position of being unable to comprehend himself in his full stature of freedom without a principle of comprehension which is beyond his comprehension." [84] Our present purpose is not to evaluate these views, but simply to suggest that there is no need of resorting to such ingenious metaphysical or theological dialectic in order to make clear man's highest preferences, such as distinguish him from the mere animal. Why not stay on the empirical level, on the level of confirmable fact? What, then, is the nature of human preference?

First, mind as preferential response is experimental in the sense that

[81] *The Intelligible World*, New York, 1929, p. 140.
[82] *The Nature and Destiny of Man*, New York, 1939, I, 124.
[83] *Ibid.*, p. 126.   [84] *Ibid.*, p. 125.

anticipatory results are compared, their consequences being noted by themselves and in relation to other consequences. This activity is objective in its intent and empirical in its drive. There are, of course, different ideational levels of choice. Making an intelligent choice is a difficult achievement. On a rather low ideational level preference is habitual. There is no clear distinction between alternative consequences. The great bulk of our choices are on this level. On a higher ideational level preferences are made through rules. Rules are guides to preferences. Being formulas that cover typical situations, they enable us to meet such situations in advance. They thus help us to deal with the complexity of life. On a still higher ideational level preferences are made through hypotheses and principles. Here one goes beyond rules. Instead of asking what one is to do, one asks why it should be done, or, in other words, what far-reaching results are expected from a given choice. Secondly, preferential response is concerned with human needs or desires. The chosen ends are ones which satisfy human desires more adequately. The "better" is the desirable rather than the desired; yet the "better" or the "best" are meaningful only in relation to a conflict of desires, and apart from this conflict there is no meaning to choice. The function of reason is not to rival desire, but rather to survey the situation impartially; the objects desired and the desires themselves are examined to the end of determining how all the desires involved may be satisfied and integrated. The desirable is not a transcendental good, unless one were to mean by "transcendental" in this context the more inclusive, that is, the comprehensive ideal of natural human desires. Of course, it is not being maintained that whenever human beings make choices they make them wisely or that the desires in every case can be integrated, but rather that the possibility exists of making wise choices and integrations. Finally, preferential activity as choice of ends and means forms a continuum. Though within a limited context one can make the distinction between ends and means, in a larger context chosen ends become means for other ends, and chosen means attain the status of ends for the time being. The person who has chosen business as his end finds it also to be the means for securing a certain place in society, while each means that is chosen for the success of his business becomes an end to be attained.

This brief account of human choice may have its limitations; yet whatever modifications one may have to introduce, one should be guided by empirical evidence, not by principles that have no empirical application.

IV

Throughout this discussion there has been hardly any reference to consciousness. Here, again, mind is anticipatory and cognitive. This phase of mind must now be considered.

Frequently mind and consciousness are considered identical. In the present discussion the notion of mind has a much wider meaning than that of consciousness. "Mind" refers to all phases of anticipatory response; "consciousness" to one phase of that response. What, then, is consciousness?

The tradition of classic empiricism has identified consciousness with the immediacy of experience. From this view of consciousness usually the consequence is drawn that mind is private, unsharable, and inaccessible to other minds. For the modern empiricist, however, with his belief that all meaningful questions of fact are experimentally approachable, the earlier usage of the word "consciousness," which conforms to its etymological meaning, is more fruitful. *Con* added to *scious* refers to the togetherness of knowledge, to participation in another's experience rather than to the privacy of unsharable immediacy. Consciousness as togetherness of knowledge, or the sharing phase of mind, takes two forms—self-consciousness and other-consciousness.

Let us first consider mind as self-consciousness. As a preliminary step to this analysis it is important to observe that by "self-consciousness" I do not mean consciousness of a spiritual entity. Such an observation never comes within experience. Still another point to observe is that experience, or the stimulus-response relation, does not necessarily involve consciousness. Having an experience, like the sensation of the color green, and being conscious of the experience are two distinct things. The concept of unconscious experience is not meaningless. It was mainly the tradition of the classic empiricists that was responsible for the neglect of the notion of the unconscious. Since they identified experience with consciousness and further identified the two concepts with unsharable immediacy, they had no place for unconscious experience. Yet many philosophers and psychologists have persistently emphasized the importance of unconscious experience. Freud argues, "Every mental act begins as an unconscious mental activity." [35] And before Freud, Schopenhauer claimed that "the will . . . in itself . . . is unconscious." [36] One need not make a mystery of unconscious experience or place it in some supernatural or subnatural realm: it is either the instinctive, impulsive activities of the organism or activities which, though they have cognition of their object, lack cognition of themselves. Frequently we see, we hear, we touch, we feel, we select, we reject, we start activities, and we complete activities without being conscious of them.

The transition to self-consciousness or introspective consciousness is a simple one. In certain cases one does not merely see a green color, but has the cognition that one sees it; in short, one knows, one is aware of having a specific mode of sensation. Similarly, when one is carried away by anger, one can hardly be said to be conscious of one's anger or to introspect one's anger; but as soon as one tries to understand what was happening to oneself, one begins to be conscious of one's anger. One begins to remember the angry words and gestures one was using, and because of them one knows that one was angry. Consciousness is not merely the experience of anger but also the cognition of the experience. The same is true of any milder experience. One may, for example, be listening to a melody leisurely, yet one becomes conscious of what one was listening to only when one begins to tell oneself, "I have been listening to so and so." What, then, are the traits of mind as introspective consciousness?

The first thing to be noted about introspective consciousness is that consciousness is relational. Consciousness is always consciousness of something. One is conscious of having the sensation of color, or of being angry, or of listening to a melody. There is no consciousness as such. The second thing to be noted is that consciousness is inspection. In conscious activity there is an attempt to know, to find out, to report what experience one has been going through. Merely to be angry is not to be conscious; but to find out that one was angry is to be conscious of that experience. Thirdly, consciousness is a specific mode of inspection: it is retrospective inspection. Introspective consciousness is always of something that has just happened; it is an early retrospection. So there is no consciousness without memory. This phase of consciousness has

---

[35] *Collected Papers,* New York, 1924-25, IV, 27.
[36] *The World as Will and Idea,* tr. by R. B. Haldane and John Kemp, London, 1885-86, II, 411.

been emphasized by Professor Whitehead: "Whenever there is consciousness there is an element of recollection. It recalls earlier phases from the dim recesses of the unconscious." [37] Similarly, Professor Holt maintains: "Whereas all so-called 'introspective consciousness' involves both retrospection (memory) and verbal report." [38] Thus, to have consciousness there must be at least two mental events: an original mental event and a later mental event, the latter happening immediately after the former and reporting it. In more behavioristic terms, introspective consciousness is had whenever an individual cognitively responds to his prior response as stimulus. Thus, one might call conscious response reflexive anticipatory response, or reflexive mind.

To the reflexive view of consciousness an important objection might be raised. How could we, one might ask, ever get the notion of a *present now* if we are conscious only of an *immediate past?* Do we not have our sensation at the exact moment we are sensing? To this the answer seems to be that since having sensation and being conscious of it are two different things, the report of the sensation, that is, consciousness, is in the present but not what is being reported. Of course, when I become conscious of my present reporting, the original reporting itself becomes a past event. There is, thus, an endless regress, but this regress does not involve us in any paradox. Psychologically the present is a durational event, part of a continuous process that has one end in the past and the other in the future; it is not an instant without duration.

Yet consciousness should not be considered something apart from the life of the organism. The organism is a going concern, a continuous process of adaptation, and in this process consciousness is functionally involved. Consciousness as reflexive response meaningfully unifies past experience with the present, and so makes possible more effective adaptation. When one becomes aware that one is angry, one tries to resume one's normal bearing.

Consciousness is also other-consciousness. Mind knows not only its own experience but also the experience of others. Everyday language indicates this possibility when one says, "I am conscious of my neighbor's predicament" or "Friends are conscious of each other's secrets." Yet, probably more than any other phase of mind, objective knowledge

[37] *Process and Reality*, New York, 1929, p. 370.
[38] "Materialism and the Criterion of the Psychic," *The Psychological Review*, XLIV (1937), 46. See also E. A. Singer, "On Conscious Mind," *Journal of Philosophy*, XXVI (1929), 561–75.

of other minds has been denied. Even empirical-minded philosophers have faltered here. Professor Lewis, whose predilections are primarily pragmatic and empirical, writes: ". . . minds are private . . . one's own mind is something with which one is directly acquainted . . . but that the mind of another is something which one is unable directly to inspect." [39] "We significantly believe in other minds than our own, but we cannot *know* that such exist." [40]

At best, knowledge of other minds is considered merely analogical. The argument runs that I, and I alone, am conscious; that certain of my bodily actions are accompanied by certain mental states. When I observe similar actions in others, I merely conclude that they, too, must have accompanying mental states. In its extreme form this argument should lead one to solipsism, a view that many thinkers find attractive, but to which no one seems willing to succumb. One need not object to the analogical argument when it is used properly, that is to say, as part of an inductive inference. But the argument has been usually used as an unconfirmable hypothesis, and as such it is factually untrue and logically useless. The argument is factually untrue, because one does not come to know others merely through analogy. Knowledge of one's self and of others arises out of the process of social interchange. The individual begins to know himself through his conception of himself in relation to others. The argument is also logically useless, because no degree of evidence can either confirm the hypothesis or refute it. If such a hypothesis is not meaningless, it can at least be considered logically inconsequential.

But the knowledge of other minds is not beyond one's grasp, nor is the nature of this knowledge merely analogical. I can know what others perceive, think, wish, or feel, and others can know what I perceive, think, wish, or feel. Here the stimulus of the anticipatory response is another mind. A few points may be mentioned in favor of this claim. First, it should be noted that the cognitive objects of mind do not exclusively belong to itself, but may also be shared by other minds. Yonder tree that you see, I too may see; the music that you hear, I too may hear; the mathematical equations that you formulate, I too may formulate. There is no object of your cognition which in time may not also be mine. To conclude that because your ideas are yours they are ex-

[39] "Some Logical Considerations concerning the Mental," *Journal of Philosophy*, XXXVIII (1941), 226.
[40] *Ibid.*, p. 232.

clusively yours is what Professor Perry calls the fallacy of "exclusive par
ticularity." There is nothing contradictory about the notion that you
ideas may also become my ideas. And it is because there are common
sharable ideas that communication is possible. The conductor of a sym
phony makes gestures; the musicians respond, not primarily to th
physical movement of the gestures, but to what the gesture means t
the conductor; and the conductor, in turn, understands the meaning o
his gestures in the way the musicians do. Here we have meanings, idea
and objects of cognition which are shared at the same time by man
minds. Secondly, it should be noted that the conative phase of mind—
its desires, purposes, feelings—is equally objective and observable. De
sires are not unobservable entities in some inaccessible realm; they ar
a certain type of observable behavior. Is one hungry, tired, or in pain
For each of these experiences the counterstimulus will objectively verif
the facts. The degree of one's hunger may be verified by the amount o
food one eats; the degree of weariness may be determined by the num
ber of hours one sleeps; and the degree of one's pain may be determine
by the amount of anodyne one takes. And, again, is one's passion in lif
music? This passion is not something hidden in one's self, but resident i
one's actions—in one's playing of a musical instrument, in one's stud
of music, in one's attendance at concerts. One's love of music is thes
and similar activities and nothing other than these activities. Finally, i
should be observed that the sensations of another mind are not beyon
the knowledge of others. We should be careful, of course, to point ou
that to know the sensation of another is not to have his sensation; fo
sensation as excitation of his nerve centers does not belong to me—I hav
a nervous system other than his. But because another individual is mor
advantageously placed in relation to his experience, it does not follow
that I cannot verify his experience. I can know another's sensation i
the same way that I can know any other event. To know fire I nee
not be fire, I need only know its consequences. The same is true of th
sensation of another individual. Has another the sensation of a color.
This question is answered experimentally by determining the intensit
and quality of his sensation. Another's experience is not beyond experi
mental verification. I can know, or be conscious of, his experience as wel
as I can know my own.

Yet in asserting that there is other-consciousness or that other mind
can be known, one need not deny the fact that in this knowledge th

observer and the observed may possess certain relative advantages. The observer has the advantage as far as the more constant and settled aspects of another's behavior are concerned. Frequently one knows the basic limitations and powers of one's friends better than they do. On the other hand, the one who is observed has the advantage as far as his specific immediate feelings are concerned, and his immediate objects of knowledge. But these relative advantages are not insurmountable and are not very important. What is more important is the fact that through consciousness the human mind gains a new dimension. Philosophers who maintain that the distinctive trait of man is consciousness state a significant truth, for it is through consciousness that an individual's past and present experiences are meaningfully related and fruitfully directed toward future behavior, and it is through consciousness that group communication, participation, and enterprise are made possible. Consciousness refers to the sharing phase of mind, and strictly it takes two minds to make a mind.

The different dimensions of mind—that is, mind as cognition, as conation, and as consciousness—have been discussed as modes of anticipatory response; but these dimensions are not isolated, they form a unity. And this unity is the whole mind. Yet this unity is not a soul, a psyche, residing in the body. Structurally the unity is the biological organism; behaviorally the unity is the integrated action. And at higher levels of integration mind attains not only unity but also its supreme achievement, freedom.

12

THE CATEGORIES OF NATURALISM

William R. Dennes

THE last half-century has seen a striking shift in what may be called the basic, as contrasted with the derivative, categories employed in naturalistic philosophy. Older interpretations in terms of matter, motion, and energy (or even in terms of substance and attribute) have given way to interpretations in terms of events, qualities, and relations (or process and character, or essence and flux). Now most contemporary philosophers have abandoned the notion that there are different and theoretically incompatible ways of knowing and that, accordingly, different philosophical positions are distinguished from one another by the fact that each of them employs some and excludes other methods of establishing beliefs as true, probable, or enlightening. How, then, are philosophical positions (such as those called naturalistic, idealistic, and so forth) distinguished from one another? Are there philosophies, or is there only philosophy?

Many gifted philosophers have lately converged upon one sort of answer to these questions. They have argued that philosophic positions are distinguished essentially by the different basic categories which they employ in interpretation, and by consequent differences in the interpretations which they develop. An examination of the relations that hold between the basic categories employed in explanatory statements and the content of those statements is therefore important for the understanding, not only of naturalistic philosophy, but of any philosophy. The recent shift in the categories of naturalism makes such an examination of the role of categories particularly important. It also makes the examination especially promising; for when the representatives of a fairly continuous philosophical tradition thus alter the categorial system they employ, we have an unusually good opportunity to determine just what effects the use of one set of categories or another has upon the theories developed in terms of them.

In what follows it will be argued quite generally that the categories basic in any philosophy cannot legitimately restrict the content of positive theories (if any) developed within that philosophy or contribute anything toward establishing the degree of probability of such theories. More specifically, we shall examine certain respects in which the recent shift in the categories of naturalism reflects a partial recognition of this situation and even prepares the way for the elimination of naturalism as a particular "ism" and its merging in the generic activity of philosophy as critical interpretation—or, more simply, as criticism.

But whatever may be the results of our examination, it will appear at the outset that positive theories (formulated in the context of a naturalistic philosophy) are expressed, not as opinions about events and their qualities and relations, but as hypotheses about what naturalists (and also most other philosophers) call the "order" and "structure," the "causes," "grounds," "purposes," and "values" of various entities, actual or merely possible. If recent naturalists nevertheless differ from philosophers of other schools and from earlier naturalists, the difference would seem to be that when pressed they construe what we may call the derivative or secondary categories, enumerated above, as names for various configurations of factors designated by such basic categorial terms as "events," "qualities," and "relations."

What, then, is the significance of the shift from such categories as matter and motion to the categories "event," "quality," and "relation"? Is it merely a verbal change, a new way of speaking? Or does the change in terminology reflect changes in the content of naturalistic metaphysics? If the latter, are the changes merely a retreat from some of the positions of traditional naturalism, or an advance to new positions? Or do the changes constitute an approach to the abandonment of anything that could be usefully distinguished as a naturalistic doctrine in metaphysics?

Even if we had forgotten the arguments of Descartes and Locke, recent semantic discussions would force us to take seriously the question whether the shift in the categories used by naturalists is merely a change in terminology. But in order to deal with the problem, it is necessary to give some attention to what we shall mean by "terms" (or "words"), by "meaning," and in particular by the term "category." If we follow carefully the Aristotelian (and recent empiricist) tradition, we shall mean by "terms," including the special class of terms called "categories," all sets of occurrences which are visible or audible or otherwise sensible [1] and

---

[1] The restriction of terms to sensible entities simply defines them as entities that are capable (as are all the terms in what are ordinarily called languages) of use in

are used as signs for entities (or sets of entities) different from themselves.

On this account of terms, no occurrence can as such be said to be a term or to have meaning intrinsic to it. There is no limit to the number or variety of sounds, shapes, motions, and so forth that may occur in the world or to their possible correlations. But none of them could be a term or could have meaning except as some agent used it to refer to an entity or a set of entities (actually occurrent or merely possible) other than itself. Where such acts of referring take place, they make terms out of the sets of perceptible entities which they use to refer, and they constitute as meanings of those terms the sets of entities (actual or merely possible) to which they are thus used to refer.

Many philosophers reject this account of terms and meanings (and with it the consequent theory of categories) on the ground that it denies (or at least neglects) meanings in those senses in which the qualities, the contexts, the causes and effects, and the values of entities are said to be the meanings (or even "the intrinsic meanings") of those entities. Others reject it on the ground that it denies the very existence of qualities and contexts. And still others reject it on the ground that it presupposes a discrimination of "atomic units," which, apart from the question whether there are in fact such units, is in any case impossible to carry out because of the dynamic interpenetration which obtains between the processes of interpreting and explaining and the objects of such processes.

These objections rest upon confusions. To be sure, a man acts within his "logical rights" if he chooses to say that the meaning of an entity (say the Botticelli *Venus*) is the integration of felt qualities, or the complex felt quality, or the expression of these qualities which the picture is experienced as being (different, no doubt, in every experiencing of it). He is equally within his rights if he chooses to say that the meaning of that entity is the wide context of artistic, technological and economic processes of which it is in certain respects a focus. And he is, again, equally within his rights if he chooses to say that an entity means its causes or its effects or both of these; as one may say that John's red face means a day's sailing (cause) or an impending desquamation (effect), or

---

communication between persons. But this restriction in no sense denies that a man *may*, in his unexpressed "private thinking," use entities (such as his own feelings) insensible by others, as symbols for anything he may choose thus to symbolize. But "thought" without any sort of symbolization would seem to be indistinguishable from revery—from any flow whatever of feelings and images.

both. Now it is fair to say, on the basis of reports available, that all experienced entities do have qualities and contexts and probably have causes and effects; also, that most of them have values, positive or negative, great or little and that in many cases and in varying degrees their qualities and values change with changes of context. But if we want to refer to any of these various aspects or relations or traits, it is usually better to call them by their more precise and usual names, (such as "qualities," "causes," "values") than to call them the "meanings" of the entities in question. And it is, in any case, experience, not any philosophical presupposition or the definition of any category (such as "meaning" or "event"), that justifies us in saying that events have contexts, qualities, causes, effects, and values. The important point to recognize in this connection is that the Aristotelian (and recent empiricist) account of meaning, just outlined, does not deny (as also it does not of itself establish) that all occurrences, including those it calls "terms" and those it calls their "meanings," are qualified, are in contexts (usually dynamic), and may have causes, effects, and values. Nor can this, or any other, conception of the nature of terms and meanings determine what specifically the qualities, contexts, causes, effects, or values of any entities (observed, imagined, supposed, or inferred) are, or are likely to be. On the contrary, it is precisely in order to facilitate the reporting, the inferring, and the interpreting of such aspects of existence that it insists that we must employ terms which, however elastic, have reference to and have some limits in their reference to the sorts of qualities and configurations that are their meanings.

But is it possible thus to demarcate the sets of entities we use as terms and the sorts of entities we mean by them? Or are the processes that make up nature (including human experience and thought) so fluid, so dynamic, so interactive that all attempts to demarcate terms and their ranges of reference distort these processes? Would it be better to describe human discourse as a kind of behavior characterized by its influence upon the other activities of the organism engaged in it and upon the activities of other organisms exposed to it than as actually describing the materials it is naïvely taken to be about?

To be sure, any stretch of thinking, while it is part of the processes of nature, is never itself that part which it is about. Nor would it make sense to wish (as F. H. Bradley apparently did at times) that it were; for if it were, it would be in no way different from "its object" and could not mean it (or anything else), or describe it, or explain it. It could only be it. But discourse is not only not identical with its subject matter; more specifically, it usually consists in processes less fluid than those it purports to be about. However, the very assertion—even the thinking—of this contrast itself requires that we should use the terms which mean degrees and sorts of fluidity with something less than unlimited fluidity. Otherwise those terms would mean all things equally, but nothing in particular.[2] If we have come to believe that many stretches of existence are more dynamic and interactive than was once supposed, let us say so and not stultify ourselves by arguing that in order to be adequate to their changing subject matter the statements of our hypotheses should themselves be as changing or as misty as the processes they are about. Three hundred miles an hour is pretty fast for a man to move, but it does not make sense to say that the expression of the ratio of the numbers of units of time and of distance should itself change pretty fast (or as fast) if it is to be an adequate expression of the speed in question.

Far, then, from denying or neglecting qualities, contexts, values, or the flux pervasive of nature and experience, the employment of terms as meaning in the Aristotelian (and contemporary empiricist) sense would seem to be unavoidable if we are to describe those very qualities, contexts, causes, effects, and values which some men have preferred to call the intrinsic meanings of entities; and it is also unavoidable if we are to formulate to any (even the smallest) degree of approximation, the very differences of dynamicity which often distinguish discourse from its objects, but which do not, as some allege, render it inadequate to (or distortive of) them.

If we follow the Aristotelian and empiricist tradition with respect to terms and meanings, what are we to say of philosophical categories, particularly of those that distinguish one metaphysics from another? Traditional metaphysicians have aimed to characterize, not restricted fields of phenomena, but some at least of the interrelations and part of the structure of the whole range of being. Like all other terms, the categorial terms they have used (such as Nature or Substance or God; matter and motion; substance, attributes, and modes; event, quality, and relation; essence and existence) have no meanings in themselves. They mean what they are used to refer to. And if various metaphysicians differ in the term (or set of terms) they use to refer to the whole range

[2] See Aristotle, *Metaphysics*, ch. iv, but especially 1006ᵃ29 to 1006ᵇ18.

of being, it would seem that all the terms so used would then share a single meaning—or else would be on all fours as having no meaning, if, as some allege, references to the whole of reality as an entity which could not have another to delimit it and must itself include the very symbols and acts of referring which are used to designate it are references to nothing. If metaphysical categories are terms used to mean all being (or the cosmos), then there is no difference in meaning, whatever the differences in sound and shape, between any set of such categories and other sets; and those who supposed there are differences of meaning between them (not to speak of different hypotheses implied by them) would be victims of a crude sort of psychological association, or indeed of a kind of verbal sleight-of-hand.

But after all, can it be that the categories of considerable metaphysical systems have been nothing but different names for all being and have thus differed, not in their meanings, but only as sounds, as shapes, as slogans, and as battle cries? No! It is much more likely that metaphysical categories have been names used, not for all being, but for specific and familiar sorts of traits and patterns of occurrences, to which metaphysicians have attributed special importance because they have hoped to show that all occurrences and all traits can be—not reduced to them— but explained by their relations to them. Categorial traits, on this analysis, are traits chosen as basic referents in procedures of interpretation and explanation in the sense that reports and hypotheses about all sorts of traits and processes are finally formulated as beliefs or suppositions about the relations of the traits and processes to be explained to the traits named by the categories. But since any relation of any B to any A is in fact equally a relation of that A to that B and may always legitimately be formulated as such, a choice of categorial traits as basic referents in explanation can make no legitimate difference whatever to the content of any descriptive or explanatory theory, but only to the language employed in formulating the theory. This will hold, whether the traits selected as categorial are widely pervasive of existence or are very rarely manifested, whether instances of their occurrence have a very wide or a very narrow range of causal consequences—indeed, it will hold, whether they are imagined traits or configurations, for whose occurrence there is no evidence, or are traits and configurations, instances of which are actually observed.

In fine, all possible entities can be described quite as adequately in terms of their relations to one sort of entity as in terms of their relations to any other—indeed, if scrupulously carried out, the accounts will be identical in content. When C is the name of any instance of a categorial entity (actual or imaginary, commonplace or rare, and much or little causally effective), and where we are in fact interested in the relations of A and B to one another, not in their relations to C, we may, nevertheless, formulate the relations in which we are interested quite as accurately as the different or similar ways in which A and B are, respectively, related to C as we can in any other way. In many cases such a formulation might be exceedingly cumbersome and might require an excessive amount of time and labor to carry it out. But that is not to say that its content would be different from that of the easier formulation. A description of the changes in position of any sidereal body in terms of its relations to the earth's axis and equatorial plane would, for example, be hundreds of times more complicated and laborious than is a description of them in terms of their relations to the plane of the ecliptic and to solar axes perpendicular to that plane. But there are no grounds whatsoever to justify the allegation that either description would (or could), because of the frame of reference employed, assert or deny anything which the other would not. If both are carried to completion, or if each is carried as far as the other, both will assert exactly the same things. And, of course, neither choice of references implies any hypothesis whatsoever about the actual relations of sidereal bodies—let alone an "hypothesis" (such as "the earth is at rest" or "the sun is at rest") the rejection of which could be implied by the other choice of references.

There are a great many objections to this thesis which deserve serious attention. To consider one of them, and briefly: Some of the highest living authorities (to whom the present writer owes much) teach that if A and B are hues—let us say, specific shades of red and green—then they are related to one another and to all other hues by their relative distance from one another (i.e., by the relative extension of the ranges of hues intervening between them and various other hues) in a "continuous" color gamut; but they are not related to C if C is, let us say, an instance of the sound called F-sharp next above middle C. Hence, it is alleged, the relation of A to B cannot in this case be formulated as relations of A to C and of B to C.

However, the instances of red and green in question must in fact stand in unambiguous spatio-temporal relations to any instance or instances of the F-sharp which one may consider—as must also all instances of other hues that differ from the specific red and green. There is, to be sure, not one chance in ten million that an arrangement of occurrent hues as spatio-temporally related to an occurrence of F-sharp would be an order, like that in the customary color cone, in which each hue is indistinguishable from either of its differing next neighbors—although the thing is not impossible. But the customary arrangement of hues in the color cone differs from any other ordering of hues in this one respect only: when it is carried out we feel no break in continuity when we run through the range from any hue to any other. That hues can be so arranged is a most important fact about them; but it is equally a fact that when hues are put in other orders we do feel discontinuities on inspecting them. Neither one of these facts can be said to determine one specific order as the intrinsically proper order, or the only order, of colors; although for most purposes descriptions of hues in terms of their relations in a continuous gamut will be found highly convenient. To say of any hue that it simply is its place in the continuous gamut, is merely to define the name of that hue. No definition or description whatsoever can actually express, or deliver to us, the felt qualities which we name red and green and yellow or those felt complex qualities which we name continuity and discontinuity in color differences. We name such qualities; but although the names may be uttered (with various sorts of accompanying ostensive indications), the qualities themselves cannot be said. But once they are named, all that can be said about their occurrences and their relations (including the specification of the conditions under which what is called continuity of difference of shades is regularly reported by observers) can be said in an account of colors that describes their spatio-temporal relations to an occurrent sound, quite as accurately as in any other account. Hence the content of any explanatory hypothesis whatsoever about hues and their felt continuities and discontinuities can be as adequately formulated in terms of such relations to an occurrent sound as in any other way.

We are thus forced to the conclusion that if traits named by categories are chosen as basic references in description and explanation, the choice cannot make the slightest logically tolerable difference in the content of descriptive statements or explanatory hypotheses which are worked out in terms of the chosen references. But there can, in fact, be no question but that men have chosen—or at least have justified (and continued in) the use of—specific sets of categories because they believed that the traits named by them were either very widespread in their occurrence (were the constituents of entities of most or all types), or were causally crucial, or were in themselves or in their effects decisively important for human beings—that is, were themselves prized or disprized or contributed fairly heavily to the enhancement or diminution of things precious to mankind. In this connection it is desirable to keep the following point in mind: How widespread in existence, how generally constitutive of "things," how causally effective, how much loved by men or how much contributive to things thus loved, any sort of trait or configuration or occurrence is—all these are questions to be seriously answered, not at all by what traits anyone has chosen to call basic or to use as basic references in explanation, but only by observation and by ordinary inductive and probability inferences from observations, reports, and other sorts of document. Nobody can legitimately alter such evidences, or the inferences from them, because of the categories which he employs. A man accustomed to using the categories of a monistic metaphysic may indeed keep his eyes sharpened to notice similarities in the same materials in which a pluralist may be quicker to perceive differences.[3] But to say that for one there are more similarities in the processes of nature than there are for the other would be no better than to say that if one is a Conservative, then a diet deficient in vitamin D does not produce rachitic children, whereas if one is a Liberal, it does. It would be no better than saying that for Fascists, *but not for other men*, there is a different and more trustworthy way of determining the influence of race upon conduct than there is for determining the influence of heat upon oxygen.

Furthermore, if different metaphysicians, operating with different sets of categories, do actually make different findings, then their different theories are not different hypotheses about the same materials, but accounts of different materials, and hence are no more in conflict, are no more to be considered as theoretic alternatives, than are, say, the

---

[3] I here deal with monism and pluralism as theories that have some reference at least—however "indirect"—to observable states of affairs. If there is any enlightenment or significance in such metaphysical "theories" as assert that, no matter what happens or is observed, it must still be referred to a single (or to a multiple) transcendent ground or source that is strictly unobservable, and must be so referred whether cumulative experience yields more similarities or more differences—if there is theoretic (as against emotional) significance in such "theories" I have not found it and must leave to others its exposition, as also the defense of the notion that it was in any such sense that considerable philosophers have really intended their metaphysics.

hypotheses of geography as against those of philology. But unlike geographers and philologists, the holders of different metaphysical theories, if they really made different findings in all situations and thus lived in totally different worlds, could never know that they thus differed, since *ex hypothesi* no one of them could ever either find himself (or show to any other man) any single instance of the difference between the traits he finds (or suppose) in existence and those that other metaphysicians find (or suppose). If he could find such a single instance he would have, as an honest man, to abate his account of being as ultimately of one sort and admit the reality of other sorts of being which are quite irreducible to the sort which had theretofore occupied him.

If the preceding analysis of terms, of meaning, and of that special class of terms called philosophical categories, is acceptable, what are we to make of the recent shift, mentioned at the beginning of this chapter and recognized on every hand, in the categories characteristically employed by philosophical naturalists?

There is no doubt that the change from matter to event as basic category reflects the recognition that materialism is a position for which there is no evidence, if by "materialism" we mean the doctrine that the ultimate constituents of all existents are extended, hard, more or less heavy, indestructible, and in motion. Indeed, if by calling any entity indestructible we mean that it is such that its nonexistence is impossible, then indestructibility is not even a conceivable trait. Its attribution is not logically possible. And if by asserting indestructibility we intend to assert a law of conservation as holding for all being, then our assertion has a worse fault than the minuteness (which has so often been pointed out) of the supporting evidence in comparison with the scope of the generalization. For our assertion is literally meaningless. Conservation, as significant in physical theory or in "common sense" discussion, is a relation between a limited system and a measure external to it. It is empty of meaning when asserted of the whole of being in relation to nothing else, and totally question-begging when construed as a relation between that whole and some entity said to be of absolutely and intrinsically constant magnitude within it.

The change also reflects the influence of the hypothesis, scientifically well-established, that nearly all ranges of existence have aspects (and important aspects) that are more fluid, more complex, and more intricately interactive than men had grounds for believing them to be in the nineteenth century and earlier. To be sure, Aristotle commonly meant by the terms we translate by "matter" and its cognates a fluid and dynamic aspect of existents. But it is probably only in the last fifty years that men have clearly realized that with respect to a world in which any alteration occurs it would be meaningless to say of any constituent of that world that it is absolutely fixed and unchanging (let alone unchangeable). For in a system in which there is any alteration whatever, it will always be quite arbitrary (logically, empirically, and factually—or, if one prefers, ontologically) to interpret the alteration as all taking place in some strands or areas which are thus contrasted with others that are said not to change. This insight is part of what is reflected by the contemporary choice of "event" as a basic category. It is an old story that there is strictly no difference in the theoretic content of the two statements that certain co-ordinates in the universe are fixed and a man's finger moves in relation to them, and that the finger is at rest and its "apparent motion" is a shift of the rest of his body and of the rest of the universe in relation to it. If anything comes to be, persists, or passses away, its doing so is a change in relation to its earlier stages and to other things [4] simultaneously existing, and could as well be described as changes in these latter in relation to it. The withering of flowers is one kind of change. It is another kind of change when they—or "the solid earth"— continue in certain configurations and in the manifestation of certain qualities. A change occurs when the complex of events and qualities which is a ten-minute section of the career of a white snowflake develops into what we call an hour section of such a career, and just as certainly as when it develops into what we call "melted" snow. In neither case, of course, could the change be said to be an alteration or destruction of the ten-minute section from which it developed. Only if there were no change whatever in the world could we say of any strand in it that it is in all respects unchanged. But in that case we could not say that anything persisted unchanged either, since where there were no change there would also be nothing of what is ordinarily meant by "time" or by "persistence."

The shift from the use of the category of matter to the use of the category of event reflects also one other change in attitude. Materialistic naturalism attached a greater or less probability to the positive hypothesis

---

[4] Lines demarcating *earlier stages* from *other things* are, of course, logically arbitrary.

that the final constituents of all things are extended, hard, heavy, and in motion, as well as indestructible. But the naturalism of events is entirely neutral with respect to—indeed, as such, it is entirely free from—hypotheses as to what are the qualities and relations of events (whether "final" or otherwise), that have occurred, are now occurring, or will occur. Its statements conform to the truism that no event (or events) can be fairly described as a complex of factors from which the factor called process is excluded. But the construction of hypotheses as to the qualities and configurations of events it leaves entirely to science; or if it performs such constructions itself, its procedure in so doing does not differ in any way from the type called scientific. But it is not thus renouncing a possible alternative. For how could anyone reach a serious opinion as to what the pattern of any range of events is except by observing what he can of it (that is, by noting the similarities, differences, concomitances, and sequences which its phases exhibit) and by making inductive inferences from such observations and from the reports of other observers (and also making "free" speculative hypotheses, but in both cases confirming inferences and hypotheses by further observations)—in short, by following the procedures definitive of science?

Our examination of the naturalistic use of the category "event" is by no means complete; but limitations of space rule out even a comparable examination of the categories "quality" and "relation." To be aware of, or to imagine, change or process is to experience differences of the kind called "qualitative." These differences must be related as in succession —as one after another—if they are to participate in constituting what is meant by change or process or event. Furthermore, if they are to distinguish what we choose to call one event from another (or, if we prefer, one phase of a more inclusive, or totally inclusive, event from other phases), they must be related either as successive to one another or as simultaneous with one another but to the right or left of, above or below, one another, and so forth. In other words, when we say that something has happened or is happening, we mean that different instances of qualities have occurred or are occurring in succession; and unless such occurrences do take place, there could be no true or probable opinions about happenings in the world. Spreads of qualities that exhibit serial orders that are distinguished from temporal successiveness are described as spatially related.

Are we justified in designating by different names—in putting in different classes—the traits called "relations" and those called "qualities"? It would seem so. For not only do traits of these two sorts often vary independently of one another—different sets of qualities often do that —but also those called relations have converses, whereas those called qualities do not. And in general what we call a relation, the holding of which is extrinsic to the qualities between which it can hold, is an entity different in type from the terms between which it can hold, although it could not "exist" or be "exhibited" apart from instances of such terms. Actually, qualities are noted, or given, in relation. This means merely that any relational structure is a relational structure, not a quality. But neither qualities nor relations nor quality-relation structures exhaust what is meant by "event," nor do we experience qualities and relations except in what we call occurrent (or imagined occurrent) instances of them.

The factors of process, quality, and relation, which contemporary naturalism takes to be the constituents of all that occurs, of all that exists, cannot be verbally defined in terms other than synonyms. But, since synonyms differ as sounds or shapes, but not in their meanings and hence not as terms, definition by synonyms is no definition at all. Of the factor of occurrence that distinguishes qualitied and related events from qualities and relations *in abstracto*, one must say, as Aristotle did of what he called ὕλη, that, as in itself indeterminate, it could not possibly exist or be conceived by itself (devoid, that is, of qualities and relations that distinguish actual occurrences from one another and from nothing). One cannot *say* strictly what one means by "event" or "quality" or "relation." But one can (and does) give ostensive definitions of quality names and relation names, and one gets responses that indicate the comprehension of such definitions by those to whom one addresses them. One can sort pencils and books and geranium and larkspur blooms and indicate which of them exhibit the qualities one means by "red," and which the qualities one means by "blue." One can put a blue book between two reds, and a red between a blue and a red, and a red pencil between two red pencils, and by appropriate indications can give an ostensive definition of what one means by the relation of "being between." Furthermore, there could be no instance of a quality or relation which is not theoretically open to inspection by any cognizing agent, whatever may be the technical difficulties in the way of accomplishing the inspection in some cases. After such definings and some further definings similar to them in kind one can construct a description, let us say, of a disk with two concentric circular bands of blue between three concentric circular bands of red. Then if one encounters (or can produce) an instance, occurrent and more or less persistent, of an object which the description fits, one is in a position to indicate what one means by a qualified and structured event, as contrasted with the description of a relational structure *in abstracto*.

The contemporary naturalist therefore believes: (1) that the three basic categories he employs designate aspects of existents which are actually given in experience; (2) that no instance of any of these aspects exists apart from instances of the other aspects, although the aspects are distinguishable by "a distinction of reason"; and (3) that he can indicate instances of the aspects meant by his categorial terms to anyone who may desire a definition of those terms. If these beliefs are correct, it follows that he is in a position to attempt, in terms of his basic categories, an empirical interpretation of concepts, hypotheses, laws, and evaluations developed in the natural sciences, in historical studies, and in aesthetic and moral judgments. If, for example, the concept of body is examined—a concept that was a basic category in earlier naturalism—the modern naturalist would ask: What do we observe, compare (including measuring), manipulate, and infer when we deal with bodies? What but configurations of qualities occurring and persisting (that is, more or less persistent) and standing in "spatial" relations to other occurrent configurations?

Whereas nineteenth-century idealists and naturalists believed that by dealing with all entities in terms of their relations to what was meant by the basic categories of spirit or of matter they were saying something about the ultimate nature of those entities—namely, that they were of the nature of spirit (or of matter) or approached that nature; the modern naturalist admits (indeed insists) that the program of dealing with all entities as qualitied related events does not of itself determine in any respect the nature of anything. The nature and the existential distribution of things can be determined only by exploring and inferring the specific sorts of quality and relation manifested by events in various regions of being.

Three sorts of question thus become crucial in an appraisal of contemporary naturalism. (1) If the use of naturalistic categories entails no positive determination (and also no restriction) upon the nature of anything, is there any justification of such categories beyond the recognition (which their use reflects) that no absolute constants can be significantly assumed and the resolution (which their use indicates) to proceed empirically and scientifically? (2) Can the derivative or secondary categories generally employed in explanation and evaluation be satisfactorily interpreted as meaning various configurations of qualitied and related events? (3) Could the secondary categories be satisfactorily interpreted in terms of fewer basic categories than the three: event, quality, and relation?

These questions are not mutually exclusive, they cannot be handled separately, and the preceding analysis of the role of categories has some bearing on all three of them. But in dealing with questions of the first sort it seems fair to add: by making serious use of the category of quality, but at the same time insisting that no categorial system can determine what qualities are manifested (or may be inferred to be manifested) in existence, or are excluded from existence, or are of importance (as causally effective or as valued for themselves or for their usual contexts), contemporary naturalism has freed itself from the objection leveled against earlier naturalism, that it excluded from existence, or was committed to neglecting in one way or another, *any* qualities experienced or imaginable, including those in which men delight as aspects of the highest achievements of the arts, the sciences, and what Aristotle called the master-art of politics. Naturalism has also thus freed itself from suspicion of dalliance with meaningless contradictions of the sort that purported to assert the identity of factors that are actually distinguished or distinguishable—for example, assertions that qualities are (or can be "reduced" to) bodies in motion, events in relation, or indeed anything else but just themselves.

Discovery (or inference) of constituents, causes, effects, and other correlatives of given qualitied events—discovery (or inference) that these constituents and correlatives probably themselves lack some of the qualities of the events of which they are supposed to be constitutive or correlative—such discovery (or inference) is not and never was in any sense a reduction of those qualitied events to a more nearly ultimate reality (or to anything else) devoid of their qualities. Nor did it in any sense imply or entail such a reduction. During the first decades of the present century various complicated theories of "levels," and of the "emergence" of the denizens of "higher levels" from "lower levels," were propounded in order to save naturalism and yet enable it to do justice to "the higher ranges of being and of value." But none of the machinery of doctrines of levels was ever needed, for the problems it was invented to solve were not genuine problems, but rather verbal confusions, as a consideration of the functions of categories could have shown at any stage.

If, for example, what are called intelligent animals exhibit traits not found in other living things, and if all living things exhibit traits not found in inanimate objects, and inanimate objects of various sorts have traits not shown by those of other sorts—no philosophical problems are thereby precipitated either as to the genesis of existents "higher" or "lower" in level or as to the compatibility of the careers of such existents in a single "intelligible" world. If we are interested in questions of genesis, philosophical criticism can neither exclude nor find any theoretical difficulty in the development of "lower" from "higher" types, or of "higher" from "lower," or the independent development of existents of all the types distinguished. We have already considered (page 279) the meaning and status of conservation principles. It is enough to state here that unless *nihil ex nihilo* or conservation laws are formulated as tautologies (and hence are empty and exclude only nothing) there is no form of either of these that is any more necessary or self-evident than would be its strict and literal contradictory. Nothing defensible in either of these principles could imply that any type of existent or of development involved problems which require theories of levels and of emergence to clear up. Philosophical analysis may well remind us, in this connection, that none of the three sorts of development here mentioned could (without self-contradiction) be construed as a *reduction* of any type of entity to any other or as an *identification* of existents of any type with existents of any other type. But which ways development has in fact taken and is now taking, what processes have been causes and of what effects, which have been conditions and which (in various senses) conditioned—these are questions to be seriously answered only by the findings and the probable inductions of science. And upon the latter, statements about the "ultimacy" of minds or bodies or about differences of level have no theoretical bearing.

If we are interested, not in questions of genesis, but in the task of explaining other than genetic relations of existents of various types to one another, then, again, no intelligible problems of priority or of ultimacy or of reduction arise for a theory of levels to resolve. The explanation of any entities will consist in hypotheses, grounded in evidence and appreciably confirmed by evidence, about the structures, qualities, and constituents of those entities, and their relations to entities of other sorts. It will make no difference whatever to the content of our explanations whether we explain mental processes by their relations to one another and to processes we call nonmental, or whether we explain nonmental processes by their relations to one another and to others called mental. Provided, of course, that we confine ourselves to stating such relations as we find or infer from specified evidence! But any other procedure would be a surrender either to mendacity or to fantasy.

Legitimate distinctions of levels are nothing more than scientific classifications of ranges of materials by their similarities and differences of qualities, structures, correlations, and values. Hence, when a "theory of levels" is offered as explaining (or as throwing light upon) such similarities and differences, mere redundancy of statement is confused with explanation or enlightenment. And when a "theory of levels" is offered as an aid in solving philosophical problems as to how entities of different sorts and of different values could develop from one another or could coexist in the same world without the reduction of the one to the other —the theory is useless because the problems themselves merely reflect confusions. To say, for example, that there are levels of being to which such categories as mind and purpose are applicable and other levels to which they are not, contributes nothing whatever to the explanation (or to the "reconciliation") of the facts that are stated when we say that some processes manifest what we call thought and purpose, while others do not, and that various relations hold between processes of these sorts. It is by the presence of the activities we call "thinking" and "purposive planning" that we define such areas or levels. These activities themselves cannot, then, be explained by referring them to the areas or levels thus defined. We describe the relations, causal and other, and large-scale and small-scale, between events and such areas, as whatever we find or infer them to be. Those relations are not explained by distinctions of level. As for "reconciliation," none is needed. For there is nothing self-contradictory and nothing "unnatural" about the fact that some ranges of existents differ more sharply and some less sharply from others or that any which develop from others should so develop.

We may say, then, that by taking seriously the category "quality" and by recognizing the limited role played by categories in developing hypotheses, naturalism is in a position to avoid the fallacies of reduction and to dispense with the clumsy apparatus of theories of levels invented to avoid such fallacies. Again, by making relation a basic category, rather than time or space or space-time, naturalism avoids possible confusions about time and space as either empty or absolute or in any way distinguishable from the actual relations of qualitied events. And finally, by paying some attention to mathematics and logic as the most highly developed symbolisms for expressing relations, modern naturalists have enabled themselves to scotch at last the foolish notion that explanations which employ mathematical methods can deal only with quantities and must either deny qualities or else denature them (and therewith experience and nature) by "reducing" them to quantities or, at the very best, relations. As a matter of fact, mathematical devices for expressing relations have always left men quite as free to apply them in dealing with relations *between* qualities (which is quite another thing from identifying the qualities with the relations) as to apply them in dealing with relations between entities of any other sort. The formulas of mathematics neither state nor imply anything whatever about their application to materials other than symbols within mathematical systems. Certainly they contain (or imply) no ukases as to what, if any, entities exist other than mathematical symbols and no ukases setting any sort of limits to what may thus exist. Mathematical formulations of serial orders, for example, themselves say nothing about either quantities or qualities. They can, however, be applied (or borrowed) quite as well to deal with reds that are between violets and oranges as to deal with feet that are between inches and yards, or ounces that are between grams and pounds. If we judge (as in many cases we may well do) that a given mathematical formulation of the relations between certain qualities ought to be rejected, the grounds should be that it states relations which do not in fact hold between those qualities. We cannot allege as grounds for rejection that the mathematical formulation as such reduces the qualities to quantities or that it has failed actually to express the qualities in question. It is, as we have seen,[5] characteristic of all symbols, not just of those called "mathematical," that they can be used to name, but in no literal sense to express, qualities.

The naturalism whose basic categories are event, quality, and relation

[5] *Supra*, pp. 271–273.

is not based upon any specific hypothesis (that is, upon any hypothesis whatever) as to what the course of natural and human history has been or will be. It implies no such hypothesis. It excludes no such hypothesis. For, on the one hand, what renders any hypothesis acceptable is, not a general philosophical position (naturalistic or any other), but the observed evidence which supports it and which must be taken seriously by truth-loving persons, whatever categories they employ in their thinking. And on the other hand, what requires us to reject any hypothesis is, similarly, evidence contradictory of it, not our general philosophical positions. Finally, when no evidence is known for or against a hypothesis, it is usually misleading to say that our general position ought to determine our attitude toward it. For a man's "general position" could not weigh on the one side or on the other unless there was some analogy, at least, between the hypothesis in question and some of the opinions that entered into his general views. If he has any evidence for his general views, it will also be in some measure evidence for or against a related hypothesis, which therefore could not be without evidence if his general views have anything to support them and have any relevance whatever to the specific hypothesis in question.

But what justification is there for calling such a philosophy, whose categories are event, quality, and relation, by the name "naturalism" rather than by any other name—or rather than to deny that it is a philosophy at all, since it professes to establish no positive hypotheses of its own? The challenge is thoroughly pertinent. Contemporary naturalism, if it goes so far as to say that nature is all, that natural processes (including those of human living) do not imply anything beyond themselves and do not require for their existence or for their explanation any grounds but the further stretches of natural processes which we observe or inductively infer to be their contexts, that in a world in which there is one event (that is, in which anything happens) we can distinguish and significantly infer or speculatively suppose nothing but further events and their relations and qualities—contemporary naturalism, in saying all this, is saying little or nothing that is positive doctrine or positive hypothesis. For by these declarations it leaves to ordinary scientific observation and inference all questions as to what the patterns of processes in the world probably are. Its spirit is in these respects very close to the spirit of traditional and more specifically materialistic naturalism. Both are protests against all philosophies which allege that events require, for their occurrence or for their explanation, reference to transcendental grounds, orders, causes, purposes, *Dinge an sich*, or the like. But contemporary naturalism recognizes much more clearly than did the tradition from which it stems that its distinction from other philosophical positions lies in the postulates and procedures which it criticizes and rejects rather than in any positive tenets of its own about the cosmos.

Naturalistic philosophy, like all philosophy, must begin its work *in mediis rebus*. The field it surveys is that of complex processes going on —processes which probably have long histories behind them and include men's efforts to explain their surroundings and themselves, to justify their values and to secure them. What insight does naturalism offer to enlighten us in these activities? That we have no methods but observation and comparison and inductively controlled hypothesis by which to reach reliable opinions about what is going on and has gone on and will go on. That nothing that goes on and no human argument implies, or even makes sense of, any notion that events require for their occurrence or for their explanation any grounds, controlling orders, laws, principles, causes, purposes, values which are anything more than further stretches of events, including such events as are themselves the formulation of causal laws or the description of other sorts of order. Even these further stretches are not required in the sense that they are logically implied, but only in the sense that so far as we have explored nature, we have found every range of events in fact embedded in contexts of such further events. Thus, there is for naturalism no knowledge except that of the type ordinarily called "scientific." But such knowledge cannot be said to be restricted by its method to any limited field of subject matter—to the exclusion, let us say, of the processes called "history" and the "fine arts." For whether a question is about forces "within the atom," or about the distribution of galaxies, or about the qualities and pattern of sound called Beethoven's Second Rasumowski Quartette and the joy some men have found in them—in any case there is no serious way to approach controlled hypotheses as to what the answers should be except by inspection of the relevant evidence and by inductive inference from it.

But if nature is to be intelligible, the critics of naturalism demand, must it not be so by virtue of an *order* that is logical or rational and is not merely whatever pattern events take in brute fact? The objection is typical of hundreds. In fact, no events whatever could fail to exhibit some order; to assert that events must have order is therefore to utter an empty pleonasm. Moreover, every possible order, as well as every occurrent instance of order, must be such that the principles of structure it exhibits are logically just as coherent, just as consistent, as any such principles could possibly be.[6] For no logical inconsistency or disorder is involved where different sections of a structure do not repeat the same pattern (unless by "the logically consistent" we mean merely the repetitive). Between different sections of a structure, or the formulas that express their patterns, there may be any amount of difference. But there could not be contradiction or logical inconsistency. If we mean by "the rational" what has such traits as logical consistency or coherence, then any series of "brute facts" is as rational as anything could be. If we mean by "rational order" an order in some specific degree congenial to man, easy for him to trace out and serviceable to his purposes, then the order of nature would be intelligible whether (in *this* sense) rational or not, and the question how rational (if at all) the order of nature is would be a question of fact to be handled exactly as we handle the question how much expansion takes place in iron when it is heated.[7]

The kinds of order nowadays loosely called "organic" are, in many ways, especially interesting and satisfying to most of us. But that is no justification for saying that where there is not such order (or to the extent to which it is deficient) there (or to that extent) there is no order and no intelligibility. Still less is it justification for arguing that there must *really* be more of such order than appears or that a transcendent reality either is such an order or induces phenomenal reality to approach it. The grounds for serious hypotheses as to the amount and kinds of organic order in the world are not "metaphysical," if that term means anything but what is ordinarily meant by "scientific."

In our discussion of the first question—"What justification is there for the categories characteristic of contemporary naturalism?"—we have advanced some way toward answering the second question also, namely, "Can the secondary categories generally employed in discourse be satisfactorily interpreted as meaning various configurations of qualitied events? We have so interpreted the categories "order" and "rational."

[6] Cf. Spinoza, *Ethics*, Appendix to Part I.

[7] I take the liberty to refer to a fuller analysis of the types of structure called "rational" and the types of activity called "reason," of the relations of these to one another, and of their relevance in explanation, in "The Appeal to Reason," *University of California Publications in Philosophy*, XXI (1939), 3–42.

If we pass on to consider the crucial category "cause," we must first observe that all that is strictly entailed by any occurrence is that occurrence itself. When we say that actually it would not occur without a cause, we mean that we believe that events generally go on only as we have observed them to go on—that is, in relation to preceding and concomitant events *more or less* uniform in type. This holds quite as much for the development of the most complex integrations as it does for simpler "linear" processes.

To *explain* anything whatever is to become as fully as possible aware of the qualities, aspects, structure that compose it, the constituents that enter into it, the causes that produce it, and the *effects* which entities similar to it usually have—including, of course, various effects upon human beings and their interests. We experience causal relations as relations of regular concomitance or sequence between events of specified types. Sometimes, in the case of human activity, the events are of the type called exertions of force and are felt as strain or effort. But nothing in experience or in events experienced either requires, or justifies, or would be illuminated by the hypothesis that causation is really some other sort of relation than that of regular correlation—that, let us say, of "enforcement" (still less entailment or logical necessitation, deviation from which could only be described in self-contradictory assertions).

As for explanation of events in terms of purpose, we do experience purpose (as against mere repetition—as in, let us say, tidal changes). But we experience it as the events of imagining alternatives when our predicament is in some respect "uneasy," of choosing one, of searching for probable ways and means to bring the chosen one into existence, and of exerting ourselves to that end. We infer purposive action in other men and animals (perhaps even in plants) when we observe instances of the sorts of speech and other behavior which, in our own careers, go with a choice among alternatives and an effort to realize whichever one is chosen.

As for values and disvalues, most naturalists follow Spinoza in defining these (but not, of course, the perfection which Spinoza defined as identical with reality) as the objects of love and hate and also in holding that no object could be intrinsically valuable, since any object can be either loved or hated or neither loved nor hated. When men have represented some values as absolutely "valid," irrespective of interests, what (except for the expression of their emotions) have they thus done but analyze

the structure of such entities as they call values and show their relations
to other stretches of existence, including various human actions? But all
stretches of existence, including various human actions, are in themselves
neutral so far as value goes (if "to be valuable" is other than a synonym
of "to be"). And they remain thus neutral, except when some positive
or negative interest plays upon them.

We turn finally to the third question: "Are all three of the basic
categories of naturalism indispensable?" Could we get along with fewer?
Such a question leads to difficult puzzles in the theory and technique of
symbolism. There is, in the first place, the problem whether terms like
"quality" and "relation" are not wholly eliminable from scientific and
philosophic discourse. In a sense they are. For if we always specify (by
names like "red," "green," "sweet," "cool," and "between," "implies,"
"causes") just which qualities and relations we are considering, nothing
seems to be added by calling them qualities and relations. In other words,
there is no quality *überhaupt*, distinct from all particular qualities, and
no relation *überhaupt*, distinct from all particular relations. But, as was
argued above, all that we call qualities seem to differ in specifiable ways
from all that we call relations. We could indicate these ways of differing
by statements about many specifically named and particular qualities
and relations, omitting the general terms or categories "quality" and
"relation." But since it is just these ways of differing which we use the
general names "quality" and "relation" to signify, we should really, by
their omission, not be eliminating the categorial terms, but only
changing the sign vehicles from two simple words to an immensely complex set of names and their combinations, which would, however, still
symbolize exactly what the terms "quality" and "relation" are used to
mean. We could, then, really dispense with one or the other of these
categories only if we proposed not to consider one phase of existence or
another. But it is very hard to imagine anything that could usefully be
called the considering, let us say, of qualities, which would not be merely
staring at them or naming them with "proper names," and yet not
a considering of them as standing in various relations. Again, relations
that merely float about and do not hold between any terms are even
harder—if not impossible—to conceive or discuss. And it would seem
that to conceive or consider any sort of configuration of qualities would
be to encounter or conceive at least one instance of it—here or there,
now or then, occurrent in fact or in imagination.

Such "secondary categories" as we have here discussed (and as other chapters examine in more detail)—*order, ground, space, time, cause, purpose, value,* and *explanation*—are employed in scientific procedure, and something like them would be needed as instruments in any explanatory activity that we can imagine. The interpretation of such categories is a traditional function of philosophy. A critical naturalism accepts the use of such categories and interprets them as meaning various sorts of configurations, all intrinsically observable, of what it calls qualitied related events. These latter are consequently its basic categories. But it holds that neither a system of categories nor any other product of philosophical activity (if philosophy is distinguished from science) can contribute to the determination of the probabilities as to what the configurations of events that comprise natural history (including human evaluations) have been, are, or are to be. If by "metaphysics" we mean a system of hypotheses about the structure of things whose probability is established by other methods than those of science, then a critical naturalism could neither be a metaphysics nor admit one. If by "metaphysics" we mean human science developed as far as possible, accompanied by (and developed in the light of) careful analysis of the categories and the methods employed in description and explanation and guided by serious judgment as to the directions of study most likely to safeguard and advance human values—if this is what we mean by "metaphysics," then a critical naturalistic philosophy would not only admit metaphysics but would also contribute to its task of analysis. And as far as he combines competence in the sciences (including the humanistic and historical) with such analysis, a naturalistic philosopher may well be called a metaphysician.

However, analysis of categories and methods used in explanation is an activity not totally different from the scientific. The determination of what people mean by the terms they use is a matter of scientific inference as much as is the determination of the probability of any opinion expressed in those terms. And if philosophical analysis pays much attention to definitions of terms and categories, with respect to which (as contrasted with material hypotheses) problems of validity cannot be raised, it is also true that no scientific explanation can be intelligible if in its actual procedure it fails to respect the difference between such definitions and hypotheses. And all questions about the superior convenience of one set of definitions (whether of categories or of any other terms) over others are questions that can be settled only on the basis of many scientifically determined probabilities.

The fruitful contribution made by philosophical analysis of categories will probably continue to be, as it has been, the correction of the confusions that operate so powerfully upon us toward making us believe that the categories we employ logically determine (at least to some extent) the beliefs we should hold and that the different categories employed in different metaphysical systems or in different sciences reflect either contradictions or else unbridgeable chasms between the different hypotheses for which there is evidence in different fields of subject matter. If such confusions, so damaging in their effects upon human practice as well as upon human theory, were ever permanently cleared away, philosophy as analysis of categories could sing its *Nunc Dimittis*, as could the art of medicine if there were no longer any impairment of desired organic functions. But in fact, particularly in the social and historical sciences and even more in applications of their results in order to justify various practical policies, there seems today to be more need than ever before for rigorous analysis of the respects in which categorial systems and points of view may be said to justify and the respects in which they may not intelligibly be said to justify (or even to affect the content of) hypotheses about matters of fact.

13

THE NATURALISM OF
FREDERICK WOODBRIDGE

Harry Todd Costello

WE are told that in the nineteenth century naturalism was an oversimplified doctrine which tried to explain away the richness of experience. But today there is a new naturalism, which does justice to the full variety of natural phenomena and human life. I am a sympathetic critic of any such program, and indeed of any philosophy which does not, as do skepticism and some forms of agnosticism, take pride in failure. I do not, indeed, like the new positivism, in so far as it is a "sour-grapes" philosophy, rationalizing its own inability to think things through by denying that unsolved problems exist. It seems to me that we have come a long way and know a great deal—not too little, but too much. We have so many pieces of the puzzle that we cannot put them all together. We are more aware than ever of the greatness of our own ignorance and must await still further gathering of information. Hence any philosophical theory that is not excessively reductionist is welcome to me.

Reductionism is always dubious, for as Bishop Butler once said, "A thing is what it is, and not some other thing," which unfortunately is far from a truism in philosophy. And it seems clear that the world is not merely "atoms and the void." Professor Royce used to tell a philosophical anecdote directed at all reductionists, from materialists to mystics. A small boy said to his elder brother, "What is the sky?" The brother was a reductionist in the making and replied scornfully, "There ain't no sky." The little one stared again at the very visible great blue vault above and finally inquired timidly, "Yes, but what is it what ain't?"

Yet at the same time we can hardly have a philosophy which leaves things entirely in their unanalyzed multiplicity. Philosophy must be partly reductionist. So even the new naturalism has at least one reductionist or liquidationist thesis: There is no "supernatural." God and immortality are myths. William James speaks of the feeling of relief which we experience when at last we give up trying to be young or slender. We say, "Thank God, those illusions are gone." So the naturalist now looks up to the great white throne, where once sat great Jove himself, and exclaims, "Thank God, that illusion is gone." But great illusions are not so easy to banish. We must take care lest our suppressed illusions come back to plague us in altered guise, like grinning fiends from out the Freudian deep.

I do not find any great unity, otherwise, among these new naturalists. Professor Dewey and Mr. Santayana are so far apart that no one can have profited by both and still be able fully to accept either. And both of them are more "idealistic," in the everyday sense of that word, than many a technically "idealist" philosopher: Hegel, for instance, whom someone has called "not merely a realist but a brutalist," or Schopenhauer, author of that pleasant little sarcasm, "If you want comfort, go to the priest. I can only tell you the truth."

And Professor Woodbridge, about whom I wish to speak further, had a third, decidedly different, philosophy. I asked him once what he thought of Santayana's thesis that mind has no causal place in the world. "When Santayana says that," he replied, "he is ignoring obvious fact for the sake of theory. The existence of his own book, lying on the table there, is evidence to the contrary." On another occasion I remember he said of Dewey, long his close friend and colleague: "I ask Dewey from time to time some simple question, such as, 'Is there not something about the past that never again changes?' Surely the state before change begins cannot itself also change." I said, "What did he answer?" "Answer!" Woodbridge replied, "Dewey defined and distinguished and qualified, in such a maze of dialectic, that not only I did not get any answer, I didn't even know where my question went to. And do you know, when he gets that way, he thinks he is being empirical."

Woodbridge's simple questions were themselves not always easy to understand. He called himself, with a bit of whimsical humor, a naïve realist, but never was naïveté more sophisticated. His questions were oracular and hinted always at a long train of previous personal thinking. I was always more interested in what he was implying or presupposing than in any answer I might have wit to make. So if the question seemed directed somewhere near me, I would respond, "But, Professor Woodbridge, just what do you mean by that question?" He could hardly deny the legitimacy of such a response. For it was said of his own teacher, the legendary Garman, of Amherst, that Garman had his students so well trained in philosophical technique that were he to say,

"Young men, do you believe in the lamp-post?" they would all come chorusing back, "But Professor, just what do you mean by the lamp-post?" Nevertheless, I do not think Woodbridge liked such a counter-question. He liked better the students who ventured a positive reply. Then Woodbridge would get a real stimulus, and after pointing out the general ignorance, stupidity, and lack of fundamental training of present-day students, he would go into a brilliant and far-ranging exposition of the whole subject involved. He did not mean to be so annihilating to the student who touched him off, for he was the kindliest of men, but he seemed to need some such stimulus to his thought.

Woodbridge running a seminar used to recall to my mind a meeting which an Irish priest once told me about. The assembled Irishmen were delighted with the principal speaker, who told them of the new day close at hand when all Ireland would be one free country. When the applause had subsided, the smiling little chairman arose, coughed, and looked around. "Would innybody like to ask the shpaker a quistion?" A moment of silence, and then somebody in the back of the room inquired, "What is to become of the north of Ireland in this new arrangement?" The startled audience looked around. Somebody exclaimed, "An Orangeman," and the fracas was on. When the police had restored order and the ambulance could be heard receding, the little chairman arose, coughed, and looked hopefully around. "Would innybody ilse like to ask the shpaker a quistion?" A Woodbridge seminar was like that. And yet it always puzzled him that he could not turn on a general discussion as one might turn on the water at the tap.

Woodbridge was a powerful personality. Those who knew him will not soon forget the square-cut face on the square shoulders, the forthright speech, the keenness, and the humor. Possibly he would have preferred to have us look at his work in the two great institutions for which he did so much—at his trusteeship of Amherst College and his deanship of Columbia University. Philosophers must be grateful for the *Journal of Philosophy* and for his long years as editor. If some of the early volumes suggested to Santayana the phrase, "the whited sepulchre," this is because no editor can print brilliant contributions which fail to arrive. And I think he helped to make a distinct improvement in the style and the liveliness of writing of philosophy in America. No one can judge whether Woodbridge might have accomplished more by writing more himself, rather than by activities as administrator and editor. Hegel, the thinker, went on correcting proof sheets while the windows rattled with the guns of Jena. And today the man of action, Napoleon, is gone; but the Europe of Marx and Lenin, of Mussolini and Hitler, was in Hegel's books. These things are hard to evaluate. Nor do I personally feel any too competent to criticize Woodbridge's somewhat fragmentary published works. I recall that somebody told me—perhaps it was Bertrand Russell—about a lecture on Bergson delivered by Bernard Shaw. In the midst of the lecture a little man near the front got more and more excited and began to gesticulate. Shaw paused, glanced down to see what was the source of the interruption, and said firmly: "Sit down and calm yourself, M. Bergson"; and then to the audience by way of apology, "I can always explain people's ideas better than they can do it themselves, and for some reason it always makes them angry." I make no such Shavian claim, and if I have any competence to speak of Woodbridge, it is that I was neither too close nor too far away to get some perspective on what he said and wrote. And I warn the reader that in what follows he will get merely my reactions to some aspects of Woodbridge's thought rather than a substitute for reading his books.

Professor Woodbridge was as fond as a preacher of having a text to expound. His interesting *Confessions* (reprinted in his collected essays, *Nature and Mind*, 1937) call attention to some of the most typical. From Bishop Butler, through Arnold, he got: "Things are what they are, and their consequences will be what they will be; why then should we desire to be deceived?" From a characterization of Aristotle by Santayana came: "Everything ideal has a natural basis, and everything natural an ideal fulfillment." From Jevons: "We can not suppose, and there is no reason to suppose, that by the constitution of the mind we are obliged to think of things differently from the manner in which they are." For Woodbridge these three texts in particular became centers for crystallizing his thinking, and indeed each text is in its way admirable. They echo the forthrightness of the man and his freedom from ordinary illusions. In other texts and at times in some favorite metaphors, for instance, the often repeated comparisons based on the conception of "Light," as in his *An Essay on Nature*, I find him becoming to me obscure.

Typical of words summing up a point of view is the word "Nature" itself. To Woodbridge, as to some of the other naturalistic philosophers, it carries a connotation of something very solid and real, an emotional unification of all things. Toward Nature they feel a natural piety, as toward the great Mother of us all. For myself, I do not feel that piety, whether expressed by a Marcus Aurelius or a Woodbridge. To me Nature seems rather a collective name for quite a mess of miscellaneous stuff. Nature should not, by some "pathetic fallacy," become a substitute for God. And if there are no gods, that is that. Let us not be "angry with them for not existing." But Woodbridge's feeling for Nature I can appreciate more than I do the attitude of those naturalist philosophers who take a spiritual pride in disillusionment: "We are the enlightened ones, we know the worst, the world is infinitely cruel." To Woodbridge the world was not thus alien to men, nor too solicitous either. It does not answer prayers, and we may be thankful that it does not answer other people's; but it does offer us material for building the better life.

For Woodbridge the realm of Nature was a region in which man could feel very much at home, as himself a part of the drama, an actor, not a mere spectator. In this sense Woodbridge could hardly have agreed with Santayana. To Santayana the life of the spirit, precious as it is to us, is a somewhat thin but delicious frosting or icing, spattered unevenly over some parts of the layer cake of essence and existence. Idealists try to live on icing and suffer from digestive disturbances and malnutrition. So Santayana quotes Goethe that "it is in the superficial iridescence of things that our life is set" (*im farbigen Abglanz haben wir das Leben*). We should not, like the rustic at the play, foolishly forget the spectator's role. Not so Woodbridge, to whom man's life and Nature were all of a piece.

One thinks rather of Spinoza. Yet I take it that the opening and the close of Spinoza's *Ethics* were not quite acceptable to Woodbridge. The emphasis on the infinity of the system of things, the awe and the acquiescence, the utter infinite greatness of Nature and the contrasted littleness of man, combined with the complete lack of arbitrariness (everything having an explanation, both what exists and what does not, in the necessity of the one great inevitable system)—all this was too extreme to fit in with observable facts. Woodbridge liked Spinoza's emphasis on structure in things, which ties them together in permanent stability. As he once remarked to me, "We can be arbitrary, as in counting by tens, but if we count by tens, casting out the nines is fixed for us by the nature of number." A system as tight, however, as Spinoza's, as unbreakable, which in the last analysis we can only acquiesce in, seemed to Woodbridge a fantastic extension of a true principle: of that structural linkage which gives skeleton and backbone to the world of Nature. Man's life is not contrasted with Nature, but neither is it submerged in the whole.

In his own presentation, the character of "the world of Light" seemed to him to reveal most nearly the essence of the natural world. He appears to mean quite literally, not the physicist's waves of radiation, but light as we experience the quality of it, its brightness and its colors. He was, of course, very well aware of the arguments which would make out that the physical world is "dark and cold and shaking like a jelly." He knew the arguments based on well-known facts: our world of color is correlated with only one octave in the vast series of radiations; the color black corresponds to no radiations at all; and so forth. But he thought these arguments overdone, the conclusions unjustified. He seems more the monist in epistemology, the "new realist," than even the famous six, the "six little realists" whom Professor Royce described as trying to sit on the monistic fence and falling off one by one into some heresy or other. For Woodbridge, as I understand him, we actually see the Dog Star out yonder, not smaller than it is, but at a distance, and not merely at a distance in space, but at a distance in time, eight years back. We see into the past. To deny this is not merely to deny that we see something that is in the past, but to deny that we ever see anything at a distance in space, the arguments being parallel. The contentions of the dualists, it seems to me, against Woodbridge's theory of perception, are very strong. But the arguments against the dualistic theory are also very strong. We are told that the physicists hold the wave theory of light on Monday, Wednesday, and Friday, and the particle theory the rest of the week. So are we situated with regard to monist and dualist theories of perception. Neither seems tenable against the arguments of the other. Yet there must be an explanation which fuller knowledge will reveal.

I can, perhaps, illustrate Woodbridge's position, through contrast, by repeating his description of a lecture by Bertrand Russell given at Columbia just before the first World War. I cannot, of course, remember verbatim, but it ran something like this. Woodbridge said: "Russell lectured to us about what we perceive when we perceive a penny. He pulled a penny out of his pocket and held it up for us to see. We gazed at it hypnotically. He turned it over and whirled it around. We followed his every move. He explained that the penny was really a series of little elliptical flat disks, each two-dimensional, which ran out toward us like buttons on a wire. In fact, there were rows of disks running out in all directions. The collection of these was the penny. He told us the penny we saw was much smaller than the penny he saw. I confess it did not look smaller to me than pennies usually are. But suddenly things grew worse. We were in six-dimensional space. Each of us, he told us, knew three dimensions of this space, and in it was a two-dimensional flat disk. This was our 'hard datum,' our penny. Other people had other three-dimensional spaces, too, in the six-dimensional space, and each of them had a little brown disk, his own precious 'hard datum,' which was his private penny. And we had somehow to get together and correlate these disk-like pennies. The collection of all of them was the only really-real penny. Though just how we were to correlate so many things we did not possess, he did not explain. Instead of that, he gave the penny a final twirl in the air and put it in his pocket, at which we all gasped. For just what it was he was putting in his pocket had by this time become an ineffable mystery." I think Woodbridge here put his finger on what is a fundamental difficulty of any monadistic dualist theory of mind, the difficulty of giving any operational definition of correlation. I recall that Russell said on one occasion that Leibniz should have been surprised to discover that "the end of his nose was a colony of spiritual beings." But surely it is just as startling to discover that the end of one's nose is a six-dimensional manifold of Russell perspectives.

May I turn aside from Woodbridge to remark that the difficulty about correlation becomes more insistent to me when I try to make out what is meant by some of our physicists as they write about relativity. I am writing here of something that puzzled Woodbridge, rather than something about which he had reached settled conclusions. The symbols used in relativity physics lead to results which unquestionably are verified by observation. But when a number of the physicists start to interpret their symbols, not merely popularly but also in their serious works, I get startling impressions that they do not always know what their own symbols mean. I think one may have symbols, one may even have verifications, and still not know how to interpret the total theory—or one may smuggle in uncriticized, as if self-evident, a very ambiguous or dubious interpretation. Woodbridge remarks that the way to understand symbols clearly is to translate them. I have a conviction that symbols which are understood can always be translated into other symbols. It does not follow that if you translate mathematical symbols into, let us say, English words, you can develop their implications in the new form (words) by deduction as exactly as in the mathematical-symbol form. Far from it. And it may be very hard even to say what you want to say. But if you do say it, you may be able to see more clearly what the results mean—not because English is the language God uses, but because any translation sets one free from the special symbols used, or does so in part.

But now let me illustrate further how this matter of correlation implies some basis of identity, reminding the reader that I am criticizing only certain vagaries, not the entire theory of relativity. May I begin with an amusing illustration of a trivial sort. I asked a group of students: "If you could suddenly jump from New York to Chicago, you would arrive an hour earlier than you started: leaving New York at 9 o'clock, you would find yourself in Chicago at 8. If you continued traveling in the same direction, could you not get back to New York on the preceding day?" To this one student solemnly replied, with the apparent full concurrence of the others, that you could do this, except that the nations had established an international date line to prevent it. I could not help being a bit sarcastic at the time about this amazing feat of international co-operation, which kept people from wandering off into yesterday or tomorrow. But I found it surprisingly hard to make these young men see that it was not "really" an hour earlier in Chicago, but the same identical time, which was called 9 in New York and 8 in Chicago, and that you do not grow younger by moving west. Then I picked up a paper by a young scientific positivist, who said, "Length is a number, and of course if the number changes, the length changes." Science knows only "pointer readings," I suppose! I had always taken for granted that it was the same length which was one and three and thirty-six, in yards, feet, and inches, the same identical length.

The new theory of addition of velocities was named the "theory of relativity." Having used the word "relativity," physicists and philosophers seem to have been thereby inhibited from thinking that space could be in any sense absolute. They forgot that Leibniz, the most famous historical defender of the relativity of space, was led to conclude that space is a confused illusion of the mind. But just what a completely relative space would be, that is not a confusion but an objective fact, is even more puzzling than the completely absolute space of which Newton apparently speaks. I do not wish to examine here the general question, but rather I would consider some illustrative cases. We are told that a length is shortened when in motion in its own direction, so nothing has an absolute length. But let us note that length is a correlation between one length and another—or to avoid the double meaning, let us say that length is a ratio between one *extensity* and another; and this ratio may have various values, depending upon the relative motion of the extensities and the operations used in comparing them. It is the same extensity which has two lengths, just as it is the same time which is 9 o'clock in New York and 8 o'clock in Chicago. It is the same man who looks smaller when one block distant than when close at my side, and likewise I look smaller to him. By "looks smaller" one means subtends a smaller angle at the observer, though in another sense, as Professor Woodbridge always insisted, he "looks" no smaller than usual, but just farther away. Of course, in terms of subtended angle there is no one angle which is his "real" size. The relativity case is very closely analogous. That it should extend to time ratios and mass ratios is indeed a bit surprising, especially since "mass" was originally an artifact to secure absolute permanence, as against the relativity of weight.

The case of time is particularly striking. We are told that a moving clock "really" runs slower than a stationary one. The interpretation that some give to this does, as Woodbridge says, "seriously raise the question whether the authors are clear in their own minds." Paul flies away and comes back, still young, and Peter has grown old waiting for him. But then it is all purely relative, and Peter may equally well be considered to have been the "little pig that went to market," so he is young and Paul is old. The theory ends in utter contradiction. Two clocks simply cannot both gain on one another and add up their gains until each is ahead when recompared. Instead of admitting the contradiction and trying a better interpretation, the relativity writers appeal to the general theory of relativity. "Maybe I can't lick you, but I got a big brother what can!" According to the general theory, if two clocks are found to differ after reunion, the fact can be explained by unsymmetrical forces. Certainly it can, and we do not need the general theory to do it. We might suppose one clock had been hit by a hammer. But the question is, why should they, or how can they, differ in a symmetrical case? It is a perfect *ignoratio elenchi*.

If it be said that no symmetrical case is possible, than that statement needs proof, for there do seem to be such cases. For example, let us consider an imaginary case like this. Suppose the earth hollowed out and evacuated of air and wells sunk from the north and south poles to the central cavity. Let us further suppose a projectile dropped from the north pole. It would speed up, then sweep across the central cavity with constant velocity, then slow down as it rose to the south pole level; and then it would fall back to the north pole again in the same way. Let us suppose another projectile from the south pole, the two projectiles provided with synchronized clocks and observers in the usual relativist way. There is no insuperable difficulty about the synchronizing of the start, and precautions taken to avoid head-on collision at the center. And supposing the experiment tried, there is no reason whatever why the clocks should not read the same when they pass, and when they repass again, for the whole situation is completely symmetrical. But for an observer on each projectile, the other clock would also seem to be running slow at the time they pass. This seeming is an observed fact, also, not an unreality. But it is not on a par with the cases, under the general theory, when there is a real asymmetry, as when one clock is in a heavy gravitational field and the other not.

We return, therefore, to this conclusion, that there is nothing in the special theory of relativity leading to a plurality of spaces and times which have to be mysteriously correlated with one another and therefore to a denial of the unity of nature. There is nothing necessarily leading to a pluralistic theory of monads or separate perspectives, like Carr's monadology or Russell's six dimensions. The different observers are observing the same world. On the other hand, the conclusions drawn by some hasty generalizers from the general theory of relativity, namely, the extreme unification which would eliminate any difference between space and time, also seems hardly justified by the formulas. Turning a yardstick into a clock by flipping it around into the fourth dimension has not yet been done. Again, some of the illustrations used by serious writers on the general theory "raise a question whether they are clear in their own minds." I read that there is no absolute rotation, although a clock on the rim of a turntable would run slower than one at the center. "For if the turn-table stood still and the rest of the universe rotated in the opposite direction, the result would, by the general theory, be the same." Surely not! Even the nearest "fixed" star would have to move faster than light, and a traveler on it would, in the terms of the well-known little poem, "go out one day in a relative way, and come back the previous night." By the theory itself complete relativity is impossible here. There does, then, seem to be something absolute about any rotation, with its set of related phenomena. A physicist of sufficient skill on the planet Venus might determine that his planet was rotating from observing these related phenomena. We may presume that he would have the aid of other whirling things to observe, such as tops or tornadoes. But operationally this would involve no reference to an absolute space, as Newton supposed, for there are no bench marks on empty space with reference to which rotation can be observed. So the absoluteness of space is not essential to the observed phenomena. But also there would be, for such an observer, who is operationally determining if his planet is rotating, no reference to the "fixed" stars, which are in fact perpetually hidden from the surface of Venus by a canopy of cloud. Both sides of the usual controversy here are alike mistaken. Operationally the stars are irrelevant, and so is absolute space, so rotation is not with reference to either.

Incidentally, this last illustration brings out what seems to me a proper use of operational definition. On the other hand, the example used by Bridgman, which Woodbridge speaks of as "impressive," namely, that distance from top to bottom of a sheet of paper is a different sort of thing from the distance from here to the sun, because operationally differently arrived at, seems to me merely muddled. The fundamental difference between the length of a page and the distance to the sun is that one is longer than the other, but they are quite comparable. The Eskimos are said to have a different name for a seal on the ice and a seal in the water, because the hunting operations called for are different. A more civilized language would note that it was the same seal in two different locations. If there are fifteen different operations by which the size of an atom can be measured, the scientist does not conclude that there are atoms of fifteen different sorts, but that the same size of the same atom is confirmed in fifteen different ways.

Returning again to the generalized theory of relativity, I find this sort of argument used. "Relativity has proved," it is repeatedly said, "that space-time is a four-dimensional manifold, and it is no longer proper even to speak of space apart from time. There is no space-at-a-particular-moment, since there is more than one set of events simultaneous with any given event." This seems to me a curious bull—not even an Irish bull, for it is not pregnant. It is just confusion. A space-at-a-time is not the old notion, it is the four-dimensional notion. If space were independent of time, it would be the same space at all times and might be linked to a particular time by various simultaneity relations. But in four-dimensional space-time, space-at-a-time becomes a necessary notion. The space of today is not the same as the space of tomorrow. Various simultaneities to one point-event involve various cross-sections of space-time at that point-event. An analogue would be to have more than one perpendicular to a line at a point in plane geometry. These complexities may be resolvable, but before drawing metaphysical conclusions you had better make sure of your foundations.

Another point where we should do well not to draw hasty metaphysical conclusions is in the relativity treatment of the finite velocity of light as if it were infinite. The light comes to us from the Andromeda nebula in some eight hundred thousand or more years, yet, by the relativity theory the causal interval is zero and there is no time lag between the event and the perceiving of it. I have spent time on such considerations here, because some one might pronounce Woodbridge's views about the unity of nature or the evident difference between space and time to be quite obsolete in the new space-time physics of today. There are surprising things in this new physics: the equation between matter and energy, the possibility of verifying a non-Euclidean geometry, and the like. But the situation is not completely revolutionized, and a good deal which we are told is new scientific fact may turn out to be actually metaphysical speculation or even confusion. So Woodbridge used to shake his head and remark: "Some of these novelties I have known for years. Others seem really new. But I am puzzled, for these relativists keep making statements which can hardly mean what they seem to say."

With that let us return to Woodbridge's discussion in what is perhaps his most striking book, *The Realm of Mind* (1926). It gives an effect of originality, even when the reader has noted that Woodbridge is close to Spinoza. For it is not the ordinary popular Spinoza. I once saw a marginal note by Charles Peirce concerning Jowett's translation of Plato. Peirce remarked that if Jowett had always written down exactly what he made out of Plato's text, he would from time to time relapse into complete nonsense. But when Jowett came to a place where he could not grasp what Plato was talking about, he put in some pleasant material of his own and cheerfully went on. The result was very satisfactory to everybody, except to the readers of Greek who could also think—not a large group. It is much the same with the understanding of Spinoza, and that is why Woodbridge can restate Spinoza in new words and make it seem at first to be something novel and startling, whether he speaks of the nature of mind or the character of the good life. In print and in conversation Woodbridge was ever praising the greatness of Aristotle, and he acknowledged indebtedness to Plato, to Locke, to Santayana, to Bacon and Hobbes. But I do not find in his published writings echoes of the very substance of these authors, as I do of Spinoza. It is with a difference, indeed, for the infinite and the absolute, which is so central in Spinoza, appealed little to Woodbridge, and in those parts which he does borrow he is not simply repeating formulas but also rethinking their meaning.

Without dwelling too much upon summary or parallels, we may note certain features of Woodbridge's characterization of mind. He begins by saying that the body thinks, just as the body walks; there is no such thing as a mind, but only forms of behavior. Woodbridge himself qualifies, even reverses, these statements later. But such statements are so typical of some types of naturalistic philosophy that we may pause to raise certain questions. If mind is behavior, it is behavior directed toward things remote, in the past, perhaps imaginary, perhaps abstract. The behavior of walking, on the contrary, involves only a co-ordination of muscles and bones in the here and now—a clearly bodily performance. The behavior of thinking probably is always linked with some activity of the brain, currents running along pathways, very complicated without a doubt, but monotonously the same sort of thing, whether we dream, or remember our childhood, or think out a logical problem. Physiological psychology, in so far as it concerns brain processes, is 90 percent introspection and 10 percent mildly plausible conjecture about the neural accompaniments. To say it is the brain or "the organism" that thinks, is to deceive ourselves with an explanation that would indeed be so simple, if only it were true, that we have a strong wish to believe it and to disregard the complexity of fact.

Professor Woodbridge further suggests that the individuality of the "inner life" of each of us is essentially due to the fact that we have different bodies. That each has such an inner life is made evident, for example, in Professor Royce's philosophical anecdote about the old colonel. The colonel had imbibed a little too much and was endeavoring to preserve a pose of great gravity in mixed company. Suddenly a rat ran across the floor and stopped directly in front of him. He looked furtively around. All eyes were in his direction. He concentrated on the rat. There it was, still there. Suddenly he blurted out, "You people think I see a rat, but I don't." If our thoughts were public property, there would be no point to the story. We must, of course, grant that individual minds are associated with individual bodies. You do see things from a different place than I; your headache I cannot feel. We laugh at the Irishman who took a strictly objective point of view about a noise in his head and insisted that he could hear it fifty feet away. So Spinoza said that every man thinks of things confusedly, not as they are, but as they affect his body. Yet I am not altogether convinced that the separateness of minds has its sole basis in the separateness of bodies. When Kant so repeatedly insists, in the famous transcendental deduction, that there is no experience unless it be synthesized under the unity of apperception, which unites always a span of time, he seems to me to be indicating something in the make-up and structure of all thinking which is not reducible to the unity of the bodily organism or the brain. I doubt if the brain ever does act as a unit or, supposing it does, whether this is necessarily relevant to the unity of experience. To me there is here a question of observable facts, and the facts do not simplify into the body as thinker. This oversimplification is indeed part of the humor in a favorite Woodbridge quotation preserved for us by Professor Randall: "Man is nothing but a tube. With the one end thereof he befouleth the ground; with the other he praiseth God."

Let us turn now to another character of thinking on which Woodbridge and, indeed, Spinoza insist. When someone raised the question one day whether there is ever such a thing as imageless thought, Woodbridge replied that the real question is whether there is any thought which is not imageless. This recalled to me a remark once made in my presence by Dr. Elmer Southard, who combined an expert knowledge of neurology and psychology with an extraordinary skill at playing chess. Southard spoke of playing simultaneous games blindfolded and playing also in three dimensions, without a board, and he said that though on such occasions he knew exactly where the pieces were on the boards, he never had any imagery at all, no mnemonic word, no picture of the boards, except occasionally perhaps a single chessman and a hand reaching for it. This was the opinion of a highly trained psychological observer. Psychologists talk of linguistic cues, of muscular tensions in the throat, and the like, and maybe there are such. I agree with Dr. Southard in not always finding such by introspection. They are certainly not what I know, for that *is* before me. Even when I think in words, I do not feel that I confuse the words with the thought. Again, there may be local signs of a qualitative sort when the skin is touched in different places, but I find I take note quite directly of the places, not of the qualitative signs, and these places are, so far as I can tell, in the space world, the world of physical nature. I remember a psychologist who was nick-named years ago "the man whose consciousness is at the end of a stick." I appreciate his insight in the matter.

The most obvious thing which is before the mind when we know something is the thing known, and as it is known. By the aid of whatever imagery we know it, what we know must itself somehow be before us. This is at once an obvious truism and a startling paradox. When I sit here in this house and think of the moon, it is the moon I think of; and if, as may be, I have a mental image, a picture of the moon, I quite clearly distinguish it from the moon itself. Of course I do not think of the moon as here, crowded between these four walls, like the mountain coming to Mahomet. But it is the moon I know, where it is, yonder in space, and not some tightening of the throat or echo of a sound. And yet I recognize that there is something more involved in this knowledge than just the moon. For there is the possibility of error. Yet even error demands a basis of contact: to be in error about this object, I must grasp this object in part in order that I may be mistaken about the rest of it. It is precisely *this* object that I am mistaken about. If truth be of descriptions, we must be able to check our descriptions; if it be correspondence, we must be able to compare the corresponding factors; if it be coherence, we seem to need more known coherence between specific facts or specific beliefs than we have; if it be success in action, we must be able to see why we succeed.

The idealist thinks he has the solution. I cannot agree. There are three factors which must be taken into account in any theory of knowledge. There is error; there is ignorance; there are individual knowers, who know at a certain time in a world which was a going concern long before they were born. When an idealist thinks his own premisses through, he ends, so far as I can see, in a denial of all three. He denies them in favor of one errorless knower who knows all in one timeless act. I agree with Woodbridge that the result is rather fantastic; one has proved too much, and the starting point has disappeared in the conclusion. As for pluralistic idealists, I doubt if they can prove their idealism without upsetting their pluralism. I do not wish to deny finally these hypotheses —the world may turn out to be a fantastic place.

There is in objective idealism, however, an emphasis on something which Woodbridge has tried to specify in his notion of "objective mind." Woodbridge expresses the hope that this is not too much like what Immanuel Kant was driving at, for he does not like Kant. I suppose he means what Kant called "possible experience," or what Woodbridge may have recollected, from student days, of Neo-Kantian readings of Kant. I would on another occasion, perhaps, say a word in defense of Kant and Leibniz, both of whom, particularly Leibniz, Woodbridge heartily disliked. But I do find myself denying that even Kant is justified in using language which suggests that "knowledge in general" or "experience in general" has some meaning, except as a pure abstraction, if it is taken apart from individual knowers. Kant's unity of apperception seems to me an essential element in my experience or in anyone's experience, but there are as many such unities as there are centers of experience. The Kantian categories seem to me a fusion, or confusion, of two separable things, the ways in which the mind functions, which ways are thinking, and the ultimate characters of things thought of. There is no necessity that I can see in the ways in which the mind functions, except as forced by the truth concerning the things it thinks about. Where the objective categories come in is something which I shall indicate later.

But let us approach the question from the angle of Woodbridge and Spinoza. Woodbridge's "objective mind" is the realm of truths and their implications. It is not so very different from Spinoza's "attribute of mind," which is all things taken from a certain angle. "The order and connection of ideas is identical with the order and connection of things," Woodbridge repeats after Spinoza, and still repeating Spinoza he adds that "ideas" are quite different from mental images or psychic stuff. This is emphatically not panpsychism. Ideas are what the intellect knows, according to Spinoza, but the intellect always knows truly, knowing all things directly as they are and without error. At this point I enter a caveat: I do not believe we ever are free from the possibility of error, nor am I sure Woodbridge would hold with Spinoza at this point. But I take it that for Woodbridge the world as an object of knowledge is the same world as the realm of Nature, except that we here stress certain other relationships, those of meaning and implication, of possibility and negativity, instead of succession and cause. Structure belongs in parallel to both realms.

Without being too sure just where I begin to insert my own thoughts in place of those of Woodbridge, I look upon this realm of "objective mind" somewhat as follows. Woodbridge's word "structure" seems to me a little ambiguous, but to indicate a very real characteristic in all concrete things. Structure is what is invariant in a process occurring in time, like a water pipe that guides the flow of water or the nodes in a vibrating string. When structures and processes are sufficiently unified to take on a career of their own, rather independent of surroundings, we may use some additional word, perhaps speak of an "organization." Proceeding backward in the direction of higher abstraction and generality, we may speak of a mathematical structure, or perhaps we use the word "system." A system seems more like a group of relations which belong together or are relevant to one another. At a still higher stage of abstraction, we may consider only the objects or things which are connected by relations, abstracting even from the quality of the relations, and then we are reduced to considering "order" or arrangement.

I was first introduced to the study of order by Professor Josiah Royce, back in the days before the new revelation by Wittgenstein and the Vienna school. Royce was interested in the new symbolic logic, having been made aware of it by Charles Peirce, who told him, "Royce, you should study logic, you need it so much." For Royce this new logic used symbols, but was not about symbols particularly. He strongly protested the effort to give precedence to the calculus of propositions, over those of classes and relations. The general logic of order was used and applied by the thinker in his syllogisms, but the logic of thinking was applied logic. We could illustrate the same ordinal structures in diagrams or could cut out models of them from paper. The science of order was also the general science, of which the mathematical sciences were specialized developments. Order was fundamental. The truths of geometry could be about lines and points, but it was their ordinal relations that counted, and quantities were only important in science because they could be ordered. Royce liked to play with another illustration of geometry, angels that sang in heavenly choirs: for any two angels, there was one and only one choir in which they both sang; any two choirs, only one angel that sang in both. There was no space in this geometry of angels, and the first book of Euclid suffered a queer sea change, but it was just as good a geometry, being the same system of order.

Of course, in this general logic of order there is a very high degree of abstraction, as in symbolic logic generally. A "relation" is not what you might think, but only the set of ordered pairs of terms which ordinarily would be considered to be related by the relation. Even true and false become T and F, and the one just as good as the other, often entirely symmetrical. It remained for those after Royce to discuss chiefly order among symbols, where whole complex propositions turned into p and q, and the relations among the truth-values of these, the aforementioned T and F, became the only relations in the world, all else being just atoms of being. Once you go as far as this, such a term as "relevance" has practically no meaning, from the point of view of such a "logical atomism." Efforts to introduce relevance, as by Professor C. I. Lewis, have not been too successful. The trouble surely has been that there has come about a confusion of a general science of order, which is prior to symbols, with a science of symbols. Royce used to say that ordinal logic and chemistry both had to use symbols, but were not about symbols. Logic as thus considered is also not about thought, as was the older logic, but the old meaning adds to the popular confusion. This confusion of a logic of order and one of symbols has created a new positivist metaphysics, a highly anemic metaphysics, even perniciously so—"logical atomism."

It has been contended by Professor John Dewey and others that the subject matter of the exact sciences, such as mathematics and formal logic, is of human invention, as are the symbols used. We define as we arbitrarily choose. We make these things. I would not wish to deny a parallelism to invention in the way we arrive at these objects and construct symbols for them. But the arbitrariness can be exaggerated. We define a circle, yet the truths about the circle are endless and to find them involves long and arduous inquiry. The value of π is not arbitrary, nor can it be made exactly equal to 3, not even by the inspired text of Holy Writ or the authoritative will of the sovereign legislature of the state of Indiana. The search for precision and rigor of proof is a genuine search, and the pragmatic value of these sciences, in their applications, is due largely to the fact that they reveal systematic connections not made by human fiat.

There may be many "logics," considered as systems of algebra. We know there are many geometries. But this sort of arbitrariness is superficial. As Willard Gibbs once remarked, a mathematician can assume anything he pleases to start from—unlike the physicist, who "has to be sane part of the time." But the reason for such freedom is the great number of possible systems, not any looseness within a system. Since a symbolic system consists often of a few symbols repeated over and over, at times one is likely to think of it as pretty much a tautology. But the system is not the "symbols" that we see, those marks on paper. What is symbolic is the way we are putting them together in more and more complex syntheses. Demonstrations then reveal a certain linkage of identity amid the constructions. One is struck by the fertility resulting from the introduction of a single new concept. Thus, for instance, from projective geometry, by the introduction of a single unit of length, all of metrical geometry can be developed: the unit being projectively duplicated wherever needed. One discovers also that the language of "exact science" may be curiously inexact and misleading: *constants* are what may be arbitrarily changed, but *variables* are not arbitrary, being what is really constant in a system.

When we try to get back to the foundations of mathematics and the logic of order, to what Professor Royce considered the new search for the "categories," the inquiry becomes more and more involved in difficulties which are due to the natural inadequacy of symbols. I recall seeing a letter written late in life by Charles Peirce, a master of the history of logic. Peirce exploded because his correspondent had written, "Things equal to the same thing are equal to each other, and therefore . . ." Peirce said very sharply that it was the height of logical stupidity to try to turn a principle of inference into a premiss and state it. Augustus De Morgan used to be similarly emphatic. Such foolishness is like that of the curate in the *Bab Ballads*, who tried to prove by the rules of Bishop Whately that "what is true of all is true of each one separately," that is, by syllogisms that the principle of the syllogism is sound. These things cannot be proved, or even stated, in the ordinary way. If one were able to state in a true proposition the law of contradiction, this proposition would normally have a contradictory, which would be the contradictory of the law of contradiction. The theory of types is merely one case of this general characteristic of logical forms, as in the example in which you cannot meaningfully say a class is a member of itself, or equally that it is not a member of itself. Logical principles cannot be directly discussed. I remember that Bertrand Russell once described the science of logic as "a science of ghosts, which deals with unmentionable things." What we find it practicable to do is usually to make a statement about symbols, such as, that it is meaningless to use symbols except in certain ways. You lay down a rule, instead of stating a true proposition, and it looks like an arbitrary fiat. But it is not arbitrary. Contradictory symbols for propositions can both find a place on the same sheet of paper, considered as marks on paper. Neither rises up to abolish the other. It is in the realm of what is symbolized that contradiction and incompatibility and impossibility are found. You choose to use symbols this way? Yes, indeed, but you are like Margaret Fuller when she accepted the universe —"Gad, she'd better."

There is a realm that symbols mean. This is the realm that Professor Woodbridge called "objective mind." He was himself not much interested in such matters as symbolic logic—and its local representatives around Columbia University. He was not so much interested in technical analysis as in direct seeing. The world in which our symbols enable us to communicate with one another is our human world. It spreads out into the whole daily world in which we live. It was at this that Woodbridge was looking. Woodbridge was an immediate empiricist, like the great philosophers whom he admired so much, Locke and Aristotle. I know it is a popular opinion that Aristotle was a speculative philosopher who misled the human race for two thousand years with wild theorizing, until modern empirical science came along to bring us back into contact with the facts. But if we inquire how Aristotle came to fall into those errors for which he has been most blamed, we shall find that he got them by direct observation, or certainly he thought that he got them in that way. That was why he felt so sure. How did he know that the heavenly bodies move in circles around the earth? Did he not see them swing nightly in circles round the pole? Or that heavy bodies fall faster than light ones? Like the critic of Galileo who let weights fall from the leaning tower at Pisa (a more authentic ocurrence than the popular reversed version), Aristotle doubtless saw how bodies fall. How did he know that moving bodies on earth tend to a state of rest? He saw it happen. In all this Aristotle was the empiricist. Modern science began with thought, not with observation, in Galileo, Descartes, Newton. The mistake of a Descartes in trying to spin the theory of the universe out of his own head was not that he used thought, but that he overlooked the great variety of possible alternatives and the weakness of the human mind in imagining what these alternatives are. These are the factors that make an empirical check on thinking imperative. Only by constant contact with facts observed can we find strength to mold and reshape our hypotheses.

There is a value in such a general picture of the natural world as Woodbridge tried to keep before him. It saves one from speculative extravagances and one-sided loss of contact with the everyday world. But such a picture is itself loaded with unrecognized thought elements. You see with the mind, not with the eye, even when you seem to yourself to be directly looking at the world around you. You might, indeed, be in greater error if you trusted the eye instead of the mind, but possible error lurks in both. Your vision can be profitably developed and criticized only by what seems to me a higher degree of detailed technical examination of fundamentals than I find in Woodbridge's somewhat impressionist picture. No man can be sure he has before him all the relevant considerations in any philosophical problem. So the philosopher needs vision, but he also needs endless self-criticism and endless alertness for the little discrepancy which indicates that he is not quite on the right trail.

I would close this discussion of Woodbridge's realm of objective mind with a word of praise for his rehabilitation of objective teleology. Since Darwin we have all been afraid to talk in teleological terms. We fear we shall be accused of appealing to some Divine plan and purpose. Yet natural products certainly do possess those characteristics which invite us to use the language of means and ends, somewhat as if it were all designed. The old lady who saw the little kangaroo look out of the big kangaroo's pocket said quite naturally, "Good heavens, what will they think of next?" Yet the kangaroo's pouch is truly a case of a means to an end, just as falling rain is a necessary means to the end of making the crops grow or the valleys widen. Woodbridge insists we have a right to this language of means and ends, without being supposed to imply a foreseen design and hence a designer. He holds that the language of teleology is as natural and accurate as the language of causality, and I think he is right, and not merely in biology.

As we have already indicated, in speaking of objective mind, Woodbridge was thinking not solely of the realm of truth investigated by the natural scientist but also of the wider realm which symbolic thinking makes possible, the whole wide range of human culture, of what Santayana calls "the life of the spirit." For Santayana, though he speaks of everything natural as having its ideal fulfillment, nature and spirit tend to fall into separate compartments; for Woodbridge, they are continuous, and all are parts of the one realm of nature, within which one may live "the life of reason." There are many mansions in the great house of the world and few high fences. All this is the kingdom of the true humanist—but perhaps we had better not enter into the controversy concerning who has the best right to the word "humanism." Woodbridge has written briefly, but with a wealth of suggestions, on many themes in the realm of human culture, of history, of classic literature, of morals. We cannot here expand on these suggestions in any adequate manner, and I shall therefore close with a brief consideration of one topic only, ethics.

In the days of American national prohibition Woodbridge once had a dream. In the first scene he is upstate, talking with an old farmer and expressing a wish for some of that good old prewar stuff. The farmer opines that it might be possible, for a proper consideration. Woodbridge offers to pay any reasonable price. The scene changes to a sandbar off Bermuda. The farmer dives into the broad Atlantic and comes up with a quart bottle of whiskey. In a flash the scene has changed again, and Woodbridge sits at his desk in the dean's office at Columbia. The farmer stands by, expectant. Woodbridge takes his chequebook and fills out one blank cheque: "Please pay to bearer one degree of Bachelor of Arts of Columbia College. (Signed) Frederick J. E. Woodbridge." On another occasion, when a student flung out the challenge, "Name something which is an absolute good, a good in itself," Woodbridge replied cheerfully, "Whiskey!" At this rather un-Spinozistic reply the student was, to say the least, "flabbergasted." I hope the reader will not be equally shocked and humorlessly record that Woodbridge must have been a heavy-drinking man and an ethical materialist. He was merely puncturing pomposities and indicating that in his opinion the goods of life are just those specific things we find to be good. We find them empirically, by trial, and in considerable numbers. We cling to what is thus found good. We compare them in retrospect. We seek to get more of them. We organize them into the scheme of our life.

In this he is really fairly close again to Spinoza, not to the Spinoza of the grand stratosphere flight at the close of the *Ethics*, but to the Spinoza of the life of "enlightened self-interest" so attractively expounded in the often neglected pages entitled, rather misleadingly, "Of Human Bondage." There are difficulties. Spinoza, it will be recalled, gets across somehow from mere self-interest to social living by an exhortation to be reasonable and by the thought that "nothing is so useful to a man as is another man," itself a favorite Woodbridge quotation. I like the empirical and specific approach to ethics, as Woodbridge sees it, without being too much impressed by Spinoza's metaphysical thesis that the good things are those which lead to "increase of our being," if this means anything more than the truism that the more we have which is worth having the fuller is our life. Nor is it wholly a truism: life may be too full, and each man must choose for himself how much he can enjoy. Each life is a separate creation in the art of living, the more self-chosen the better; and why should lives be alike? But everyone should have a chance to find out what he is capable of and can enjoy, and also have a chance to work toward it. It takes many sorts of people to make a world. The totalitarian leader would force each life, not merely his own, into the common mold of a servant of the state. You say, "Why shouldn't he, if that is what *he* wants?" The reply is that the society built on these principles defeats itself in the end. As Spinoza said, no society can be permanently strong that sends its best citizens into exile or to the scaffold because of their nonconformity. Originality and diversity are precious to a state. But I see no refutation possible of the value of any sort of life, save in this, that some sorts of life are self-defeating, as are the selfish, the irrational, the bigoted, and the domineering.

Woodbridge will never be an influential philosopher, as is his colleague John Dewey. In the university Dewey was a quiet teacher, lacking all the arts of teaching save one, that he inspired many a young man to think for himself by showing how it could be done. In a lecture Dewey was thinking through the subject as he went along—thinking in public— perhaps to remark at the close, with a certain naïveté, that he had got considerable enlightenment from the lecture that day. Dewey is a modest man, and hence the complaint of a Chinese student, "I came around the world to hear Dewey talk about Dewey, and he speaks of Locke and Rousseau and John Stuart Mill, but he never speaks of Dewey." But Dewey outside the classroom has come to stand for a certain point of view and certain ideals. For better or for worse, certainly for better in many instances, these ideals have become a force in American life. The imprint of Dewey's thought is on all our normal schools. It shapes the lives of millions of school children here and overseas, though they may never hear his name. From Woodbridge there came no such influence, except on the smaller group that met him face to face. A great personality—that was something you felt at once. A wise man, yes, a regular Dr. Johnson of philosophy—a little too brusque at times, too prompt to settle a complex puzzle by kicking a stone. One wishes he had devoted a great mind to the more technical development of his philosophy, and had let someone else handle the transient problems of an administrative dean.

14

NATURALISM IN AMERICA

Harold A. Larrabee

THE career of naturalism in America is the history of the slow growth
of an attitude rather than of a specific philosophical doctrine. It has
meant the gradual development and spread of a point of view that is at
once naïve and sophisticated. Those who have come to share the naturalistic outlook, while they may differ in many details, tend to begin with
whatever confronts the human observer in his complete daily living and
to endeavor to frame a satisfactory account of it in its own terms. They
agree, that is, in rejecting the aid of congenial but unverifiable myths
masquerading as literal truths. It should not be necessary to point out
that naturalism, in the words of Santayana, "may find room for every
sort of psychology, poetry, logic, and theology if only they are content with their natural places. Naturalism will break down, however, as
soon as words, ideas, or spirits are taken to be substantial on their own
account, and powers at work prior to the existence of their organs, or
independent of them." [1]

This approach implies a willingness, even an eagerness, to face all the
facts in any situation with a minimum of distortion by personal desires
or prejudices. If there is any way to avoid it, we must not deceive ourselves. History must not be read in terms of what we wish it might have
been. This is not to make the absurd claim that bias can be wholly eliminated, but rather that it can be, and on naturalistic premises it must be,
acknowledged and guarded against. To be credited with any degree of
consistency, therefore, the naturalistic historian must begin his account
with the frank admission that American philosophy in the usual sense
of the doctrines professed in our colleges and publications has been,
throughout most of its history, theological and idealistic—the very
opposites of naturalistic. Professor H. G. Townsend is substantially correct in declaring that the dominant motif in American philosophy to date
has been idealism in the sense of the belief that "the visible is no whit
more real than the invisible, in fact that the invisible kingdoms furnish

[1] George Santayana, "Dewey's Naturalistic Metaphysics," *Journal of Philosophy,*
XXII, 674.

the foundations for the visible."[2] In its common religious renderings, this view is the antithesis of naturalism; and it enjoyed what amounted to a metaphysical monopoly on this continent for at least two hundred and fifty years. But what it permeated so completely was American speculation in the academic sense. It was not so fully in control of American thought in general, and still less of American living. That is another way of saying what philosophers are sometimes reluctant to admit, that technical philosophizing has been comparatively uninfluential in determining the course of American life. It explains in part the paradox that naturalism has been, at one and the same time, a major unreflective assumption of everyday existence in America and, until recently, one of the minor tendencies in American academic philosophy.

There were naturalistic forces at work in this country long before their overt manifestations in the philosophy of the closing decades of the nineteenth century, and to ignore them is to make the present vigor of that point of view historically unintelligible. Naturalism is no sudden overnight growth in America; neither is it a mischievously transplanted foreign importation. Its spread has been world-wide, because scientific enlightenment and technological control cannot be permanently hemmed in by geographical or political boundary lines. But it has roots in American soil, roots which run deeply into our national past. They are to be traced in two main directions: (1) in the conscious and articulate intellectual life of the rude young country, where they appear first as sporadic and scattered protests against the prevailing supernaturalism, often as arrogant mouthings of premature syntheses, but in time more solidly based upon a clearer understanding of the sciences; and (2) in the overpowering influence, largely anti-intellectual, of the immense opportunities for the immediate exploitation of the physical foreground by the previously unprivileged masses toward the new goals of widespread material comfort, increased self-esteem, and a degree of democratic control. Europeans have continually confused the keen American interest in technology with a belief in some brand of philosophical materialism. Far more important than any theory has been the practical materialism of Thomas Jefferson's conviction that "the business of life is with matter."[3]

Science in the intellectual sphere and commonsense "American ma-

[2] H. G. Townsend, *Philosophical Ideas in the United States*, New York, 1934, p. 4.
[3] G. Chinard, *Jefferson et les idéologues*, Baltimore, Md., 1925, p. 282.

terialism" in the environmental—these are the two major themes in the progress of American naturalism from its early rejection in theory and partial acceptance in practice by the more intellectually influential of the seventeenth-century colonists to its present wide adoption in both practice and theory by their present-day successors. Taken together, the two influences—one naïve, the other sophisticated; one welling up through the masses, the other percolating down from a handful of savants—have spelled the gradual but inexorable secularizing of American life and thought, primarily a process, still far from complete, of bringing American public pronouncements into line with American private practices. For our professed philosophies have endlessly refuted naturalism, while our practiced philosophies have steadily confirmed it.

Almost from the first, the two tendencies, the economic and the scientific, have interacted and reinforced one another, but haphazardly and unevenly, so that only in the present century have they begun to find partial expression in the works of our major philosophers. For the last four hundred years the peopling and industrializing of the Western hemisphere and the rearing of the vast edifice of modern science have proceeded simultaneously. Supernaturalism has thus been subjected to a double assault: the direct attack of science, which has undermined its philosophical foundations; and the indirect attack of impersonal worldly progress, which has crowded it out of modern living. As nearly everyone is now aware, the scientific spirit has had to win its way inch by inch against bitter opposition; and it is still unhappily insulated from direct contact with most of our social problems, so that our notions in all the realms of value—aesthetic, ethical, religious, economic, and political— have lagged far behind our technological advances. In the slow and painful process of readjustment of our philosophical principles to the floods of new scientific knowledge and the demands of machine-age living, America has had some special advantages and disadvantages. Most of them flow from the cardinal fact that ours is a society of fortunate *émigrés*, with an imported culture already shaped by millennia of internal and environmental pressures in Asia and Europe, but exposed, in America, to a novel set of material circumstances. We have been obliged to import the greater part of our theories from abroad; yet we have been extraordinarily at liberty to discard whatever we could not immediately utilize in practice here at home.

At the moment of initial transfer from the old world to the new, there was already under way what Santayana calls the "many-sided insurrection of the unregenerate natural man, with all his physical powers and affinities, against the regimen of Christendom," with its resulting disintegration of otherworldliness. Man had been taught for centuries that he was not at home within this universe and certainly did not deserve a better one. Naturally it took some time to make him feel at home in a merely mundane setting, but yet by no means contented with its actual condition. As far as professed philosophies were concerned, the chief events which accelerated the process continued to take place on the mother continent. The struggle between science and religion in America, intellectually speaking, has been largely a belated chapter in the history of Western Europe. On both continents the direct impact of scientific thinking altered the private reflection of a small handful of the elite, but the masses seldom questioned the familiar dogmas. If, however, we turn our attention from the ways in which theory affects practice to the ways in which practice gives rise eventually to theory (or cancels it), we shall find that the tables are reversed. Here the main accelerating factors were no longer European. The release of the torrent of pioneer energy upon the wilderness by the universal hope of individual ownership of "land in the woods" was a new thing in history, and it made new men. American opportunity, optimism, and material abundance were factors with which Oriental and European systems of supernaturalism had never had to deal en masse.

Fashions in speculative thought might still be exported from static Europe to dynamic America, but now they must take their chances in the hurly-burly overseas; and fashions in living in comfort for the multitude began to be set in the New World rather than in the old. Theological doctrines which had all the appearance, at least, of defeatist rationalizations of earthly scarcity, frustration, and despair could hardly retain their hold in a land which had turned out to be one of plenty and of hope. Buoyant optimism and predestined damnation by the wholesale do not permanently mix; abject dependence based upon a belief in total depravity is no abiding posture for an army of continent-conquering extroverts. The time-honored protestations of belief in other-worldliness and miraculous intervention continued for an unconscionably long period to be characteristic of American public utterances, but everyday life was conducted in terms of an orderly and improvable physical environment. The colossal discrepancy was veiled by the middle class mores of

Protestant capitalism, the open compromises with mammon which had resulted from the Puritan attempt to moralize profit making in the name of Christian stewardship.

It was thus that millions of Americans lived, as it were, naturalistically, long before a few philosophers among them began to make theoretically and systematically explicit the underlying premises of American enterprise. For many generations the "new men" were content with the old thoughts, especially in the domain of the abstract, which did not particularly interest them anyhow. "American opinion," as Santayana has pointed out, "is largely pre-American." Native philosophizing, even in imitation of foreign models, was a long time in getting started on this too-busy continent. Practical pioneering against the "down drag of the wilderness" absorbed the time and energy which might have gone into theoretical adventuring. The pressing interests of theology, politics, and business between them left little scope for reflection for its own sake. Alexis de Tocqueville's often-quoted dictum concerning the total absence of interest in philosophy in America in 1835 was a young aristocrat's exaggeration based upon a slight acquaintance with American intellectual life; [4] and yet Woodbridge Riley's counterclaim that "there was no important intellectual movement of Europe which was not reflected in some measure among thoughtful minds in America" [5] fails to carry much conviction when one remembers the isolation, the obscurity, and the cultural impotence of most of our early philosophers. Many foreign schools of thought have been reflected in America; but merely to be reflected is hardly to gain a firm foothold or to exert a decisive influence upon our intellectual life.

When, in the last century, after many false starts, American philosophizing ceased to be merely a provincial copy of the European article, it had to get under way in a transplanted society which had already been exposed to other and more violent influences. The main thought patterns of America in matters of action had been shaped by the laissez-faire commercialism of the Eastern cities and the individual libertarianism of the ever-advancing Western frontier; while those of expression had been molded into that famous Genteel Tradition which a missionary combination of church, school, and college had spread from New England and the Middle Atlantic States to the evangelized South and West. In the

[4] A. de Tocqueville, *Democracy in America*, New York, 1845, II, 1.
[5] I. Woodbridge Riley, *American Philosophy; the Early Schools*, New York, 1907, p. 13.

academic world, the chief institutional medium of intellectual influences, science and philosophy were still the prisoners of religious respectability, save in a few exceptional institutions; and metaphysical inquiry was almost exclusively the province of the theologically minded. The scientists won their freedom first; but they used it, for the most part, to go about their own business of specialized research and to stand aloof from dangerous controversies wherever possible. As long as they were let alone in their laboratories, their attitude was to "let the preachers preach." The liberation of philosophy was long postponed by the predominantly theological training of the teachers of that subject, the effects of which have persisted into our own era. The result has been to widen the gulf between the official American professions of faith, which have continued to be couched in terms of evangelical idealism, and the hardheaded practices of business and applied science, which have been carried on in other worlds of scornful realism.

Naturalism in American thought has run the whole gamut of popularity from execration to acclaim. As in Europe a few decades earlier, it began in an atmosphere of intense hostility as the feared and detested party of opposition to the entrenched theology of the academic world, and as the authentic, though wholly unauthorized, voice of American practice, itself quite innocently nonphilosophical. By contrast with the extravagant claims and promises of the philosophies which preceded it, naturalism seemed at first to be composed of little more than negations and renunciations. In addition, it incurred all the handicaps which accrue to an unpopular minority that dares to state publicly some of the concealed premises of a smug and satisfied majority. Its first great task was polemical, to free itself from its medieval fetters and to deprive its jailers of their powers of censorship. More than once, in the heat of battle, some of its adherents stooped to noisy iconoclasm and the metaphorical hurling of dead cats into sanctuaries. But with the collapse of supernaturalism and its idealistic props under the triple impact of evolution, industrial urbanization, and modern war, naturalism found itself face to face with the new responsibilities of reconstruction and re-education. The new and prodigious prestige of the name of science did not at all insure a wide and deep understanding of the significance of scientific method, but often only a "vulgar scientism" instead. Having been preserved from its enemies, who heaped abuse upon science, naturalism had now to be saved from its friends, who praised and misused it.

Jean-Jacques Ampère, who visited America in 1851–52, in discussing the prospects for Comte's positivism in the United States, predicted that it would thrive *dans le pays positif par excellence*.[6] Yet more than half a century was to elapse before this "positive" country produced a major naturalistic philosophical system, the work of a transplanted Spaniard who was a poet rather than a scientist. Why the long delay? The answer requires, on the one hand, a consideration of the dependence of naturalism upon the free development of the sciences, and, on the other, an understanding of the relatively easy circumstances of life in America in the last fifty years, which have permitted the survival of obsolete religious and social traditions in our convention-bound colleges. One does not have to be an orthodox follower of Comte to recognize that a mature and tenable naturalism in philosophy was impossible until the biological and social, as well as the physical sciences, in intent at least, had become positive. Naturalism has always thrived to the extent that science has been increasingly understood and reflected upon; it has withered whenever science has been isolated or misconstrued. Sometimes it has been metaphysical and dogmatic, capitalizing the results of science at a given period as if they were definitive, and soon appearing narrow and out-of-date. Recently it has become methodological and tentative, making no attempt to define away the aesthetic side of man's nature in terms of his theoretical interests. Obviously an adequate account of the career of naturalism in America would have to include an outline of that neglected subject, the history of American science and its impact upon our intellectual life, together with a realistic study of the economic and social background of our colleges and universities. Little more than glimpses of either can be afforded within the compass of this essay.

COLONIAL PERIOD

In spite of all the exaggeration of the earlier New England historians, it still remains true that the chief formative influences upon the intellectual life of the colonies radiated from that tiny northeastern corner of the country. They were aggressively antinaturalistic to such an extent that the account of their ultimate enfeeblement-from-within forms an essential chapter in the prehistory of American naturalism. The dispute over the relative importance of the economic and religious motives in

---

[6] J. J. Ampère, *Promenade en Amérique*, Paris, 1855, I, 364.

the colonization of America is endless and unprofitable; but few historians any longer question the extreme concentration of the religious motive in one time and place, namely, in the Great Migration of English dissenting Protestants of many shades of sectarian opinion to New England between 1620 and 1640. Whether these settlers, mainly drawn from the "will-making classes" (and below) of the eastern counties of England, amounted to one-fifth or one-third of all those who left the country for the New World during those two decades, it is evident that they came primarily because of religious discontent with the rule of Archbishop Laud, further aggravated by the decline of the cloth trade. But that such pious rather than "carnal" purposes were unique in the colonies they were well aware, and they never ceased to dwell upon the fact.[7]

At the same time thousands of other Englishmen, to say nothing of Frenchmen, Spaniards, and Dutchmen, drawn by "the age-old lure of substantial things," were pouring into the West Indies and the American continent with no such earnest disclaimers of profit seeking. If predominantly economic motives were the exception in New England, certainly they were the rule almost everywhere else. But we know that even among those who took part in the attempted founding of the truly Holy Commonwealth there were some whose "main end was to catch fish." The leaders of the Boston theocracy set their faces firmly against the direct pursuit of earthly riches, which were "but a Loan from the great God" until the day of final accounting. It was "the insatiable desire after land and worldly accommodations" which tempted good Christians to "live like heathen." A church member, said John Cotton, must "bee a man deadhearted to the world." Yet, at the same time, he must "bestir himself for profit," since idleness was even worse than greed. In the eyes of Cotton Mather it was "the most concealed and yet the most Violent of our Passions," to be sternly repressed by law. Those who neglect to increase the wealth that is entrusted to them will find it taken away; for "if we are Unfruitful after all 'tis but Reasonable that we should be deprived of those Means." [8] Add to this conception of Christian diligence in both heavenly and earthly callings, the Puritan emphases upon fecun-

---

[7] See John Winthrop, *Conclusions for the Plantation in New England*, 1629, p. 8; John Higginson, *The Cause of God*, 1663, p. 11; Increase Mather, *Necessity of Reformation . . . Agreed upon . . . in the Synod at Boston*, 1679, p. 6; Cotton Mather, *Some Considerations on the Bills of Credit . . . in New England*, 1691.

[8] Cotton Mather, *Durable Riches*, Boston, 1695, pp. 13–14; Increase Mather, *loc. cit.*; John Cotton, *Christ the Fountaine of Life*, London, 1651, pp. 119–20; and Cotton Mather, *Bonifacius; an Essay upon the Good*, Boston, 1710, p. 10.

dity and thrift, and it becomes apparent that even bleak New England was bound to witness the eventual accumulation of about the same surplus of material goods that would have been piled up by a policy of unconsecrated selfishness.[9]

The inevitable "commercialization of the North" took time; and yet as early as 1640 acute observers had begun to scent the polluting growth of a prosperous and sinfully independent Boston merchant class. By 1674 Samuel Torry found "the very heart of New England . . . changed and exceedingly corrupted"; while two years later Edward Randolph reported thirty traders in Boston alone with fortunes of ten to twenty thousand pounds.[10] From that time on, the steady piling up of capital to the point of luxury by the upper economic group evoked a series of lamentations by the clergy over the rising tide of "sensuality, licentiousness, libertinism, carnality, pride." But their shrill complaints were wholly ineffectual; for it was this rising merchant class, which, as the founding of the Brattle Street Church in 1698 was to show, the theocracy could neither control nor ignore, that was soon to lay bare the fatal paradox of Puritan economics. The medieval monastics had openly renounced the normal economic struggle-for-existence in their attempts to realize holiness here below; but the Puritans, no less agonizingly sincere, sought to do business as usual in the sight of God and to His glory. They worked more diligently than worldlings, treating the external world "as though it were real"; and yet they sought to convince themselves and others that their hearts were not truly set upon any of the trivialities of earthly prosperity. Their zealous attempt to regulate commerce by a bourgeois interpretation of the Mosaic law ended in failure, although the preachments continued long after holiness had degenerated into respectability. Economic self-restraint plus industry, in the cities at least, yielded the wealth which it professed not to aim at; and wealth in turn proved to be morally unmanageable by frail and selfish mortals, just as the Puritans feared that it would. Thus, by the end of the colonial period the foremost American stronghold of professed immaterialism had become a fortress of materialism in practice.

In intellectual matters, also, something of the same internal disintegration set in. The Englishmen of New England were medieval Protestants,

[9] See Perry Miller, *The New England Mind*, New York, 1939, pp. 40–44, for an excellent discussion of Puritan "other-worldliness" and the economic motive.
[10] T. J. Wertenbaker, *The First Americans, 1607–1690*, New York, 1927, pp. 71, 110, 112; and Perry Miller, *The New England Mind*, pp. 471–84.

the spiritual heirs of scholasticism and the Reformation and, to a lesser extent, of Renaissance humanism. They had left Europe before the mathematical method had revolutionized scientific inquiry, and thus before science had given proof of its immense utility in the conquest of nature. Such few known regularities of physics as they recognized were Aristotelian, could be reversed or interrupted at any time by divine decree, and were worthy of study only as symbolic of God's purposes. There was nothing fundamentally wrong about the investigation of nature as long as it was conducted in the right spirit, that is—in strict subordination to the saving of souls. By many of the Puritan divines science was regarded, says Perry Miller, "as a part of faith itself, a positive declaration of the will of God, a necessary and indispensable complement to Biblical revelation." Nevertheless, it was an undertaking full of peril for the unwary, the danger being, as John Cotton expressed it, that the inquirer might become "very quick sighted in points of nature, but very dull and heavy in matters of Religion and grace." Cotton Mather's recommended query of all history: "What can I see of the Glorious GOD in these occurrences?" was also the keynote of the Puritan approach to science.[11]

This meant in practice that nature was regarded as a reservoir filled with spiritual meaning, a potential treasury of hints concerning what God might have in store for sinful mortals and the elect. Since "the actual government of the minutest event, the rise of the sun, the fall of a stone, the beat of the heart, was under the direct and immediate supervision of God,"[12] both the dividing line between supernatural miracle and natural happening and that between the spiritual and the corporeal became somewhat blurred. Everything was from God's hand; but some things were orderly and regular in their normal states. These came to be regarded as "natural," and relatively devoid of cosmic importance. But, from the twentieth-century point of view, all these distinctions were *within* the supernatural. As time went on, however, miracles became rarer, and "the conviction grew that God abided by His laws." This was the opening through which the mathematical formulations of Coper-

[11] Cotton Mather, *Manuductio ad ministerium,* Boston, 1726, p. 39. See also Theodore Hornberger, "Puritanism and Science," *New England Quarterly,* X, 503–15, and the same author's *Science and the New World,* San Marino, Calif., 1937, p. 13.
[12] Perry Miller and Thomas H. Johnson, *The Puritans,* New York, 1938, p. 8; and Perry Miller, *The New England Mind,* ch. viii.

nicus, Descartes, and Newton entered Puritan thought and supplied the philosophical foundations for an ever-encroaching deism.

The Puritan attitude toward science, as well as toward wealth, was an unstable compromise: neither was important; both were dangerous; yet neither was to be entirely shunned. In terms of empirical inquiry, science could hardly have been expected to thrive in harassed and isolated frontier settlements. A few amateur scientists, such as John Winthrop, Jr., Thomas Brattle, Paul Dudley, Jared Eliot, Thomas Robie, Leonard Hoar, the Mathers, and Doctors William Douglass and Zabdiel Boylston made collections or recorded observations admixed with old wives' tales. It was Dr. Boylston who gave the colony "its first rational understanding of scientific medicine" in the smallpox controversy of 1721; and there is a reminder of the fact that America, thanks to the absence of fixed academic traditions, took the lead in the introduction of experimental science into the world's universities, in the career of John Winthrop IV, second Hollis professor of mathematics and natural philosophy in Harvard College at the age of twenty-four. Winthrop was the founder, in 1746, of the first American laboratory of experimental physics and a conspicuous representative for forty years of the new rationalism of Newton, confidently reconciled with Holy Writ, which was soon to gain a foothold in Bostonian intellectual circles.[13] Skepticism about demonic possession developed soon after the excesses of the Salem witchcraft trials; and Copernican astronomy in the colleges and in almanacs began to rob the sky of some of its major terrors. So great was the prevailing confidence that all scientific discoveries could not only be brought into line with the Bible, but would also positively support what needed no such buttressing, that few of the seventeenth-century orthodox seem to have been aware of the beginning of the slow process of attrition by which the vast areas claimed by supernaturalism were eventually to be whittled away to the vanishing point. A sermon by an English clergyman quoted in the *American Weekly Mercury* of Philadelphia in 1722, however, denounced smallpox inoculation as tending "to anticipate and banish Providence out of the world," an accurate descrip-

[13] F. E. Brasch, "The Royal Society of London and Its Influence upon Scientific Thought in the American Colonies," *Scientific Monthly*, XXXIII (1931), 353, 453-57; "Newton's First Critical Disciple in the American Colonies—John Winthrop," in History of Science Society, *Sir Isaac Newton, 1727-1927*, Baltimore, 1928; and F. Cajori, *The Early Mathematical Sciences in North and South America*, Boston, 1928, pp. 98-99. The above-mentioned John Winthrop, Jr., eldest son of the governor, was John IV's great-grand-uncle.

tion of that inexorable replacement of fanciful causes by tested ones which was to pave the way for the triumph of naturalism.

It is a mistake to lay much stress upon the differences, during the colonial period, between New England and the rest of the country in the broad matter of conventional religious beliefs. Yet the Middle Atlantic and the southern colonies, where "people took themselves less seriously" than in New England, enjoyed from the start a milder theological climate, due in part to a greater sectarian heterogeneity and cultural cosmopolitanism. This freer atmosphere lessened some of the discouragements which science had to face, without adding materially to its encouragements. The wealthy planter class which emerged in the South after the introduction and spread of Negro slavery adopted a mode of living patterned upon that of the English country gentry with whom they kept in touch. Among the latter it was becoming fashionable to dabble in plant collecting or magnetism, but on the whole the model of well-bred leisure which they supplied could hardly be called intellectual. The amateur scientists of the pre-Franklin era south of New England comprised a small group of the educated who had little in the way of popular fame or support. Botany was far in the lead as the favorite colonial science, attracting the interest of such men as the Reverend John Banister, Dr. John Clayton, Dr. John Mitchell, James Logan, Dr. John Tennant, Mark Catesby, Dr. Alexander Garden, William Byrd, and the native-born John Bartram. Most of these enthusiasts had brought their scientific leanings with them from abroad; and the number who were physicians is strikingly large in view of the extremely backward state of medical science in colonial America.

Astronomy also had its devotees; chief among them was David Rittenhouse of Philadelphia. But the subject that was to sweep both botany and astronomy from the center of the scientific stage at the middle of the century was electricity, and its amiable sponsor was Benjamin Franklin. It is easy to dispute about Franklin's stature as a philosopher outside the field of ethics, but as a popularizer of science and quasi-naturalism in his day in America he ranks as a commanding figure. The scientific hero of two continents, he was the new Prometheus whose tolerant skepticism, guarded though it was, made the world safer for dozens of lesser heretics. As Poor Richard he was also the first major prophet of openly secularized Puritanism, "less concerned with the golden pavements of the City of God than that the cobblestones on Chestnut Street in Philadelphia should be well and evenly laid . . ." [14] He saw through the increasing incompatibility between the naturalistic presuppositions of the business and political morals practiced by the descendants of the Puritans and the idealistic ethics which they continued to preach; and, unlike them, he dared "to change the preaching." By openly asserting that earned wealth might lead toward some of the virtues instead of away from them, Franklin became the patron saint of American business in the eyes of those who, unfortunately, could not see beyond his instrumentalist ethics to the humane ends which he had in view; just as he became the patron saint of science in the eyes of those who could not see beyond its immediately useful applications. Thus, at a time when, after the fervor of the Great Awakening, godliness was again rapidly declining, he united in the popular imagination the two main secularizing tendencies that were ultimately to furnish the broad foundations of American naturalism. Neither a great theoretical scientist nor a typical American business man, Franklin like Francis Bacon was a scientific promoter par excellence, who reached the peak of his endless curiosity only a few years before his death. As he wrote to James Bowdoin of Boston in 1788: "Our much regretted friend Winthrop once made me the Compliment, that I was good at starting Game for Philosophers; let me try if I can start a little for you." [15] But the scientific hunt which Franklin sought to initiate during forty years of intellectual ambassadorship was soon to encounter many obstacles in addition to the interruptions caused by the struggle for American independence.

REVOLUTIONARY PERIOD

As far as the fortunes of naturalism are concerned, the Revolutionary era presents a paradox that is likely to deceive the unwary observer: actual scientific accomplishment was almost at a standstill; yet popular faith in the supposed results of science and doubts about the old-time religion enjoyed a mushroom growth. In spite of the war's paralyzing effect upon the nonpractical varieties of reflection, a striking change of climate for the warmer in intellectual circles seemed to give promise of great things to come. For a while it almost looked as if the hour of liberation of science and philosophy from theology might be at hand. In the

[14] V. L. Parrington, *The Colonial Mind*, New York, 1927, p. 178.
[15] A. H. Smyth, ed., *The Writings of Benjamin Franklin*, New York, 1905-7, IX, 652-53; and H. W. Schneider, *The Puritan Mind*, New York, 1930, pp. 248-53.

light of colonial religiosity more than one student of our history has expressed amazement at the relatively secular, cosmospolitan, anti-clerical mood of the war period, only a scant third of a century after the Great Awakening. It is difficult, for example, to think of a notion much further removed from Calvinism than the individual's natural right to the "pursuit of happiness" as a proclaimed national ideal. In terms of leadership, the United States of America came into being in an age of religious indifference and unbelief. The dominant figures—Washington, Franklin, Jefferson, John Adams, Thomas Paine—as well as many lesser lights, were deists or strongly influenced by deism.

The groanings and thunderings of the clergy need not be taken at their face value,[16] but there can be little doubt that, in the eyes of the pious, infidelity in all its many guises—deism, sensationalism, material-ism, skepticism, and atheism—seemed about to sweep both the army and the country into the waiting arms of Satan. Among the educated the change of intellectual climate merely reflected the rise of the cult of science and the accompanying decline of religious ardor among the upper classes of Europe. Its chief source was commonly supposed to be the Encyclopedists of France, but the actual channels by which the ideas of men like Descartes, Bayle, Diderot, Rousseau, Voltaire, Gassendi, and Montesquieu reached America were more often the works of such English writers as Locke, Newton, Hobbes, Shaftesbury, Collins, Til-lotson, Boyle, Clarke, Bolingbroke, Hume, and Hartley. It was the spread of the English versions of deism before the Treaty of Paris in 1763 that paved the way for a certain amount of French skepticism after that date, rather than the other way around. There had long been a steady seepage of mild liberalism into the northern colleges and pulpits; and the multiplication of dissenting sects in the Old Lights-New Lights schism which followed the Great Awakening had further weakened the colo-nial churches.

Even more destructive of godliness were the political and economic interests which diverted attention from salvation to state building. The temper of the times had become political; and the debates about the future of the new republic were carried on, for the most part, in terms of a robust materialism. Perhaps the best commentary on the essential

---

[16] H. M. Jones, *America and French Culture, 1750–1848*, Chapel Hill, N.C., 1927, pp. 377–85; and V. Stauffer, *New England and the Bavarian Illuminati*, New York, 1918, pp. 76, 97–102.

boredom of the period with all religion is the fact that, even though it was semipolitical in nature, deism as a religious sect could thrive only in a few centers for a brief season. "The American liberal, while a republican in politics, was unable to accept republican religion." [17]

In its many varieties, from enlightened and respectable Anglicanism or Unitarianism to radical free thought for the masses, deism was "anticlerical theism," a halfway house between naturalism and supernaturalism. There was, in other words, a general tendency among deists to hold that, in the words of Shaftesbury, "Deity is sufficiently revealed through natural Phenomena." A popularized version of Newton's orderly universe of natural law, which man could exploit for his own benefit by the use of his reason, filled the foreground; while God retreated into the distant background as "proprietor" or "great first cause." In America, as in Europe, deism as a mode of thinking, rather than as a single system of thought, came to be taken for granted among the educated, but with even less inquiry into its deeper implications. Metaphysics was scornfully regarded, both as having no practical value and as too closely associated with religious obscurantism. A few militants, such as Ethan Allen, Thomas Paine, and Elihu Palmer earned unbridled calumny by their angry frontal attacks upon miracles and Scriptural literalism; but for many of the educated who shared it, the deistic temper was a mildly skeptical attitude easily superimposed upon nominal church membership. Little scientific knowledge and no real comprehension of the scientific spirit were needed to maintain a sophisticated contempt, sometimes well dissembled, for the "Gothick phantoms" which were still, unfortunately, so necessary for manipulating American public opinion.

Deism and materialism (together with republicanism in politics) were lumped together by those who feared both, but the actual links between them were largely coincidental. "Contrary to common assertions both then and now," declares Professor Koch, "the movement to establish deism as a religion in America had little to do with philosophical materialism." The single exception (outside the South, not treated by Koch) was John "Walking" Stewart, a conceited Englishman who came to Philadelphia in 1796 and whose quasi-materialism was practical, not metaphysical.[18] Nevertheless, the wide prevalence of deistic tendencies

[17] G. A. Koch, *Republican Religion*, New York, 1933, p. xii.
[18] *Ibid.*, pp 148–67, 287.

in revolt against Calvinism undoubtedly afforded philosophical naturalism, in the form of Anglo-French sensationalism, its first brief opportunity to take root in America. But the galaxy of "medical materialists" who revolved about Philadelphia, the focal point of French influence (John Adams, not without sarcasm, said that it considered itself "the pineal gland of the United States"), including Cadwallader Colden, Joseph Priestley, Thomas Cooper, and Dr. Benjamin Rush, were not to prove equal to the task of laying a solid scientific foundation for a well-thought-out American naturalism that could resist the onslaughts of hostile criticism. While bold and ambitious in their system building, they were sadly lacking in originality and thoroughness; and the crude science which they borrowed from England and France was wholly inadequate to the demands which they made upon it. Inconsistent attitudes of relativistic skepticism about the views of others, combined with dogmatic absolutism about one's own, were all too common. It was an age of overconfident "reason," of premature syntheses, and of few laboratory experiments. Amid the excitements of nation building, thinkers were in haste to proceed from dogmatic general theories of human nature to specific practical applications in education or politics. The long-run results to their reputations were not surprising: obscurity and neglect in some instances, misunderstanding and abuse in others.

The versatile Colden, an Irish-born Scot who came over with a medical degree from Edinburgh in 1710, at first devoted his acute powers of observation to Linnaean botany. Turning, about 1750, to speculative physics, he produced, during a lifetime filled with political and business interests, a series of works which became less and less consistently materialistic. A follower of both Hobbes and Newton, he involved himself in the dualistic compromises of the latter's deism and ended by approaching panpsychism. Although Colden rose to prominence in New York politics, his philosophical writings were "unknown and unhonored" in the colonies. At the other extreme of notoriety were the celebrated scientist and Unitarian clergyman Joseph Priestley and the truculent Thomas Cooper, who took refuge in America in 1793–94 and were constantly involved in controversies that exposed them to the coarsest abuse. When Thomas Jefferson proposed Cooper as the "corner-stone" of his new faculty at the University of Virginia, "the very mention of his name aroused such a storm among the clergy that the appointment had to be withdrawn"; and later, in spite of his services to the states-rights cause, Cooper was "tried" for atheism and ousted, at the age of seventy-five, from the presidency of the College of South Carolina. That the bitterness which he aroused followed him even after his death may be seen from the inscription on his tombstone in the Trinity Episcopal cemetery at Columbia, South Carolina, which begins: "Erected, by a Portion of His Fellow Citizens, to the Memory of Thomas Cooper . . ."

Where others had equivocated, Cooper, who was entirely familiar with French as well as British materialism, came out flatly, albeit dogmatically, for the complete explanation of mental phenomena from the properties of the "corporeal organized system." Half a century before Comte's positivism reached this country, he argued that "the faculties of the soul have no existence; they are words only, the counters employed in reasoning, convenient signs of arrangement like plus and minus." Yet his views, "conceived in a decidedly Gallic section of the South, exerted not a fraction of the influence of the later Comteanism of the north." [19] Cooper would gladly have translated Cabanis, but feared, as he wrote to Jefferson in 1814, that "the public would not bear it. Too much light is apt to blind us. Then again who would read it except some few young physicians, who would lose all their practice if they were known to approve of it." [20] It was his confident belief that eventually "the progress of accurate physiology" would expose the "inanities" of Scottish realism and New England immaterialism; but a century was to elapse before man as a biological organism could become, as Cooper desired, the starting point of a convincing philosophy in the hands of a James or a Dewey. The medical man of the period who was the most successful in escaping both obscurity and calumny was the philanthropic Dr. Benjamin Rush, a materialist in his working hypotheses, but also addicted to introspection, whose influence upon his many Southern students at the University of Pennsylvania could hardly have been other than equivocal.

Medical materialism, for all its promise, lacked institutional auxiliaries and organization, as well as the needed influx of new blood in the form of immigrants with superior education. Outside the University of Pennsylvania it did not gain a foothold in any of the older colleges. Their clerical presidents saw to that. But it did bid fair, for about two decades,

[19] I. W. Riley, *American Philosophy; the Early Schools*, p. 416.
[20] G. Chinard, *Jefferson et les idéologues*, p. 231.

to establish itself on the irreligious frontier, many thousands of miles from Europe. Under the stimulus of revolutionary liberalism and incipient nationalism, new colleges, relatively free from direct ecclesiastical influence, were being projected, especially in the South. One of the most remarkable of these rising foundations was Transylvania University at Lexington, Kentucky, first established as a seminary in 1783. Control of the new public institution was bitterly contested by two factions: the strict Calvinist Presbyterians and their allies and the liberal "infidels" of the relatively wealthy classes in the few large towns. In 1817 the liberals, swept into power by the rising tide of republicanism, forced the election of Horace Holley, a Boston Unitarian minister, as president. During the decade of his enlightened leadership Transylvania won a national reputation; and "perhaps the majority of Kentuckians of note during those years were at one time or another associated with the university." [21] Large sums were expended for scientific books and equipment, which had to be brought across the Atlantic and then by pack horse over the Alleghanies.[22] On a faculty which included such prolific writers on science as Constantine Rafinesque and Dr. Charles Caldwell, was a gifted young alumnus named Dr. Joseph Buchanan, appointed in 1809 as Professor of the Institutes of Medicine in the proposed medical school at the age of twenty-four, only five years after his arrival, with but fourteen months of previous schooling, as a rustic student from Tennessee. In anticipation of the opening of the school in 1812, Buchanan prepared a course of lectures embodying "a metaphysical investigation of human nature" to precede the medical subjects; and, when the opening was delayed, he decided to publish them in book form. They appeared in Richmond, Virginia, in 1812, under the title *The Philosophy of Human Nature*—the first native American treatise on physiological psychology, and "perhaps the most systematic presentation of the case in behalf of materialism that the country had yet afforded.[23] Frankly admitting his reliance upon Locke, Hartley, Hume, and Erasmus Darwin, the young writer could hardly have been expected to succeed in his ambitious attempt to materialize mind by demonstrating

[21] R. L. Rusk, *The Literature of the Middle Western Frontier*, New York, 1926, I, 58–60; and Niels H. Sonne, *Liberal Kentucky, 1780–1828*, New York, 1939, *passim*.
[22] T. G. Johnson, Jr., *Scientific Interests in the Old South*, New York, 1936, pp. 34–40.
[23] I. W. Riley, *American Philosophy, the Early Schools*, p. 379.

the indissoluble connection between psychical and physical processes. He did, however, thoroughly arouse the ire of the orthodox by presenting in print a coherent alternative to Calvinism as the basis of sound moral character. Meanwhile, the Kentucky Presbyterians, enlisting the aid of the Baptists and the Methodists, were venomously using "every device conceivable" to destroy the Holley administration and with it the hopes of leadership of frontier infidelity. When they succeeded, in 1827, Transylvania paid the penalty for its "free, inquisitive, excited spirit" of inquiry in a revival-ridden community by thirty years of decline to complete ruin; and frontier higher education became the function of the small and safe denominational college.

The high hopes aroused by Thomas Jefferson's challenge to the clerical rulers of America's colleges in the founding of the University of Virginia also largely failed to be fulfilled. Although Jefferson had known Destutt de Tracy, Cabanis, and other French idéologues and had written to correspondents, "I am a materialist; I am an Epicurean," his moderate deism was "just as remote from the mechanistic materialism of d'Holbach and La Mettrie as from Calvinism and predestination." Yet, because of his supposed propagation of infidel French doctrines of "terror, atheism, and free love," Jefferson was calumniated as few Americans have been before or since.[24] But, aside from purely political hatreds, it was his eudaemonistic deism (and worse) that was feared, not the secularized science which he hoped would pervade the atmosphere of the University of Virginia. Moreover, the impressive enrollment figures in the science courses given at that institution offer little proof that large numbers of the students who took them became openly skeptical. The zealous reconcilers of natural science with the truths of revelation soon managed to render scientific curiosity as harmless and infidelity as odious there as elsewhere in America. Empirical naturalism was not even strong enough to be recognized as their real enemy: "the dialectic of Christian apologetics in the South was until 1861 aimed principally at the rationalism of the eighteenth century rather than at the scientific revolution of the nineteenth." [25] Jefferson's great services in lending prestige to free scientific inquiry were probably more than offset, dur-

[24] P. L. Ford, ed., *The Writings of Thomas Jefferson*, New York, 1899, X, 143; G. Chinard, *Thomas Jefferson*, pp. 522–23; and H. M. Jones, *America and French Culture*, pp. 395–97, 406–7, 550–59.
[25] T. G. Johnson, Jr., *Scientific Interests in the Old South*, pp. 13–16, 40.

ing his own lifetime, by the abuse that was heaped upon his political and religious views. Infidel democracy, even with the third President of the United States as its leader, could not wrest the key positions in the country's intellectual life from the entrenched supporters of respectable federalism.

ROMANTIC PERIOD

So sharp and so general was the American reaction to the French Revolution and its aftermath, turning public sentiment away in horror from all forms of unbelief toward a re-energized Protestantism, that it virtually closed the national mind for the greater part of the nineteenth century to all philosophies except religious versions of realism and idealism. So violent was the counterattack upon deism that it left no tenable middle ground between evangelical fervor and odious infidelity. To this revulsion in popular feeling many factors contributed: the Reign of Terror dismayed even the most advanced freethinkers on this side of the Atlantic; an emerging nationalism made all obviously imported notions unwelcome; and new techniques of proselyting enabled the churches to reconquer the frontier, where sects now succeeded "in inverse ratio to their intellectual attainments, and in direct ratio to their emotional appeal." [26]

In the colleges, where the clergy in positions of authority had managed to ride out the tempests of adolescent agnosticism, the students who were not swept away by revivalism were assured that natural religion led to conclusions identical with those of revelation; and of the forty thousand who were graduated before 1855, at least one-fourth became ministers. That the new abhorrence of deism did not extend to the study of science is evidenced by the action of President Timothy Dwight of Yale, who both depicted in lurid terms the foul plottings of the French Illuminati against Connecticut Christianity and introduced advanced natural science courses into the Yale curriculum. He epitomized the propaganda of the clergy against deism (the method known today as "smearing") in two discourses to the seniors in 1797, during which he reviewed and attacked both the views and the personal characters of ten British deistic writers, adding: "So evident is the want of morals on the part of Infidels, in this country, generally, that to say—'A man is an Infidel'—is understood, of course, as a declaration that he is

[26] R. L. Rusk, *The Literature of the Middle Western Frontier*, I, 46.

a plainly immoral man." [27] Morality was held to be the basis of civilization, and evangelical religion was the basis of morality.

Thanks to the frontier revivals, orthodox evangelical Christianity (what is now known as "fundamentalism," and a far less intellectual affair than Puritanism) reached the zenith of its power in the interval between the Revolution and the Civil War, when America turned its back upon the Atlantic and with gusto and bluster began the great task of westward expansion in earnest. The loose, minimum, secular form of government devised in the Age of Reason now released upon the land's incredible riches an incalculable flood of energy and acquisitiveness. Matters soon reached the point where Professor Jonathan Pearson of Union College was moved to inquire in his diary on March 30, 1836, "Who ever heard an American speak ten words if 'Dollar' was not one of them? His mind is an arithmetic of loss and gain." [28] Nothing could have been more gross than the materialism of the successive land booms in the West and the first big factories in the East; and yet the contemporaneous intellectual pronouncements were laden with spiritual unction. Unleashed greed quickly draped itself in the middle-class garments of respectability and church-membership. The raw and sprawling continent had found an authentic voice in the rhetorical rhythms and crashing crescendos of Walt Whitman; but, lest it acknowledge to itself its own hearty vulgarity, it acclaimed instead the clipped sententious dicta of Emerson and the lofty professorial domesticities of Longfellow. Only Hermann Melville attempted in vain to challenge the sentimentalism of the 1850's with a naturalistic philosophy of morals.

When the first stirrings of consciously independent American philosophizing, aroused by Anglo-German romanticism, began in the lay movement known as transcendentalism, naturalism was lost in the shuffle of utopian enthusiasms. The New England Unitarians and their successors took over the analytical negations of the deists, but added mystical affirmations which infused the chilly mechanism of Newtonian physics with aesthetic ecstasy and moral earnestness. They held that it was folly to split the world into its component parts, "to see the world by piece," if that meant losing sight of the whole. "Science at its best, they believed, was their friend, not because it could ever find out anything essential

[27] T. Dwight, *The Duty of Americans, at the Present Crisis*, New Haven, Conn., 1798, p. 82.
[28] Codman Hislop, "Jonathan Pearson's Thinking Books," *New York History*, XIX (October, 1938), 372.

about matter, but for the reason that it was constantly finding out the most amazing 'correspondences' and 'emblems' of spiritual truth." [29] In the academic world, however, the prevailing doctrines were still those of Scottish common-sense realism, spread by the "Presbyterian glacier" from its central ice cap at Princeton, an "eminently safe philosophy which kept undergraduates locked in so many intellectual dormitories, safe from the dark speculations of materialism and the beguiling allurements of idealism." [30]

Through such layers of prejudice, preoccupation, and fear of unpopular theories, the embryo naturalisms of Europe, still dogmatically framed in terms of Newtonian mechanism, could hardly penetrate. As early as July, 1824, a young Frenchman who had dreamed eight years earlier of emigrating to "that fortunate land," America, sent to the aging Jefferson the first published sketch of a new system of social physics that was to be "entirely positive, and detached from all theological and metaphysical notions." The author, an obscure *Polytechnicien* named Auguste Comte, who had derived the key ideas of positivism from his master, Henri de Saint-Simon, was just on the point of emerging angrily from anonymity and strike out for independent fame. He had taken "the modern Socrates," Benjamin Franklin, as his model in matters of conduct, and he saw in the creation of the American republic the chief precedent for his ardently advocated renovation of European society.[31] Later he became convinced that the New World might also become a fertile field for the new faith and a source of personal subsidy, provided only that the Protestants, "the spontaneous enemies of positivism," could be redeemed from their deplorable hypocrisy and anarchism.[32]

Yet it was through the liberal clergy of these same despised Protestants that the first tidings of Comte's system reached American shores. In the autumn of 1844 the Reverend William Henry Channing discussed the *Cours* with his friends Theodore Parker, George Ripley, and Orestes

[29] Odell Shepard, *Pedlar's Progress*, Boston, 1937, 254–55. For the same view of science as symbolic in colonial New England, see Perry Miller, *The New England Mind*, p. 213.

[30] W. Riley, *American Thought*, New York, 1915, p. 120. Scottish realism had the added advantage of justifying the divine right of private property, according to Ralph L. Gabriel, *The Course of American Democratic Thought*, New York, 1940, pp. 147–50.

[31] R. L. Hawkins, *Auguste Comte and the United States, 1816–1853*, Cambridge, Mass., 1936, pp. 6, 9, 14.

[32] A. Comte, *Cours de philosophie positive*, Paris, 1841, V, 598.

A. Brownson; and in 1849 another Unitarian, the Reverend James Walker, later president of Harvard, clearly foresaw that the law of the three stages meant that "Religion, as well as metaphysics, is destined to die a natural death;—not by being denied and confuted, but by being ignored; not by the answer given to religious questions, but by the fact that the time is coming when no religious questions will be asked." [33] A less alarmist and more extensive criticism came from the pen of the Reverend Joseph Henry Allen in 1851; but these few New England Unitarians could hardly correct the general impression that Comte was just another French materialist, whose genetic approach to the allegedly eternal truths made him an especially dangerous heretic. This fear was heightened by the publication in the same year of the first book written in the United States under the influence of Comte, a blasphemous and anonymous work (by one James O'Connell) entitled *Vestiges of Civilization*. Theological predilections and scientific deficiencies vitiated the one serious and prolonged attempt by an American to decipher the "ten thousand pages of abstruse reasoning" published by Comte before 1854. George Frederick Holmes, who made it, combined a too-penetrating insight into some of Comte's personal weaknesses with an equal blindness to some of the Frenchman's real virtues; and in any case his readers in the *Methodist Quarterly Review* were hardly predisposed to give positivism a friendly hearing.[34] Those Americans who could appreciate Comte's scientific accomplishments were evidently, with a very few exceptions, repelled by the synthetic religious trappings with which the Grand Priest of Humanity insisted upon bedecking them. William Mitchell Gillespie, professor of civil engineering at Union College, irked Comte by seeking to salvage for readers of English what was thought to be mathematically valuable in the first volume of the *Cours*, omitting what he called "the peculiar 'Positive philosophy' of the author." Comte claimed that the deletions were because of "the Protestant censorship, against the will of the translator"; but this is unlikely in view of Gillespie's notorious lack of reverence for any form of tradition or authority.[35]

Comte's direct influence in America was small, in spite of his pathetically exaggerated notions to the contrary. Before 1853 not a single Amer-

[33] R. L. Hawkins, *Auguste Comte and the United States, 1816–1853*, pp. 14–17.
[34] *Ibid.*, chs. ii–iii.
[35] W. M. Gillespie, *The Philosophy of Mathematics*, New York, 1851, p. vii, *Dictionary of American Biography*, VII, 288–89.

ican "accepted the positive philosophy without reservation, and not a single one accepted the Religion of Humanity at all." The American apostle of religious Positivism, English-born Henry Edger, "after five years of earnest efforts, succeeded in making only ten converts, four of whom were his wife and three of his children." Aside from the fact that Edger chose to preach the authoritarian doctrines of the new cult in Josiah Warren's ultra-anarchistic village of Modern Times, Long Island, there were so many reasons why the notions of the "second career" repelled Americans that "it would almost seem that Comte, with malice prepense, had sought to create a system in which there would be elements objectionable to as many classes of American society as possible."[36] Other European social reformers with naturalistic leanings fared little better than Comte. The agnostic Icarian communities inspired by Etienne Cabet, in Texas and Illinois, dragged out a precarious existence from 1848 until 1895. Robert Owen's decline as a leader is commonly dated from his open attack upon religion on August 21, 1817; and his New Harmony, in Indiana, was quickly disrupted by internal dissensions aroused by itinerant preachers. The Fourierist phalanxes, in spite of their compromises with orthodoxy, were soon under the usual attack as "unchristian." Yet, in the face of all their practical misfortunes and mismanagements, they attracted many choice intellects in the decade from 1840 to 1850. In all these scores of hopeful reform enterprises of "the stammering century," however, it was the utopian goals of the rival formulas, not their philosophical presuppositions, which received the most attention.[37]

While these numerous prophets of earthly as well as heavenly paradise filled the air with their competing gospels, a vast amount of quiet spadework in laying the foundations of the sciences in America was going on in relative obscurity. Not only were the separate disciplines being split off from philosophy one by one; they were also being cultivated by men trained here at home in partial independence of Europe. In July, 1816, Benjamin Silliman of Yale launched the pioneer journal of general science (and the arts) in this country with the remark that

[36] R. L. Hawkins, *Positivism in the United States, 1853–1861*, Cambridge, Mass., 1938, chs. ii–iii; and pp. 208–12. For Comte's possible later influence in America, see ch. xv, "The Religion of Humanity," in R. L. Gabriel, *The Course of American Democratic Thought*, esp. pp. 183–84.

[37] See W. A. Hinds, *American Communities*, Oneida, N.Y., 1878; J. H. Noyes, *History of American Socialism*, Philadelphia, Pa., 1870; and M. Hillquit, *History of Socialism in the United States*, New York, 1910.

"the devoted cultivators of science in the United States are comparatively few; they are, however, rapidly increasing in number." The limited clientèle of his *American Journal of Science* during its first thirty years may be estimated from the fact that the number of its subscribers fluctuated between six and seven hundred, barely meeting expenses.[38] By 1847, however, Silliman could boast that "multiplied labors of many hands have produced great results," especially in the fields of organized exploration and observational astronomy. Of the latter, President Barnard candidly remarked in 1876: "Half a century ago such a thing as an astronomical observatory was unknown in the United States. At present the number (not fewer than thirty . . . probably more) is considerably greater than the necessity." [39] The average college undergraduate of the fifties, however, probably shared the disgust of young Andrew D. White of Yale, "that any human being should give his time to pursuits so futile" as chemistry.[40]

In co-operative tax-supported scientific activity the state of New York, whose succession of savants in public office, begun by Colden, had been continued by De Witt Clinton and the amazingly versatile Dr. Samuel Latham Mitchill, set the pace for the rest of the country with its epochal Natural History Survey of 1836–43. The little group of devoted field-naturalists on its staff, who battled the perils of the wilderness and of popular suspicion with equal fortitude, seemed to the newly arrived Agassiz of Harvard to provide "the best nucleus for post-graduate instruction in science to be found in the United States"; and despite the failure of the proposed University of Albany in 1851, the quickening influence of the New York Survey was felt in a dozen directions.[41]

America's inventors, however, continued to overshadow her scientists. Besides such giants of ingenuity as Morse, Whitney, Howe, and McCormick, there were contrivers of the whittle-and-tinker variety at nearly every crossroads. The country could also boast some able scientific investigators before the Civil War; but their work did little either to forward the cause of deism, to aid the spread of such imported natu-

[38] E. S. Dana and others, *A Century of Science in America*, New Haven, Conn., 1918, pp. 30, 42, 44.
[39] T. D. Woolsey and others, *The First Century of the Republic*, New York, 1876, p. 297.
[40] A. D. White, *Autobiography*, New York, 1905, I, 290.
[41] Dixon Ryan Fox, "The Rise of Scientific Interests in New York," *History of the State of New York*, New York, 1937, IX, 99–123.

ralisms as positivism, or to supply the basis for an indigenous naturalistic philosophy. The prime reason for this was that their prevailing patterns of thought about the universe were surprisingly similar to those of their early colonial predecessors. Although Newton had replaced Aristotle, empirical inquiry was still carried on within an axiomatic a priori framework of supernaturalism.[42] Even those who were not actively devout seem to have regarded the new knowledge either as something quite apart from philosophy and religion or else as ultimately reconcilable with the traditional beliefs. President Barnard only stated the almost universal assumption when he declared that "it is in the nature of things impossible that science and religion should be in conflict, since truth, which is the aim of the one, is also the substance of the other, and truth can never be inconsistent with itself."[43] On the surface, intellectually speaking, the middle of the century was the darkest hour just before dawn. Deism was steadily declining, but underneath, the slow, steady fact-digging of the scientists (many of them quite unaware of the implications of their own discoveries, or discreetly silent about them) was undermining the last supports of the vested orthodoxy and clearing the ground for the foundations of something different. It took, however, the triple earthquake of Darwin, the panic of 1857, and the Civil War to bring the ancient structure down; and to arouse both scientists and philosophers to a belated realization that supernaturalism had overstayed its era and that a new America—urban, industrial, and secular—was on the way.

THE MACHINE AGE

In the year 1869, America was in the midst of the most roaring, spectacular material development that she had ever known. Exploitation and expansion were the order of the day . . . everyone was making money and expecting to make more . . . the clank of machinery and the clink of dollars silenced religion, letters, and the arts.—S. E. MORISON.[44]

The Civil War now appears, as Charles A. Beard has pointed out, as the second American Revolution. The victory of the North was the triumph of diversified "free" industry and agriculture over a planter's

---

[42] For example, *The Religion of Geology and Its Connected Sciences*, Boston, 1851, by the Reverend Edward Hitchcock, president and professor of natural theology and geology in Amherst College.

[43] T. D. Woolsey and others, *The First Century of the Republic*, p. 337.

[44] *Three Centuries of Harvard*, Cambridge, Mass., 1936, p. 323.

society on a slave basis. Wheat, iron, and shoes had conquered King Cotton. In terms of quickly exploitable land, the country was rapidly filling up. During the four decades from 1860 to 1900, fourteen million European immigrants poured into America; and from 1900 to 1920, another fourteen million came in. The frontier in the old sense was vanishing. The trend to urban industrialism began, accelerated by the almost incredible tempo of American inventiveness, which shot the total of patents from a mere 36,000 in 1860 to 676,000 in 1890 and to 1,347,000 in 1925. The individual ingenuity of inventors in solving what seemed to be merely local problems resulted in a vast enlargement of the scale of industry and commerce through quantity production and swift communication. The joint-stock-company device, which had made many of the early colonies possible, was now adapted to the needs of the new era of big business. Already, in 1873, a Congressional investigating committee, the first of a long series to come, was reporting that "the country is fast becoming filled with gigantic corporations wielding and controlling immense aggregations of money and thereby commanding great influence and power."[45] Once the lesson of economic concentration had been learned, the "age of dinosaurs" in business began; and within half a century the nation's broad distribution of property was virtually turned upside down, with roughly one-fifth of the population, instead of the former four-fifths, in effective key control of the means of industrial production. Labor was compelled to begin thinking nationally also. Its first serious revolt, the railroad strike of 1877, came as a shock to the complacency of the "robber barons" and their less affluent admirers; but Marx's prophecy, in hailing the re-election of Lincoln, that just as "the American War of Independence initiated a new era of ascendancy for the middle class, so the American Anti-Slavery War will for the working classes," was not to be fulfilled for another generation or two. The new industrialism encountered a mentality that was emerging, not from European feudalism, but from the optimistic and untrammeled life of the frontier; and that fact made it possible for the American dream of individual economic opportunity for all to survive into the postfrontier days of trusts and monopolies. The resulting gospel of wealth, harmonizing "competitive acquisitiveness with the fundamental moral law," became "the formula which permitted the Church

[45] S. E. Morison and H. S. Commager, *The Growth of the American Republic*, New York, 1930, pp. 662–67, 688–92, 695–98, 714–23.

to make peace with popular materialism," and thus to insure the eventual decadence of American ecclesiasticism.[46]

In the first half of the century the work of such determined educational crusaders as Horace Mann and Henry Barnard had assured the secular character of American public elementary education. And now, amid the graft and scandals of the Gilded Age, with typical American inconsistency, there began a veritable renaissance of higher education, made possible in part by the diversion, under exceptionally astute leadership, of a rivulet of the golden flood of profits into the coffers of the colleges and universities. By 1928 the total endowments of institutions of higher learning in America exceeded one billion dollars, while a few years later the total number of college students, which had stood at twenty-three thousand in 1873, passed the million mark. The pattern of modern American scholarship was traced in the decades between the Civil War and the World War, when both endowments and student bodies doubled and redoubled, and teaching was revolutionized by the lecture and elective systems and the home-grown graduate school. New and relatively secular institutions, such as Johns Hopkins, Cornell, and the Massachusetts Institute of Technology, to say nothing of the scores of land-grant foundations, arose to rival the older schools. In spite of the stubborn opposition of the classicists, the teachers of science, partly through alliances with industry based on technological usefulness, began to increase in numbers and influence. The new academic prosperity, much of it in the form of "expiatory benevolence" dispensed by the boards of philanthropic foundations, by providing economic support for a growing array of secular investigators, materially weakened the monopoly which the theological educators had so long enjoyed.

It was in these same decades of an ever-expanding academic universe that philosophy as a college subject was to assume its modern shape in America; and yet it would be folly to argue that it has been chiefly molded by economic and social influences, from most of which it has been carefully insulated. While America was blissfully surrendering to the inventors and promoters who were to take it over and make it over, its academic spokesmen went on complacently repeating their stock homilies and abusing or ignoring the very thinkers who might have shed some light on what was occurring. Secular influences began, however, to lift some of the fear of clerical censorship of the teaching of

[46] Ralph L. Gabriel, *The Course of American Democratic Thought*, pp. 153–58.

philosophy by making it a highly specialized lay affair; yet they were also to shape the apprehensive, middle-class outlook of most college teachers of philosophy by continuing to hold them paternalistically responsible for the guidance of the youths entrusted to their care. Yet one college after another dared to elect its "first president not a clergyman"; and financial acumen replaced godliness as the prime qualification for membership on boards of trustees. The immediate outcome, as far as naturalism was concerned, was to permit most professors of philosophy to shift from outright apologetics to a respectable German idealism that was almost equally out of touch, not only with the issues raised by the laboratory sciences for revelation, but also with those generated by the emerging social studies for entrenched plutocracy. Being sophisticated followers of Kant, Fichte, or Hegel, they might permit themselves a tolerant contempt for the "narrowness" of Darwin and Spencer; but they could afford a complete ignorance of Comte and Marx.

The most important single event in the history of modern naturalism in America, as in Europe, was the publication in 1859 (in America in January, 1860) of Charles Darwin's *Origin of Species,* although its revolutionary significance for philosophy was not to be fully grasped for another fifty years. "It came into the theological world like a plough into an ant-hill. Everywhere those thus rudely awakened from their old comfort and repose swarmed forth angry and confused." [47] Among them were many professors of philosophy, led by Bowen of Harvard, who vied with theologians like Hodge and Duffield of Princeton in heaping upon the new biology the same abuse that had long been the portion of all "infidel philosophy." [48] Unhappily, the men who were regarded as the country's leading scientists disagreed among themselves, with the great prestige of Louis Agassiz arrayed on the side of the creationists. As defenders of Darwin there were only the cautious botanist Asa Gray and the geologist William B. Rogers. With the appearance of Darwin's *Descent of Man* in 1871, the controversy reached a new peak of violence, the brunt of the fighting being borne outside the colleges in lyceums and publications by such doughty popularizers as Edward L. Youmans, John W. Draper, John W. Powell, and John Fiske. In conflict with opponents as bitter and vituperative as the fundamentalists of the

[47] A. D. White, *A History of the Warfare of Science with Theology in Christendom,* New York, 1890, I, 70.
[48] Sidney Ratner, "Evolution and the Rise of the Scientific Spirit in America," *Philosophy of Science,* III, 106–16.

period, it is hardly surprising that evolutionary naturalism itself became at times a fighting creed or that its defenders developed a "war psychology" that was alien to the scientific spirit. In the long "warfare between science and theology," both sides were guilty of intellectual atrocities; and there is little of permanent value to be culled from the rancors of a controversy that was bound to end in the complete defeat of the creationists.

Having failed in their first attempts to denounce and deny, the next move of the theologically-minded was either to reconcile or to belittle. A far-flung army of industrious compromisers, from James McCosh and Henry Ward Beecher to Joseph Le Conte and John Fiske, endeavored to show that evolution "properly understood" only confirmed creation and design "properly interpreted." Fiske made especially heroic efforts to clear his widely read *Cosmic Philosophy* of any taint of materialism, atheism, or Comtism. In his hands Herbert Spencer's evolutionary system took on "the undertone of the deep ethical purpose" which Fiske discerned in the universe. Others found contempt an even easier posture of defense than compromise; and where the college atmosphere had been sufficiently "drenched with Hegelianism," scientific categories and discoveries were dismissed as "vicious abstractions from the organic unity of experience."

But such myopia was not quite universal; at least one American saw something of the task of philosophical reorientation that lay ahead. An obscure teacher of mathematical physics at Harvard, in 1874–75, named Chauncey Wright, caught sight of what needed to be done in the direction of that speculative development of evolution which his fellow scientists, motivated "mainly by a desire for peace with Theology and Philosophy," hesitated to undertake. A keen student of the British empiricists from Bacon to Darwin, Wright celebrated the stark "cult of the fact" as against poetry and conventional metaphysics and attacked all those who strove to create a new theology from the theory of evolution. Universal causation he held to be the foundation principle of science: ". . . the constitution of nature is written in its actual manifestations; and needs only to be deciphered by experimental and inductive research; it is not a latent invisible writing, to be brought out by the magic of mental anticipation or metaphysical meditation." Wright bade fair to bring a new positivistic rigor into American thinking and foreshadowed many of the doctrines which his more famous companions were to develop: tychism, pragmatism, and the genetic approach to mind and knowledge. But since he chose to exercise his extraordinary critical powers mainly in intimate conversation, his influence was felt almost wholly through his fellow members of "The Metaphysical Club" of Cambridge, including William James, C. S. Peirce, John Fiske, and the future Justice of the Supreme Court, Oliver Wendell Holmes. To these "romantic cosmologists" he appeared as tough-mindedness incarnate, the club's "boxing-master," who delighted to pummel the tenderer athletes. Undoubtedly he possessed the insight and acumen that might, if only they had been systematized and exercised to the full, have made him a pivotal figure in American thought; but his premature death left the promise of his penetrating reviews and articles unfulfilled.[49]

Another New Englander who falls within Santayana's category of "private gentlemen whom the clergy and the professors could not deceive" is Henry Adams. A skeptical liberal after the grand style of the eighteenth-century *philosophes* and "a Darwinist because it was easier than not," he declares in his *Education* that "by rights, he should have been a Marxist, but some narrow trait of the New England nature seemed to blight socialism, and he tried in vain to make himself a convert. He did the next best thing; he became a Comtist, within the limits of evolution." [50] His effort to bring into a single focus the unity of the Middle Ages and the multiplicity of the onrushing power age took the form of a naturalistic philosophy of history, worked out with the aid of hardly more than an amateur's grasp of the Phase Rule of Josiah Willard Gibbs of Yale.

In seeking to utilize mechanical, rather than biological materials, Henry Adams was almost alone among the American naturalists of his period; and in even toying with the idea of Marxism, he was most exceptional among Americans of his generation. For although Karl Marx had acted as correspondent for Horace Greeley's New York *Tribune* in 1861–62, few people in this country, except the German exiles who formed the core of the early socialist movement, were acquainted with his major writings. A theoretical materialist such as Joseph Dietzgen was virtually unknown outside the small circle of readers of his German

[49] C. Wright, *Philosophical Discussions*, New York, 1878, pp. xvii, 376; G. Kennedy, "The Pragmatic Naturalism of Chauncey Wright," *Studies in the History of Ideas*, III, New York, 1935, 475–503.
[50] H. Adams, *The Education of Henry Adams*, Boston, 1918, p. 225.

party newspaper. As late as 1907 one of the earliest critics of Marx in America, Professor E. R. A. Seligman of Columbia, broached the subject of the study of scientific socialism as one which had as yet received little or no attention in American academic circles. Among professional philosophers, no American devoted serious attention to Marx until the recent studies, much influenced by the instrumentalism of John Dewey, by Professor Sidney Hook.

One of the reasons for the American neglect of Marx was the fact that this country was breeding its own native substitutes in the persons of such naturalistic social scientists as Lewis Henry Morgan, Lester F. Ward, Thorstein Veblen, William Graham Sumner, and Charles A. Beard. As a result of their labors, the new disciplines of anthropology, economics, government, and sociology, at the formative period of their most rapid expansion, were given a strongly naturalistic bent. Theory and practice, however, were seldom abreast of one another. Lewis Henry Morgan, who was a stern, conventional upstate New York capitalist, Labor-hater, and fanatical dry, offered the ironical spectacle of delighting Friedrich Engels with a pioneer classic of anthropology, *Ancient Society*, written "in a manner that might have been used by Marx himself." [51]

In American academic philosophy "the first decade of the present century," writes Professor W. P. Montague, "was a time of change and insurgency." [52] Several sorts of profound dissatisfaction, both epistemological and practical, with the prevailing idealism began to make contact with the new interest in science aroused by the evolution controversy. As a result there emerged the twin revolts known as pragmatism and realism, and for idealism a swifter debâcle than anyone would have believed possible. The essential hollowness of the Genteel Tradition and its smug remoteness, both from the world that science was discovering and from the actualities of American living, were suddenly and effectively exposed. At first both of the new movements tended to take up positions midway between the extremer forms of nineteenth-century naturalism and idealism. But their vigorous polemical bombardments had the effect of completely demolishing the prestige of ideal-

---

[51] Friedrich Engels, *Der Ursprung der Familie, des Privateigentums und des Staats, in Anschluss an Lewis H. Morgan's Forschungen*, 1884. English translation from 4th German edition, Chicago, 1902, p. 26.

[52] W. P. Montague, "The Story of American Realism," *Philosophy*, XII, 141; also included in the same author's *The Ways of Things*, New York, 1940, pp. 230–61.

ism, thereby clearing the field for its relatively undamaged opponent. It was not merely that it became evident that man's privileged position in the cosmos and all the defensive idealisms which had sought to bolster it must now be abandoned. Henceforth all inquiries and debates must be carried on in new terms and in a new setting: as themselves developing activities of growing human organisms mutually adapting and adjusting themselves to their changing physical and cultural environments. Psychology had shifted from the philosophical to the biological sciences. Once thinking and valuing became envisaged as natural events in no way exempt from the orderliness of the world in which they occur, a whole host of "perennial problems" became meaningless or devoid of interest. It was, above all, a revolution in the direction of moderating philosophical demands, expectations, pretensions, a giving up of several romantic dreams—the theological dream of spiritual absolutism based upon divine favoritism toward man, and the academic dream of a world that was guaranteed to live up to the platitudes of a baccalaureate sermon.

Just as the Civil War killed transcendentalism, so the first World War and its disillusioning aftermath precipitated the downfall of the feebler Roycean idealism which had succeeded it. A vigorous naturalistic movement in American literature aided in making the reading public aware of the sweeping change in the climate of opinion. By the nineteen-thirties it became evident that idealism and an inclusive naturalism had virtually exchanged places and that the latter was likely to become the dominant American philosophical temper of the mid-century. To list the thinkers who under various banners contributed to this general outcome would be to call the roll of most of the American philosophers and psychologists of the present century.

The sudden overturn in prestige, however, brought with it the necessity of a change of strategy from attack to defense, and the acceptance of new and sobering responsibilities for philosophical reconstruction, for which no American naturalist was fully prepared. Few of them possessed scientific training sufficient to enable them to keep pace with simultaneous advances on so many fronts. The new social sciences, moreover, were still in a state of flux; while physics, the main reliance of the older naturalisms, was in the midst of a violent internal revolution. Needless competition for favor among rival brands of specialized knowledge ensued; and it has taken some time for the pragmatic or genetic or experimental naturalists, relying upon the biological-social sciences and their motivating interests, to make common cause with the realistic or structural or logical naturalists, who have taken their departure from the more fully positive fields of mathematics and physics—to say nothing of the poetic naturalists following in Santayana's train. Consequently the established American naturalisms of the present century are either mixtures, embracing too many legacies from past controversies, or else, as Professor Randall expresses it, "as yet programs rather than achievements." [53]

It is this effort to assimilate the vast resources of contemporary science to the best of the humanistic tradition, infusing the whole with an awakened social consciousness, that explains the good-natured charges exchanged by the two elder American philosophers who have constructed major naturalistic systems, George Santayana and John Dewey. The latter, trained in Hegelianism and consumed with practical social passion, was accused of "half-hearted and short-winded" naturalism by the former, a poetic materialist with a fondness for timeless essences, whose naturalism was characterized in turn as "broken-backed." [54] Now, no American or guest of America has presented more persuasively than Santayana in his five-volume *The Life of Reason* (1905–6) the best of that Greek theory of nature and morals which stems from Aristotle; and yet it is now recognized that his later *Realms of Being* (1923–40) contains dualistic elements which tend to divorce both the realm of essence and the mind from the all-inclusive natural setting of his earlier works. John Dewey, on the other hand, the evolutionary foe of absolutism and the quest for certainty, assumes a biological background for human social behavior, only to become so absorbed, as a moralist, in experience, that the structure of nature tends to become veiled in the "luminous fog of immediacy."

This is not in any way to minimize the signal services of Dewey and Santayana, to whom, along with F. J. E. Woodbridge, M. R. Cohen, R. B. Perry, W. P. Montague, R. W. Sellars, and many others, contemporary naturalism in America owes so much. After some two hundred and fifty years of repression and vilification at the hands of the antinaturalists, it has at last emerged to a position of relative academic

[53] In Horace M. Kallen and Sidney Hook, editors, *American Philosophy Today and Tomorrow*, New York, 1935, p. 425.
[54] *Journal of Philosophy*, XXII, 680, and XXIV, 57.

prosperity and respect. In most of the leading institutions of the country, at least, it can no longer plead censorship as an excuse for its shortcomings. Science, indeed, has long since replaced theology as the popular fetish in all but the most sheltered localities. Nevertheless, American scientists, as a class, cling to various forms of intellectual and moral isolationism. While practicing naturalists in their laboratories, they are still quite blissfully unmindful of the wider implications of their methods, and of what the latter would produce if adapted to the investigation of other subject matters. In consequence, they often try to make up for what they are told are the limitations of their particular specialties by displaying a childish credulity with respect to everything else. Then, too, it has not been the relentlessly self-critical method of science applied to all our problems, to which the public has looked with such great expectations, but rather to its supposed technological program of scientific "magic," with the result that an abstraction standing for science in general has been foolishly blamed for not making wars and depressions impossible. Once more science has been made into a narrow cult to which men have looked for a substitute for their lost religious security, rather than a liberating spirit and universal instrument by which the human adventure may be carried forward on all fronts with cumulatively increasing prospects of eventual success.

Meanwhile, from the dark shadows of the Occident and the Orient alike, the forms of new irrationalist oppressors have come forth to do battle for the privilege of shaping the future of mankind; and a chastened America is once more being thrust into a possibly messianic role among the nations. For ours is still the country where daily living, for the masses of men, has most pointedly belied the allegedly impassable gulf between the material and the ideal, even though their actual advances toward the good life have so far been halting and often inept. But if the land of noble dreams of liberty and justice for all is not to disappoint a hard-pressed humanity, those ideals must be given a firmer intellectual foundation than heretofore, in a more realistic and tough-minded understanding of man's continuity with many-storied nature, as well as of his natural capacity to pursue those imagined ends which are not "vain." Such a renunciation of romantic myths, when not carried to a drab extreme, may enhance rather than diminish his store of values. Here is naturalism's present opportunity, and that concluding note of sober hope without which no history would be American.

15

EPILOGUE: THE NATURE
OF NATURALISM

John Herman Randall, Jr.

In Baldwin's *Dictionary of Philosophy* there are listed some thirty-seven different meanings for the term "Nature" in philosophic discussion, and should the spirit move him Mr. Lovejoy could doubtless specify many more. "Nature," in fact, is the oldest idea in the Western intellectual tradition. It is the Latin version of the Greek φύσις; and legend has it that philosophic reflection arose in the Greek world when certain bold thinkers in Asia Minor began to criticize their inherited beliefs by speculating on the φύσις or "nature" of things. Greek wise men early wrote books "On Nature." But what they were actually writing about has been a subject for debate ever since Aristotle attempted to set forth what they should have been doing; and it is a theme for vigorous controversy among scholars today.

The defense of "nature" and what happens "by nature" against the idealistic followers of Plato and against the mechanistic thought of Democritus is the major theme of the Aristotelian writings. The founder of atomistic thinking, Empedocles, insisted in a famous line that there is no "nature," but only a mixing and unmixing of things; yet the outstanding document of ancient mechanism is devoted to setting forth "the nature of things," and delineating "Nature's aspect and her law." The great Stoic philosophy, so influential down to the present day in forming man's conception of his own "nature," saw in the adjustment to a cosmic "Nature" the highest wisdom. And so the story goes: not a thinker in the Western tradition has failed to give his own distinctive interpretation to "nature" and to find an appropriate place for it in his own body of ideas.

In the light of this familiar situation, for a group of thinkers to proclaim their common devotion to "naturalism" is by no means self-explanatory. As Mr. Boas points out, the term is vague; its employment may be a mere fashion of the day, in this our own country, covering a multitude of intellectual sins—or at least heresies. The usage is hardly fashionable abroad, even in England; though the temper it is here made to stand for is much less rare than the designation. And as Mr. Dewey's citations make clear, those who dislike this temper and attitude are far from discriminating in their contemptuous application of the label "naturalism" to almost every tendency in modern thought.

Yet for all the many varied and confusing overtones that twenty-five centuries of history have added to the theme of nature, and for all the doubts, expressed here by Mr. Costello, whether present-day "naturalists" exhibit much unity of thought, the reader has surely found in these essays a community of temper, of method, and even of general outlook, rather remarkable in any group of writers so crotchety and individualistic as professional philosophers. Whatever different views "naturalism" has meant in the past—and it has meant many—these thinkers employ it to name a position which both negatively and positively is not lacking in precision. And whatever the propriety of the particular term to indicate this position—and here the reader may suspect that some of the contributors would really prefer a more methodological designation, like "experimental" or, more broadly, "empirical"—at least the writers are clear what they mean by the word. The methodological terms, alas, have had as confusing a history.

I

"Nature," in fact, has normally been employed as one term in an intellectual distinction: "the natural" has been set over against something else, some other realm of being. In Greek thought the great contrast between "nature" and "law" or "convention," first developed by the Sophists, was broadened by Aristotle into the distinction between "nature" and "art," the whole of man's intellectual activity. In the thirteenth century Nature was injected, by those dissatisfied with the traditional Augustinian concern with the soul and God alone, into the Platonistic hierarchy of realms of being; the Natural was contrasted with everything in that hierarchy above man's sensitive soul, with the Supernatural. In an altered climate of opinion, German thought reformulated this antithesis as that between the Natural and the Transcendental: what was natural was merely empirical. An earlier modern tradition, to whose formation John Locke largely contributed, opposed Nature, which it read in wholly Newtonian terms, to Man, whose conscious experience in particular clearly did not lend itself to elucidation in the categories of the science of mechanics. When these professed "empiricists" had managed to bifurcate Nature, in Whitehead's now classic phrase, into a conjecture and a dream, they were left with an experience quite literally supernatural, and a nature whose status and very existence had grown problematical—a confusion neatly illustrated today by Bertrand Russell, and by the unwilling outcome of Santayana's inconsistent thought.

This double antithesis, between Nature and the Supernatural or Transcendental on the one hand, and between Nature and Man or human experience on the other, still governs present-day usage of "the natural" as a term of distinction. It is reinforced by our common employment of "natural science" to designate those methods and procedures which have been so successful in bringing knowledge of and power over what is not "supernatural," or "distinctively human." Conversely, those anxious for various reasons to assert the existence of a "Supernatural," or to insist on the unique and distinctive character of man or of some portion of his being—his soul or mind—have been led to try to restrict the application of the methods of "natural science" to what is "merely natural," and above all to attempt to disparage their intrusion into human affairs. The unfortunate consequences in ignorance and failure in that field, springing from this divorce of two realms of being, Mr. Dewey has here once more vigorously set forth.

"Naturalism" came into vogue as the name for a recognized philosophic position during the great scientific movement of the nineteenth century, which put man and his experience squarely into the Nature over against which he had hitherto been set. The obliteration of the gulf between the nature of the "natural scientist" and human life was then associated with the discovery of the facts of biological evolution and of the descent of man. "Naturalism" was consequently identified with evolutionary thought and with theories of the biological "origin" and "genesis" of the various aspects of human experience. Mr. Dewey, the only writer here who has lived through that intellectual revolution in his own lifetime, often phrases his position in such genetic terms, inquiring how this or that phase of human experience "arose" out of a previous nonhuman biological nature. But Mr. Nagel is probably much more typical of the younger "naturalists" here speaking in being much more skeptical of the possibility of such speculative anthropology, or of its explanatory value could it be achieved—though of course neither he nor the others presume to question the facts of man's biological ascent from primordial protoplasm.

But such an inclusion of man within Nature by no means originated with the theory of biological evolution. To say nothing of Greek thought, it had been vigorously and consistently proclaimed during the seventeenth century—Mr. Dewey mentions Aristotle and Spinoza, and he might well have included Hobbes. And the attempt to carry through this inclusion in detail was one of the major tasks of Enlightenment philosophizing, though it had then become complicated and confused by the empiricist view of human experience as a screen shutting man off from access to Nature. It has now grown clear that the fundamental importance of evolutionary thought, like that of those earlier naturalisms, lay primarily in its methodological significance: there was to be no sharp difference in intellectual methods in treating man and the other aspects of the Nature of which he was taken to be a part. In Miss Lavine's excellent phrase, naturalism has come to mean not so much a continuity of genesis as a continuity of analysis. Even for Mr. Dewey it is manifest that this is the nub of the matter.

Now naturalism, in the sense in which it is maintained in this volume, can be defined negatively as the refusal to take "nature" or "the natural" as a term of distinction. As Mr. Lamprecht well points out, it is opposed to all dualisms between Nature and another realm of being—to the Greek opposition between Nature and Art, to the medieval contrast of the Natural and the Supernatural, to the empiricist antithesis of Nature and Experience, to the idealist distinction between Natural and Transcendental, to the fundamental dualism pervading modern thought between Nature and Man. For present-day naturalists "Nature" serves rather as the all-inclusive category, corresponding to the role played by "Being" in Greek thought, or by "Reality" for the idealists.[1] In this sense, as Mr. Dennes recognizes, naturalism, in becoming all-inclusive,

[1] Mr. Schneider's suggestive proposal to revive the traditional normative usage of "nature" and "the natural," in Aristotelian contrast to "the accidental" and "the artificial," and to give "the natural" a concrete and specific meaning as the fruitful, has much to recommend it. And in truth such collective and denotative concepts as Being and Reality have found it hard to avoid becoming terms in a distinction of value. Whether Mr. Schneider would go so far as to advocate "Nature (loud cheers!)" is left unanswered. But as he admits, this normative usage is hardly established in present-day naturalistic thinking, and aside from his paper none of the essays in this volume even suggests it. Some, like Mr. Costello's, seem definitely hostile to the idea.

ceases to be a distinctive "ism." It regards as "natural" whatever man encounters in whatever way—Nature, as Mr. Costello puts it, is a collective name for "quite a mess of miscellaneous stuff." Naturalism thus merges in the generic activity of philosophy as critical interpretation—the examination of the status of all these varieties of "stuff" in Nature—or in Being, or in Reality—and the discovery of their various relations to each other and their respective functions in man's experience. Positively, naturalism can be defined as the continuity of analysis—as the application of what all the contributors call "scientific methods" to the critical interpretation and analysis of every field.

But while naturalism, refusing to admit impassable gulfs and dualisms, either ontological or methodological, holds that everything encountered by men has some natural status in Nature, this does not mean that naturalism can absorb all the philosophic theories of what man encounters and in that sense cease to be a distinctive position. It is indeed fundamentally opposed to all those theories and interpretations which assert dualisms and gulfs and, as Mr. Dewey's polemic makes clear, remains their active antagonist so long as they are flourishing. As Mr. Costello insists and Mr. Lamprecht cogently argues, there is no room for any Supernatural in naturalism—no supernatural or transcendental God and no personal survival after death. There is room for religion, to be sure, since that is an encountered fact of human experience. Mr. Lamprecht wisely takes religion as a descriptive rather than a eulogistic term; most religions, doubtless, are sadly in need of criticism and reformation. There is room for celebration, consecration, and clarification of human goals; there is room—*pace* Mr. Dewey!—for man's concern with the eternal and with what Plato calls "the deathless and divine." But for naturalism eternity is no attribute of authentic Being, but a quality of human vision; and divinity belongs, not to what is existent, but to what man discerns in imagination.

Thus naturalism finds itself in thoroughgoing opposition to all forms of thought which assert the existence of a supernatural or transcendental Realm of Being and make knowledge of that realm of fundamental importance to human living. There is no "realm" to which the methods for dealing with Nature cannot be extended. This insistence on the universal and unrestricted application of "scientific method" is a theme pervading every one of these essays. Its basic position in naturalistic thought is well set forth by Miss Lavine:

The naturalistic principle may be stated as the resolution to pursue inquiry into any set of phenomena by means of methods which administer the checks of intelligent experiential verification in accordance with the contemporary criteria of objectivity. The significance of this principle does not lie in the advocacy of empirical method, but in the conception of the regions where that method is to be employed. That scientific analysis must not be restricted in any quarter, that its extension to any field, to any special set of phenomena, must not be curtailed—this is the nerve of the naturalistic principle. "Continuity" of analysis can thus mean only that all analysis must be scientific analysis.

And Mr. Dennes puts this controlling methodological principle:

There is for naturalism no knowledge except that of the type ordinarily called scientific. But such knowledge cannot be said to be restricted by its method to any limited field of subject matter—to the exclusion, let us say, of the processes called history and the fine arts. For whether a question is about forces "within the atom," or about the distribution of galaxies, or about the qualities and pattern of sound called Beethoven's Second Rasumowski Quartette and the joy some men have found in them—in any case there is no serious way to approach controlled hypotheses as to what the answers should be except by inspection of the relevant evidence and by inductive inference from it.

II

Now this reliance on an unrestricted scientific method and the consequent rejection of any form of supernaturalism or "extranaturalism" —the term is Mr. Dewey's—were the distinguishing features of the philosophic position which in the nineteenth century came to be known as "naturalism," and indeed of the long line of predecessors which that position discovered. In the words of Mr. Dennes characterizing contemporary naturalism,

Its spirit is in these respects very close to the spirit of traditional and more specifically materialistic naturalism. Both are protests against all philosophies which allege that events require, for their occurrence or for their explanation, reference to transcendental grounds, orders, causes, purposes, *Dinge an sich*, or the like. But contemporary naturalism recognizes much more clearly than did the tradition from which it stems that its distinction from other philosophical positions lies in the postulates and procedures which it criticizes and rejects rather than in any positive tenets of its own about the cosmos.

Indeed, the popular meaning which "naturalism" still bears, and which it retains in antinaturalistic circles, has been derived from the scientific materialism of the nineteenth century—a body of ideas founded on a reductive analysis of all processes to the motion of masses, on the mechanistic dogmas of nineteenth-century physics, and on the materialistic metaphysics which regarded the scientific enterprise as the simple discovery of the physical and biological laws "governing" events. That reductive analysis, those dogmas, and that materialism have very largely disappeared from the store of scientific ideas today, and that conception of the scientific enterprise itself has been profoundly modified. Yet, as Mr. Dewey notes, the two antinaturalistic schools, the frank supernaturalists and the transcendentalists, both "identify naturalism with 'materialism,' and then employ the identification to charge naturalists with reduction of all distinctively human values, moral, aesthetic, logical, to blind mechanical conjunctions of material entities—a reduction which is in effect their complete destruction."

In view of the nineteenth-century usage of "naturalism" to designate the scientific materialism of evolutionary thought, a usage still lingering on in the semi-educated mind, this identification has, perhaps, more of historic justification than Mr. Dewey here admits—though he adduces abundant illustration to show that "the identification thus permits antinaturalists to substitute name-calling for discussion of specific issues in their own terms and in their connection with concrete evidence." To be sure, very few of the responsible scientific materialists of the last century, even in the heyday of mechanistic reduction, could regard the polemics of the antinaturalists as directed against other than a travesty of their real views. As Mr. Dewey points out, "since 'matter' and 'materialism' acquired their significance in contrast with something called 'spirit' and 'spiritualism,' the fact that naturalism has no place for the latter also deprives the former epithets of all significance in philosophy."

Now, it is a legitimate question whether an attitude and a method so different from that of the nineteenth-century "materialistic naturalists" as that which controls the thinking of the present essays might not be subject to less misinterpretation and confusion were it to call itself by another name. This is as it may be; naturalism is far more than devotion to a mere term. However, it might equally well be asked what right that transitory and rather provincial body of ideas has to claim a monopoly of devotion to scientific thinking and hostility to supernaturalism. Surely the power and scope of Nature had been discerned long before; and the Aristotle and Spinoza to whom so many of these contributors owe so much can fairly be said to have made clear the main outlines of a naturalistic procedure and attitude, long before the nineteenth-century reduction of all processes to the motions of matter. And it is plain that many of these essays desire to preserve at least some continuity with the great protagonists of scientific thinking of the last two centuries, however anxious they may be to correct their insights by a later sophistication. Finally, it may well be doubted whether such anti-naturalists as Mr. Dewey allows to speak would show more understanding to men enlisted under any other banner.

Whatever the label, however, the major fact stands out: the "new" or "contemporary" naturalism these writers are exploring stands in fundamental opposition not only to all forms of supernaturalism, but also to all types of the reductionist thinking which up to this generation often arrogated to itself the adjective "naturalistic," and still is suggested by it to the popular mind. Second only to the unanimity with which these writers reject supernaturalism and acclaim scientific procedures is their agreement that the richness and variety of natural phenomena and human experience cannot be explained away and "reduced" to something else. The world is not really "nothing but" something other than it appears to be: it is what it is, in all its manifold variety, with all its distinctive kinds of activity.

Human life in particular displays characteristic ways of action which have no discoverable counterpart in the behavior of any other being. Man's searching intelligence, his problems of moral choice and obligation, his ideal enterprises of art, science, and religion are what they inescapably are. Nothing could be clearer on this point than Mr. Krikorian's treatment of mind, Mr. Edel's discussion of ethics, Mr. Vivas's analysis of the aesthetic experience, or Mr. Lamprecht's study of religion. Whatever criticism some of the beliefs connected with these enterprises may call for, as activities that men perform because they are men and not another kind of being, they are no illusions or "mere appearance." Inquiry can find out much about them, about their conditions and consequences, their functions and values; but what it finds is an addition to our knowledge of what they are, not the amazing discovery that they are not, or ought not to be.

The fundamental antireductionist thesis of this present-day naturalism, distinguishing it sharply from the materialistic naturalism of the last century, may be stated: Intellectual analysis may discriminate hitherto unknown factors and structures in a subject-matter, but it can never validly take away from or destroy the subject-matter it sets out to explore. Mr. Lamprecht phrases this principle: "The nature of anything may of course be, and probably always is, much more than it is empirically found to be. But the point of the argument is that everything is at least what it is given as in experience." Whatever faults these naturalistic thinkers may possess, they cannot be legitimately pilloried as philosophical "nothing-butters."

Mr. Dennes here explains more technically how present-day naturalistic philosophy has abandoned as basic categories "matter," "motion," and "energy"—the controlling ideas of philosophic materialism —for others which enable it the better to avoid the treacherous fallacies of reduction.

Contemporary naturalism has freed itself from the objection leveled against earlier naturalism, that it excluded from existence, or was committed to neglecting in one way or another, any qualities experienced or imaginable, including those in which men delight as aspects of the highest achievements of the arts, the sciences, and what Aristotle called the master-art of politics. Naturalism has also thus freed itself from suspicion of dalliance with meaningless contradictions of the sort that purported to assert the identity of factors that are actually distinguished or distinguishable—for example, assertions that qualities are (or can be "reduced" to) bodies in motion, events in relation, or indeed anything else but just themselves. Discovery (or inference) of constituents, causes, effects, and other correlatives of given qualitied events—discovery (or inference) that these constituents and correlatives probably themselves lack some of the qualities of the events of which they are supposed to be constitutive or correlative—such discovery (or inference) is not and never was in any sense a reduction of those qualitied events to a more ultimate reality (or to anything else) devoid of their qualities. Nor did it in any sense imply or entail such a reduction.

III

This temper and attitude, at once antidualistic and antireductionist, has indeed in this generation been increasing rapidly in all the Western philosophic traditions. But, as Mr. Larrabee suggestively points out, there has been in recent American social and intellectual experience much that has given it a peculiar power in the thinking of our own countrymen. Contemporary naturalism may well claim to be a distinctively American philosophy; and the intellectual inspiration of these writers, however deeply rooted their thought may be in the classic traditions of the West, has come to them through a group of great American thinkers.

The identification of "naturalism" with the double protest, against nineteenth-century materialism as well as against supernaturalism and transcendental idealism—and in that sense the christening, if not the begetting, of the "new" or "contemporary" naturalism—was primarily the responsibility of that cosmopolitan spirit whose influence has been exerted almost wholly on American philosophizing, Santayana. Santayana's *Life of Reason* is pervaded with the naturalistic spirit of Greek thought in general and of Aristotle in particular, well summed up in the characterization of the latter which Mr. Costello reminds us Woodbridge loved to quote: "Everything ideal has a natural basis, and everything natural has an ideal fulfilment."

These five volumes, especially the latter four, have become a classic document of the new naturalism. The first, it is now clear, contained implicitly the seeds of those new dualisms, Platonic and Lockean, which his later *Realms of Being* develop so charmingly and so tantalizingly. For it now appears that Santayana himself in writing the *Life of Reason* was deflected somewhat from his controlling bent by his preoccupation with Greek thought. His underlying adherence to a combination of Spencerian materialism and mechanism with a Platonic realm of timeless and nonexistent essences has brought the not-undeserved charge that his professed naturalism of those days is now "broken-backed." Santayana, indeed, is the Moses of the new naturalism, who discerned the promised land from afar but still wanders himself in the desert realms of being.

So great was the influence of the *Life of Reason* on the older naturalists of our generation—on men like Woodbridge, Wendell T. Bush, and Morris Cohen—that it may be somewhat surprising that these present essays reveal so little of Santayana's presence and mention his name so rarely. This is due, it would seem, to the fact that he has known little and cared less about the living currents of scientific thought; while the naturalism of these younger men is nothing if not scientific method critically aware of its assumptions and implications. Santayana was willing enough to accept the scientific ideas of his youth; they saved him the trouble of engaging in the fruitless task of so much of modern thought, the attempt to resist the encroaching attack of science upon cherished illusions. But scientific methods and procedures in any technical sense have always meant nothing to him; and the revolutionary changes in fundamental scientific concepts our generation has witnessed have left him untouched. Democritus of old, indeed, would have served his purposes as well, freeing him for his self-appointed role as moralist of the natural life of man. There is much irony in the fact that Morris Cohen could nevertheless say of such an essentially unscientific mind that he has written the best book extant upon science as an intellectual enterprise.

It is significant that Mr. Lamprecht here makes the most explicit and serious reference to Santayana: for Santayana's naturalistic interpretation of religion, whatever its rather Catholic limitations, is undoubtedly his most substantial and permanent contribution to present-day naturalism, the one in which his vertebrae are most sturdily connected. But Santayana's broader influence, in emphasizing the concern of naturalistic thought with precisely those ideal enterprises of human culture like art and religion which philosophic idealism had attempted to pre-empt and toward which the earlier naturalism had taken a largely negative or even hostile attitude, has been incalculably great.

That John Dewey's lifelong preoccupation with scientific methodology has made his "experimental naturalism" the great inspiration of the present generation of naturalistic thinkers in this country, is obvious on almost every page of these essays. His concerns and problems touch the very heart of their own philosophic drive; they still speak his language, though their intellectual experience has been very different from that of his pioneering efforts. What is indeed remarkable is not that he bears the scars of battles long won which they never had to fight, and still occasionally belabors points they can now afford to take for granted. It is rather that a man who felt the full impact of evolutionary thought in his own lifetime, and pulled himself out of Hegelian idealism by his own bootstraps, should still be in the very forefront of the methodological conflicts of the present day. Fortunately Mr. Dewey is here to speak for himself, in what is characteristically the most aggressive paper in this volume, carrying the battle into the heart of the enemy's camp. No other evidence is needed that naturalism is a fighter's creed, and a creed worth fighting for.

It is worth remarking that, great as is their debt to Dewey and their respect for his leadership, no one of the thinkers here included is a professional teacher of "education" or so much as mentions, save in passing, his profound influence on educational theory. Their naturalism is not the "naturalism" of Rousseau—or Babbitt—and their concern with Dewey's thought is not that complacent acceptance of a gospel that marks so many a student of the "philosophy of education" in these United States. In the words of the contrast once made by Mr. Schneider, they have studied what Dewey studied as well as Dewey's works, they have not studied Dewey alone. In consequence, it is fair to say that they understand Dewey, they do not merely repeat his phrases. The extent of their understanding is measured by the degree to which they here discuss, not Dewey's experimental naturalism, but "specific issues in their own terms and in their relation to concrete evidence."

Dewey's naturalism represents a Hegelian concern with the intellectual problems of human culture, rendered pluralistic and concrete by saturation in biological thought and devotion to scientific methods and procedures. He found liberation from the dualisms that have marked so much of modern thinking through the two great nineteenth-century intellectual movements that emphasized an ontological and methodological continuity, left-wing Hegelian idealism, and the evolutionary sciences of life and of man. His friend and colleague, Frederick J. E. Woodbridge, found his inspiration rather in the naturalism of the classic tradition and of Greek thought, the naturalism of Aristotle and, he insisted, of Plato, and of the last great Aristotelian, Spinoza. Indeed, Dewey's own appreciation of the superiority of the Greeks to modern dualisms, so marked in his writings from *Experience and Nature* onward, seems to have been greatly extended and deepened through his discussions with Woodbridge.

Woodbridge's devotion to the classic tradition gives his naturalism a rather different stamp from Dewey's, as Mr. Costello well brings out in his affectionate and penetrating account. Woodbridge's habit of mind was profoundly empirical: he used to insist that he was the only man he knew who could actually learn from experience, and he accused Dewey of too great a reliance on the dialectic he handles so expertly. He was fascinated by the British empiricists, especially Locke and Hume, and he admired their temper and attitude of mind as much as he distrusted their metaphysics. Yet he never found congenial the language of the philosophies of experience, which Dewey has developed with such consummate skill; he much preferred to think in terms of the language of the philosophies of Being.

In consequence, on all his philosophic reflection there was the imprint of an ontological and realistic cast of thought, that allied him closely with Morris Cohen. He was proud to call himself a metaphysician, in the legitimate Aristotelian sense of that controversial term. Though he was greatly impressed by mathematics and logic, he had little concern with methodology, and much impatience with the attempt to translate all philosophic issues into purely methodological terms. When the gospel of the logical positivists burst upon the philosophic world, he first claimed great sympathy with their intentions and attitude; he had himself been one for years. In later disillusionment he concluded that they were trying to do with words what John Locke had done with ideas, and were involved in the self-same muddles and confusions.

Woodbridge's use of the language of Being rather than of experience often makes his naturalism seem more different from Dewey's than it really is. Dewey, of course, finds that ontological language far from congenial; where he occasionally attempts to employ it, largely under Woodbridge's influence, the difference between them seems to shrink to minor proportions, and Dewey's own fundamental realism stands out clearly—his "functional realism," it might be called.

This realistic emphasis of Woodbridge appears in a number of the essays here; for over half the contributors were students of his—he was a consummate teacher—and reveal the strong impress of his powerful intellectual personality. Much as they have learned from Dewey, it is clear to the discerning reader that most of them owe their fundamental naturalism to Woodbridge. Since Woodbridge's writings were regrettably slender, and seem not to convey to the uninformed reader what they hold for those who know through personal acquaintance their background and can appreciate their overtones, it has seemed an act of clarification as well as of intellectual piety to include Mr. Costello's discerning study.

These three figures on the American philosophic scene, Santayana, Dewey, and Woodbridge, typify the major personal influences contributing to the thinking of the new naturalism illustrated in this volume. Many other names, of course, as Mr. Larrabee points out, might be mentioned. Several of the contributors have been students of Morris Cohen; and all of them, with every other present-day naturalist, owe him a large debt for the sanity, sobriety, and critical skill with which he has brought his immense erudition to bear in support of the naturalistic philosophy. Some of the writers here, notably Mr. Dennes, Mr. Edel, and Mr. Nagel, show that they have absorbed much from the insights of the logical positivists, which they interpret in a uniformly naturalistic fashion.

The rather solitary figure of Whitehead deserves at least some mention among the pioneers of contemporary naturalism, for he has argued brilliantly and powerfully against dualisms and in favor of a continuity of analysis. But there is considerable hesitation about the consistency of his somewhat dubious naturalism: Mr. Dewey, for example, here expresses a rather widespread suspicion of the principle of concretion. In any event, it is difficult to discern much that these writers have learnt specifically from Whitehead, and many of them would not be too comfortable if found in the company of his speculative philosophy.

IV

But much as this new naturalistic temper and attitude owes to these pioneering thinkers of the last generation, it is really the culmination of a much older and wider movement of ideas. And so important is it, for an understanding of the position within which the present writers are operating, to grasp the significance of their combination of hostility to both supernaturalism and reductionism, that it is worth while attempting to place this larger movement in a broader historical perspective.

Anyone familiar with the Anglo-American philosophic scene today is aware that there has taken place a genuine revolution in thought—a revolution so fundamental that many have said, not without hopeful relief, "Modern philosophy, thank God, is at last over." Woodbridge used to add that this event could be dated about 1895—a remark that puzzled those listeners who failed to realize immediately that this was the year he saw the light. But Woodbridge was after all typical of a large number of younger thinkers at that time. And it is true that the controlling problems and answers of the modern period have been rapidly giving way to others. Not only have the traditional systems of the nineteenth century lost most of their power; the basic issues from which they arose have receded into the background. For a hundred years "modern philosophy" was divided into the two periods, Before and After Kant. Today the unquestioned assumptions common to both have been examined and rejected; the problems they generated have been judged unreal and irrelevant; and the major philosophies of the whole modern age, aside from their incidental insights, have for the present "post-moderns" become largely historical exhibits.

Superficially, this means that our generation has seen the passing of nineteenth-century post-Kantian idealism; Mr. Larrabee dates its demise from the disillusionment of the first World War. Philosophic idealism is still maintained in England and America, but by only a handful of men of outstanding ability; and most of these have so reconstructed the position as to transcend it. But more fundamentally we have seen the passing of the problem to which philosophic idealism was a solution: the nineteenth-century religious problem, which dominated so much of men's thinking about ultimates a generation ago. How can man and man's interests and values be given a cosmic significance, in the face of a science steadily undermining the traditional Hebrew-Christian guarantee of man's central place in the cosmos? And the passing of this problem has carried with it not only philosophic idealism, which sought that significance outside the so-called "realm of science," but the evolutionary philosophies as well, of Spencer, Bergson, James, and the rest, which sought it inside the scientific world; and nineteenth-century mechanism and materialism, the negative answer to the whole question.

In a still deeper sense, our generation has seen the passing of the problem that has dominated the whole of "modern philosophy"—the conflict of the moral and religious tradition with newer scientific concepts and techniques, the clash between a knowledge of the ends of action in the familiar moral, religious, and artistic fields, and a novel knowledge of natural processes. This is the typical problem of the struggle between two conflicting types of knowledge for men's allegiance. In such a competition the "problem of knowledge" in general naturally assumes a controlling and central metaphysical importance. And this "problem of knowledge" has in successive forms dominated modern philosophy, ever since Aristotelian science began in the twelfth century to compete with the traditional Jewish and Christian wisdom. It has lasted in some version until the present-day acceptance of an enlarged and deepened science and scientific method as the one type of knowledge and truth.

During the earlier modern period Western civilization possessed a science that described Nature in terms that at worst denied all reality to man's religious, moral, and artistic life and experience, and at best left them unintelligible and irrelevant. With such an obviously inadequate set of scientific concepts and procedures, it is little wonder that sensitive men sought for these enduring interests another place in a further non-scientific and supernatural "realm." Kant's philosophy is the classic expression of the dualism thus springing from the methodological inadequacy of the methods of Newtonian science—which Kant identified with "pure reason." If this methodological dualism is dead today, it is because our scientific method has been extended and deepened until we no longer need to abandon it in dealing with the intricate problems of human culture.

Today we are at last in possession of a science that insists on the importance and reality of all man's experience and enterprises, and has developed concepts that promise to render them all intelligible. In consequence we are now able to erect for ourselves philosophies that can find a natural and intelligible place for all human interests and aims, and can embrace in one natural world, amenable to a single intellectual method, all the realities to which human experience points: symphonies as well as atoms, personality as well as reflex action, religious consecration as well as the laws of motion or the equations of the field theory. These contemporary and "post-modern" naturalistic philosophies are thus a direct function of the present maturing of the scientific enterprise.

The temper made possible by present-day science is of course no wholly novel attitude. Greek thought was also, in its major strains, predominantly naturalistic. The Greeks saw man living in a world that sustains and responds to his interests. They regarded him as an animal that can know, and the world as a habitation that can be known. For them man can choose from this world what he finds to be good, and organize these goods into the Life of Reason; the world offers such goods, along with evils to be rejected—it provides the materials for the Life of Reason, and sustains man's efforts to attain it through his intelligence. For the great Athenian thinkers, the world exhibits what later came to be called a "logos," a rational structure or system. And this structure is not only "logical," lending itself to man's discourse and understanding, a structure of ideas, forms, or intelligible aspects; it is also teleological, a system of ideals and ends, of valuable aspects.

The Greek relation of man to his world is an intelligible interaction between an intelligent and valuing organism and an intelligible and valuable system of nature. It is a joint co-operation of powers, of the power of man to know and choose, and of the power of the world to be known and chosen. Man's living and knowing, his moral choosing and artistic production, are natural events and activities in such a world; they express in fact the operation of its highest powers. The concepts in terms of which nature is understood are concepts capable of making living and knowing intelligible: they are biological or teleological, and logical. The world and human life are to be understood in the same terms: through the distinctions between powers and their operation, or potentiality and actuality, between regularity and contingency, between quality and individuality, the universal and the particular, ends and means, organisms and their functioning. The world as a whole, the sum of all natural processes, is to be understood as making human living and knowing possible, as furnishing the materials for the organization of the Good Life. Man leads an existence, precarious, to be sure, but not impossible, in a universe that responds to his activities and is to be construed in terms appropriate to those activities.

In the Hellenistic age this naturalistic attitude and temper gave way to one quite different. The denaturalization of man and of human experience took place by successive stages, until it reached the form transmitted to the West in Pauline and Augustinian Christianity. But the thirteenth century saw a markedly successful attempt to revive the naturalism of the Greek tradition, within the framework of Augustinian supernaturalism. In the compromise of St. Thomas there is reintroduced the old Greek idea of a continuity between Man and Nature—no longer is there a gulf, no longer is the thinker's concern with the soul and God alone, no longer is the body the prison-house of the spirit, but once more the organ of human functioning. Experience became again a natural event, a relation between different parts of Nature, between an experiencing organism and an experienced world, generating knowing and the choosing of goods.

Into this revived though unstable Greek view, seventeenth-century science introduced a revolutionary set of ideas, which ushered in a new process of the denaturalization of man and human experience. It transformed the conception of Nature into a purely mechanical system of tiny billiard-balls following the laws of dynamics. But it left man—or at least the essential part of his being, his "mind"—much as he had been conceived before, as a knowing and valuing being. Now, however, he was living in a world stripped of all intelligible and valuable structure. Between man, his "mind" and experience on the one hand, and Nature on the other, there yawned a chasm. Man's only relation with such a world must be exclusively mechanical: when the small billiard-balls hit him on the head, he could see stars.

Thus human experience was removed from Nature and made "subjective": its locus was in man, in a separate substance, "mind," not in Nature at all. It was the mechanical effect of Nature upon and in man's "mind," not a co-operation of natural powers. The varieties of human experience, religious, artistic, moral, even intellectual, became quite literally supernatural—they were in no sense natural processes. Man's "mind" was no longer a natural function, but an independent substance with an extranatural status. The teleological, functional, and logical concepts appropriate to human experience were now wholly irrelevant to the purely mechanical concepts appropriate to Nature. Conversely, human life and "mind," as Mr. Krikorian points out, grew quite unintelligible in terms of such a mechanistic science—even the existence in man's experience of the science of mechanics itself became an enigma. In the course of a century's development of the implications of these ideas, this latter dialectical problem naturally became crucial.

Three major positions were held upon this problem of science, though strictly speaking the terms in which it was set permitted no answer. First, science was taken as a logical and mathematical system, directly accessible to "mind." But this system of science was left hanging, with no intelligible relation to the purely mechanical and alogical Nature it purported to express. This was the view of modern rationalism. Secondly, if men insisted that it was the mechanical world that after all was known, man's only relation to it became that of seeing stars when it impinged mechanically upon him. Science was thus not a logical system but a succession of stars seen—more technically, of ideas or impressions. This was the view of the modern empiricists. Thirdly, if it were pointed out that science is, nevertheless, a logical system, the conclusion was inescapable: it must be a logical system of stars seen, and it must have its locus, not in a presumed "external world," but in man. This is the view of the Kantian critical philosophy, the most consistent answer to the dialectical problem posed by the assumptions of "modern" thought. But Kant still left a chasm between the realm of nature, science, and "pure reason," and man's moral, religious, and artistic activities—his thought remains the classic modern expression of a thoroughgoing dualism and supernaturalism.

Now this gulf between man and Nature, this characteristic dualism of modern thought—this sophisticated supernaturalism, what Mr. Dewey calls "extranaturalism"—was during the nineteenth century gradually overcome from both sides. It was overcome, by men concerned primarily with the realm of human activities, in philosophic idealism, which thus stands historically as the first major stage in the transcending of the characteristic modern form of philosophic supernaturalism. For idealism, man's experience, religious, moral, artistic, and intellectual, is once more the clue to the nature of the universe. Man is again living in an intelligible and valuable cosmos. The chasm between human life and the world has disappeared; the world man really dwells in once more exhibits a "logos," an intelligible system of values; man's interests and concerns have a genuine home in the "real" world.

But the idealists were fleeing from the "realm" of natural science, with which they identified "nature," to the "real world," a wholly different "realm." Hence for them natural science was left as one single isolated human activity, in a separate and narrow "realm" of nature. The methods of natural science were taken as applicable only to this restricted realm; a different intellectual method was demanded for the rest of the "real world" to which other experiences pointed. The most complete idealistic system, that of Hegel, included everything but natural science: it had no real understanding of physics and its methods—a rather large omission, to be sure, which was accentuated by those who unlike Hegel himself relied on his imposing synthesis as an apologetic for traditional religion.

During the century, however, one important strand of idealistic thought became increasingly scientific in its intellectual methods, and gradually embraced the categories and the experimental analysis of science, especially of the social sciences. This combination of the Hegelian emphasis on continuity and against dualisms of every sort with the methods and concepts of biology and anthropology led directly to the contemporary type of antireductionist naturalism. It is interesting to note that Dewey exemplifies this transition in his own intellectual growth, and also that the specific idealist against whom he developed critically his own thought was the most scientifically minded of them all, Lotze.

While this process of the working-out of the idealistic position toward a scientific methodology was going on, the natural sciences were themselves extending their scope to include man—in the great flourishing of biological thought stimulated by the evolutionary theories—man's mind —in the newer experimental psychology, whose fruits for a naturalistic view construing mind as a complex set of specifically human activities, Mr. Krikorian so well sets forth in his elaboration of a functional behaviorism—and man's activities—in the rapidly developing social sciences, especially in the most critical of them all, anthropology. In this extension of scientific treatment to the new fields which the earlier Newtonian mechanics had been unable to handle satisfactorily, the concepts of science were naturally enlarged, and its methods generalized into a complex and flexible set of procedures and standards.

The net result of this vigorous scientific enterprise of the century was to bring man back into Nature once more: experience became once again an interaction of natural processes. Conceived in biological terms, it was now taken as an interaction between an organism and its environment, an affair of responses to stimuli; conceived in social terms, it was construed as the complex interactions between the individual and his cultural setting, an affair of education and of social and cultural reconstruction in the broadest sense. Thus from their side the scientists were arriving at the same general view of the status of man in the world that the more scientifically minded idealists were reaching from theirs. And again Mr. Dewey beautifully illustrates this strand of intellectual development.

Viewed in this extended perspective, and in the light of the great intellectual movements of the nineteenth century, contemporary naturalism thus represents at once the culmination of the idealistic criticism, and of the natural sciences of man and human culture. It carries on the idealistic emphasis that man is united to his world by a logical and social experience. But it rephrases the idealistic scheme of man's activities and environment in biological and anthropological categories. While like the idealists it makes them all amenable to a single intellectual method, it reformulates that method in experimental terms. At the same time, contemporary naturalism is rooted in the natural sciences, extending their content and scope, and expanding and rendering more flexible their methods to include a treatment of even those human activities formerly set apart as "spiritual." With those sciences it reads Nature once more as exhibiting an intelligible pattern or structure of natural activities, and of goods, ends, and qualities, as well as of purely mechanical motions. With them, it views human experience as a complex natural process in such a Nature—as a biological and social response to a Nature that sustains human living and knowing and loving.

In the light of these two major strands that have united to form contemporary naturalism, its double opposition to supernaturalism and to reductionism should now be clearer. It can be described equally as the concern to treat the total subject-matter of idealistic metaphysics, with all its sensitivity to the complex range of human culture, in terms of a scientific and experimental method; or as the carrying of scientific methods into all the areas of human experience.

In its fundamental attitude, in its basic metaphysical position, contemporary naturalism is thus back once more with the naturalistic world-view of the Greeks. But it has increased its resources to include all that men have learned since the ancients. It now possesses in great detail a knowledge of the structures or ways of behaving of things, and the elaborate set of techniques and standards of inquiry and verification that constitute the scientific enterprise, the most potent instrument the wit of man has yet devised for analysis and control. For it, man is still what he was for the Greeks, an intelligent and valuing animal living in an intelligible and valuable world. He now knows something about the nature of that world, and is beginning to learn how to make it serve his ends.

V

Most of the essays in this volume point out that the naturalism they are adopting is not so much a system or a body of doctrine as an attitude and temper: it is essentially a philosophic method and a program. It undertakes to bring scientific analysis and criticism to bear on all the human enterprises and values so zealously maintained by the traditional supernaturalists and by the more sophisticated idealists. Today there is no further intellectual need to defend the Good Life, with its component artistic, moral, and religious activities, against a reductionist philosophy that would deny it all validity. As naturalism reads the scientific enterprise, such activities are now recognized as integral natural processes with an assured status in the universe whose structure science has begun to reveal to us.

Freed from the necessity of either defending or denying the existence of its subject-matter, naturalistic philosophic criticism can hence go on to explore the possibilities of art, religion, and of human relationships in the richer world science is disclosing and technology bringing to pass. Above all, philosophic thought faces the problem of working out the organization and adjustment of the various strands of human living, of formulating a conception of the Good Life adequate to present-day resources and to our bitter needs, and elaborating a program for bringing its achievement nearer. Mr. Hook here illustrates, with the fundamental ideal or instrument of democracy, how naturalism would marshall its resources for this task; and he as well as Mr. Dewey makes plain the obstacles which antinaturalism would set in the way. The task is notoriously more difficult today than ever before; it is no easy emancipation from sweat and blood and tears that naturalism offers. The materials to be organized are of surpassing intricacy, and the complexities of adjustment are truly apalling. But the intellectual problems are at least not made insoluble by contradictory premises and futile negations; they are not dialectical, but practical and critical, and intelligence can hope to make some headway with them.

Science furnishes the method of experimental analysis and criticism; but the scientific philosophies of the past, for all their narrow penetration, have possessed such a paucity of facts about human life, and so few sensitive insights into its bewildering range of values. They have left out so much of experience—they have been, for all their intensity, so meager and bare, so Puritanical. The idealists may have lacked scientific knowledge and techniques. But it is often hard not to feel that they have possessed most of the human wisdom. One has only to compare Augustine, Dante, or Goethe, with Descartes, Hobbes, or Hume—or to place the treatment of the problem of human freedom by the major German idealists, with their sense of the complexity, the discrimination of the many factors involved and their attempt to reconcile collectivism and social control with individual autonomy, side by side with the cavalier nonchalance of Herbert Spencer, or even John Stuart Mill.

The idealists appear to have the edge on insights, on the discrimination of values, on the appreciation of the richness and variety of the factors demanding organization. They lack the ability to deal with the complex values they recognized by means of the experimental techniques found so effective in the natural sciences—they were unable to criticize those values in terms of the conditions of their attainment and the consequences of their pursuit—because they were rebels against the narrow and dogmatic science of their day, and not unnaturally distrusted its methods.

But in revolting against the transcendental, supernatural, and non-scientific world-view and metaphysics of nineteenth-century idealism, naturalism cannot afford to overlook its human wisdom and insights—even as it cannot dismiss as valueless the rich store of human experience embodied in the great supernaturalistic philosophies of an earlier past. Naturalistic philosophizing must become as rich as the idealistic philosophies by incorporating the facts and experiences they emphasized within its own more adequate framework, and bringing its best critical thought to bear on organizing and adjusting them within the pattern of the Good Life.

It must, for example, assimilate the genuine values of the personalistic and theistic philosophies to its own scientific thought and temper: it must take over what is actually valid in the "spiritual life" of the great religious visions. It must really interpret, clarify, and criticize the facts and values of man's moral, religious, and artistic experience, and not merely try to analyse them away. Many of the essays here included attempt just such an essential task. Mr. Vivas does it for the "aesthetic transaction," Mr. Lamprecht for the religious life, Mr. Edel and Mr. Hook for man's moral choice and political idealism; while Mr. Strong incorporates and explores the vision of history. The reader may judge for himself the inspiration a naturalistic approach can bring to such sympathetic and constructive enterprises.

VI

By this time it should be clear that to adopt a naturalistic method is the starting-point of genuine philosophizing, rather than the solution to all its problems. Hitherto the stress has been put on the community of temper and approach shared by the contributors. But within a naturalistic framework there is room for distinctive emphases, for the debating of genuine philosophic issues. It is hence far from surprising that upon the common ground of naturalism there should still be raised many of the perennial questions that have exercised philosophic reflection in the past.

Mr. Larrabee mentions the difference of emphasis, at times sharpened into a philosophic issue, which has for several decades divided American naturalistic thinkers. Those starting from a special experience and concern with mathematics and mathematical physics have emphasized the fundamental importance of logical structure in Nature and in man's scientific knowledge of it; they have tended to develop their naturalism along the lines of a logical or Platonic realism. Those starting rather from the biological, psychological, and social sciences have emphasized process and activity as the setting within which such structures can be discriminated; their naturalism has become "instrumentalistic" and functional. The issue may be phrased: Are mathematics and physics to furnish the ultimate categories and methods through which explanation is to be sought, or is physical science to be taken as having a biological setting, in the behavior of living beings adjusting themselves to their environment and actively manipulating it, and a cultural setting, in which it functions in specific ways as a social institution, itself a natural, objective process of interaction between groups of men and their environment?

Till the last decade this seemed perhaps the most important division of opinion within naturalistic thought. Structuralists like Cohen and Woodbridge could not stomach the functional setting within which Dewey located the structures of natural processes; it seemed essentially irrelevant to what they saw. From the side of mathematics, Whitehead attempted a reconciliation—as he explained, he was trying to "de-anti-intellectualize" Dewey, by discriminating a more flexible and pluralistic set of structures within natural processes. The informed reader may be surprised that this issue plays so slight a role in the present essays. In part it may be due to the accident that so many of their authors happened to be students both of the structuralists, either Cohen or Woodbridge, and of the functionalist Dewey.

But in a deeper sense the reconciliation has already been effected in present-day philosophizing. The philosophies of physics have been forced by their own subject-matter—the field—to adopt temporal and functional categories similar to those the biological and social sciences had already derived from theirs. Today, in fact, if we can take these essays as illustrative, we can fairly claim to have reached a synthesis between the structural categories of mathematics and physics and the functional categories of biology and the social sciences. There is already a common emphasis on the ongoing processes of Nature, on the emergence of novel ways of acting, on the genuine creativity and productivity of the life of the universe—and on a pluralistic, functional structure flexible enough to do justice to the immense variety of types of natural process. Mr. Dennes has underlined the shift in the basic categories of naturalistic metaphysics to event or process, quality, and relation; he develops technically the consequences of the emphasis on process and temporal change which so many of the other essays signalize.

There is a second issue between naturalists, already touched upon here, which does appear in these pages. Denotatively, it can be said to arise between a naturalism whose inspiration is fundamentally Greek, and one strongly influenced by evolutionary thought. The latter tends to construe the relation between the different types of activity encountered in the world in terms of their temporal genesis in the evolutionary process. In general it sets high store by genetic analyses. The former, true to its Aristotelian inspiration, prefers to read those relations as obtaining between factors discriminated in an experimentally observable subject-matter. It employs rather a functional or operational analysis. It finds genetic considerations to throw less light than the discovery of actual operations and functionings; it leads easily to a general operational attitude.

Both Cohen and Woodbridge were keen critics of the excesses of the genetic method of the evolutionary enthusiasts; they have transmitted their suspicion to many of their students. Mr. Dewey's evolutionism, especially when under the influence of G. H. Mead, has put much more emphasis on various types of genetic analysis—though he would in fact pretty much agree with the specific criticisms advanced by Woodbridge. Reliance on a functional rather than a genetic analysis has been reinforced, for this generation, by the operational interpretation of scientific techniques and procedures, of which Mr. Nagel here gives a sober and critical version. Both Mr. Dennes and Miss Lavine, in their critiques of reductionism, take occasion to grow rather caustic over the notion of "emergent evolution," the product of combining a genetic analysis with rejection of reductionism; and Mr. Nagel more temperately presents an even more devastating dismissal. Whether these criticisms would touch Mr. Dewey today is doubtful; and even Mr. Krikorian, who offers a discrimination of levels in Nature, makes no special temporal claims.

But though one may well agree with Mr. Nagel that speculative theories of emergence are of little value, the problem presented by biological and human evolution remains. And an analysis of experimentally—or historically—ascertainable geneses seems more intimately bound up with an analysis of the functionings and operatings of things than either Mr. Dennes or Mr. Nagel would seem to allow. Mr. Dewey has recently come to call his own type of analysis "genetic-functional," thus stressing the continuity between causes and consequences, or means and ends. And Mr. Strong, taking his point of departure from Woodbridge, develops the explanatory value of historical knowledge.

In this connection it is well to observe that the concern with a functional analysis and with the means-end relationship has led nearly all present-day naturalists to recognize the importance of what Woodbridge called "natural teleology"—a point which Mr. Costello here defends valiantly. From the time of Spinoza and Hobbes through the Darwinian period, the older naturalism overlooked natural teleology in its hostility to explanation in terms of "purpose," conscious or unconscious. But present-day naturalists, though finding no evidence that ends operate apart from human action, recognize that ends are nonetheless achieved through natural means, and that a concern with means and ends is fundamental for human understanding. Teleology, in fact, is implicit in the very notion of process, which is defined by the exhibition of such a functional structure.

The third issue between present-day naturalists has been mentioned a number of times; it must have impressed the reader of these pages. For the moment, it appears as the major difference between naturalists, as here illustrated by the contributors. Superficially, it is their attitude toward the gospel of logical positivism. But none of those here whose language and procedure reveal the influence of that rather dogmatic school on their thought exhibits the specific features that seem to awaken the ire of certain of their fellow contributors. Those very positive apostles of the unity of science, it has become notorious, have scarcely achieved a unity of philosophy; and like so many who have despised metaphysics, they severally display a whole gamut of metaphysical positions. Some of these are definitely reductionist; and some even carry terminism to a clear supernaturalism with regard to language. Needless to say, neither of these vagaries is here illustrated.

The underlying difference seems to occur between those naturalists who approach philosophic issues directly, either with the Greeks in the language of Being, or with the moderns in the language of experience; and those who translate all issues into methodological terms—between, broadly, the experimentalists and the logicians. In a sense this is the strictly contemporary version of the older issue between functionalists and structuralists. Logical terminism, in this sophisticated and technical rendering, has saved the logicians from the difficulties of a Platonic realism, only to plunge them into the equal problems of a purely linguistic analysis which at times loses sight of natural events in a maze of words. A methodological concern has always been strong in Dewey; and those who have already absorbed his sturdy functionalism have been able to construe formal logic and mathematics, as elaborated with expert proficiency by the positivists, in the light of the role they play as instruments employed in scientific procedures. Mr. Nagel has been peculiarly successful in developing such a functional terminism, and using it to make clear how the formal sciences can be at once conventional and not arbitrary—conventional in their free manipulation of postulates, yet not arbitrary because controlled by their function in experimental inquiry. And both Mr. Dennes and Mr. Edel are in the end sufficiently good Aristotelians to confine their terminism within functional bounds.

In the last analysis, realism and terminism, when sufficiently critical and sophisticated, seem rather alternative ways of construing the same facts than opposed positions to be debated—alternative languages, as it were. Mr. Dennes argues cogently—against Mr. Pepper, one suspects—for such an interpretation. And in truth between a functional terminism and a functional realism there is little ultimate difference. It is the terminist, however, who seems to find it hard to realize the fact. Mr. Nagel, it is worth remarking, makes excellent use of his terminism to provide a place within the naturalistic framework for the formal and mathematical procedures of the exact sciences. So heavily, in fact, does he emphasize them, that the confirmed "experimentalist" may suspect him of being a rationalist wolf in sheep's clothing. But the scientifically minded reader, who may have grown suspicious of the way in which most of the other authors rather cavalierly identify "scientific method" with experimentation, will find in his careful analysis by far the fullest and most exact account of what the others rather elliptically refer to as the "experimental method." He makes explicit the fact that the devotion of naturalists to scientific methods does not include any hostility to rational thinking—as was assumed recently by a rather naïve supernaturalist who entitled one of his chapters "The Encroachment of Scientific Method upon Thought."

VII

Naturalism, indeed, is not unsympathetic to the genuine values on which the antinaturalists have heroically insisted. It is convinced that it feels them as strongly and understands them better than their protagonists. And this brings us to a final problem, especially worth raising in these times of conflict and strong conviction. From the standpoint of the disinterested appraisal of the traits of Nature, it is important to recognize the setting of the ends of human activity amid other natural processes, in co-operation with which they must function. Truth is the discernment of the systematic, structural aspect of Nature, which conditions the appearance of events, and can be used as the means to human ends. Good is the system of valuable aspects of Nature, the organization of experienced goods into a reasonably harmonious whole.

But for scientific practice, for the achievement of the Good Life, Truth and Good are supreme objects of attainment, the only test we have of beliefs and values. In human living, for the men who strive after them, they function as transcendent; they are instrumentally, or, in Miss Lavine's phrase, "functionally absolute." To see those structures in their natural setting—to take an Aristotelian, biological view, or to take the cultural view of the sociology of knowledge—is to see the function of the tests of specific truths and goods; it is to be able to criticize and improve concrete beliefs and particular values. But to feel them as ultimate—to aspire to Platonic ideals of Truth and Good—is characteristic of action; men crave working standards of truth and good on which they can count. In human practice it is only natural that men should feel such standards as imperative, elevated above the rest of Nature, "absolute" or self-contained, "deathless and eternal."

This is faulty metaphysics: standards have their natural setting, in terms of which they are warranted. But humanly speaking, it is, as we all realize these days, sound practice. This human need has been the great bulwark of idealisms and supernaturalisms: the imperatives men crave have been read as the deliverance of Reason, as the dialectic of history, as the voice of God. This demand of human practice must and can be satisfied within naturalism. Men must have a faith in ultimate principles of scientific verification, in ultimate standards of human conduct—"ultimate" in the sense of what Miss Lavine calls an "objectivity norm." Men cannot live, to say nothing of living well, in a kaleidoscopic shift from one belief to another, or from one enjoyment to its successor.

But they can live by the carefully built-up body of procedures of testing and verifying beliefs which forms the scientific enterprise. They cannot live well by any other Truth. What Truth—of self-proclaimed revelation, of mystic insight, of rational self-evidence, of hypnotic leadership—can claim to be more deserving of confidence and allegiance than that which relies on all available evidence drawn from the public experience of mankind? What Good can men pursue with the assurance that when won it will not turn to dust and ashes, but one forged in the painful experience of the efforts of common men engaged in the enterprise of associated living? What Church, or what Party, can proclaim a Truth or a Good which measured by its power—and it is the politics of power we are discussing, the power to bring knowledge and wisdom and to render men steadfast in their devotion—can compare with the principles of scientific verification of which Mr. Nagel is here speaking, and which Mr. Hook is here bringing to bear on human conduct? *Non est potestas super terram quae comparetur ei.*

How, then, are men to combine a genuine devotion to these functionally transcendent organizations of values in science, art, conduct and religion, with the readiness to revise them in the light of their actual operation in human experience? It is an insistent and patent fact that men need both faith and intelligence: they need a critically and intelligently held faith in the standards by which they judge. They need an emphasis on ideals or standards in practice, and on their context and setting in criticism. Naturalism must combine the wisdom of Plato with the sanity of Aristotle. Is there any other enterprise in our vexed world today where this combination has been successful save in the practice of scientific inquiry? Assuredly, the antinaturalists are right: our world is perishing for want of faith. The faith we need, the faith that alone promises salvation, is the faith in intelligence.

INDEX

Aberrations, social, 193
Abnormality and its forms, 126 ff., see Unnatural, the
Absolute, the: and Community, 134
Accidental sequences distinguished from normal processes, 126 ff., 130
Adam and Eve legend, 9
Adams, Henry, 64n, 349
Adams, John, 332, 334
Aesthetics, ancients little concerned with, 148; basic error of modern theories, 116; central problem: misunderstandings to be intercepted, 101; experience of, defined, 100 ff.; experience of pure attention: standard for measure of ordinary experience, 118; factors that determine acceptance of art, 105-15; a form of cognition? 105; interest in philosophy of, 136; no place for emotion, 103; suspension of belief, 117; three modes from which aesthetic experience distinguished, 96-99; use of term, 99 f.; what success or failure depend upon, 115
Agassiz, Louis, 343, 347
Agnosticism, 28
Alien world, 29 f.
Allen, Ethan, 333
Allen, Joseph Henry, 341
"All possible worlds," logical relations as invariants of, 214-17
Ambivalence, 86
America, history of the growth of naturalism in, 319-53; Colonial period, 325-31; effect of economic opportunity and success in secularizing life and thought, 320 ff.; its possibly messianic role among nations, 353; Machine age, 344-53; Revolutionary period, 331-38; Romantic period, 338-44; two main directions in which roots in the past can be traced, 320
Ampère, J. J., 325
Analysis, continuity of, 184 (see also Continuity); genetic-functional, 379; of mind, 188; of social dynamics, 204n; of validity, 191 ff. (see also Validity)

Ancient Society (Morgan), 350
Animal response, 258
Anthropological dating, 163
Anthropology, 356, 373
Anthropomorphic conception of God, 31
Anticipatory response, mind as, 252-69; see also Mind
Antinaturalism, degrading view of nature and human nature, 9; founders, 1; language barrier, 4; point of agreement and co-operation between non-naturalism and, 2; relative bearings of naturalism and, 5-16
Antinaturalists, attitude toward scientific method, 3, 10; charge against naturalists by both schools of, 360; manifesto by Princeton group, 7, 11
Appearance and reality, 143
Apprehension, vivid, 103
Approval and disapproval, degrees of, 92
Archaeological dating, 163
Aristotle, 11, 65, 66, 69n, 73, 85, 91, 92, 125, 134, 142, 145, 147, 149, 284, 298, 307, 344, 352, 354, 355, 357, 361, 363, 365, 378, 382; Aristotelian and empiricist tradition re terms and meanings, 271, 273, 274, 280, 282; assertions of things taken for granted: ideas re motion, 146; formulation of the principle, 212; influence of, 1; observer or speculative philosopher? 314; relation to Church, 1; virtues defined, 67
Arnold, Matthew, 27, 298
Art, distinguished from nature, 355, 357; factors determining acceptance of, 105-15; factors which make intransitive response possible, 108; great, 117, 119; relationship between perfection and significance, 115 ff.
Art as Experience (Dewey), 100
Assertions of things taken for granted, 146
Atheism, 28
Attention, aesthetics an experience of pure, 118; intransitive, 106 ff.
Augustine, Saint, 2, 9, 134, 172, 355, 370

Bacon, Francis, 331
Bacon, Roger, 138*n*
Baldwin, James Mark, 354
Balfour, Lord, 180
Banister, John, 330
Bankruptcy of civilization, 43
Barnard, Henry, 343, 346; quoted, 344
Bartram, John, 330
Baur, 180
Beard, Charles A., 166, 181, 344, 350
Beauty, in the form of an object, 100; relation of cognitive or moral values to, 117
Beecher, Henry Ward, 348
Behavior, life as purposive, 245 ff.; mind as, 307
Being, concept of, 355, 357, 358; metaphysical realm of, 55; Woodbridge's use of the language of, 366
Belief, suspension of, 117
Bell, Clive, 116
"Belong and not belong," 212, 213
Bentham, 69
Bergson, Henri, 5, 6, 150 f., 256, 298
Berkeley, 145
Biased anticipatory response, 258
Big business, age of, 345 ff.
Biology, experimental procedure, 246
Bloch, Engels' letter to, 148*n*, 152
Body, relation to mind, 307 f.
Bosanquet, Bernard, 249
Botanists, amateur, 330, 334
Bowen, C. D., 347
Boylston, Zabdiel, 329
Bradley, F. H., 273
Brattle, Thomas, 329
Bridgman, P. W., 137, 305; quoted, 192 f.
Broad, 244
Brownson, Orestes A., 341
Buchanan, Joseph, 336
Burtt, Edwin Arthur, 137, 148
Bury, J. B., 181
Bush, Wendell T., 363
Butler, Bishop, 295, 298
Byrd, William, 330

Cabanis, 335, 337
Cabet, Etienne, 342
Caldwell, Charles, 336
Calkins, Mary W., 134
Campbell, Norman Robert, 137
Capitalism and its influence, 323, 345 ff.
Carr, Herbert Wildon, 304
Categories, are all three basic, indispensable? 284, 292 f.; basic, 271, 293;

change in, and its significance, 271, 279; functional terminism, 380; metaphysical, 274-79; of event, 271, 279 ff., 289 ff.; of naturalism, 270-94; of quality, 271, 277, 281 f., 284 ff., 292; of relation, 271, 281 f., 275 ff., 287, 292; secondary, 271, 293; structural and functional, 377 f.; three crucial questions concerning, 283 f., 288, 290, 292; *see also* Language; Terms
Category, meaning of term, 271
Catesby, Mark, 330
Cause and effect, 19, 129; category, 271, 291, 293
Certainties, moral, 37
Change, 141 f.; alteration of existents, 280; dialectic of changes, 174; produced by processes of inference, 145; reality of quality and, 147; substitution of one ruling minority for another, as basis of historical, 62 f.
Channing, William H., 340
Cherniss, Harold, 140
Chesterton, G. K., quoted, 8
Choice (preference), 262 f.; as an act of choosing, 74, 91; difficulties of interpretation, 82; first-order and second-order, 72 ff.; interpretation of ethics in terms of, 69 ff.; means-end phases of, 74 ff.; search for causal elements or necessary conditions of, 93
Christianity, *see* Religion; Theology
Chronology, defined, 167
Circularity, objective validity charged with, 193, 194
Civilization, bankruptcy of, 43
Clash, term, 86, 89
Clayton, John, 330
Clinton, DeWitt, 343
Clocks, differ in a symmetrical case? 303
Cognition or intelligence, mind as, 252-58; aesthetic experience a form of? 105; memory, 256; perception, 255; relation to conation, 259-62; thought, 257; three types of response, 253 ff.
Cognitive or scientific situation, 97
Cohen, Morris R., 352, 363, 364, 366, 367, 377, 378
Coherent, term, 86, 89
Colden, Cadwallader, 334, 343
Colleges and universities, early intellectual lag, 335, 337, 338, 340; enormous endowments and resulting renaissance of education, 346; new, freed from direct ecclesiastical influence, 336, 337,

346, 347; philosophy's modern shape, 346; students, statistics, 338, 346
Colonial period in America, 325-31
Colors, in terms of their relations, 276
Communication and laws of thought, 226
Community, the: and Absolute, 134
Compatible, term, 86, 89
Comte, Auguste, 170, 173, 347; derivation of his positivism, 340; emergence in United States, 325, 340 f.; influence there, 341
Conation or interest, mind as, 258-64, 268; biased anticipatory response, 258; cognitive element in relation to, 259-62; preferential response, 262 f.
Conclusions, reasonable: democratic methods of reaching, 59
Conditioned, defined, 19
Confessions (Woodbridge), 298
Configurational organization, procedure of, 170 ff., 179, 182
Conflicting, term, 86, 89
Consciousness, mind as, 264-69; other-consciousness, 266-69; self-consciousness, 264-66
Conservation, meaning and status, 279, 285
Consistency, logical, 217
Consistent, term, 85, 89
Constancy, 82, 84
Consultation and communication, mutual, 59
Continent and incontinent, 91
Contingent world, 34
Continuant configuration, 172, 174
Continuant past, 161
Continuities, reconstruction of, 160
Continuity, principle of: employment of scientific method, 183, 185, 206, 207, 208; from matter to mind, 247; significance of naturalism lying chiefly in, 183-209, *passim;* summation of implications which sociological study of knowledge has for, 206 ff.
Continuity of analysis, 184, 367; naturalism defined as, 357, 358
Continuity of historical events, 157 f., 159 ff.
Contradiction, 214, 313
Contradictory ideas of philosophers, 134
Contradictory, term, 85, 86, 89
Contranatural, 130; *see also* Unnatural
Cooper, Thomas, 334 f.
Corporations, 345

Correlation, 301 ff.
Corruption of natural man, doctrine, 2
Cosmic laws and democracy, 47, 63 f.
Cosmic Philosophy (Fiske), 348
Cosmological argument, 32
Cosmology, 148
Cotton, John, 326, 328
Cours (Comte), 340, 341
Criticism, categories of, 115

Darwin, Charles, 93, 347; influence in America, 347
Dating procedures, 162 f.
Death, and decay, 129; survival after, 295, 358
Decline of the West, The (Spengler), 160
Deformity, 128
Deism, counterattack upon, 338; prevalence of, in early America, 332 ff.; Unitarian interpretations, 339
Democracy, analysis of, to discover whether it rests upon theological or metaphysical truths, or can be justified from naturalistic standpoint, 44-64; and metaphysics, 51, 53; and preferences: as a hypothesis, 51, 56; and religion, 51; as a way of life, 48-51; asservations that naturalism is destructive of values of, 9; causes of failure, 43-44; clarification of meaning of, 46 ff.; characteristics of present-day failure of nerve, 40-43; distinguished from totalitarianism, 48; feasibility of, 47, 61-64; grounds for justification, 51-61; philosophical presuppositions, 47; principle of equality analyzed, 49 f.
Democritus, 45, 65, 139, 145, 354, 364
De Morgan, Augustus, 313
Depravity of human nature, 2, 9
Descartes, 19, 167, 271, 314, 329
Descent of Man (Darwin), 347
Design argument, 131
Destutt de Tracy, 337
Determinism vs. free will, 90
Dewey, John, 45, 65, 76, 100, 103, 110, 185, 198, 255, 296, 312, 350, 355-80 *passim;* "Antinaturalism in Extremis," 1-16; and Santayana, 296, 352; as teacher and intellectual philosopher, 317, 365; creator of a major naturalistic system, 352; experimental naturalism of, 364 f., 366; on the significance of

Dewey, John (*Continued*)
naturalism in the principle of continuity, 183
Dialectical materialism, 148
Dialogues concerning Natural Religion (Hume), 34
Dietzgen, Joseph, 349
Discourse, term, 273
Discussion of Human Affairs, The (Beard), 166, 181
Disvalues, *see* Values: Valuing
Divinity, 358; *see* God
Doctrines, defined, 23; *see also* Theology
Douglass, William, 329
Draper, John W., 347
Driesch, Hans, 246
Dualism, Kant's thought the classic modern expression of, 372
Duality and the strife of systems, 143
Dudley, Paul, 329
Duffield, 347
Duhem, Pierre, 240
Durkheim, Emile, 190
Dwight, Timothy, 338

Economic and moral, line drawn between, 14
Economic opportunity and success and its effect upon American thinking, 320-53 *passim*
Edger, Henry, 342
Education (Adams), 349
Einstein, Albert, 137
Eliot, Jared, 329
Emerson, Ralph Waldo, 339
Emotion, 15, 104; controls of, 16; not a trait of aesthetic experience, 103; music as stimulant, 113 f.
Empirical equivalence, rule of, 157, 158, 159 ff., 165, 172, 174, 176, 181
Empiricism, Aristotelian and empiricist tradition re terms and meanings, 271, 273, 274; check on thinking, 314 f.; meanings, 18; method taken seriously by naturalists, 18; of Woodbridge, 365; a philosophy congenial to democracy, 51
Empiricists' view of science, 371
Encyclopaedists, 28, 332
Ends, pursuit of, as ends-in-view, 252, 258; systematization, 75, 77; term, 74; test is its functioning as an end, 77; *see also* Means-end relationship
Engels, Friedrich, 350; letter to Bloch, 148*n*, 152

Environment, materialism in environmental field, and its influence upon American thought, 320-53 *passim;* nature as, 122; relation with organism, 251
Epistemology, 148
Equality, concept of, 49 f.
Essay on Nature, An (Woodbridge), 298
Eternity, 358
Ethical democracy, equality the principle of, 49
Ethics, descriptive and normative statements, criticism of choices, 71 f.; good things of life, 316; interpretation of terms, 66-79; interpretation as in rules of law, 70-72; naturalism's ethical theory and its sources, 65-95; need have no finally delimited subject matter, 69; no distinctively ethical statements, 73; problem of verification, 79-89; relation of ethical to nonethical systems, 89-95; self-interest, 316
Ethics (Hartmann), 66*n*, 67
Ethics (Spinoza), 299, 316
European schools of thought reflected in America, 322, 323, 332, 337, 340, 342
Events, can secondary categories be interpreted as meaning configurations of qualitied and related events? 284, 290 f.; category of, 271, 279 ff.; continuity of, 157 f., 159 ff., 177; order in, 289 f.; reconstructed in their interconnections, 162; sequentially reconstructed, 159
Evidence, demand for, 40 ff.; experiential, for religious beliefs, 46
Evolution, emergent, 378; impact of theory in America, 347 ff., 378; importance, 181; man included in the natural sciences, 373; panevolutionism, 184; paths to acceptance of, 151; problem presented by biological and human, 378; term naturalism identified with, 356
Evolution and Ethics (Huxley), 28
Excluded middle, principle of, 225
Existence, nature as, 121, 122
Experience, consciousness identified with the immediacy of, 264; emergence and differentiation: three modes other than aesthetic, 96; an interaction of natural processes, 373; moral or practical, and scientific or cognitive, situa-

tions, 97, 99; religious, 98; aesthetic, *see* Aesthetics

Experience and Nature (Dewey), 365

Experiential evidence for religious beliefs, 46

Experimentalism, as guiding procedure in approach to mind, 242, 252; to unsolved biological problems, 246

Experimentation, method, 380

Explanation, 291, 293

Expression theory, 111, 113

Expressive vehicle distinct from expressed meaning, 115

Extensities, 303

Extra-naturalism, 359, 372; *see also* Supernaturalism

Fact-statements, evidence a question of relevance, 164; how established in historical writing, 156, 164; not substitute for perspicacity, 180

Fallen estate of man, doctrine, 2

Familiar, the, 107

Fear and hate, 15

Feeling vs. evidence, 41

Fichte, 145, 347

Fiske, John, 347, 348, 349

Fourierism in America, 342

Four Stages of Greek Religion (Murray), 40

Franklin, Benjamin, 330 f., 332, 340

Free Man's Worship, A (Russell), 28

Free will, 141; vs. determinism, 90

Frege-Russell view of arithmetical truths, 235

French Revolution, 338

Fresh perception, 107

Freud, Sigmund, 264

Fuller, Margaret, 314

Functionalists, 377 f., 380

Fundamentalism, 339

Futuristic response, 253

Garden, Alexander, 330

Garman, 296

Gateway of History, The (Nevins), 178

Geological dating, 163

Gibbon, Edward, 166

Gibbs, Josiah Willard, 313, 349

Gillespie, William Mitchell, 341

Gobineau, Arthur de, 5

God, an ideal or a supreme value, 35; "what God wills" as interpretation of right, 68*n*

God, existence of, affirmed the timeless ground of the temporal world, 34; arguments for, rejected as failing in empirical warrant, 36; in the sense of a person, can be determined only by empirical evidence, 31; James's will-to-believe argument, 31, 33; meaning of phrase, 30; naturalistic standpoint, 30, 45, 295, 358; a necessary premise for democracy? 53; theism a matter of great moment, 30; the three traditional arguments, 31, 32

Goethe, 299

Good, distinction between apparent and real, 73; interpretations of "a good" and "good for," 67 ff., 74-78

Good and Truth as supreme objects of attainment, 381 f.

Good Life, the, 374-76, 381

Gray, Asa, 71, 347

Gré, Gerard de, 188, 199

Great Chain of Being (Lovejoy), 151

Greeks, functional or operational analysis, 378; naturalism back again with world-view of, 374; naturalistic attitude and temper, 369 f., 374; theme of "nature" and "the natural" in thought of, 354, 355, 357

Greeley, Horace, 349

Greene, Theodore M., 112, 118

Ground, 271, 293

Guggenheim, Mrs. John Simon, 96*n*

Hartmann, 67, 92; quoted, 66

Hate and fear, 15

Hegel, 134, 145, 148, 150, 297, 347; idealism, 296, 364, 365, 372; theory of history, 156, 172

Helmholtz, 244

Hindu beliefs, 53

Hippias Major, 148

Hippocrates, 14

Hippocratic Corpus, 137

Historical-knowledge materials, 154-82; conflicting opinions re contribution of, 178; dating procedure, 162 f.; fact —, knowledge —, and relation-statements, and speculative supposition, defined, 156; historical understanding, 176-82; limitations accepted by historians, 177; materials of reconstruction, 159-64; narrative and comparative organization, 169-76; orientation of the historian, 164-69; working distinction between prehistory and history, 162

History, definitions, 156; science of, 155; why written, 168 f.
History of Philosophy, A (Windelband), excerpts, 135, 136
Hoar, Leonard, 329
Hobbes, 36, 65, 67, 90, 307, 334, 357
Hocking, W. E., 242
Hodge, 347
Hoernlé, R. F. A., 249
Holley, Horace, 336
Holmes, George Frederick, 341
Holmes, Oliver Wendell, 349
Holt, E. H., 253, 266
Hues, in terms of their relations, 276
Human beings, adaptation transformed to adaptability, 258; as creature, natural: as artificer, beyond nature, 122; causes of good or evil nature, 62; contrast between the natural and the spiritual self, 2; cruelty and oppressions, 6, 15, 56; democracy's regard for potentialities of, and treatment of, 49, 57-59; de-naturalization of human experience and, 370; free, and an end in himself, 6; importance and reality of their experiences and enterprises, 361, 369; inclusion in the natural sciences, 373; inclusion within Nature, 9, 11, 29, 356 f., 369, 373; lack of knowledge about Nature and, 128; moral and social consequences of degrading view of Nature and, 9 ff.; principle of equality, 49 f.; Truth and Good as imperative standards, 381 f.
Humanism, 6, 316
Hume, David, 32, 34, 145, 365
Huntington, Ellsworth, 154
Huxley, Thomas Henry, 28, 151
Hypotheses, historians', 164, 171, 174, 176

Ideal, God as an, 35
Idealism, dominant motif in American philosophy, 319; downfall of Roycean, 351; Hegelian, 296, 364, 365, 372; lack of basis, 9; objective, 310; passing of philosophic, 368; rise of realism and pragmatism a debâcle for, 350; swing toward a scientific methodology, 372 f.
Idealists, human wisdom of, compared with scientific philosophies, 375
Idealization of desires, 144
Ideas, after they prove false or unsatis-

factory, 148 f.; as anticipated operations, 257; conflict of, resulting problems, 140; cannot be separated from total intellectual life of a period, 136, 138, 153; defined and evaluated, 24; definitions, 310; fundamental questions about, 141; responses to, 119; stratification, 150; survival, 139, 144; test of new, 152
Identity, principle of, 225
Ideologie und Utopie (Mannheim), 186
Imageless thought, 308
Immanent meaning, 100, 102, 112, 118
Immigrants in America, 321, 345
Immortality, 295, 358; as a presupposition of democracy, 52, 53
Inappropriateness, 127
Inaugural Address (Bury), 181
Inconsistency, logical, 217
Indestructibility, 279
Individual, *see* Human beings
Inductive generalizations, 234, 235
Inductive truths, logical principles as, 218 ff.
Industrialism, 345
Inference, principles of, 215, 224, 226 ff.; processes of, 145; valid, 219
Inner life, individuality of, 307
Insight, historian's, 180
Institutions, religion embedded in, 21
Instrumentalism, 25
Instrumentalistic naturalism, 377
Instrumentality-assertions, 80
Intellectual chaos, 205
Intellectual culture, history's aid to, 178
Intellectual import of religion, 22, 23 f.
Intellectual life, 23, 24; in America from its beginning to the naturalism of today, 319-53 *passim*
Intelligence or cognition, mind as, 252-58; resoluteness and, compatible, 60; *see also* Cognition
Interest or conation, mind as, 258-64; *see* Conation
Intransitive attention, 106 ff.
Introduction to the History of History, An (Shotwell), 166
Introduction to the Study of History (Langlois and Seignobos), 177
Introspective consciousness, 254, 265 f.
Intuition, 55; historian's, 180
Inventors, 343, 345, 346
Irrational numbers, use in physical measurement, 238
Irrelevant, the, 127

James, William, 5, 23, 64, 128, 133, 134, 143, 144, 256, 295, 349; influence upon liberal theology: fundamental concerns, 32 f.; will-to-believe attitude, 31, 33

Jefferson, Thomas, 320, 332, 340; abuse heaped upon political and religious views of, 337; University of Virginia, 334, 337

Jevons, William Stanley, 298

Jowett, Benjamin, 306

Judgment, alterations with changes of temporal perspective, 168; conative, 260, 262

Judgments about historical events, 155, 156, 164, 180; of presentness, 166

Justification of logical laws, 231 f.

Kant, Immanuel, 32, 81, 134, 145, 308, 310, 347, 369, 372; as dividing line of modern philosophy, 368; definitely an antinaturalist, 2, 5

Klineberg, Otto, 193

Knowledge, distinguished from speculative supposition, 158, 160; meaning, 105; sociological analysis, 183-209 (*see entries under* Sociological); togetherness of, 264

Knowledge-statement, defined, 156

Koch, G. A., 333

Labor, 345

Langlois and Seignobos, 171, 177; quoted, 177, 178, 180, 181

Language, importance of terms and, 4; necessary truths contained in, 230 f.; of teleology, 315; principles prescriptive for the use of, 225 f., 228, 230, 232; relation to subject matter, 240; *see also* Categories; Terms

Latta, Robert, 249

Laws of thought, 218, 224, 225 ff.

Le Conte, Joseph, 348

Legal rules, interpretation of ethical rules by, 70-72

Leibnitz, G. W., 214, 301, 302, 310

Levels, theories of, 284 ff.

Lewis, C. I., 267, 312; quoted, 118

Life, as purposive behavior, 245 ff.; matrix in which mind functions, 243-52; mechanistic conception, 244 ff.

Life of Reason, The (Santayana), 66, 352, 363

Light, 298, 300; velocity, 306

Locke, John, 271, 307, 314, 355, 363, 365, 366

Loeb, J., quoted, 245

Logan, James, 330

Logic, continuity the primary postulate of naturalistic theory of, 183; rules of inference conventional but not arbitrary, 227-28; laws and language, 232; of order and of symbols, 311 ff.; positivism, 295, 340 ff., 366, 367, 379 f.; terminism, 380

—— without ontology, 210-41; grounds for accepting logical laws, 231 ff.; limitations of certain narrowly empirical approaches to, 212, 217-24; logical relations as invariants of all possible worlds, 214-17; regulative role, 212-17

Logic: the Theory of Inquiry (Dewey), 185

Logical atomism, 312

Logical principles, ontological interpretation, 212-17; as inductive truths, 218 ff.; as prescriptive, 225

Logical relations in ethical statements, interpretation, 85 ff.

Logic of Modern Physics (Bridgman), 137

Logico-mathematical concepts and principles, operational interpretation of notions of, 212, 224-41

Lotze, R. H., 373

Love, natural and artificial, 125; powers of strife and, 142

Lovejoy, Arthur O., 142, 151, 188, 354; quoted, 187

Lucretius, 122, 123, 124, 131

McCosh, James, 348

McDougall, William, 5, 257, 259

Machine age in America, 344-53

Magnitudes of physical properties, 236 ff.

Man, *see* Human beings

Mandelbaum, Maurice, 193; quoted, 165, 187

Mann, Horace, 346

Mannheim, Karl, 186, 191, 194, 200, 206

Maritain, J., 243; quoted, 6

Marx, Karl, 15, 174, 347; correspondent for Greeley's *Tribune*, yet little known in U.S., 349; quoted, 345; recent studies about, 350

Marxianism, 65, 89, 93, 148*n*

Materialism, American strivings and success and their influence upon thinking,

Materialism (*Continued*)
320-53 *passim;* economic factors, 15; naturalism represented as a variety of, 11; scientific, of nineteenth century, 360; significance of term, 3, 279

Mathematics, formulas for expressing relations, 287; function of, in inquiry: discussion of uses of two mathematical ideas in measurement, 233 ff.; human invention, 312; magnitudes of physical properties, 236 ff.; Mill's view of arithmetic, 234; propositions of arithmetic, 234 f.; real number system, 235 f.; *see also* Logico-mathematical concepts and principles

Mather, Cotton, 326, 328, 329

Matter, shift from category of, 271, 279 ff.; significance of term, 3

Mead, G. H., 378

Meaning, account of terms and, 271 ff.; distinction between organization and intrinsic value of, 115; embodied in object, 101; how embodied immanently, 102; immanent, 100, 102, 112, 118; referential, 102; response to, 253

Meaningful discourse, 221

Means, interrelatedness of, 130; mind as anticipatory response, 252; term, 74

Means-end relationship, 74 ff.; causality, 78; language, 315; preferential activity as choice of, 263; temporal reference, 77; the two aspects of purposive action, 250, 252; *see also* Ends

Measurement, discussion of the uses of two mathematical ideas in, 233; *see also* Mathematics

Mechanical process, 123

Mechanism, 123; conflict with purpose, 245, 247, 250; life as purposive behavior within medium of, 245 ff.; meanings and types, 244

Medical materialists in early America, 330, 334, 335

Melville, Hermann, 339

Memory, as a mode of cognition, 256; meanings, 256; no consciousness without, 265

Mental habits, 148

Merton, Robert K., 190, 206

"Metaphysical Club, The," of Cambridge, 349

Metaphysical Foundations of Modern Science (Burtt), 137

Metaphysical spiritualism, 9; *see* Idealism

Metaphysics, as foundation of democracy, 44, 53-56; categories, 274-79; conception of, 54; logical atomism, 312; theories not entailed in scientific method, 42; two meanings, and attitude of critical naturalism toward, 293; two species, 54 f.

Method, in historical work, 155

Meyerson, Emile, 142, 147, 148

Michels, Roberto, 62

Mill, J. S., 69, 80, 234, 375; psychological atomism, 218, 221; quoted, 218

Miller, Perry, 328

Mills, C. Wright, 197; quoted, 198

Mind, analysis of, 242; analyzed as behavior: three dimensions of response, 252 ff.; as cognition or intelligence, 252-58; as conation or interest, 258-64; as consciousness, 264-69; attribute of, 310; locus of human experience in, 371; matrix in which it functions, life, 243-52; naturalistic view, 242-69; objective, 310, 311, 314; types of analysis of, 188; Woodbridge's characterization of, 306 ff.; *see also entries under* Cognition; Conation; Consciousness

Minorities, ruling and historical changes, 63

Mitchell, John, 330

Mitchill, Samuel Latham, 343

Modern, historian's designation, 167

Modern Times, L. I., 342

Monism, 278*n*, 300

Montague, W. P., 350, 352

Moral and economic, line drawn between, 14

Moral and social consequences of degrading view of nature and human nature, 9 ff.

Moral consciousness, an element of religion, 26

Moral ideals, as hypothesis? 56; defined, 57

Morality, implications of term, 29; relation to theism, 36

Moral law and wealth harmonized, 326 f., 345

Moral or practical situation, 97

Moral theory, medieval theology's, 1

More, Paul Elmer, 27

Morgan, Lewis Henry, 350

Morgan, Lloyd, 257

Morison, S. E., quoted, 344

Morris, C. W., 188

Mosca, Gaetano, 62, 63
Mother, analogy of nature as, 124
Motion, 146
Murray, Gilbert, 17; quoted, 40
Music, as an object of aesthetic perception, 113 f.; significance, 119 f.
Mythological conception of things, 26

Narrative and configurational organization, 169–76, 179, 182
Natural, the: as a term of distinction, 355, 357
Natural History Survey of 1836–43, 343
Naturalism, analysis of natural and unnatural values and disvalues, 130–32; and the religious view of life, 17–39 (*see also* Religion); and the sociological analysis of knowledge, 183–209; antisupernatural doctrinal conclusions, 45 f.; attitude toward metaphysics, 293; categories, 270–94; contrast between charges brought against, and facts of the case, 5–16; conception of the Good Life, 374–76, 381; concomitant phases as the sciences grew, 93; confirmed by our practiced, and refuted by our professed, philosophies, 321, 324; differences concerning logical and mathematical principles employed in inquiries, 210; differences of emphasis within framework of, 376–81; differences of outlook and resulting gradual development, 319, 352; distinction from other philosophical positions, 289; ethical theory and its sources, 65–95; history of, in America, 319–53 (Colonial, 325–31, Revolutionary, 331–38, Romantic, 338–44, Machine age, 344–53, periods); importance of clarification of terms and discussion of language, 4; importance of Darwinism to, 347 ff.; manifesto declaring free scholarship endangered by, 7, 11; naturalistic view of mind, 242–69; nature of, 354–82; new, and nineteenth century, 295; no place for spiritualism in, 3; of Frederick Woodbridge, 295–318; older and wider movement of ideas of which it is culmination, 367–74; philosophical, and its ancestry, 1; present position of prosperity and respect, 353; respect for the conclusion of natural science, 2; scientific materialism of nineteenth century, 360; significance of, lying in principle of continuity, 183 ff.; social sciences given a naturalistic bent, 350; stands or falls with its acceptance of a strictly empirical method, 36; summary of what there is, and is not, room for in, 358, 361; tenacity of opposition to, 200, 208; the term and its implications, 18, 132, 356 ff.; theory of aesthetics, 96–120; three major personal influences, 363–66; three questions now crucial in an appraisal of contemporary, 283 f., 288, 290, 292; type of, expressing temper of modern mathematico-experimental science, 212; when and by whom, major system produced, 325; whether democracy can be justified from standpoint of, 44–64
Natural sciences, basis for unity of social sciences and, 189; contemporary naturalism rooted in, 374; idealists turning from, 372; inclusion of man in, 373; period of, 136; term, 356; *see also* Evolution
Natura rerum, 122, 123 f., 132
Nature, concepts of, 121–32 *passim*, 242; consequences of a degrading view of human nature and, 9 ff.; design argument, 131; exclusion of man and his works from, 122, 370; has it a plural? 121, 123; inadequate concepts and scientific procedures concerning, 369 ff.; inclusion of man within, 29, 356 f., 369, 373; naturalness a matter of degree, 127; order in, 289 f.; Puritans' view of, 328; and the natural: terms, their origin, meaning and usage, 122, 354 ff.; what is excluded as unnatural? 121; why singular, 123 f.; Woodbridge's feeling toward, 298 f., 306, 315, 316
Nature and Mind (Woodbridge), 298
Nature and Sources of the Law, The (Gray), 71
Necessary truths, 216, 224, 230 f., 232
Neill, Thomas P., quoted, 5
Nerve, failure of: characteristics and causes, 40–44
Nevins, Allan, 178
New, the, 107
New England, commercialization and resulting wealthy class, 327; formative influences upon intellectual life, 325 ff.; Unitarians, 339, 341
New Harmony, Ind., 342
Newman, Cardinal, quoted, 1, 14

Newton, Isaac, 302, 305, 314, 329, 333, 334, 340, 344, 369, 373
New York Survey of 1836-43, 343
Niebuhr, Reinhold, 41, 262
Nietzsche, Frederick, 56
Noncontradiction, principle of, 216, 217, 225, 230
Nonnaturalism, 123; point of agreement and co-operation between antinaturalism and, 2; terms affected by inheritance of, 4
Norm, nature as a, 125
"Normal aesthetic perceiver," 106
Normal processes distinguished from accidental sequences, 125 ff., 130
Norms, directional, 201; presentational, 195; types, 196 f.; validity norms, *see* Validity

Object, of aesthetic experience, 100 ff., *passim;* of moral and of cognitive situations, 97, 99; of religious experience, 98
Objective mind, 310, 311, 314
Objective validity, 193 ff., 203
Objects, meanings embodied in, 101
O'Connell, James, 341
One, the: ambiguity of term, 143
Ontological argument, 32
Ontological interpretation of logical principles, 214 ff.
Ontology, logic without, 210-41 *passim; see entries under* Logic; Logicomathematical
Operational definition, 305
Order, category, 271, 289 f., 293; logic of, 311 ff.
Organization, relation to purpose, 249
—— configurational: and narrative, 169-76, 179, 182
Origin of Species (Darwin), 347
Origins, defined, 177
Other-consciousness, 266-69

Paine, Thomas, 332, 333
Palmer, Elihu, 333
Panevolutionism, 184
Panpsychism, 247 f.
Pareto, Vilfredo, 62
Parrington, V. I., quoted, 331
Parsons, Talcott, 190
Past, continuant, 161
Patents, statistics, 345
Patterns of organized responses, 102
Paul, Saint, 2, 9, 56, 134, 370

Peace must respect all peoples, 16
Pearson, Jonathan, 339
Peirce, Charles S., 198, 306, 311, 313, 349
Penny, Russell's lecture on, 300
Pepper, Stephen Coburn, 380
Perception, 147, 188, 255, 300
Perfection and significance in work of art, 115
Periods, of science, 136 f.; of philosophy, 138 f., 153
Perry, R. B., 256n, 258, 268, 352
Perspective of temporal reference, 166 ff.
Philosophers, conclusions re contradictory ideas of, 134; expressive of certain ages, 135 f.; influence of predecessors: processes of inference, 145; relationships, 133, 150; self-evident assertions, 146
Philosophical positions, 207
Philosophical presuppositions of philosophy, 47
Philosophical schools, 134, 136, 138
Philosophy, American, mostly theological and idealistic, 319; as idealization of one's desires, 144; difference between science and, 135; groups and periods, 138 ff.; history, 133-53; modern period, 367 ff.; modern shape as a college subject, 346; naturalism a minor tendency until recently, 320; naturalism confirmed by our practiced, and refuted by our professed, philosophies, 321, 324; of science and of aesthetics the two present prevailing interests, 136; problems of, 138 ff., 148; proto-philosophies, 147, 148; reorientation foreshadowed by Wright and Adams, 348 f.; scientists peculiarly aware of, 137; shifts in meaning of terms, 142; summation of knowledge about history of, 152 f.; tendency of a time identified with philosophical ideas, 136, 138, 153
Philosophy of Human Nature, The (Buchanan), 336
Physical properties, magnitudes, 236 ff.
Physics, "reduction" of ethics to, 90; *see also* Relativity
Plato, 1, 27, 35, 69n, 86, 125, 134, 140, 145, 151, 259, 306, 307, 354, 355, 358, 363, 365, 381, 382; use of myths, 26
Pleasure, as an end, 77; as the interpretation of good, 69, 80
Plentitude, principle of, 151
Plotinus, 145

Poetry, religion in terms of, 26, 27
Political influences during Revolutionary period, 332
Ponendo ponens, principle of, 224, 226
Poor Richard, 330
Positivism, 295, 366, 367, 379 f.; Comte's introduction to America, 340 ff.
Positivists and democracy, 44
"Possible worlds, all," 214-17
Powell, John W., 347
Practical or moral situation, 97
Pragmatic naturalism, 126
Pragmatism, 24; rise of, 350
Prall, David Wight, 100
Pratt, James Bisset, 32
Prediction (charting) of forward course, 176, 179
Preference, 262 f.
Preferences and democracy, 51, 56
Prehistory and history distinguished, 162
Presentational norms, 195
Presentness, historian's judgment of, 166, 167
Priestley, Joseph, 334
Principia Mathematica (Whitehead and Russell), 227, 234
Principle, the: interpretation of, 212 ff.
Principles, discussion of formal and two senses in which commonly asserted, 224 ff.; logical, as principles of being as well as principles of inference, 215; *see also kinds*, e.g., Inference; Noncontradiction
Problems, philosophic, 138 ff., 148
Process, category of, 280, 281, 282, 379
Propositions, 218, 234; and beliefs distinguished, 189
Protagoras, contemporaries, 139
Proto-philosophies, 147, 148
Psychological atomism, 218, 221
Psychological possibility of democracy, 61
Psychological terms, translation of, 90
Psychologism, error of, 101
Puritans and their influence, 325 ff.
Purpose, 271, 291, 293; conflict with mechanism, 245, 247, 250; life as purposive behavior, 245 ff.; relation to organization, 249; two aspects, 250

Qualitative nature of a thing, 19
Quality, category of, 271, 277, 281 f., 292; reality of change and, 147; theories of levels, 284 ff.

Rafinesque, Constantine, 336
Randolph, Edward, 327
Rational, category, 290
Rationalism, view of science, 371
Real, the: identified with the ideal or with the actual, 125
Realism, functional, 380; rise of, in America, 350
Reality, and appearance, 143; concept of, 357; of quality and change, 147; sense of, 118; sense-perception not evidence of, 146, 147; a value term, 54
Realm of Mind, The (Woodbridge), 306
Realms of Being (Santayana), 352, 363
Real number system in measurement, 235 f.
Reason, Life of, 369
Reason, Social Myths, and Democracy (Hook), 48*n*, 63*n*
Reasonable conclusions, democratic methods of reaching, 59
Reasoning, 257
Recognition, response, 103
Redemption, 2, 9
Reductionism, 295, 361, 378; the antireductionist thesis, 362, 372; major strands uniting to form opposition to supernaturalism and, 367, 372-74
Referential meaning, 102
Reflection and subject-matter, 25
Reflexive meaning, *see* Immanent meaning
Reflexive mind, 266
Regularities in environment, 210
Regulative principles, choice between alternative systems, 228
Relation-statements, defined, 156; judgments of connections with fact-statements, 165
Relations, category of, 271, 281 f., 292; ordinal, 311; of traits and processes, 275 ff.; symbolisms for expressing, 287
Relativism, social, 197, 198
Relativity, 124, 132; "theory of," 302; physics, 301 ff.
Religion, as a mode of aesthetic experience, 98; as a way of life, 20, 22; conflict with science, 11, 17, 344, 348, 368; curious notions, 27; dangers in a too-intense zeal and in formulating a universally acceptable religion, 38; doctrinal conclusions, 37; experiential evidence for, 46; importance, 21, 30; influence of medieval Christianity,

Religion (*Continued*)
1 f.; its many results, 21; older forms of naturalism hostile to, 17, 28; other meanings, 20; passing of problem of, 368; postponement of religious commitment, 39; relationship between theology and the religious way, 22 ff.; Santayana's interpretation, 364; summations of virtues of, 37; suspension of belief, 117; theocratic forms of government supported by institutional, 52; two elements: a moral consciousness and a poetic or mythological conception of things, 26; whether democracy rests upon belief in, 44, 51-53; why room for, in naturalism, 358; *see also* God; Theology

Renaissance, the, 149 f.

Republican government, Kant's belief in, 6

Res naturae, 122

Resoluteness and intelligence compatible, 60

Response, 119; disinterested, 116; mind as anticipatory, 252-69; patterns of, 102; what constitutes aesthetic, 103

Revolutionary period in America, 331-38

Rhythm, 110

Richards, I. A., 117

Rickert, Heinrich, 177, 179

Rignano, Eugenio, 251

Riley, Woodbridge, 323

Ripley, George, 340

Rittenhouse, David, 330

Robie, Thomas, 329

Rogers, William B., 347

Roman Catholic Church, 5, 8; doctrine of corruption of nature, 2; interpretations of medieval, 1; persecutions and oppressions carried on by, 6; valuation of the soul, 14

Romantic period in America, 338-44

Ross, W. D., 67; quoted, 66

Rotation, absolute, 304

Royce, Josiah, 134, 247, 259, 261, 295, 300, 307, 311, 312, 313, 351

Rush, Benjamin, 334, 335

Russell, Bertrand, 28, 298, 300, 304, 314, 356

Russell, Whitehead and, 227, 234

Sabine, George H., 189; quoted, 190

Saint-Simon, Henri de, 340

"Same attribute," 212, 213

"Same respect," 212

Santayana, George, 26, 27, 33, 55, 65, 132, 296, 297, 298, 299, 307, 316, 323, 352, 356; and Dewey, 296, 352; conception of religion, 25 f., 35, 37; creator of a major naturalistic system, 352, 363 f., 366; quoted, 319, 322, 349

Schelling, 134

Schelting, von 193, 199; quoted, 186, 194

Schopenhauer, Arthur, 144, 145, 265, 296

Science, conflict with religion, 11, 17, 344, 348, 368; difference between philosophy and, 135; Franklin as a popularizer of, 330; in the intellectual sphere, as influence upon American thinking, 320-53 *passim*; intellectual and moral isolationism, 353; of history, 155; philosophies of the past compared with those of idealists, 375; Puritan attitude toward, 328, 329; spadework in laying foundations in America, 342; three major positions held upon problem of, 371; *see* Natural sciences; Social sciences

Scientific knowledge of material conditions, relevance to interpretations of history, 154, 155

Scientific method, antinaturalist attitude toward, 3, 10; attack upon, a flight from responsibility, 43; empiricistic interpretation of logic based upon inadequate conception of, 221; failure of nerve exhibited as loss of confidence in, 40 ff.; insistence on application of, 358, 359; Jefferson's services in lending prestige to free inquiry, 337; pleas for exemption, 41; principle of continuity's appeal to, 183, 185, 206, 207, 208; swing of idealism toward, 372 f.; *see also* Empiricism; Experimentalism

Scientific or cognitive situation, 97

Scientists, awareness of philosophy, 137; disagreement about Darwinism, 347; in early America, 329, 330, 334

Seignobos, *see* Langlois and Seignobos

Self, *see* Human beings

Self-consciousness, 264-66

Self-evident, the, 146, 147, 148

Self-interest, 317

Self-knowledge, 79, 84

Self-maintenance, 251

Seligman, E. R. A., 350

Sellars, R. W., 352

Sense of reality, 118

Sensory perception not evidence of reality, 146, 147

Sextus Empiricus, 137
Shaftesbury, 333
Shaw, G. Bernard, 298
Sheldon, W. H., 143*n*
Sherif, Muzafer, 195; quoted, 196, 205
Shotwell, James Thomson, 166, 171
Sidereal bodies, relations, 276
Sidgwick, Henry, 80
Significance, and perfection in work of art, 115; of music, 119 f.; of philosophical problem, 141; term, 120
Silliman, Benjamin, 342
Singer, E. A., 266*n*
Social and moral consequences of degrading view of nature and human nature, 9 ff.
Social dynamics, analysis, 204*n*
Social equality, phrase, 50
Social existence and thinking, connection between ways of, 175
Social forms, religion built into, 21
Social reformers, European: in America, 340, 342
Social relationships, harshness and oppressions, 6, 15, 56; less cruelty in democracies, 58
Social responsiveness to "valid" knowledge, 206
Social sciences, 372, 373; basis for unity with natural sciences, 189; divorce of comparative studies of continuities and, 170; in America, 345 f.
Social scientists, Karl Marx, 349 f.; American, 350
Social values, redirection of, 94
Sociological analysis of knowledge, 183-209; cognitive validity, 191 ff.; concrete contributions of, as a special science, 200 ff.; critics' convergence of views, 186 ff.; review of its implications, 206 ff.; tenacity of opposition to, 200, 208; types of approach, 201 f.
"Sociology of Knowledge, The" (Merton), 190
Socrates, 74, 139
Sophists, 355
Soul, and its value, 14; immortal, as a presupposition of democracy, 52, 53
Sound stimuli, 119
Southard, Elmer, 308
Space, category, 276, 293; relativity, 302, 304, 305
Speculative supposition, defined, 156; distinguished from knowledge-statement, 158, 160

Speier, Hans, quoted, 189
Spencer, Herbert, 5, 28, 347, 348, 363, 375
Spengler, Oswald, 160
Spinoza, B., 1, 124, 131, 145, 291, 317, 357, 361, 365; extent of Woodbridge's acceptance of, 299, 306, 307, 308, 310, 316; quoted, 247; no place in naturalism for, 3
Statistical norm inadequate for a theory of nature, 125, 130
Stewart, Houstan, 5
Stewart, John "Walking," 333
Stimson, Miss, 149
Stratification of ideas and interests, 150
Strife, of systems, 143; powers of love and, 142
Structuralists, 377 f., 380
Structure, 299, 311; objective, of the system of fact, 232
Subjective conditions of aesthetic experience, 106, 107
Subjective science, history a? 180
Subject-matter and reflection, 25
Sumner, William Graham, 350
Supernaturalism, cruel events that occurred with sanction of, 6; findings of science denied when in conflict with creed, 11; Kant's thought the classic modern expression of, 372; major strands uniting to form opposition to reductionism and, 367, 372-74; "the natural" contrasted with, 355, 356, 357; no room in naturalism for, 45 f., 295, 358, 359, 361; of Roman Catholic Church, 1; prevalence of, in early America, and its gradual undermining by science and economic progress, 319-53 *passim; see also* God; Religion; Theology
Suppositional response, 254
Survival after death, 295, 358
Suspension of belief, 117
Symbols, in relativity physics, 301; logic of, 311 ff.; role of symbolic constructions, 221, 223 f., 226
System, term, 19, 311

Taylor, A. E., 34
Teggart, Frederick John, 169
Teleological argument, 32
Teleology, implicit in notion of process, 379; rehabilitation of objective, 315
Temporal reference, perspective of, 166 ff.
Tennant, John, 330

Terms, account of meanings and, 271 ff.; designating logical relations in ethical statements, 85, 89; functional terminism, 380; importance to naturalists of language and, 4; interpretation of, ethical, 66-79; shifts in meaning of philosophical concepts, 142; *see also* Categories, Language

Theology, a dominant motif in American philosophy, and its gradual undermining, 319-53 *passim;* colonial Puritanism, 325 ff.; indifference and unbelief during Revolutionary period, 332 ff.; James's influence upon, 32 f.; medieval, 1 f.; reaction during Romantic period: fundamentalism, 338 ff.; relationship between religious way, and doctrinal theories and beliefs, 22 ff.; term, 23; *see also* God; Religion

Theophrastus, 137

Theory of History (Teggart), 169

Things and their attributes, logical principles about, 230

Thomas Aquinas, Saint, 6, 32, 34, 370

Thought, as a mode of cognition, 257, 258; connection between ways of thinking and social existence, 175; empirical check on thinking, 314 f.; imageless, 308; laws of, 218, 224, 225 ff.

Three Dialogues (Berkeley), 146

Time, category, 276, 293; continuant processes, 159; relativity, 192, 302, 303 ff.; tendency of a: relation to philosophical meditation, 136, 153

Tocqueville, Alexis de, 323

Torry, Samuel, 327

Totalitarian states, 48, 58

Townsend, H. G., 319

Toynbee, Joseph, 154

Traits, categorical, 275 ff.

Transcendental, antithesis between nature and, 355, 356, 357

Transcendentalism, 339, 351, 356, 360

Troeltsch, Ernst, 179, 180

Truth, 200; and Good as supreme objects of attainment, 381 f.

Ultimate values, 85

Unconscious experience, 264

Uniformities in environment, 210

Unitarians, 339, 341

United States, naturalism in, *see* America

Unity, aesthetic, 108 ff.

Universals, whether they have a natural existence, 121

Universities, *see* Colleges and universities

Unnatural, the: as a criterion for value judgments, 123; its forms, 127-30; meaning, 122; must be perceived as essentially pluralistic, 126; nonnaturalism, 2, 4, 123; things imagined, 121; uses: unnaturalness a matter of degree. 127; theory of values and disvalues, 130 ff.

Urban, Wilbur Marshall, 262

Uselessness, 127

Utilitarians, 65, 69, 80

Valid inference, 219

Validity, advantages of a normative schema, 197 f.; analysis of cognitive, 191 ff.; cognitive elements socially responsive, 204; distinction between the norm, the validating act, and the resultant established validity, 192; method for establishing validity of logical principles, 219 f.; norm defined, 195; norms, 192, 193, 196; objective, 193 ff., 203; types of demand upon norm, 199

Values, act of choosing or valuing, 91; actualization of, 88; causal examination of, 93; democracy grounded in metaphysical realm of, 55; discovery of varieties, 92; discussion of natural and unnatural values and disvalues, 130-32; incompatibility of specific, 89; naturally instituted by human beings, 13; reality a value term, 54; redirection of, 94; term without precise analysis, 79; terms having reference to values and acts of valuing, 85, 89, 271, 291, 293; ultimate, 85; verification of ethical statements about general, 80 ff.; valuing and disvaluing, conditions leading to employment of the terms, 86-88; not contradictory acts, 86

Veblen, Thorstein, 350

Velocities, addition of, 302

Verification in ethics, analysis of the problem, 79-89; instrumentality-assertions, 80; of general and singular statements, 80 ff.; statements involving logical relations, 85 ff.

Vestiges of Civilization (O'Connell), 341

Virginia, University of, 334, 337

Virtues, defined, 67
Virtuous and vicious, 91
Vitalism, 245-47

Walker, James, 341
War, attempts to hold rise of naturalism accountable, 15
Ward, James, 28, 247
Ward, Lester F., 350
Warren, Josiah, 342
Washington, George, 332
Watson, D. M. S., 251
Wealth harmonized with moral law, 326 f., 345
Whately, Bishop, 313
White, Andrew D., 343; quoted, 347
Whitehead, Alfred North, 34, 35, 37, 266, 356, 367, 377
Whitehead and Russell, 227, 234
Whitman, Walt, 52, 339
Will, mind as, 258; *see also* Conation
Will-to-believe, 31, 33

Windelband, Wilhelm, 139, 140*n*, 177, 179; quoted, 135 f.
Winthrop, John, Jr., 329
Winthrop, John IV, 329
Wittgenstein, Ludwig, 311
Woodbridge, Frederick J. E., 295-318, 352, 363, 365 ff., 377, 378, 379; administrative and editorial work, 297, 318; characterization of mind, 306 ff.; closeness to Spinoza, 299, 306, 307, 308, 310, 316; description of Russell's lecture, 300; empiricism, 314, 365; ethics, 316; feeling for Nature, 298, 306, 315, 316; great personality, 297, 318; influence, 317, 318; language of teleology, 315; on relativists, 303, 306; oracular questions, 296; quoted, 154; seminar, 297; writings, 297, 298, 306, 366
Worshiper and object, 98
Wright, Chauncey, 348

Youmans, Edward L., 347